I0147987

END OF DAYS

ALSO BY CHRIS JENNINGS

Paradise Now

END OF DAYS

RUBY RIDGE, THE APOCALYPSE, AND THE UNMAKING OF AMERICA

CHRIS JENNINGS

L B

LITTLE, BROWN AND COMPANY

New York Boston London

Copyright © 2026 by Christopher Jennings

Hachette Book Group supports the right to free expression and the value of copyright. The purpose of copyright is to encourage writers and artists to produce the creative works that enrich our culture.

The scanning, uploading, and distribution of this book without permission is a theft of the author's intellectual property. If you would like permission to use material from the book (other than for review purposes), please contact permissions@hbgusa.com. Thank you for your support of the author's rights.

Little, Brown and Company
Hachette Book Group
1290 Avenue of the Americas, New York, NY 10104
littlebrown.com

First Edition: February 2026

Little, Brown and Company is a division of Hachette Book Group, Inc. The Little, Brown name and logo are trademarks of Hachette Book Group, Inc.

The publisher is not responsible for websites (or their content) that are not owned by the publisher.

The Hachette Speakers Bureau provides a wide range of authors for speaking events. To find out more, go to hachettespeakersbureau.com or email HachetteSpeakers@hbgusa.com.

Little, Brown and Company books may be purchased in bulk for business, educational, or promotional use. For information, please contact your local bookseller or the Hachette Book Group Special Markets Department at special.markets@hbgusa.com.

Book interior design by Marie Mundaca

ISBN 9780316381949
Library of Congress Control Number: 2025949512

Printing 2, 2026

LSC-C

Printed in the United States of America

CONTENTS

CONTENTS

For Corrine

THE END

APOCALYPSE HANGS ON the horizon like a never-setting star, irradiating the present with its lurid glow. Some people can hardly look away. For a time, it lit Victoria and Randall Weaver's entire world.

The Weavers had been bracing for the End since at least 1983, when they left Iowa and brought their three young children to a high, forested ridge in North Idaho, overlooking Ruby Creek, the Kootenai River valley, and the rest of God's green, fallen creation.

Now, on a pale, late-August morning in 1992, the great cosmic struggle had finally arrived at the base of their mountain. They knew this day would come and had prepared in every way they could imagine. They had prayed and armed themselves. They had run tactical drills and canned gallons of berries, green beans, and sauerkraut. The root cellar was stocked with cornmeal, potatoes, and peanut powder.

How could they have known that Armageddon would begin with the killing of their yellow Labrador?

———

Summer closes hard in the Idaho panhandle, but that morning was warm and dry, the air astringent with pine. All three of the Weavers' dogs were restless, whimpering and pacing in the rocky yard that lay between the cabin, Vicki's menstrual shed, and the high granite prom- ontory from which the family surveyed the road that switchbacked up from the meadow below. Maybe the dogs had scented a deer. Fresh game would be welcome; the family was down to their last couple jars of preserved venison.

The Weavers owned twenty steep acres near the small logging community of Naples, just south of Bonners Ferry, not far from the Canadian border. Their cabin was a neat plywood rectangle with a porch at each end and a corrugated steel roof. Randy and Vicki had constructed it themselves in the winter of 1984, while eight-year-old Sara babysat little Rachel and Samuel in a rented trailer down the hill. Even though it was built on the cheap by a pair of amateurs, the house was well-framed and snug against the harsh northern winters. A woodstove brought from Iowa kept the upstairs sleeping loft warm. There was a trickling year-round spring a quarter mile downhill, but no plumbing. Their only power came from a generator. On that August morning, two kitchen gardens were in full, late-summer swing.

The place was built according to the bare-bones logic of life in the wilderness with young kids and little money—as well as the convic- tion that the End was coming soon. Randy explained to neighbors that the cabin would not need to last more than a few years. Excluding a bright patch of zinnias blooming by the front door, some Bible verses posted behind plexiglass on the porch, and a laminated sign with the words "New World Order" slashed out within a red circle, only the loca- tion of the home suggested a more romantic, less practical cast of mind.

Instead of building downhill beneath the spring, where the land leveled off and a truckload of lumber or groceries might be driven up to the front door, the cabin was perched on a little knoll at the very crest of the ridge, amid an outcropping of large boulders. This dra- matic layout had come to Vicki Weaver in a vision when the family was still living in Iowa, before they had even glimpsed Idaho or the Selkirk range of the Rocky Mountains. She told Midwestern friends that God had revealed an image of her and Randy living out West on a mountaintop, surrounded by children with biblical names, safe with their guns and supplies, while the world below sank into tribulation. In 1983, before they even started framing the house, Randy pointed up to his land and told a neighbor, "Armageddon is going to end on that hill." They reckoned they had about three years.

Vicki had long felt drawn to the rule-bound, cast-iron faith of the Old Testament. She kept pork out of her kitchen, secluded herself each month while "unclean," and, for a time, scrubbed their home of graven images. In letters to family and friends, she drifted into the antique syntax and *whithersoevers* of the King James Version.

She and Randy had both grown up in the flatlands of central Iowa, among gridded county roads, church potlucks, and slow rivers. Like previous generations of American dissenters, they went West looking for empty space and proximity to the divine. Vicki's visions and a road trip through the Mountain West led them to a place that matched the drama and severity of their faith. In North Idaho, the family became a denomination unto themselves, alone in the wilderness with their awesome God, like a tiny splinter tribe of Israel.

For some, the voice of God rings most clearly in high places. The Weavers' boulder-strewn ridgetop was the type of landscape where you could picture Moses receiving the law, or Abraham guiding Isaac up an escarpment with kindling and a sharp blade. When she first saw it, Vicki immediately knew that this high, craggy place was where Yahweh, as the family addressed their creator, intended them to ride out the calamitous End of Days.

Reporters and federal agents would later call their home a fortress, a compound, a fortress-like compound, or a log cabin. It was none of those things. Perched up on fir pilings, with views all the way to Canada and Montana, the homestead resembled nothing so much as an oversized fire lookout.

The Weavers were certainly on the watch. They monitored their driveway for feds, the county sheriff, a growing list of double-crossing neighbors, and other agents of what Vicki called the "One World Beastly Government." They saw conspiracies everywhere, some petty and local, others world-historical. The groan of a truck downshifting to climb the final, steep stretch up to the cabin invariably sent Randy and the kids running, guns in hand, to the immense granite boulder that overlooked the road.

Since the late 1970s, Randy and Vicki, like many Christian fundamentalists, had also been keeping watch over world events, scanning headlines for proof that a very old story about the end of the world was finally coming true. The evidence for this prophecy, a still-lambent artifact of the late first century, seemed to be piling up. Demonic control of the government, the rise of the Illuminati, the Masons, the Trilateral Commission, the Zionist-occupied government (ZOG): the agents of evil seemed to be gathering in plain sight, readying for the global order that the Bible rather plainly says will command the nations at the end of time.

A lot of people believe these things. The Weavers took them more seriously than most. At the base of their long, rutted driveway, a sign heralded the coming judgment. In vine-like letters, painted neatly on two strips of plywood, it paraphrased the prophet Isaiah, using a Hebrew name for Jesus: "Every Knee Shall Bow To Yahshua Messiah."

As the dogs paced fretfully on that late-August morning, the Weavers breakfasted on eggs and potatoes. Vicki, then forty-three, carried ten-month-old Elisheba, their fourth child, periodically nursing the baby. Based on Vicki's reading of scripture, their Sabbath began Friday at sundown. Since the twenty-first was a Friday, the family planned to spend the following day relaxing. Their routine was familiar and hemmed-in, like a family on lockdown. For almost eighteen months, none of them had left the property or even strayed very far from the cabin. Yet it had, on the whole, been a fairly happy time. At a glance, one might not have guessed the reason for this homebound exile: Randy Weaver was a federal fugitive.

The way his family saw it, Randy had been set up — tricked by an agent of ZOG into selling two illegally modified shotguns. For a decade, Randy and Vicki had been saying that something like this would happen. In 1983, Randy told a reporter that, in the final days, "God will remove his restraining hand from Satan." The authorities will then stir up disorder, root out dissenters, and coax the population into submission to a One World Government.

Even under this looming threat, the Weavers went about their daily business calmly. After finishing their breakfast, the three older kids — Sara, Samuel, and Rachel — did their morning chores and goofed around with the dogs. They took turns in the outhouse, a two-seater with fur-covered seats.

Vicki, the petite matriarch whose faith, zeal, and competence bound the family together, moved around the cabin in a long white nightgown, cradling baby Elisheba.

Randy, a short, wiry man with dark, deep-set eyes and a hand-some, angular face, changed into camo pants and a T-shirt. Taking a break from his morning rounds, he stopped to roll a cigarette from a bright yellow pouch of Top and share it with his friend Kevin Harris. Harris, who was twenty-four, had lived with the family off and on for almost nine years, sometimes staying for months at a time, sometimes just visiting for a few days on his motorcycle. He was a quiet, thoughtful young man who had first run away from home at fourteen. With the Weavers, he had found a sense of family and belonging. When he was up on the ridge, he slept on the porch or in the living room and acted as a helper and sidekick to Randy, working on the house or cutting neat, high-stacked cords of hot-burning tamarack for Vicki's kitchen stove. He was an unofficial big brother to the Weaver kids, who all adored him. That morning, he was planning to do some work on the log cabin he had started building lower down on the property.

Around 10:45 a.m., Sam's big yellow Lab, Striker, began barking anxiously over by the pump house. He was a smart, useful animal. The previous winter Sam had rigged up a sled and harness so Striker could haul water across the snow.

After sniffing the air for a while, the dog heard or scented something worth chasing. "Hey Dad, come out here," Sam shouted. "Striker is really raising Cain." The dog lit off into the woods by the lower garden. As he ran into the trees, his barking grew more intense. Buddy, a small brown border collie who was tied up near his doghouse, started to bark frantically.

As was their routine, Randy, Kevin, and Sam grabbed guns and rushed out to the overlook rock to see who might be coming up the road. Sara, who was sixteen and shared her mother's intense faith, trailed behind. Ten-year-old Rachel came last, toting a rifle on each shoulder. Under the tutelage of their father, the kids had practiced this drill many times. Peering down from the rock, they saw no sign of visitors. Randy later testified that he hoped Striker was onto a deer or an elk.

Samuel took off after his dog, jogging across the dry meadow and down into the woods. He was fourteen but looked ten, with freckles, a slight overbite, and a freshly shaved head. He weighed less than eighty pounds and his voice had not yet dropped. He carried himself seriously. He was Sam, never Sammy, and liked to impress visitors by reciting scripture or facts memorized out of the encyclopedia. His favorite book was *The Last of the Mohicans*. He seldom went outside unarmed. Trotting behind Striker, he wore jeans, a flannel shirt, and a sheepskin vest with antler buttons that his mother had made. He carried a light .223-caliber rifle and wore a holstered .357 pistol. Kevin Harris followed close behind him, with a heavy bolt-action hunting rifle and a .22 pistol on his waist. They followed Striker in single file down a narrow, overgrown trail and cut through a field of ferns.

Randy went downhill, too but took a different route, following an old logging road that curved around the bottom of the property where it would intersect with the trail Sam and Kevin had taken. He carried a shotgun and wore a 9mm pistol on his hip. The girls lingered for a while on the overlook rock before drifting back toward the cabin, where Vicki sat in a chair on the front porch beside stacked boxes of canning jars. She watched Elisheba learning to toddle inside a playpen.

———————

Among the scrubby pines beside the logging road, like one of Vicki's nightmarish visions made real, were three men in full camouflage, their faces hidden behind sheer black balaclavas. Each carried a submachine gun.

Now, with the dog charging straight for them, the men took off running downhill, keeping parallel to the road but staying in the scattered light of the forest. They rushed from tree to tree, sidestepping, running backward, spreading out, leapfrogging past each other. None of them wanted to turn their back on the heavily armed family up the hill. As they retreated, Striker's barking grew louder and more insistent.

The three men, William Degan, Larry Cooper, and Arthur Roderick, were deputy US marshals, all members of the Special Operations Group, or SOG, an elite tactical unit within the US Marshals Service. Along with another three-man team that was elsewhere on the ridge that morning, Degan, Cooper, and Roderick had been hiking around the Weaver tract since before sunrise. They used night vision goggles to check on hidden cameras, swap out batteries, and scout surveillance locations for an upcoming mission: an elaborate and expensive scheme to apprehend Randy Weaver away from his permanently armed children. They were just wrapping up for the day when Striker gave chase.

Following the sound of the dog's barking, Randy came around a bend in the logging road that served as the bottom of the family's driveway, carrying his shotgun in one hand. Confronted with the sight of their fugitive all alone in the road — the precise situation that the marshals had spent more than a year trying to orchestrate — one of the officers stepped out of the trees, hoisted his gun, and yelled, "Freeze, Randy!" Weaver spun on his heel, shouted "Fuck you," and took off uphill. No shots were fired. "I realized immediately," he would write shortly thereafter, "that we had run smack into a ZOG/New World Order ambush." As he raced toward the cabin, he shouted for Sam and Kevin to come home.

A moment later, Striker came trotting down the overgrown game path with Sam and Kevin following close behind. As they emerged into the grassy spot where the trail intersected the logging road — a spot that would come to be known as the Y — Sam and Kevin saw a tall, thin man step out of the pines and briefly move from side to side in front of the leaping dog.

Seeing the man at a distance, Kevin claimed to have mistaken his sheer balaclava for a beard and taken him for a neighbor. Kevin's first instinct was to call off Striker so that the man wouldn't get scared by the dog, who had a tendency to playfully nip at people's hands.

The man in the mask — Deputy Marshal Roderick — was worried that the dog would draw the armed men directly to him and the other two retreating marshals. After a bit more dancing back and forth with the dog, he shot Striker. The big yellow dog yelped and fell dead in the road.

Seeing Striker go down, Sam wheeled on Roderick. In his high, boy's voice, he screamed: "You shot my dog, you sonofabitch!" He fired his rifle into the woods without hitting anyone.

A bit up the ridge, Randy heard Striker's yowl followed by Sam's gunshots. He fired his shotgun twice into the air, hoping to both draw attention from Sam and Kevin and summon them home. He tried to reload, but, in his frenzy, jammed the gun. Unholstering his pistol, he fired a long series of shots into the air while jogging uphill toward the cabin. Between shots, he heard Sam shout, "I'm coming, Dad!"

Later, the Weavers would plausibly insist that they came down the hill the way they did — Sam and Kevin taking an upper path, Randy coming along the road below — because it was the best way to bag a deer, with one person to flush the animal and another to block its likely escape route. "Bird-dogging," Kevin called it. But to the marshals, who had watched hours of footage of the Weavers running drills with their weapons, it felt like a tactically sophisticated assault.

Returning fire, one of the marshals, most likely Larry Cooper, shot Sam. One bullet shattered the wooden stock of his rifle and almost severed his skinny arm. As Sam spun to run uphill toward his family, a second bullet caught him square in the back. The boy fell forward into the loose dirt.

Seeing Sam go down, Kevin Harris hoisted his heavy thirty-aught-six hunting rifle and fired once into the trees, aiming for a spot where he could make out little puffs of smoke and the flash of spent casings. He hit William Degan in the center of the chest and heard him shout, "I'm hit. I'm hit."

Cooper fired on Kevin, letting off two three-shot bursts. Kevin dropped into the thick brush without being hit. It was only then, he later claimed, that the masked men finally identified themselves as US marshals. Kevin scrambled to his feet and sprinted up the road for the cabin, stopping briefly to grope at Sam's neck for a pulse. There was none.

———

Quiet descended. It had all happened in less than a minute. Cooper hurried over to Bill Degan, who was lying on his side behind a stump, his mouth full of blood. Ripping off layers of tactical gear, Cooper searched for a place to apply pressure. The entry wound on

Degan's chest was small and clean, but his back was a wet mess. Over his radio, Roderick called for help. The other three-man team on the ridge, which included their medic, raced toward the logging road, their shoulders braced for incoming fire.

Up the hill, Randy had joined Vicki and the girls on the over-look rock. They listened anxiously to the chaotic, echoing sounds of several different guns—the sharp report of Sam's light rifle, the low boom of Kevin's 30.06, the muted clanking bursts of the marshals' suppressed submachine guns.

Vicki and the girls began desperately shouting for Sam and Kevin to hurry home. Randy set down his jammed shotgun, took Sara's semi-automatic Ruger from her and emptied the entire magazine into the sky. At last, Kevin came running up the hill, winded and missing his hat. Everyone frantically asked about Sam. "Sam is dead," was all he could manage.

The Weavers exploded into grief and anger, sobbing and firing their guns into the air. "We went berserk," Randy later said. Vicki wailed "Yahweh! Yahweh!" over and over.

With the stutter of more and more gunshots echoing off the rocky gullies, the five marshals now huddling around Degan's dead body took cover behind nearby boulders, believing that they were under assault from above. They later testified that they were truly being shot at, with the trees and dirt around them popping with incoming fire. In the immediate aftermath of the confrontation, both the Weavers and the marshals used the word *ambush* to describe what they had experienced.

Up at the cabin, Sara changed out of her shorts, putting on camo pants and reloading the gun that her father had emptied. Vicki pulled on jeans. It had been about half an hour since the initial shots were fired. She and Randy walked down the road to collect their son's body, half expecting to be shot themselves. Kevin had told them that he was pretty certain he had hit one of the masked men.

For a few minutes Randy and Vicki sat on the ground beside

Sam, kissing their boy and screaming curses into the woods. Eventually, Vicki picked up the shattered rifle and Randy scooped Sam's light body out of the dirt and carried him up the road. Kevin came to help Randy up the final stretch. Sara spread a blanket over a mattress in Vicki's shed and they stripped off Sam's bloody clothes. They inspected his wounds, cleaned his body, and covered him with a sheet. When they were done, they returned to the overlook rock with their guns.

In the afternoon the weather turned gray. A cold, late-summer rain began to fall. The family left the rock, bringing food from the root cellar and gallons of water into the cabin, preparing for the attack that they felt certain was coming soon.

From near the bottom of the ridge, in a flat grassy expanse known locally (for reasons long forgotten) as Homicide Meadow, they could hear the sound of car doors slamming and the idle of big diesels. Drawing the denim curtains that Vicki had sewn herself, they gathered blankets in the middle of the room and hunkered down together, away from the windows. After a while, Vicki took Elisheba in her arms, collected her Bible, and went up to the sleeping loft. In her diary she recorded the death of her son. Sam and Striker were shot, she wrote, by "servants of the New World Order."

As it became dark, they heard the faint keen of sirens rising up from the highway that traced the valley floor. "Sirens from everywhere," Randy said, "sirens, sirens, all around below down the valley."

AMERICAN APOCALYPSE

"Watching, waiting, and working for the millennium... has become, even more than baseball, America's pastime."

— *Leonard Sweet*

IN A LARGE-SCALE telephone survey conducted in 2021, nearly three decades after the bloodshed at Ruby Ridge, 15 percent of Americans told researchers that the media, Wall Street, and the United States government had fallen under the control of a Satan-worshipping cabal of pedophiles. Among self-identified Republicans and white Evangelicals, the portion that believe in this cabal rose to a full quarter. An even larger share anticipated that a violent "storm" would be coming to wash away the corrupt elites. Today, the number of Americans who profess faith in the core QAnon cosmology — more than thirty million as of 2021 — is about equal to the number of white evangelical Protestants.

The prevalence of this dark worldview can seem wholly contemporary, a product of the message-board fever swamps in our age of frenzied unreality. Yet a separate query in the same survey from

2021 carbon-dates this intellectual artifact with surprising precision, revealing a much older lineage. A tenth of all Americans, and half of those who believe in the satanic cabal, claimed that the COVID-19 vaccines contain tiny microchips that are intended to serve as the "Mark of the Beast" — the identifying brand that will be forced upon humanity just before the end of history according to the Book of Revelation, a phantasmagoric vision recorded in the first century that serves as the final book of the New Testament: "And he causeth all... to receive a mark in their right hand, or in their foreheads: And no man might buy or sell, save he that had the mark, or the name of the Beast, or the number of his name... for it is the number of a man; and his number is Six hundred threescore and six."

For two thousand years, the scenario sketched in Revelation has captured imaginations and focused passions, offering a terrible, thrilling story on which to graft the anxieties and fears of the day. The narrative that modern readers have wrung from Revelation's bewildering parade of images — a many-horned dragon, a blood-drinking harlot — is basically a political story: an account of creeping globalism, scheming elites, violent comeuppance, and a final, cleansing worldwide war.

A specific version of this tale has long circulated through the American body politic. From the Fundamentalist awakening of the early 1900s, to the John Birch Society of the '60s, to the Christian survivalism of the '70s and '80s, to the militia boom of the '90s, to the more recent rise of QAnon and its far-reaching successors in the Trump era, endtimes prophecy and the conspiratorial vigilance that it generates have pressed upon American life, and not just at the fringes. In 2010, a Pew survey reported that 41 percent of all Americans expected Christ's eventual return. Among self-declared Christians, 47 percent claimed that the Second Coming will "probably" or "definitely" happen by the year 2050. When the field was narrowed to white Evangelicals, that proportion climbed to 58 percent.

Regardless of whether or not the United States was ever, as some insist, a "Christian nation," Protestant Christianity has undoubtedly

been the dominant cultural influence on America's founding and subsequent history. Any substantial change in the vast churn of popular
religion will exert pressure on the wider culture and politics of the
republic. The rise of apocalyptic faith that took place over the course
of the twentieth century is more than some esoteric matter of doctrine. It represents a complete inversion of how a large and highly
activated portion of the citizenry thinks about history, the future, and
the basic purposes of human endeavor.

If the promise of everlasting life is, in Marx's famous formulation,
"the opium of the people," then the Apocalypse is their amphetamine,
with all the manic clutter that the word implies. Into the relentless,
story-generating combine that is the human mind, endtimes prophecy feeds heroes, villains, urgency, plot, and a sense of an ending.
It provides a feeling of direction that alleviates the impression —
uncomfortable for all, unbearable for some — that things aren't really
going anywhere. The true believer has the passion of a dozen ordinary
citizens and regards all opponents, no matter how benign, as agents
of evil. Bumper stickers proclaim the bummer tidings: "The Storm is
here," "The only way out is up," "It's later than you think."

While politics and faith inform each other in ways that are
impossible to untangle, belief in the endtimes narrative laid down in
Revelation practically demands a worldview defined by conspiratorialism and a permanent filibuster against consensus reality. Refracted
through the lens of doomsday prophecy, every news item is evidence
of a cosmic war raging behind the scenes — a literal, zero-sum battle
between good and evil. It is a belief system that dramatizes and sanc-
tifies the commonplace impression that things are getting worse.

Apocalyptic faith cannot, on its own, explain the ongoing crackup of
American civic life, but it is nevertheless a potent and habitually overlooked ingredient in the blend of forces — material, demographic,
cultural, spiritual — that have delivered us to our baffling present.

Along with the immense number of American citizens with explicit ideas about the identity of the Antichrist, the role of Israel in the Second Coming, or the significance of the number 666, there are many more with a vague yet deeply internalized apocalyptic sensibility: a belief that conspiracy is the true engine of history, that a cosmic struggle between light and dark is playing out just beneath the surface of things, and that civilization is rushing toward some final cataclysm. For more than a century, this very outlook—the same apocalyptic faith that sent the Weavers up their ridge and into a senseless stand-off with the federal government—has coursed through American life like an underground river, occasionally welling to the surface to perplex those of us who cannot hear the thrumming beneath our feet.

The word *apocalyptic* often serves as a catchall for the overheated, antidemocratic style and conspiratorial fixations of the American right. Ironically, that handy metaphor obscures the extent to which those attitudes and that style have their roots in literal beliefs about the capital-a Apocalypse. While this troubling, unwieldy presence in our national life goes by many names—"the paranoid style," "the slow civil war," "the indigenous American berserk"—its roots are not as hazy or inexplicable as we often imagine. Like any other intellectual tradition, it has its own pantheon of thinkers, organizers, and heroes—little-remembered men (almost invariably they are men) like John Nelson Darby, Cyrus Scofield, Hal Lindsey, John Todd, William Potter Gale, Gordon Kahl, and Robert Jay Mathews. It is a lineage that can be traced all the way back to patient zero himself: the first-century Jesus follower known as John, who recorded the vision that became the Book of Revelation on the Aegean island of Patmos.

Before Waco, Oklahoma City, the militias, the Bundys, the Three Percenters, Charlottesville, Q, the Plandemic, the Steal, January 6, or Jeffrey Epstein, there was the place that we call Ruby Ridge. The Weaver tract was actually on Caribou Ridge, but it was within the Ruby Creek drainage and "Ruby Ridge," the accidental coinage of one reporter, sounded better. With its storybook glint of something red and faceted, the name stuck. Like Lexington Green, Valley Forge, Harpers Ferry, the Alamo, Mountain Meadows, Watts, or Kent State, the name of the place came to stand for a brief spasm of violence, which in turn came to stand for something about who we are as a people. With Ruby Ridge, as with those other cases, the haze of contingency, accident, and context gradually burned off, leaving only a morality play in its place: the actors performing Innocence and Valor over on one side, those playing Tyranny and Infamy on the other.

———

On the afternoon of August 21, 1992, as news of William Degan's death arrived in Washington, DC, the collective attention and energies of American law enforcement turned, like a vast bureaucratic murmuration, toward the woods of North Idaho. Control of the Weaver case, which had already passed from the Bureau of Alcohol, Tobacco, and Firearms (ATF) to the US Marshals, now moved to the FBI, which called up the Hostage Rescue Team, its most elite and well-armed tactical unit. They mobilized under the false impression that they were heading into an active gun battle with religious zealots intent on the murder of federal agents.

As the Weavers drew their curtains and prepared for ZOG to kill them off, trucks began rolling into Homicide Meadow. The FBI, with support from the Marshals Service, the Idaho State Police, the local sheriff, and the ATF dug in, as if for war. Within a few days there were three hundred people in jungle camo hustling around amid olive-drab mess tents and mobile command centers. On both sides of the siege, the militarization of American civilian life that began in the wake of Vietnam — the hardware, the clothes, the tactics, the language — was on full display.

A bit further down the road, a large encampment of protestors materialized, separated from the makeshift federal base by a cordon of yellow tape and a thin rank of policemen. As word of the siege spread, people poured into Naples to take a stand against the New

World Order. It was a gathering of the tribes for the anti-government right — fundamentalist preachers, gun rights activists, white separatists, skinheads, old guard neo-Nazis, anti-tax protestors, and conspiracists of every variety. As the siege ground on and the news filtering down from the mountaintop got worse, plenty of less politically activated citizens came, too, all of them enraged by this outlandish display of federal muscle.

The siege (or "standoff," depending on the angle of one's sympathies) became a media circus of the sort that is now commonplace: a slow-motion tragedy broadcast in real time. The year 1992 was early days for cable news. Live on-site transmission was still a novelty. It had been a year and a half since the vicious beating of Rodney King by members of the Los Angeles police had become national news because a curious plumber stepped onto his balcony with a new Sony Handycam. Two years after Ruby Ridge, one hundred million Americans watched live as O. J. Simpson's white Bronco cruised slowly down an empty freeway.

———

The facts of the Ruby Ridge affair, when maximally compressed, make no sense. An unemployed man, living in the wilderness to separate his family from civilization, commits a petty crime, into which he was possibly entrapped. In response, the full force and fury of the world's most powerful government — snipers, helicopters, commando teams, rooms full of lawyers, a shotgun-wielding robot — comes down upon his family, costing three lives, millions of tax dollars, and the good faith of countless citizens. Randy Weaver's trifling offense and the government's overwhelming response are perversely asymmetrical. What else can this be but a tyranny rendered brutal and vindictive by unchecked power?

Except that is not how it happened. Right up until the brief span of seconds in which William Degan and Samuel Weaver were both killed, the glacial pace and scale of the effort to get the fugitive Randall

Weaver before a judge attests to a government so scrupulously devoted to its own codes that it would spend immense sums and countless man-hours to avoid even the possibility of gunplay, while upholding the basic notion that if you're indicted for a crime you need to come to court, regardless of how tightly you clutch your rifle. Willfully unenforced laws revert to what they were all along: a bunch of nifty ideas that somebody set to paper. If the statute in question is about enforcement itself (i.e., once charged, you come to court), the reversion from law to mere words is as abrupt as the breaking of a spell—carriages zapped into pumpkins.

The exhaustive official postmortem of Ruby Ridge—a sprawling federal trial, a huge DOJ investigation into what went wrong, weeks of Senate hearings, internal reports by every agency involved, reports about those reports—proceeded from the premise that it does not really matter what the Weavers believed. Official after official intoned some version of "we don't punish citizens for their beliefs," before hurrying to the inevitable coda: "no matter how reprehensible." The government's analysis rightly focused on its own errors. History, however, is not a criminal trial. What the Weavers read, and believed, and said were at the very heart of what happened at Ruby Ridge, and what continues, at an accelerating clip, to go wrong between American citizens and their government.

Today, the ten-day siege occupies that ambiguous borderland dividing history from news. For many, Ruby Ridge is a vaguely recalled headline, something from the lost but familiar world of Ross Perot, the LA riots, and A Current Affair. The news footage has the magnetic haze of old videotape, but the haircuts, the guns, and the politics could be ours. In actuality, the late summer of 1992—before the Internet, cell phones, and 9/11; a decade closer to the fall of Saigon than the fall of Kabul—truly is a foreign land. It was 1992 when Francis Fukuyama smiled upon American victory in the Cold War and, like a more thoughtful Vicki Weaver, glimpsed something like an approaching "End of History." History rolled on in some surprising directions, but it seems to keep looping back, bolstering the grandiosity of Fukuyama's infamous title in ways he might not precisely have intended.

Coming at the end of the Cold War, as the millennium coasted irritably to its finish, Ruby Ridge (briskly concatenated by Waco and the bombing in Oklahoma City) seemed, at the time, like a tragic valediction. A new age of prosperity and peace — *boredom* even — was settling upon the United States. With its arcane Fundamentalism and its trappings of Vietnam and Nazism, the mess in North Idaho looked like one last gasp of the blood- and ideology-sodden twentieth century. As it turned out, the forgetful, becalmed End of History was a mere interlude. Three decades on, Ruby Ridge looks more like the start of something than its finale.

PART I
LEVEL GROUND

Behold, I come as a thief. Blessed is he that watcheth...

— *Revelation 16:15, KJV*

CHAPTER ONE

HOME PLACE

COMPARED TO THE uplands of North Idaho, the green, mellow expanse of the American Middle West seems an unlikely place for premonitions of apocalypse to creep into the human heart. In Iowa in the 1970s, there was no great pestilence upon the land; no tyranny hounded the faithful; and the blood-dimmed tide had not been loosed upon the plain.

Around the edge of Cedar Falls, the college and ag town where Randy and Vicki Weaver settled after their marriage in 1971, the prairie was held at bay by strip malls, leafy redbrick neighborhoods, and a patchwork of soy, corn, and pasture. Grain prices were up. Credit was loose. And the John Deere plant across the river in Waterloo was cranking out grass-green combines as fast as farmers could sign loan papers.

There was, as always, the usual cycle of local botheration and calamity — tornados and cancers, frozen crops, depressions, sudden reversals of fortune — but nothing to herald the Final Things. In the broad sweep of history, it was a remarkably placid time, especially out there on the fruited plain, snug in the grassy center of a still-ascendant American empire.

All the same, restless minds furnish their own evidence. Visions of judgment and cabal spring just as often from everyday disenchantment as from earthquakes and persecutions. Something in the drift of the times had a large portion of Americans unnerved by dark expectations. For many of them, including the Weavers, an ancient story was close at hand to give shape to that dread.

Long before Randy and Vicki felt called to separate from the world, they were energetic farm kids from pious, deeply rooted Iowa families. Like many American Protestants of their generation, they grew up within a rich ecology of millenarian traditions. They came together, fell in love, and forged their shared faith in the late 1960s and early '70s, swept along by a national wave of prophetic faith and the roiling conspiracism that inevitably follows in its wake.

Their consuming beliefs about the New World Order, Babylon, the Beast, ZOG, and the approaching End did not arrive in any single epiphany. There would be no Damascene strobe or rending of the veil. The young seekers were borne along gradually, book by book, tract by tract, cassette by cassette. Delving into a well-established intellectual tradition — a set of ideas, thinkers, and texts with roots in the theological debates of the middle nineteenth century and earlier — the Weavers gradually became part of a subculture that has long thrived within American civic and religious life.

———

Victoria Jean Jordison was born on the family farm in Coalville, a tiny settlement outside of Fort Dodge, in North Central Iowa. Her great-grandfather Samuel had immigrated from Northern England to dig coal from outcroppings along the banks of the Des Moines River. The railroads were just then stitching the continent together, creating new demand for fuel as well as the means of carting it off. When the easy pickings had been hauled away, the black seams were chased underground, with narrow shafts sunk into the prairie. Colliers like Samuel Jordison mined the coal for 90 cents a ton.

In 1878, thirteen Coalville miners and their families gathered to establish a small branch of the Reorganized Church of Latter-day Saints, an offshoot of the larger Mormon Church that was blooming in the West. Samuel was one of the congregation's first presidents.

Early Mormonism's embrace of personal revelation made for a volatile and fractious religious movement. In the years since 1844, when "prophet, seer, and revelator" Joseph Smith was murdered by an Illinois mob, sixty-five separate Smith-based denominations have been established. The Coalville miners belonged to the largest of several early breakaway sects. It had been founded by a group of Saints, including Smith's widow Emma, who declined to follow Brigham Young to the valley of the Great Salt Lake. The Reorganized Church remained in the Midwest, rejecting both Young's leadership and the controversial doctrine of plural marriage. In 1860, these dissenters organized themselves under the prophetic authority of Joseph Smith III, who had been eleven when his father was shot.

In 1900, with Samuel Jordison in the lead, the Coalville miners built a white clapboard church beside a large shade tree. They also established a branch of "Zion's Religio-Literary Society," a reading group devoted to studying scripture and prophecy. In a report to church authorities, they celebrated the presence of various spiritual "gifts" within their community, including angelic prophecies delivered in unknown tongues. Each year, the Coalville Saints tithed a portion of their meager wages to RLDS headquarters in Independence, Missouri, helping fund the construction of a massive upward-spiraling temple.

By the time the coal beds tapped out in the early twentieth century, the Jordisons were earning their living up on the face of the land. They raised hogs, cattle, corn, and soy on a hundred and sixty fertile, windswept acres. The white farmhouse Samuel built and bequeathed to his descendants was far enough from the town of Fort Dodge that it did not get hooked up to power lines until 1949, the year that Samuel's grandson David and his wife Jeane had their first child, Victoria.

Two more children, Julie and Lanny, followed. The Jordisons were a close-knit, hard-working family. They often gathered for large mid-day meals cooked by Jeane and her two daughters. For fun, they took long road trips to the mountains, camping and fishing along the way.

As a teen, Vicki was small, with a wide, rabbity smile that showed all her upper teeth. She had dark eyes and a neat helmet of curled black hair. Within a family of hard workers, she was the fastidious perfectionist. She was strong-willed but distinctly, proudly feminine, the sort of girl who was always eager to help in the kitchen and never got into any trouble. Her younger sister Julie, who deeply admired her, described Vicki as "prissy." On the farm, she had a special knack for indoor chores. She could sew, cook, preserve, or mend anything.

At Fort Dodge Senior High in 1967, only the faintest hints of the new youth culture could be detected. A few boys wore paisley shirts, but not one of them had hair that grazed his ears. In the fall, the junior lettermen were hazed during Twerp Week. The girls learned to cook spaghetti in home ec. Even within this context, Vicki Weaver was notably straitlaced. With her homemade clothes and small cross necklace, she looked, as certain teens do, both too young and too old for her age. She received straight A's, did 4H, and was elected vice president of the Future Business Leaders of America, helping oversee that year's big project: printing a telephone directory of the whole high school. She was particularly close with her father, David, who took great pride in her skills with a sewing machine.

If the piney scarps of North Idaho are a landscape fit for the Hebrew patriarchs, then the rolling expanse of Iowa — among the greenest, most fertile places on the globe — is very much New Testament country. With its intimate farming communities organized around low-slung churches with carpeted sanctuaries, it was a place where religion meant consolation and stability, not fear and trembling. Jeane Jordison, who chaperoned her daughters' 4H group, was a Congregationalist, but David remained committed to the church of his grandfather and a hereditary line of prophets descended from Joseph and Emma Smith. (Until 1996, the RLDS was led by someone with the last name Smith.) It was this faith that held sway in the old white farmhouse. On Sundays, while Jeane stayed home cooking, Vicki and her younger siblings joined their father for RLDS worship. Afterward, David went to Bible study and the kids did RLDS Sunday school.

Cut off from the expanding Mormon Church in Utah, the Reorganized Latter-day Saints kept faith in the Book of Mormon and Joseph Smith's vision that his Saints represent a chosen people with their own holy covenant, an American Israel with a special role in the coming Kingdom of God on Earth. By the time Vicki was a teen, the RLDS liturgy had begun to drift toward something like the evangelical mainstream, but the church continued to teach a doctrine of unmediated revelation between believers and their God. While the LDS church in Salt Lake City is led by anointed prophets who routinely announce divine revelations, it discourages lay members from seeking prophetic messages beyond those relevant to their personal lives. The RLDS church, which renamed itself the Community of Christ in 2001, took a less hierarchical approach to revelation, calling its entire body of believers "a prophetic people."

With the sanction and encouragement of his church, David Jordison liked to settle into his favorite chair on Sunday afternoons to puzzle over current affairs in light of prophecy, flipping through dog-eared copies of the Bible and the Book of Mormon. Long before Vicki began to have visions of the coming End, she had a casual domestic intimacy with the thrilling notion that the ancient past and the cataclysmic future press upon the present from either end.

In her senior year of high school, Vicki met a wiry, gregarious college freshman named Randall Claude Weaver. At the time, everyone called him Pete. When he was a boy, Randy's family lived fifteen miles outside the small farming community of Villisca, Iowa, best known as the site of a grisly 1912 massacre. (Six adults and two children were murdered with an ax. The killer was never identified.) His parents, Clarence and Wilma, were native Iowans, both descended from Germans who came west to farm the prairie. Clarence and Wilma met at a Church League dinner, married in 1937, and had three daughters — Marnis, Roberta, and Colleen — before Randy came along in 1948.

The Weaver household was strict, tidy, and pious. Wilma ran the home, babysat neighbor children, and candled eggs. Clarence, who sold Chevrolets, was deeply patriotic, but leery of a federal government that had allowed his parents to lose their farm during the Depression years. Unlike Vicki, Randy grew up in rented houses. He played Little League baseball and took genuine pleasure pledging allegiance to the flag each morning at school. By the time he was seven, Randy was raising hens and selling eggs. On Saturday mornings, he listened to the *Lone Ranger* on the radio. At ten, he received his first BB gun. A series of rifles and shotguns followed. His delight in firearms never faded, gradually becoming central to his identity and politics, with guns becoming synonymous in his mind with both freedom and safety.

In 1959, when Randy was eleven, Clarence took a job selling feed and fertilizer for the Walnut Grove Company and moved the family to a gabled, two-story house in Jefferson, a slightly larger town than Villisca, with elm-lined streets, lots of churches, and no bars. Randy wasn't much of a student, but he was an easygoing, confident kid. He delivered the *Des Moines Register* and obsessed over cars. Despite his small frame, he was a good ballplayer. In winter, he played pickup hockey on a flooded parking lot. Midway through the 1992 siege that would make him famous, an AP reporter canvassed Randy's old classmates. They were baffled by the turn his life had taken. "He was so easy to talk to and fun to be with," recalled one old friend. "Everyone liked him real well." "He was fun-loving," said another classmate. "Wherever there was fun, he was part of it."

Wilma and Clarence were Presbyterians, more or less, but over the years of Randy's childhood, they attended a variety of conservative evangelical churches — Presbyterian, Baptist, United Brethren, and others — seeking a communion that matched their own zealous calling. It was a common pattern for American fundamentalists, for whom the ardor of a good preacher might trump generational and denominational ties to the local parish. Even in a place where almost everyone took church seriously, the Weavers were known as an especially religious family. In Clarence Weaver's household, strong faith was a matter of filial obligation. "[Randy] always believed in God, always did right by Him," his father said. "We didn't stand for anything less." Warmed by his father's pride, Randy took church more seriously than school. In 1958, when he was ten, he stood up one Sunday morning to declare that he had been reborn in Christ. Clarence wept.

As in the Jordison home, certain notions about the Apocalypse were part of the intellectual furniture of Randy's childhood — central to the teachings of every church in which Wilma and Clarence prayed. In these churches and the Presbyterian youth group which Randy attended through high school, he would have learned the core Christian doctrine that God oversees the long pageant of history and will someday bring it to a close. The very notion that history *has* a purpose or that it will reach some sort of conclusion — be it utopian, cataclysmic, or both in succession — may be one of Christianity's defining contributions to Western thought. The question of when and how the world will end preoccupied the very first believers.

In the Book of Matthew, the opening text of the New Testament, written in Greek sometime in the late first century, Jesus's followers press him on the matter. "What shall be the sign of thy coming, and of the end of the world?" Standing in an olive grove across from the Jerusalem Temple, Jesus gives a fairly straightforward response, listing specific portents they should watch for: earthquakes, the persecution of the faithful, stars falling from heaven, the rise of false prophets.

With his answer, Jesus (or at least the author of the Gospel) endorsed a series of millenarian prophecies recorded in the Old Testament Book of Daniel, thereby blending the new doctrine with a long-established Jewish tradition about the end of history.

Near the end of Jesus's answer about the signs of the end, he made an exciting promise. "When ye shall see all these things, know that it is near, *even* at the doors. Verily I say unto you, This generation shall not pass, till all these things be fulfilled." In other words, at least some of the people gathered around him in the olive grove would live to see the final defeat of evil and the triumphant establishment of God's Kingdom on Earth. With that prophecy stubbornly unfulfilled — at least in any literal way — competing notions about the End have come and gone over the intervening two thousand years.

Around the same time that Vicki's great-grandfather emigrated from the north of England to dig prairie coal and pray his latter-day gospel, a new set of ideas about the End arrived in the United States from Great Britain. Over the course of the early twentieth century, those ideas would sweep through American churches, dividing congregations, spinning off new denominations, and transforming American religious life.

————

In 1966, Randy graduated high school. Along with a friend from Jefferson, he enrolled at Iowa Central Community College, commuting forty-five minutes each way to Fort Dodge. To cover expenses, he loaded flats of soda onto a truck. Off hours, he drank Schlitz and crawled the main street in a red Mustang. When the academic year started, he took a job driving a bus for the Fort Dodge school district. It was there that Vicki first noticed him.

When she graduated high school the following year, she also enrolled at Iowa Central. During a party at a local ballroom, she was dancing with a boy named Nick when Randy brashly cut in. A quarter century later, lying on an FBI cot with his arm swollen from a gunshot wound and his family shattered, Randy recalled the exact moment they had met. Vicki had looked so "pretty," he told the gaggle of police and medics hovering over him. "Jesus Christ, the first time I saw her, if I ever thought this was gonna happen, I'd have never broke in on a friend of mine dancing with her. I'd have let Nick have her."

Randy and Vicki were soon dating. They were a well-matched set, a pair of good-looking, strong-willed, conservative kids. Like Vicki, Randy was short and compact—five foot eight, 140 pounds. He had blue eyes and a wry, joshing way about him. Despite his farm boy manners, he regarded the world through a squint that gave him a slight air of rebellion. Plus, he had that Mustang. When his job driving the school bus ended in June, he went to work on a road crew.

When school started up again, Randy Weaver was gone. In the fall of 1968, he dropped out of Iowa Central and enlisted in the army. He was twenty. The war in Vietnam was near its peak. It had been nine months since the Tet Offensive, when news footage of street fighting in Hue and Saigon shocked many Americans out of their illusions about the war's progress.

Nobody was burning their draft card in Fort Dodge, but Randy stood out for his eagerness to fight global communism in the rice paddies of Indochina. Brimming with the Bible-soaked patriotism of his boyhood, he jumped at the chance to get out of Iowa, join the fight, and make something of himself.

Basic training—the buzzcut and vaccinations, the jogging and pushups, the endless rifle cleaning—suited Randy just fine. He was used to long days of outdoor work and he didn't mind taking orders. At Fort Leonard Wood, in the Missouri Ozarks, he trained as a combat engineer, learning to build fortifications, operate heavy equipment, and deal with explosives. A childhood spent hunting small game and a natural delight in firearms earned him marksmanship awards on the .45-caliber pistol and the M14 and M16 rifles.

Randy was athletic, competitive, and handy with big vehicles, all of which made him good at being in the army. After basic training, he went on to Advanced Infantry Training. He earned his parachut-ist badge and qualified for the special forces, commonly known as the Green Berets. (His discharge papers, a document known as a DD-214, indicates that his "occupational specialty" was "Combat Engineer" and that his last assignment was to the 7th Special Forces Group.)

As the death toll mounted in Vietnam, support for the war cra-tered. While the quagmire spread in every direction, President John-son and General Westmoreland claimed that victory was in sight. May of 1968, while Randy was still in training, was the deadliest month of the war for US forces. Westmoreland responded by requesting another 200,000 troops for deployment.

Despite the army's insatiable need for men and Randy's eager-ness to join the fray, he was never deployed. With mobilization hap-pening on such a large scale, qualified soldiers were needed to serve stateside. Randy was promoted to sergeant and received a National Defense Service medal, but remained in the United States working as an engineer.

On leave in 1970, Randy hurried back to Iowa to find serious, dark-eyed Vicki Jordison. She had graduated from her two-year degree program and gone to work as a secretary at Sears.

Randy showed up in Fort Dodge looking fit and sharp in his crisp uniform and buzzcut. He and Vicki went out most nights during his leave. When he returned to base, she promised to visit. Soon, she made the trip to North Carolina and came home with an engagement ring. By then, troop drawdowns had begun.

Randy was honorably discharged in October of 1971, having never seen combat. Over the course of three frustrating years, he came to regard the army as a mess of mismanagement and corrup-tion. Like many Americans, he blamed a squeamish public and a feck-less bureaucracy for the disaster in Vietnam. Before long, he would change his mind about the virtues of the entire enterprise and the nature of American power itself.

As Randy's gung-ho patriotism curdled into something darker, popular notions about the Green Berets also grew more ambivalent. The public image of the army's most elite fighters had once been exemplified by John Wayne's campy 1968 blockbuster *The Green Berets* (produced in conjunction with the Johnson administration) and Barry Sadler's chart-topping 1966 hit "The Ballad of the Green Berets" ("Trained to live off nature's land / Trained in combat, hand-to-hand / Men who fight by night and day / Courage take from the Green Berets"). In the wake of Vietnam, Wayne's beefy commandos were replaced on the silver screen by the likes of Colonel Kurtz and Captain Rambo: fictional Green Berets who had been driven off the rails by the corruption of their government and its dissipated, inscrutable aims.

This shift in public perception would prove consequential to the fate of Randy Weaver and his family. Although he never actually saw combat, his status as a Green Beret would be mentioned at the top of practically every media dispatch from Ruby Ridge. When the US Marshals commissioned a threat assessment of the Weavers, it focused on Randy's elite training, suggesting, without any evidence, that he, like the fictional John Rambo, might have booby-trapped his land. For Randy's supporters, his special forces pedigree added considerably to his mystique. To this day, Weaver is regularly identified as "a Green Beret from Vietnam."

A month after Randy's discharge, he and Vicki were married at the First Congregationalist Church of Fort Dodge. She was twenty-two. He was twenty-three. To satisfy all parties, the ceremony was co-officiated by a Congregationalist and an RLDS minister. Randy wore a pink ruffled shirt and a tuxedo with a white carnation in the buttonhole. His buzzcut had gone shaggy and he had managed to grow a mustache and sideburns. Vicki wore a great quantity of white lace. The short, churchy hairdo she had worn through high school had given way to abundant dark curls.

The newlyweds moved into a small apartment in Cedar Falls, two hours east of Fort Dodge. Given Randy's success in the army, law enforcement seemed like a natural next step. He wanted to try for a job at the FBI which, in the early '70s, was still closely associated with J. Edgar Hoover's zealous anti-communism and opposition to the civil rights movement. Randy applied for G.I. Bill benefits and enrolled in the criminal justice program at Northern Iowa University. Vicki took another job as a secretary, but her main ambition was to start a family as soon as possible.

Not long after their wedding and the move to Cedar Falls, Randy and Vicki were swept up by an exciting opportunity to transform their lives. Amway was the first American company devoted to what is now called network marketing. The premise is that "distributors" pay the company for the privilege to sell its products. Theoretically, they make money by recruiting friends and family to do the same, thereby creating a financial pyramid upon which fresh cash is conveyed perpetually upward. The actual products — soap, cleaning supplies, and other household necessities in those early years — are mostly beside the point, just Amway-branded versions of goods available elsewhere, often for less money. Amway's real product is a potent rhetoric of success, Americanism, faith, and community. The pitch is that hard-working distributors can make it rich and "get free," without having to work for someone else. Since it takes a bit of spare cash to buy in, Amway — the name is an elision of "American Way" — is not for the truly hard up. It is pitched to people who might make a decent living some other way but remain afflicted by a persistent sense of unfulfilled potential. The company's lingo of self-empowered entrepreneurship and its promise of fast, lavish fortunes rests on the notion that every American is, in Steinbeck's famous phrase, just a "temporarily embarrassed millionaire."

Eager to kickstart their lives and easily carried away by big plans and an exciting story, Randy and Vicki were ideal candidates. They went all in. Just a few years before they started testing the patience of their loved ones with harangues about the Illuminati and the Book of Revelation, they preached the gospel of soap and self-reliance with breathless zeal. The culture and language of Amway owes a great deal to the world of evangelical revivalism. Success depends entirely on effective proselytizing. Ascending the "pin-levels" from Silver, to Emerald, to Diamond, to Triple Diamond, to Platinum, means vending to your "downline" the same hope (some would say credulity) that lured you in the first place. Richard DeVos, who cofounded the company in 1959 before helping to bankroll the ascent of the modern Christian Right, said that Amway is built on the four "fundamentals" of freedom, family, hope, and reward. To succeed, he exhorted distributors, "you've got to believe." Being good at that sort of belief means having an unusually strong capacity to resolve cognitive dissonance. It also means being willing to tune out, or even draw strength from, the skeptics and scoffers in your life.

Given that the company depends on the generation of faith among its customers and its more-than-passing resemblance to a church (some apostates say "cult"), Amway, and the swarm of multilevel marketing schemes that copied its model after the Federal Trade Commission tried and failed to outlaw its business practices, have proved especially popular among Evangelicals and Mormons. Connections are often made at church, and Amway's circuit of motivational speakers includes notable evangelical preachers. The distributor's pitch, delivered over cheese and crackers in the living room, is often buttressed with abundant quotations from scripture.

The fundamentalist leanings of many Amway sellers were revealed when Proctor and Gamble, the company's biggest rival in the soap trade, took Amway to court because its distributors were telling customers that P&G was officially tied to the Church of Satan. In what appeared to be a coordinated campaign, Amway distributors claimed that the president of Proctor and Gamble had gone on the Phil Donahue Show and openly admitted his Satanism. (He had not.) Amway sellers also spread a theory that P&G's trademark—a crescent moon and thirteen stars — was filled with hidden satanic symbols, including the 666 mentioned in Revelation. In a memorable legal filing, P&G was obliged to assert that "Procter & Gamble has never supported Satan, the Church of Satan, or any similar religion or entity in any manner whatsoever." Eventually P&G just changed their logo.

Back in Coalville for their first Jordison family Thanksgiving as a married couple, Randy set up a film projector in the living room and subjected the whole clan to a two-hour presentation about the tremendous opportunities awaiting them. Randy and Vicki's approach to selling Amway set the pattern for what was to come. Vicki, the straight-A student and perfectionist homemaker, studied the catalogs and issues of *Amagram* magazine, becoming expert in Amway's elaborate catechism of products, sales levels, and benefits. Randy, the excitable son of a Chevy salesman, made the pitch.

Like most Amway distributors, the Weavers' dreams of climbing the ladder to wealth and independence never went anywhere. As soon as good paying work came Randy's way, they threw in the towel.

In the early '70s, the agricultural economy of the Great Plains was experiencing a rare boom. For decades, technological advances in seed, fertilizer, and equipment had been generating large grain surpluses, driving prices ever downward. That changed abruptly in the early '70s, when the USSR, suffering from a series of bad harvests and a brutal 1972 drought, negotiated a deal to buy American corn and wheat on credit. Henry Kissinger and other Cold Warriors in the Nixon administration leapt at the possibility of getting the Russians hooked on American exports. As things turned out, American policy experts vastly underestimated the USSR's need for grain. The Soviets were soon buying up huge quantities of American corn and wheat, acquiring more than a quarter of the harvest. The surge in demand caused grain prices to double in 1972 and triple the following year.

John Deere, which operated a large complex in the industrial town of Waterloo, just across the river from Cedar Falls, ramped up production to meet rising demand. In 1973, after just two quarters at Northern Iowa University, Randy dropped out to take a well-paying job tending factory equipment at Deere & Company. Vicki, still working as a secretary, plied her considerable domestic energies into preparing for the children she eagerly awaited.

They weren't even thirty, but with two incomes and no children the Weavers were able to buy a home for $26,000. The white ranch house was one of the nicest on the block, set back from the four-lane thoroughfare of University Avenue by a square of close-cut lawn.

The couple dove into their new suburban life. They went door to door, visiting with neighbors and impressing everyone with their faith and generous manners. Randy was often in the front driveway, a cigarette in his lips, while he tinkered with a rotating collection of fun, impractical vehicles: the red Mustang, an orange Corvette, a Triumph roadster, a lime-green Datsun, a snowmobile, a Harley.

Vicki, whose life would be directly shaped by an intimate relationship to certain texts, spent her free time lost in literature. The trick of rummaging a historical figure's bookshelves for insight can make for thin biography, but with someone like Vicki Weaver, the books really do tell much of the story. Aside from the occasional Marxist or Freudian, few people live so entirely in relation to texts as devout fundamentalists. For Vicki, a biblical literalist with a highly mythic sensibility, the line separating what she read and how she experienced the world was almost nonexistent.

From her father, she inherited a passion for science fiction that prefigured her devotion to endtimes prophecy. She devoured sci-fi classics like H. G. Wells's *A Dream of Armageddon*, in which the main character is tormented by dreams about the future. He sees a world consumed by war while he and a companion watch from a clifftop home. In his dreams, he sees real places he has never been, implying that some sort of prophetic power is at play. As the world of his

39

dreams descends into "wreck and ruin," a totalitarian army sweeps across the planet, gunning for him.

Whether or not David Jordison and his daughter knew it, their shared interest in sci-fi was a natural extension of their faith. The RLDS is too small to have generated any research on the subject, but studies indicate that Mormons consume (and produce) science fiction at a much higher rate than other Americans. Mormon authors have been blending sci-fi with their faith since the nineteenth century and have produced classics in the genre. Hits like *Battlestar Galactica* and *The Expanse* even feature Mormon theology in essential plot points. One explanation is that Joseph Smith's cosmology shares qualities with speculative fiction. In the *Pearl of Great Price*, a canonical LDS text which Smith claimed to have translated from an Egyptian scroll, God's throne is said to be located near a distant planet called Kolob. "We believe in miracles and angels and ancient prophets and redis-covered Scripture," observed LDS author Shannon Hale, "so maybe it is almost natural for us to dive into these other stories."

Like many fledgling anti-government types, Vicki had a meaning-ful, early encounter with Ayn Rand's *Atlas Shrugged*. The novel, pub-lished in 1957, is set in a near-future United States that has descended into ruin at the hands of assorted unionists, bureaucrats, and mooch-ers. Rand's heroes are a collection of free-thinking entrepreneurs who retreat to a Rocky Mountain valley called Galt's Gulch to watch the world, deprived of their genius and vigor, unravel. The novel's steamy sex scenes and sharp denunciations of American society have long appealed to a certain breed of precocious young thinker. Most of them, one critic observed, make their first and last visit to Galt's Gulch "sometime between leaving Middle-earth and packing for college." In his famous review of *Atlas Shrugged*, the anti-communist intellectual Whittaker Chambers, who ought to have been an ideal reader, expressed alarm at the book's undercurrent of fascism. "From almost any page," he wrote in *National Review*, "a voice can be heard... commanding: 'To a gas chamber — go!'"

Randy was never much of a reader, but he listed *Atlas Shrugged* among his favorite books, placing it alongside titles like *None Dare Call It Conspiracy*, an influential "exposé" of the "New World Order" being orchestrated by a cabal of Bolsheviks and international financiers.

The search for secret knowledge travels in one direction. The more Vicki read, the more she was drawn to obscure titles about esoteric or hidden information. In 1995, three years after the siege, Randy explained the evolution of their beliefs on the floor of the US Senate. "My wife and I, if you knew us and followed us from the late '70s, even before that the early '70s, through 1992, you would see change after change after change after change, we studied and read, we were, you might say, on a search for 'the truth.'" In service of that search, Vicki read *Babylon Mystery Religion* and *Satan's Angels Exposed*, both of which claim to expose dangerous truths about an ancient, supernatural struggle taking place behind the scenes of ordinary life. Her private syllabus led from bestsellers, to evangelical-press prophecy guides, to far-right magazines, to mail-order cassettes, to mimeographed tracts. Taken as a whole, these works comprised an underground canon of the conspiracist far-right in the 1970s and '80s, much of it pitched directly to Christian fundamentalists. Decades before the advent of *Infowars*, YouTube, or 4chan, this material, at once entertaining and alarming, spread apocalyptic and conspiratorial ideas with astonishing efficiency.

By the mid-'70s, the Weavers began to consider adoption. As Randy told it, Vicki wanted a kid and he wanted a Corvette. Right after he bought the car, Vicki discovered she was pregnant. Sara was born in the winter of 1976, a healthy baby girl with her mother's thick, dark hair. Randy traded in the Corvette for a station wagon. Two years later, Samuel came along.

It was a hectic, encumbered chapter of their lives — the proverbial long days and short years of early parenthood. Two decades later, after the family had been shattered by violence, it would come to resemble a Kodachrome idyll of suburban peace and plenty. Randy was the handy, always-goofing dad, making the kids squeal at breakfast by flashing a raisin-bran-caked grin. Vicki was the patient, all-capable mother — self-consciously old-fashioned and feminine. "She was the kind of mother who didn't yell for her kids to come," recalled neighbor and friend Carolee Flynn. "She would walk over and get them." The kids raced Hot Wheels in the carpeted basement while "Itsy Bitsy Teenie Weenie Yellow Polkadot Bikini" and "The Purple People Eater" wore themselves smooth on the turntable. During the long Iowa winters, Randy and the kids dug snow caves in the backyard. In the summer, Sara and Samuel ran screaming beneath the sprinkler, while new Schwinns lay beached at the edge of the lawn.

On weekends the family drove the station wagon out to the Jordison farm in Coalville. The kids climbed into the hayloft looking for barn cats and stuffed themselves with cherries in the orchard. On summer evenings, the whole extended family lingered outside, the heavy Midwestern air loud with insects. Randy called Vicki "Ma." She called him "Weaver."

CHAPTER TWO

THE TURN

AND SO THINGS might have stretched on through the cycle of years, had there not been something restless at work inside the Weaver home. Randy and Vicki had new cars, a steady income, and a growing family. Vicki, who drew energy from domestic challenges, finally had two little kids to feed, wash, and chase. Yet this suburban existence gradually came to feel flimsy — even unreal. They had not traveled far across Iowa, but the ranch house on University Avenue would never accumulate the grounding weight of the Jordison farm in Coalville, where generations had been raising children, crops, and hogs for more than a century. During those mid-'70s summers, Rod Stewart and Conway Twitty dominated the hit parade in Iowa, but Vicki's favorite song was "Flowers on the Wall," the Statler Brothers gently unhinged ballad to staying inside and coming apart.

For a pair of seekers raised in conservative, pious families, church was the obvious place to go looking for transcendence. As a couple, Randy and Vicki grew more preoccupied with religion than either of them had been on their own. Rather than fix them sleepily to the present, parenthood seemed to intensify their appetite for something loftier. At first, they repeated the pattern of Randy's folks, sampling different denominations as they tried to square their questing faith with institutions chiefly devoted to binding people into community. For a long stretch, they settled into the padded pews at Cedarloo Baptist, a new, single-story brick church halfway between Cedar Falls and Waterloo. But the Weavers craved something harder and more exciting than the consoling rhythm of Sabbaths and holidays. Eventually, they found it.

Like millions of other American Evangelicals then and since, Randy and Vicki became preoccupied by the relatively small portion of the Bible's thirty-one thousand verses devoted to the endtimes. The faith which the Weavers gradually embraced — one that places the Apocalypse and its prelude at the very center of the religion — not only transformed the lives of Randy and Vicki, it has fueled some of the most extreme forces within American life, even as most non-Christians (and a large portion of mainline Protestants and Catholics) remain wholly ignorant of the basic story.

The biblical episode in the olive grove, in which Jesus plays the twin roles of prophet and prophesied, comes at the very outset of the New Testament. It is often called the "Little Apocalypse," to distinguish it from the Bible's three more substantial descriptions of the End. The first two, which long precede Christ's earthly ministry, are contained within the Old Testament books of Ezekiel and Daniel, both of which were written during eras of brutal persecution for the Jews. The author of Ezekiel identifies himself as a Jewish priest held prisoner in Babylon in 592 BCE, around the time Nebuchadnezzar destroyed the Temple in Jerusalem. The Book of Daniel dates from the second century BCE, when Judea was besieged by Antiochus IV of Syria, who endeavored to wipe out Jewish observance altogether and installed a statue of Zeus in the Temple. But, like a shady antiques dealer scuffing up a modern piece to increase its value, the author of the book tells the story from the perspective of the sixth century BCE, in the court of Babylon. This backdating allows Daniel's author to "predict" the past — presenting a long stretch of established history as the result of keen future vision.

The third and final apocalypse canonized in the Bible is the one that would exert the greatest pull on the Weavers and the millions of other Americans who have come to believe that they are living through the final days of history. The Book of Revelation (also known as The Apocalypse of John) is a short, confounding text. Written about six decades after the crucifixion, when Judaism and the nascent Jesus movement were just starting to part ways, it became, after many years of controversy, among the last books accepted into the canonical New Testament.

Closing out the Christian Bible, Revelation is a testament of violent and bitter resentment. It makes for a discordant coda to everything that precedes it. Unlike most of the New Testament, it is not an epistle to believers, a record of Jesus's teachings, or an instructive fable. In just fourteen pages (in the King James Version) it recounts the terrifying vision of a man who identifies himself as John, who says he is a Jesus follower living in Asia Minor.

Revelation is modeled closely on Daniel, which had inspired an entire subgenre of apocalyptic texts, all following a fixed template. The basic form involves the appearance of some supernatural being who leads the narrator to a heavenly realm where he is shown an alarming preview of future events. Typically, these visions end with the narrator returning to the present with an urgent warning. (As one theologian has noted, Dickens's *A Christmas Carol* is a perfect secular exemplar of the form.)

When John wrote his Apocalypse, the Roman Empire was trying to shore up its authority in the Eastern Empire by spreading the Imperial cult, which celebrated the emperor Domitian as a living god. John and his Jesus-worshipping companions rejected this state religion and preached defiantly about their martyred Messiah and his imminent return. To Roman authorities, this constituted treason. Persecutions followed. John, who was likely born in Judea, was (probably) exiled to Patmos, a small, sun-bleached island in the Aegean, between modern-day Greece and Turkey. (He has long been confused with the apostle and Gospel writer named John, but they are almost certainly two different men.) It was on Patmos that he had the vision that would, two thousand years later, conquer the minds of Randy and Vicky Weaver.

The action starts on the Sabbath. John is standing on the beach when he hears a trumpet-like voice from the sky. The end is at hand, it announces. "Come up hither and I will shew thee things which must be hereafter." John is lifted into the air, to see what's coming. From there, the narrative advances by strange leaps, like the groggy recitation of a nightmare that cannot find easy translation into words.

Christ first appears to John as a lamb and sets about opening seven seals on a scroll held by God. Each broken seal cues up a new catastrophe on Earth. There are locusts with human faces, long hair, and scorpion tails. A star called Wormwood splashes to Earth and poisons the oceans. John eats a small book that tastes sweet but gives him a stomachache. A woman "clothed with the sun" goes into labor. A seven-headed, ten-horned dragon paces beneath her, waiting to devour her baby. An immense "Beast," also with seven heads and ten horns, rises out of the sea. With the help of a charismatic human leader—long identified as "the Antichrist," although that term is not in John's text—the Beast, whose power comes from Satan, rules over all "tongues and nations" for forty-two months. A new global government, led by the Antichrist, requires everyone to get the Beast's name (represented by the number 666) branded on their hand or forehead if they wish to buy or sell anything. The new global authority goes to war against those holdouts who refuse the mark.

A series of plagues sweep the globe. The Beast's subjects break out in sores. They chew their tongues in agony. A "great whore" rides up on a seven-headed monster sipping from a golden cup "full

German engraver Albrecht Dürer's fifteenth-century woodcut rendering of the Beast from the Book of Revelation, part of his series *The Apocalypse*.

of abominations and filthiness of her fornication." As in an editorial cartoon, her forehead is labeled: "Mystery Babylon the Great, the Mother of Harlots and Abominations of the Earth." Next comes a vivid sequence, long beloved by certain preachers, depicting the destruction of decadent Babylon. The merchants, who have "waxed rich through the abundance of [the whore's] delicacies," wail as their silks and cinnamon go up in flames.

At last, the final battle is joined. Jesus rides in on a white steed, a far cry from the humble donkey that was his previous mount. He has returned to Earth as a warrior king to "rule with a rod of iron." His eyes are flames. His vesture is dipped in blood. His tongue is a blade. "If it is imagery," D. H. Lawrence wrote of Revelation, "it is imagery which cannot be imagined." How, for instance, are we to picture a lamb — the actual baby sheep seen in John's vision — opening the seven wax seals binding the scroll? With its hooves? Its little teeth? Others find a special appeal in John's heavy-metal prose. Hunter S. Thompson called it "language that will peel the skin off your back."

Leading a heavenly army dressed in white linen and mounted on white horses, Christ clashes with earthly armies from the kingdoms of "Gog" and "Magog," who have united under the banner of the Beast's government to attack Jerusalem. War is total. Blood rises to the height of the horses' bridles. Birds descend from heaven to eat the flesh of the dead. None of the tender love of the Gospels can be found here. It is smiting and gnashing, top to bottom.

When the dust settles, the Beast, his false prophet, and their followers are cast into a sulfurous lake. Satan is locked inside a bottomless hole for a thousand years. All human beings — the living and the dead — are then sorted. For the saved, it's eternal life. Everyone else reports directly to the pit.

With human history concluded, eternity commences with a vast, bejeweled city surrounded by gates made of pearl, winched down to Earth from the sky. "And I John saw the holy city, new Jerusalem, coming down from God out of heaven, prepared as a bride adorned for her husband." And with that, the long saga that began naked in an orchard wraps up in the manner traditional to comedies, with a wedding party — "the marriage supper of the lamb" — between God and His elect.

———————

While much of the New Testament is concerned with the inner lives of believers, Revelation is full of what can only be called politics. Along with its dread menagerie of monsters and dragons, John's kaleidoscopic vision is crowded with alliances, conspiracies, economies, and wars. Sin and salvation are global affairs. Wealth and power are determined by faith. God deals with "nations," as much as with individuals. Alongside the approaching End, John's loudest theme is the antagonism between Christ's people and the state, or at least any state that precedes the earthly reign of Jesus and His martyrs.

Historians of religion have a fairly clear sense of what this was all supposed to mean for John's intended audience of Jesus followers in Asia Minor. While the Babylonian Empire was already in ruins when John wrote, it was, among Jews, a general synecdoche for subjugation and enslavement. For John, it is obviously a stand-in for Imperial Rome. His angelic guide says as much: "the seven heads [of the Beast] are seven mountains" (i.e., Rome, city of seven hills). The angel, evidently the sort who likes to spell things out, further explains that the Beast's ten horns represent ten kings, interpreted variously down through the centuries, but most recently taken to represent some sort of Rome-like alliance of nations (the USSR, the EU, or the UN) that will come to dominate global affairs (and oppose Israel) during the latter days. The whore labeled "Mystery Babylon" seems to represent the state-enforced Roman religion known as the Imperial cult. The Beast most likely represents the emperor Nero, infamous for his zealous persecution of early Christians. Although Nero was already dead by suicide when Revelation was written, a widespread superstition held that he would eventually return to life (or come out of hiding) and resume harrying the faithful. That would explain why the Beast is described as having died and then returned to power with a wound on his head. Using gematria, a then-common system for translating names into numerals, it is possible to extract the number 666 from "Nero Caesar."

If Revelation was simply about Rome and its imminent comeuppance — "anti-Roman propaganda that drew its imagery from Israel's prophetic tradition," as the scholar Elaine Pagels puts it — then the prophecy was a bust. Instead of being obliterated for crimes against the one true God, the empire was officially Christianized with the conversion of Emperor Constantine.

None of that has particularly mattered to readers since John's own time. In the two millennia since it was written, Revelation has lived a life of its own. People in wildly different historical moments have read John's bloody seaside frothings and reached the same conclusion: this is about *now*. "Babylon" is a perennial stand-in for the sinful metropole where nonbelievers dwell in swank licentiousness. Or, if it is not an actual place on the map, it is a general term for false belief made manifest as an oppressive political order.

Antique visions of the future — be they utopian or dystopian, apocalyptic or millenarian — betray a lot about the moment in which they were set to paper. Revelation was written during an era when the followers of Jesus were a precarious, persecuted sect. It was a time when someone like John of Patmos was more likely to think of himself as a Jew whose Messiah had come (and would soon return) than as a "Christian." That sense of embattled solidarity shines through in Revelation's merciless sorting of humanity into the saved and the damned, often in ways that align with nationality or ethnicity.

For the uninitiated, Revelation's ardent worship of power and rigid distinction between the elect and damned (including, in John's view, the substandard Christians within his own community in Asia Minor) contrasts with the unto-all-nations universalism that made the Gospels so radical.

To read Revelation as a nonbeliever is to confront the astonishing fact that this gory fever dream serves as the epilogue of the most widely read book in human history. There it sits, quietly smoldering between the pebble leather covers of the King James Version or the waterproof plastic favored by many contemporary editions. Every day it is tucked into purses, backpacks, and gloveboxes. It rests on the nightstands, coffee tables, and laps of dentists, schoolchildren, and world leaders.

"If you say in the first chapter that there is a rifle hanging on the wall," Chekhov wrote, "it absolutely must go off." Disseminated so widely across time and space, and claiming, with the full wind of both Testaments at its back, to be a true chronicle of future events, how could such a ballistic bit of prose fail to occasionally detonate?

For most of the last two millennia, Jesus's clear-cut statement that the timing of the End is unknowable — "But of that day and hour knoweth no man" — has rendered speculation about the endtimes a fairly abstract pursuit, at least for most believers. Historically, the vast majority of Christians have read prophecy as a symbolic account of events playing out slowly over the course of history. The authors of Daniel, Ezekiel, and Revelation were not taken as soothsayers or fortune tellers. Rather than a literal account of things to come, prophetic texts provided preachers with a storehouse of resonant phrases, mysterious ellipses, and evocative metaphors that could make meaning out of suffering. The prophecies, wrote the scholar Norman Cohn, "were devices by which religious groups, at first Jewish and later Christian, consoled, fortified, and asserted themselves when confronted by the threat or the reality of oppression." Don't worry, the prophets console, the tables will turn; Babylon will fall. Likewise, at times when religious obedience seems to be on the slide (i.e., all the time), the prophets deliver a jarring summons to first things. A dread tribunal is coming. Gird your soul. Not for nothing are trumpets one of the most consistent images in prophecy.

Theologians of a more mystical bent take an even less literal view, recasting the Apocalypse as a metaphor for spiritual progress. As early as the second century, these texts were being interpreted as allegories in which the coming millennium was a spiritual state, not a material utopia, and the Beast was a stand-in for generalized notions of evil and persecution. Augustine, the most influential and profuse theologian of early Christianity, read John's global war as a meditation on the inner struggle toward grace and as a metaphorical sketch of events unfolding slowly through history.

At the Council of Ephesus in 431 CE, a gathering meant to land on some sort of consensus Christian theology, the notion of a literal earthly millennium (the thousand-year earthly reign of Christ promised in Revelation) was declared unorthodox, and various millenarian texts were purged from the canon. Roughly a thousand years later, Martin Luther went so far as to claim that Revelation was "neither apostolic nor prophetic," consigning John's vision to an appendix of his famous translation, although (tellingly) he was happy to reach for it to tar the pope as the Antichrist.

Randy and Vicki Weaver were not the sort to dwell in the beguiling mysteries of metaphor and allegory. Inside the tidy house on University Avenue, they, like many others, became obsessed with a highly literal reading of Revelation. They debated "signs of the times" with friends and Vicki's father David. As they were drawn deeper into what Billy Graham called "the thrilling doctrine," a bright constellation of TV shows, paperbacks, and AM radio programs was there to guide them, all claiming to prove how John's account of the End was finally, truly, at long last, coming to pass. Some portion of Christians have always been preoccupied with the End, but the volume of prophecy-oriented media available to Randy and Vicki in the early '70s was something new.

———

Until the early twentieth century, American religious and intellectual life was overwhelmingly shaped by various Protestant denominations and their traditional teaching that history, at least since the resurrection, forms a long triumphal march of progress. The basic story goes like this: As the Gospel spreads across the globe, moral and material conditions will gradually improve, eventually culminating in the reign of heaven on Earth and some sort of Second Coming. Armageddon might be scheduled for some time after that, but worldly perfection is coming first and it is going to take a long time. This view is known as *post*millennialism because it places the dramatic events of the Apocalypse *after* the thousand years of God's kingdom on Earth. This was the view of things preached by Jonathan Edwards, the signal voice of the Great Awakening and the most influential American divine of the colonial era. God's kingdom, Edwards taught, was going to be built up through faith and good works: "preaching of the gospel and the use of ordinary means of grace."

This was the theology of a confident faith, one that regarded its own triumph as inevitable, without the intervention of supernatural violence. If Revelation's frightful chain of images — the Beast rising from the sea, the dragon, a world-destroying war — are not to be expected until after the millennium, there is hardly much point in quibbling about them while life on Earth remains manifestly unperfected.

This assumption — that history is slowly tending toward perfection — was the dominant view of American Protestants between the Revolution and the Civil War. It was woven so deeply into early American thought that it was practically invisible. Even before British Puritans arrived with their conviction that North America was a place set aside for divine purposes, Christopher Columbus obsessed over his role in the coming millennium. "God made me the messenger of the new heaven and the earth of which he spoke in the Apocalypse of John," wrote the Italian admiral while bobbing at anchor off the New World. "[A]nd he showed me the spot where to find it."

With varying degrees of fervor and literalism, this postmillennial outlook and its implicit enthusiasm for the future was shared by a wide array of American Christians, from the powdered-wigged Deists who framed the Constitution to the foot-stamping revivalists of the Second Great Awakening. Quite a few took it as a mandate for material and moral progress — an invitation to build up the millennial kingdom with their own hands. Under the influence of postmillennial beliefs, Protestants of the eighteenth and nineteenth centuries led all the major reform movements of their time. For better and worse, millenarian hopes provided the theological ballast for the Revolutionary War, manifest destiny, abolitionism, the temperance movement, female suffrage, and the so-called social gospel with its focus on urban poverty. This was a faith that mingled easily with nationalism, flattering Americans with the notion that their young, lightly peopled republic would be ground zero for God's millennial paradise.

Surveying the social and technological advances of their own times — and overlooking some of its darkest horrors — many Evangelicals of the 1830s and '40s were convinced that they stood at the crack of a dawning golden age. "America in the early nineteenth century," wrote the religious historian Ernest Sandeen, "was drunk on the millennium."

For those inclined to a more rationalist outlook, this account of God's plan dovetailed easily with eighteenth-century Enlightenment notions about the inexorable march of reason and science. Step by step, in the fullness of time, planning and technology would lead to the end of all want and suffering.

In its most zealous form, this view of history inspired a wave of utopian colonies intent on literally raising New Jerusalem upon the fresh soil of the New World, often through novel schemes of mutual aid or social liberation. Closer to the mainstream, Whiggish politicians invoked the millennium to spark enthusiasm (and raise taxes) for such practical "internal improvements" as the digging of canals and the construction of public schools. The spirit of Christian millenarianism was even subsumed into various explicitly secular political projects, with theorists on both the left and the right envisioning history as an inevitable progression that leads (perhaps dialectically, perhaps through revolution) toward a golden age of justice and abundance.

———————

There were always exceptions to this optimistic view of God's plan. Cotton Mather, for instance, reflected the outlook of many Puritans when he speculated about apocalyptic portents in his own time, claiming that the imminent conversion of the Jews and destruction of the Catholic Church would herald the Second Coming. A half century later, during the chaotic years of the French Revolution, a portion of American and British Protestants became convinced that the end-times sequence described in Revelation had begun. In 1798, prophecy watchers claimed that the expulsion of Pope Pius VI from Rome mirrored scenes in both Revelation and Daniel.

Starting in the aftermath of the Civil War and gathering speed in the first decades of the twentieth century, the postmillennial consensus that had suffused American Protestantism with a confident, reformist tenor began to fray. Among a large portion of believers, it was replaced by a far less sanguine reading of prophecy, one that was hostile toward the very notion of progress, if not the future itself. A majority of American Protestants, the Weavers eventually among them, gradually became convinced that the world was not being perfected through revivalism or good works. The only real progress to be expected would arrive with the galloping return of Christ and his iron rod. In the meantime, dark forces were definitely in the saddle.

From the outside, this sea change within American Protestantism might look like an intramural squabble within that rather large segment of the population which believes that the Bible has something useful to say about the future. It is not. The prototypical postmillennialist might think and behave a lot like a civic-minded reformer — casting about for canals to dredge, lyceums to organize, and social ills to ameliorate. On the other hand, an apocalyptically minded *pre*millennialist — that is, one who expects the Apocalypse to arrive *before* God's reign on earth — is likely to oppose, on reasonable religious grounds, anything that smacks of human progress. The consequences of this shift in how a great many people think about the future have been far-reaching.

The religious faith of millions inevitably impinges on the public sphere, but not all beliefs impinge equally. It is possible to maintain absolute faith in the resurrection, the cycle of reincarnation, or the proposition that North America rides atop a great tortoise, without those beliefs having much effect on civic or political life. You can embrace such beliefs while still rendering unto Caesar all those things that need rendering. But if a core tenet of your faith is that life on Earth is racing toward a violent conclusion and that most earthly authorities are a front for an evil conspiracy to rule the globe, your relationship to the state and your fellow citizens will surely be affected.

CHAPTER THREE

HAVE YOU HEARD THE BAD NEWS?

IN THE UNITED States, the turn from the old build-the-millennium optimism to a more apocalyptic style of faith began quietly, with hermeneutic squabbles over ancient Greek and Hebrew texts at stodgy summertime prophecy conferences in the Northeast. Before long, however, the new prophetic ideas bred a schism that spread rapidly through American churches.

Conservative white Protestants were already in a rebellious mood. By the close of the nineteenth century, mainline denominations were increasingly oriented toward a liberal, modernist theology that sought to reconcile the Bible with a more naturalistic view of the world, especially following Darwin's shocking challenge to the creation story. Liberal theologians were emphasizing the moral teachings of the Gospel over supernatural events like the Virgin Birth or a bodily Second Coming. At the same time, a new approach to reading scripture — known as Higher Criticism — emphasized the role of historical context and human authorship in the creation of the Bible. To many, these changes felt like an effort to demote their awesome Lord (and his infallible Word) to some sort of a philosopher-poet with a lot of nice things to say about the poor.

Tensions that had been simmering since at least the 1870s came to a boil in the 1920s with what historians now call the "Fundamentalist controversy." It is impossible to say whether it was the modernizers or the reactionaries who had strayed further from the shared turf of denominational Protestantism, but only one side — the conservatives — consciously donned the mantle of insurgency. Predictably, the two groups drove each other to further extremes as they caricatured one another: smart-aleck infidels on one side, holy-rolling hicks on the other. As it happened, both camps had their own impressively credentialed exegetes, equally versed in Greek and Hebrew.

It was into this fractious atmosphere that a new interpretation of the endtimes arrived, touching a lively nerve. Those new ideas — or, more precisely, a reformulated admixture of various old ideas — first appeared in Great Britain in the 1820s, but they were imported to the United States in the aftermath of the Civil War, right around the time that Vicki Weaver's great-grandfather sailed from Northern England to dig prairie coal.

The chief importer was Mr. John Nelson Darby, a caustic Anglo-Irishman with a dark gaze, generous muttonchops, and a messianic sense of certainty. Other theologians had written things similar to Darby, but he did more than anyone else to transform the way American Protestants thought — and continue to think — about the coming End.

It would be hard to identify another individual who has held more sway over American thought while being so little known. Despite generating several million words on the subject of prophecy, Darby wrote very little about himself. Even among his direct intellectual heirs, a group that arguably includes the bulk of conservative Evangelicals, his name is mostly forgotten. A proper full-scale biography of the man still has not been written.

Photograph of John Nelson Darby taken in the garden of the Palais Eynard, Geneva, 1840.

Darby's father made a fortune selling munitions during the Napoleonic Wars, and young John Nelson was raised in privilege on a Sussex estate, the eighth of nine children. He graduated from Trinity College Dublin, literate in Greek, Latin, German, and Hebrew. Deciding against a career in the law, he was ordained in the (Protestant) Church of Ireland. He promptly quit the church over what he saw as its theological corruption and joined a radical evangelical sect centered in the port city of Plymouth.

The Plymouth Brethren, who defined themselves in opposition to the state-aligned Anglican church, were loosely organized in local chapters. In the tradition of countless breakaway sects throughout Christian history, they aspired to recreate the spontaneous, egalitarian spirit of the primitive church, as described in the Book of Acts. Instead of Sunday services, they gathered for sessions of collective Bible study, usually in the parlor of some wealthy supporter.

Like so many other dissenters and come-outers, the Brethren continuously subdivided into ever smaller competing groups. Darby assumed command of the "Exclusive Brethren," based in County Wicklow. Under his unbending leadership, the Exclusives came, in the view of Donald Harman Akenson, the leading contemporary historian of Darbyism, to resemble a cult more than a traditional denomination. The group was defined, Akenson writes, by "tight discipline, compelling propaganda, stealth proselytism, and [Darby's] charismatic individual leadership."

As a young preacher, Darby remained in constant motion, relentlessly walking back and forth across Ireland—and eventually traveling throughout France, Germany, Switzerland, Italy, New Zealand, the West Indies, Canada, and, especially, the United States—to spread his novel reading of prophecy. And what did this dour young man think about during all that time on the road? Mostly how wrong everyone else was.

Darby was a full-time doctrinal mutineer: a writer of brusque corrections, a striding one-man Reformation. With his eyes fixed firmly on Armageddon, he made no effort to establish any sort of lasting institution. Despite the stunning triumph of his ideas in the United States, his approach was not the tent revival or camp meeting that have defined America's great spiritual awakenings. His charisma worked at close range. He favored days-long sessions of biblical exposition with groups as small as two or three. He was not an inspired preacher, but he possessed a stern, Old Testament air of authority and a preternatural command of scripture that left people, including some of America's most prominent churchmen, feeling as though they had brushed up against the truth. Even so, it would fall to others to popularize his ideas.

Darby's big contribution to theology was a distinctly modern one. Using only his own "literalist" reading of the Bible, he took the unruly, gnomic morass of ancient prophecy and boiled it down into a pseudo-empirical system for understanding world events. To the nonbeliever, this resembles a category error, like using the *Iliad* as a guide to Turkish beaches, or *The Waste Land* as a military history of World War I. Adherents of this reading—what came to be known as "premillennial dispensationalism" after Darby's death—illustrated his theory with math, charts, and great cascades of footnotes.

To accomplish his act of reverse alchemy—transmuting the fevered visions of ancient prophets into something like a flowchart—Darby dusted off two old and obscure ideas. The first was the notion that divine history is divided into distinct eras or "dispensations," during which God's relationship to His creation shifts in fundamental ways. (The Greek word translated as "dispensation" is *oikonomia*, meaning something like "style of keeping house," as if God were a fickle inn-keeper who periodically rewrites the house rules.) Each dispensation ends with humanity's failure to satisfy the Creator's expectations.

There are seven:

- Creation through the apple.
- The fall until the flood.
- The Rainbow Covenant until Abraham.
- The era of God's special covenant with Abraham and Israel.
- Moses receiving the law until the crucifixion.
- The resurrection until Armageddon. (*You are here.*)
- Christ's millennial reign on Earth.

Darby's second big idea was that scripture, when read properly, foretells a dramatic supernatural event: the sudden snatching up of all true Christians into the clouds, where they will meet Jesus. This "Rapture" (the word does not appear in the Bible), will arrive without warning, just before the end of the sixth dispensation. With all true believers beamed to safety, the brutal events described in John's Apocalypse will commence, starting with a period of "Tribulation" during which the Antichrist will rise to power and lead a new, global government. After seven years, the Tribulation will conclude with a world-consuming battle in the valley beneath Mount Megiddo, near the city of Haifa. (This sequence is described in Revelation, albeit more elliptically.)

To Darby and the millions of Christians who took up his scheme, the Second Coming is not some misty allegory for the triumph of Christ in the hearts of men. The End will come fast and unbidden, with a great deal of violence and the bodily return of Jesus. Trying to improve things in the meantime, cannot shift God's plan. In fact, such efforts can only help to conceal the operations of the Antichrist, who will accumulate power by preaching peace, progress, and international comity. The only thing to do between now and the End is win souls and avoid accidentally supporting evil. All the old millenarian stuff—good works, material progress, peace on earth, goodwill toward men—are, in the words of one early Darbyite creed, just "unchristian delusion."

Along with dividing history into distinct eras, Darby's system split humanity into three groups: Israel (the Jews), The Church (true Christians), and The Nations (everyone else). Darby advanced the notion that the Jews are history's great timepiece. Their failure to recognize their Messiah had the effect of hitting a cosmic snooze button, thereby delaying the Second Advent for two millennia. (This explains why, in the Book of Matthew, Jesus seems to promise a swift return that has not yet come to pass.) If you want to know where things stand on the countdown to the End, simply look to the Jews. Only once they are in position, can Christ return. The prevalence of this notion would greatly influence American foreign policy in the Middle East, in turn shaping domestic politics. As a result of the prophetic conviction that modern Jews need to return to Palestine for the Second Coming to commence, political American and British Evangelicals began lobbying for Jewish resettlement in the Holy Land even before the advent of Jewish-led Zionism at the end of the nineteenth century.

Darby did not give much credit to his forerunners, but none of this was wholly original. The division of history into separate dispensations had been performed before, notably by Joachim of Fiore, a twelfth-century Italian abbot whose ideas helped inspire Dante's *Inferno*. More broadly, Darby's literalist reading of the endtimes echoes the bated hopes of the first Christians, who had been promised earthquakes, falling stars, and the speedy return of their murdered Messiah.

As for the Rapture, great volumes of ink have been spilled debating its intellectual vintage. To millions of adherents, it is plainly scriptural. Doubters regard it as a modern heresy, with some claiming it as the invention of a mentally disturbed teenaged girl in the 1830s. What is undeniable is that, prior to the nineteenth century, few people believed in the notion that Christians would be taken out of the world in advance of Armageddon. It was John Nelson Darby who put into circulation the idea that Jesus will return not once, but twice: first to remove the Church, and then again to lead the charge at Armageddon. The idea of the Rapture allowed believers to accept a literal reading of Revelation with the consoling assurance that they will be spared John's parade of monsters and bloodletting.

Whatever Darby's sources and influences, his gift as a theologian was to put everything together in a way that spoke to modern, literal-minded Christians. Compared to the contortions of mainline preachers, who were trying to reconcile scripture with a series of destabilizing scientific breakthroughs (e.g., the fossil record and the theory of evolution), Darby's pat certitude made the vagaries of ancient prophecy sound like its own sort of science.

Amid his writing and traveling, Darby not only forged a new eschatology, he also helped form a new style of worship. While he worked with the zeal of a prophet, he insisted that his scheme was the mere product of close reading. He sifted through the Bible like a conspiracy hunter hopscotching through microfiche, plucking out a word or a number here, placing it alongside something else written centuries later in a different language, triangulating off some third scrap of text, and connecting the dots with great spools of interpretive string. The Bible might be the literal and inerrant word of God, but it did not surrender its truths lightly.

In the fall of 1862, Darby sailed to North America to visit groups of Brethren immigrants who had settled in Ontario and Iowa. Over the next two decades, he made six more missions to North America, spending a total of seven years on the road in the United States and Canada. His all-consuming purpose was to broadcast his theory as widely as possible. He visited with ministers and parishioners of many

different churches, encouraging them to abandon their denominational loyalties. The goal, as the Brethren liked to say, was to "gather
churches out of churches." That is precisely what he accomplished.

———————

As he wound his way through the United States, Darby's anti-
institutional faith resonated with American Evangelicals, many of
whom were already coming around to a more literal way of reading
scripture. His ideas found early traction among Baptists and Presbyterians, whose Calvinist roots predisposed them to the notion that no
amount of human effort could budge God's plans.

In the United Kingdom, the Darbyite charge petered out, with the
Brethren continuously splintering. But in the United States, the popularity of Darby's theory exploded in the wake of the Civil War. After
four years of wholesale carnage in local cow pastures, the old notion
that history is tending inevitably toward perfection made no sense.
The new apocalyptic faith — which held that things are *supposed* to be
coming undone — met the moment. The church, as one prominent
minister put it, is not here to "tinker and patch up a world system
which God has doomed, and which the Son of God will sweep away
at his coming." If Americans had formerly been drunk on the millennium, the hangover had arrived. Dwight Moody, a leading evangelist
of the new era, wrote, "I don't find any place where God says the world
is to grow better and better... I find that the earth is to grow worse
and worse."

Darby's abstruse, difficult writings were given a decisive boost
when Cyrus I. Scofield, a Confederate veteran turned drunk, turned
lawyer, turned preacher, assembled a "reference Bible" that installed
Darby's interpretive system directly into the margins of the Good
Book itself. Scofield, who had experienced a conversion while in
prison, devoted himself to spreading a literalist, Darbyite reading of
scripture. The Scofield Reference Bible, printed by Oxford University
Press in 1909, sold as many as ten million copies, quietly turning

Darby's theory into orthodoxy for many Americans. Readers who never even learned the name John Nelson Darby absorbed his novel scheme from the margins of their Scofield Bibles.

———

A crisis was coming. As early as 1878, the *New York Times* covered a prophecy conference on the Upper East Side, reporting that "the sounds of the theological war are already in the air." In the face of large-scale Catholic immigration, rapid urbanization, and the widespread acceptance of Darwinism, the newly apocalyptic theology bred schisms within almost every major denomination, dividing American Protestants over the importance of prophecy and the very nature of the future. The change Darby sparked would become, in the words of one historian, "the most resilient popular theological movement in American history."

Adherents eventually came to be called "fundamentalists." While that term has since come to mean strict belief in any doctrine, at the time it specifically referred to a new type of Protestant. It came from *The Fundamentals*, a popular series of religious pamphlets published between 1910 and 1915 by Lyman Stewart, an oil magnate from Los Angeles who had plowed his wealth into aid work before being converted to premillennialism, after which he devoted his fortune to spreading the new theology. Three million copies of his collected pamphlets were printed and sent for free to anyone who might want a set. As a self-applied designation, *fundamentalist* was first used in 1920 by a Baptist minister named Curtis Lee Laws, who expressed the pugilistic spirit of the movement by defining *fundamentalists* as those who are willing "to do battle royal for the faith." There were other components that defined Fundamentalism, but the prospect of an imminent Apocalypse was by far the most potent: the stick of dynamite tucked in among all the other theological boilerplate.

Among other things, the fundamentalists emphasized a "common-sense" approach to scripture, a modern version of the Reformation's impulse to sidestep clerical expertise. While fundamentalists celebrated "plain reading," the effects were far from plain, especially when the "every-stroke" literalism that Darby and others preached was turned loose on the dizzying phantasmagoria of ancient prophecy. "How did people who set out to preserve commonsense reading of the Bible get tangled in such obscure readings?" wrote the historian Garry Wills. "They could hardly avoid it, since the plain sense is the wildest one where eschatology is concerned."

Seminarians and leading churchmen, even some stalwarts of the conservative camp, were sometimes slow to adopt the new ideas, but ordinary believers thrilled to the notion of an imminent End.

By the 1920s, the endtimes had become one of the main lines dividing American Christians. "How the Higher Critics have sneered at Bible Prophecy," wrote the fundamentalist theologian Arno Gaebelein, feeling vindicated by the outbreak of World War I. In the early years of the Fundamentalist movement, that "sneer" — often real, always felt — came from some of the best-known voices in the country, men like Sinclair Lewis, whose hit 1929 novel *Elmer Gantry* depicted a fundamentalist pastor as a randy, drunken mountebank. If any individual can be credited with shaping the negative impression outsiders had of the new fundamentalists, it was the journalist H. L. Mencken, who somehow missed the presence of many erudite theologians within the movement — those anti-intellectual intellectuals — when he cast Fundamentalism as a triumph of "the booboisie."

With Lewis, Mencken, and their millions of readers having fun at the fundamentalists' expense, believers felt as if the whole world was arrayed against them, even as they overran many of America's largest denominations. The fundamentalists established their own seminaries, assumed leadership within many existing churches, and split congregations into opposing factions. Bolstered by the passion of several wealthy lay believers, the new faith — often misleadingly styled "old-time religion" — spread rapidly.

Ironically, this change in how a portion of Americans thought about the End burst into public view during the Scopes Trial of 1925, a controversy over the start of history, rather than its conclusion. The trial in Dayton, Tennessee, became one of the first great American media circuses and served, for many Americans, as an introduction to the Fundamentalist movement. Under the pretense of a legal cross-examination, Clarence Darrow, the most famous lawyer in the land, and William Jennings Bryan, a populist firebrand and three-time candidate for president, engaged in a public, line-by-line analysis of Genesis. While half of Americans might have chuckled at Darrow's wry questions about when snakes first lost their legs, the other half only heard the chuckling. One consequence of H. L. Mencken's event-defining coverage of the trial was that Fundamentalism became associated with the rural South, when in fact most fundamentalists lived in the North and the West.

Gradually, Darby's account of the End (and the signs of its approach) became the dominant story that white Evangelicals told themselves about the future. With the Scofield Bible in one hand and the daily paper in the other, believers combed world affairs for events that seemed to echo ancient visions of doomsday. The outbreak of a global war in 1914 seemed to prove beyond any doubt that the world was not on the glide path to millennial perfection. For those awaiting the imminent return of the Lord, the most exciting side effect of the Great War was the 1917 Balfour Declaration and the bloodless capture of Ottoman-controlled Jerusalem by British forces. The Jews could now be restored to Palestine, just as Darby's reading of the prophets had promised. "Now for the first time," Cyrus Scofield rejoiced, "we have a real prophetic sign."

Over the course of the twentieth century, John of Patmos's inscrutable, fervid vision—squeezed through Darby's hermeneutics—seemed to keep coming into sharper focus. The formal establishment of Israel in 1948, a cold war against an explicitly godless empire, and the inauguration of the European Common Market and the United Nations were all greeted as fulfillment of John's ancient prophecy.

With decline understood as the first law of history, pretty much all social change came to resemble the work of sinister forces. Every conceivable form of progress—from female suffrage, to the rise of the welfare state, to desegregation—looked like mounting evidence of the coming End. This led to some peculiar places. Under the widespread assumption that the battle of Armageddon would be nuclear, preachers like Jerry Falwell opposed disarmament on biblical grounds. Even genial Billy Graham—"America's pastor"—was compelled by his dispensationalist beliefs to refute Martin Luther King Jr.'s hopeful preaching. In reaction to King's "I have a dream" speech, Graham responded the only way an honest dispensationalist could. "Only when Christ comes again," he said, "will the little white children of Alabama walk hand in hand with little black children."

Faith and race are sufficiently intertwined in the United States that it is impossible to untangle the extent to which resistance to integration drove the rise of Fundamentalism from the ways in which Fundamentalism, as it spread in the early twentieth century, entrenched existing racial divisions. Either way, as the religious historian Matthew Avery Sutton writes, Black churches "had almost no role in shaping the broader premillennial movement." In the 1920s and '30s, as Fundamentalism spread, white Evangelicals (with the exception of some Pentecostals) did not give Black Protestants much reason to join their ranks. The older postmillennial outlook—famously expressed in Rev. King's claim that "the arc of the moral universe is long but it bends toward justice"—remained the operative eschatology in most Black churches. The story of a long, hard march from slavery to liberation that animated much of the civil rights movement—with its potent analogizing to the children of Israel—only makes sense under such an outlook. This theological divide is just one of many reasons why, as King observed, "eleven o'clock on Sunday morning is one of the most segregated hours, if not *the* most segregated hour, in Christian America."

A century and a half after Darby's novel reading of prophecy first arrived on American shores, widespread belief in the coming

Apocalypse continues to press upon the mood and politics of the nation, channeling the springs of public opinion and shaping cultural forces in ways only distantly related to theology. Few things, it turns out, exert more gravity on the present than the story that citizens carry around about the future. It is one of the great flukes of American intellectual history that a tiny, cultlike sect from High Victorian County Wicklow gave rise to the beliefs that would, over many decades, conscript a sizable share of citizens into a permanent revolution against modernity.

This was the theology with which Randy and Vicki Weaver were raised and into which they dove headlong during the early years of their marriage. While other, darker elements were later folded into their faith, the endtimes story contained within John Nelson Darby's reading of prophecy would remain at the core of their worldview.

Inside the house on University Avenue, Randy and Vicki watched hour upon hour of religious programming on their small kitchen television, especially Jerry Falwell's *Old Time Gospel Hour*. Falwell's cheery, patriotic brand of dispensationalism claimed a special role for the USA in the runup to Armageddon, an event he expected to arrive within his lifetime. (He died in 2007.) As Fundamentalism was subsumed during the middle of the twentieth century under the older, more capacious banner of "Evangelicalism," Falwell helped guide prophetic ideas out of obscurity and into mainstream denominations and suburban living rooms like the Weavers'. In doing so, he linked a style of faith that had once been skeptical of earthly politics with movement conservatism, building up the modern Christian Right and forging an unlikely alliance between those who would stand athwart history yelling "Stop" and those who would leap in front of it, crying "End!"

As endtimes faith became inextricably mixed up with anti-communism, fundamentalists, who as late as the '50s had been at the fringes of the American right, became the indispensable bloc of the Republican party. Billy Graham, for a time the most influential and respected Evangelical in the world, preached that the Antichrist was Russian and that Armageddon would take the form of a war between the USA and the USSR that would climax in the Holy Land. In 1951, Graham boldly claimed that the End would probably come within a year. Later in his career, he kept the timing vague. "We are living the latter days. I sincerely believe that the coming of the Lord draweth nigh."

Fascination with the endtimes surged during the '70s. Not since the nineteenth century had so many Americans taken such a keen interest in prophecy. *Newsweek* declared 1976 to be "the year of the evangelical." While mainline denominations continued to dwindle, fundamentalist denominations like the Southern Baptists grew rapidly. This shift coincided with a population boom in the Sunbelt, where Fundamentalism had already gained much purchase.

For those Americans who did not approve of the liberalizing cultural upheaval of the 1960s, things seemed to be truly out of control.

On the same small TV where the Weavers watched Jerry Falwell fulminate against godless communism and dark secular forces, they watched Jim and Tammy Faye Bakker's *Praise the Lord* (*PTL*) program and Pat Robertson's *700 Club*. Robertson blended charismatic faith (including live broadcasts of faith healings) with Republican politics. His own prediction was that the seven-year period of Tribulation would commence in 1982.

The Weavers absorbed all of this. "When we moved in here, they were common, ordinary people," said Carolee Flynn, who had moved next to the Weavers in 1976, becoming close friends with Vicki and a sort of extra grandmother to the children. "I think a lot of this came from watching *PTL* on television. They got to studying and researching extensively by the hour inside that home until they knew more than an ordained minister."

CHAPTER FOUR

THE THRILLING DOCTRINE

ONE AFTERNOON IN 1978, when Vicki was almost thirty and happily occupied with motherhood, she came home with a paperback copy of Hal Lindsey's *The Late Great Planet Earth*. Initially published eight years earlier, the book's cover showed an image of the earth spinning alone in black space. It resembles the iconic earthrise photo on the cover of the *Whole Earth Catalog*, with one telling difference: on Lindsey's book, the precious blue home planet trails a massive plume of flame, like a meteor streaking across the cosmos.

More than all the other apocalyptic and prophetic material that the Weavers would consume over the years — and they consumed a lot — Lindsey's slim page-turner would change the course of their lives. They were not alone. Among the many feisty tribunes of doom who emerged in the 1960s and '70s, nobody reached a wider audience than Hal Lindsey.

Born in Texas in 1929, Lindsey had studied business, served in Korea, and then worked as a tugboat pilot in the Mississippi Delta. Sometime in 1956, he heard a sermon on the endtimes and committed his life to the electrifying prospect of an imminent End. He enrolled at the Dallas Theological Seminary, which had been founded in 1924 by dispensationalist Presbyterians associated with Cyrus Sco-field. The school remains a major center of American dispensation-alism. It has been called "the intellectual and ideological 'Vatican' of the movement." After graduating, Lindsey preached at UCLA, Berke-ley, and San Francisco State as part of the Campus Crusade for Christ, an organization funded by Amway founder Richard DeVos.

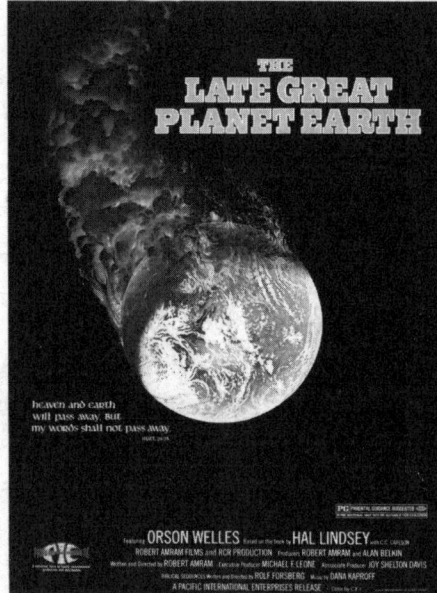

Poster art for *The Late Great Planet Earth* movie, 1978.

By the late '60s, Lindsey was running a communal home in an old frat house near UCLA called the JC Light & Power Company, training young evangelists in Bible studies and prophecy. The Light & Power house was part of a nationwide movement of young, self-described "Jesus freaks" who were being gleaned from the burned-over edges of the counterculture. They blended aquarian affect — sandals, beards, acoustic guitars — with fundamentalist (and often charismatic) the-ology. Alongside the Bible, *Late Great* would become the movement's most important text.

Lindsey preached with an easygoing Texas lilt and, at least during the 1960s and '70s, peppered his sermonizing with youthspeak and puns. In his book, the pre-Tribulation Rapture is "the ultimate trip." The whore of Revelation, dressed in her red toga, is "Scarlet O'Harlot."

Lindsey himself was no longhair. Although he was born in Texas, he was a pure product of the Southern California Bible belt, that palm and sunshine cradle of the aerospace industry and the modern Christian Right. He sported a bushy mustache and wore his hair sleeked up in a well-fixed televangelist coif. Rather than the baggy brown suits favored by the fundamentalist old guard, he wore Hawaiian shirts.

The book that would eventually exert such influence upon Vicki and Randy Weaver had its inception in 1969, when Lindsey set out to adapt his lecture notes into a book (although he left much of the actual writing to his co-author, Carole C. Carlson). The result, *The Late Great Planet Earth*, adapts John Nelson Darby's prophetic framework to the geopolitics and culture wars of 1970s America. From the dry stuff of Darby's dispensational schema, Lindsey confected a glossy tale of global intrigue and carnage. In that sense, he owes as much to the bracing violence of John's original Apocalypse as to its more scholarly modern interpreters.

The prose is melodramatic and schlocky, combining the cheeky idiom of tabloids with the thrills of an action movie. Lindsey claimed that his imagined audience was a cynical youth. Indeed, *Late Great* sidles up to the reader like a groovy youth pastor, offering mind-blowing secrets.

Despite Lindsey's slick presentation, his message was the same as that of every scraggly-bearded street prophet to ever don a sandwich board: The End Is Nigh. Specifically, he claimed that the Tribulation would commence sometime in the '80s, with Armageddon following seven years after that. How did he know that time was finally up? Well, in the olive grove discourse recorded in the Book of Matthew, Jesus implies that the Jews will be resident in Judea when He makes his triumphal return to Earth (as they were at the time He was speaking).

It was mostly from this scrap of text that Darby and others had determined that the restoration of the Jewish diaspora to Palestine was a necessary precursor to the Second Coming. When Jesus said, "This generation shall not pass, till all these things be fulfilled," what He *really* meant was that the endtimes could only commence one generation *after* the restoration of the Jews to the Holy Land. Estimating a generation to be four decades, Lindsey determined that the apocalyptic sequence of Rapture, Tribulation, and Armageddon would begin about forty years after the 1948 establishment of Israel. Expressing the complicated "affection" that American fundamentalists possess for the Jewish state, Lindsey calls Israel "the fuse of Armageddon."

Having determined that the endtimes are imminent, Lindsey, like others before him, saw evidence wherever he looked. "Gog," the evil kingdom mentioned in Ezekiel and Revelation, must be the USSR. The ten-horned Beast, which historians interpret as a thinly veiled proxy for Imperial Rome, is actually the then ten-state European Common Market. As for the "Babylon Mystery Religion" with which the Antichrist will ensorcell the nations, Lindsey saw it in the rise of spiritism, false prophets, Wicca, New Age–ism, astrology, and the drug culture. Seeing college kids doing yoga on the quad, Lindsey flatly asserts that they are "indulging in a primitive sort of sun-god worship," picked up from the idolaters in Big Sur. He claimed that the sorcery mentioned in ancient prophecy was really about drugs. He relates the story of a young Christian frat boy who had "blown his mind" on acid. "I've been taking trips and I've really seen God," the young man supposedly told him. "Only this God is the King of Darkness — this is the one we worship."

Lindsey explains that the Antichrist, who is already out there somewhere, slouching toward his awful purpose, will be greeted as a peacemaker, calling for internationalism and economic cooperation. This man will be deified by the masses before forcing everyone under his sway to accept the Mark of the Beast. As the Tribulation reaches its climax, Lindsey writes, the Antichrist's reign "will make the regimes of Hitler, Mao, and Stalin look like Girl Scouts weaving a daisy chain."

Sun salutations, European trade deals, and an ingathering of Jews between the Jordan and the Mediterranean were all important signs, but the real-world development that truly convinced Lindsey and his millions of readers that they were living in the endtimes was that, starting in 1945, the world-devouring conflict described in Revelation was, for the first time in history, a material possibility. Armageddon was coming and it would be nuclear.

As Lindsey tells it, a confederacy of Arab and African states, China, and the USSR will invade Israel, where the Antichrist will somehow have inspired the rebuilding of the long-destroyed Temple. This invasion will trigger a nuclear conflict that brings in the United States, which, *Late Great* concedes, is not mentioned in ancient prophecy.

Lindsey found an interesting solution to the problem of applying a literalist reading to the overtly symbolic language of endtimes prophecy. He argues that the ancient prophets described their visions as best they could, but that they simply lacked the vocabulary to describe calamities destined to unfold in the 1980s. Horses with lion heads that spit fire? That was a first-century man's best effort to describe the mobile rocket launcher that God had shown him. Falling stars? That must be ICBMs. Fire and brimstone that melt the flesh? Surely that's nuclear fallout. As for Revelation's locusts with human faces, a Green Beret friend told Lindsey that it was a perfect description of Cobra helicopters spraying poison gas. Much of *Late Great* is taken up with lists of armaments. For all his doomsaying, Lindsey takes a boyish delight in the details of military hardware, lingering over the missiles and bombers that author and historian Mike Davis called the "hot rods of the apocalypse."

If the two traditional functions of prophecy have been to console the downtrodden and admonish the wayward, Lindsey struck upon a third. He doesn't reassure or scold so much as he excites. In a rhetorical style that would partly define conservatism in the current age, he managed to deliver dreadful tidings in a way that got the crowd whooping. His blend of politics and prophecy, delivered in breathless, *isn't-it-all-so-obvious* prose, reenchants the world, turning modern life into something like a sci-fi blockbuster, full of hidden clues, dark conspiracies, and gathering speed. Again and again, he writes how "exciting" and "thrilling" it all is.

In the first century, John of Patmos had his bloody vision of Christian retribution and conquest. In the nineteenth century, John Nelson Darby hammered that vision into a pseudoscience for literal-minded Christians. In the twentieth century, Hal Lindsey burnished Darby's system into a product of mass entertainment and mass persuasion. Americans ate it up.

———————

The Late Great Planet Earth was published in 1970 by Zondervan, an evangelical press in Michigan. It sold so well that it was picked up by the trade publisher Bantam Books, where it continued to sell about twenty thousand copies a month into the '80s, despite the fact that Lindsey had pumped out half a dozen other bestsellers in the meantime. Quickly spilling beyond the prophecy shelves of Christian bookshops, it was sold alongside diet books, astrology guides, and bodice rippers on the spinning racks in drug stores, airports, and supermarkets.

The doomsday trade has always been brisk. Cheaply printed prophecy almanacs were ubiquitous in the Middle Ages. The first bestseller in the New World was Michael Wigglesworth's 1662 poem "The Day of Doom: or, A Poetical Description of the Great and Last Judgment." One of out every twenty residents of the Massachusetts Bay Colony owned a copy. During the golden age of televangelism and the "electronic church," when the Weavers were inside their ranch house, glued to *PTL*, TV ministers seemed to prosper in direct relation to the urgency and specificity of their prophetic warnings. Who could resist tuning in to hear Billy Graham host a special titled "Are the Last Days Almost Here?" The centrality of apocalyptic speculation to white, evangelical faith was probably not a matter of cynical financial calculation, but when you hit a note that gets the congregation jumping, you keep singing it.

Even with the airwaves and bookshops crowded with doomsayers, Hal Lindsey stood out for his success. The superlatives pile up. *The Late Great Planet Earth* was the best-selling nonfiction work of the entire 1970s, outselling everything except the book it purports to analyze: the Bible. Scholars now reckon that it is the most widely read apocalyptic text ever. At one point, Lindsey had three separate titles on the *New York Times* bestseller list. Bible scholar Bart Ehrman claims that Lindsey, who was running a rather slapdash YouTube ministry at the time of his death in 2024, was "probably the single most read author of religion in modern times." Among other distinctions, he was the first prominent commentator to identify then-candidate Barack Obama as the Antichrist, a notion that, according to polls, one quarter of voters believed in 2012. By one recent tally, *Late Great* has sold more than 81 million copies.

The book proved popular among readers like Randy and Vicki, who grew up steeped in fundamentalist theology, but it also spoke to people without much previous exposure to endtimes prophecy. *Late Great* was likely a key text in Bob Dylan's 1978 conversion to evangelical Christianity. Traces of its prophetic scenario are littered across Dylan's three overtly Christian records.

The Book of Acts says that an outpouring of prophecy will be a sign of the impending Second Coming. By that logic, *Late Great*'s runaway success was hailed as a certification of its prophetic accuracy—a theological version of McDonald's "Billions and Billions Served" or "50,000,000 Elvis Fans Can't Be Wrong." In 1978, the year Vicki brought home a copy of *Late Great*, the cover boasted "More than 9,700,000 in print!" Beneath that came every publisher's favorite jacket copy: "NOW A POWERFUL MOTION PICTURE." The movie adaptation is fittingly hallucinatory, starring a late-career Orson Welles, who wanders the Holy Land, contemplating the skull of a bygone prophet, like Prince Hamlet gone badly to seed. Interspersed with Welles's gravelly soliloquies are Pythonesque reenactments of the Hebrew prophets and stock footage of marauding hippies, sheiks in aviators, saucer-eyed Hare Krishnas, Chinese military parades, and mushroom clouds galore. Combined, the book and the film did in the 1970s and '80s what the Scofield Bible had done at the start of the century: mainstreamed Darbyite theology among people who maybe never heard the name John Nelson Darby.

Hal Lindsey in the movie version of *The Late Great Planet Earth*, 1978.

One of the virtues of Lindsey's writing is that, by compressing the endtimes drama into a seven-year window that is forever on the brink of commencing, breathless predictions of the End (and book sales) can be maintained for years. More than a century before Lindsey's success, in October of 1844, tens of thousands of followers of a New York preacher named William Miller waited on Northeastern hilltops for a Second Coming that failed to materialize. After what the press gleefully dubbed "the Great Disappointment," American prophets, Lindsey among them, grew more cautious about so-called date-setting. (The Seventh-Day Adventist Church was born from the ruins of Miller's wildly popular movement.)

While many of *Late Great*'s prophecies have now clearly passed their expiration date, the book successfully predicted the constellation of beliefs and fixations that would define right-wing politics in the first quarter of the twenty-first century, even after the main drama at the center of the book—the Cold War—came to an end. Lindsey's claim that international socialism was an instrument of the Antichrist led him to condemn entangling international alliances. His rejection of the social gospel led him to rail against welfare. His speculation about which nations (Arab, African, Asian) would make up the Antichrist's coalition stems from fairly overt racism. (*Late Great* features a chapter titled "The Yellow Peril.") The book spins a worldview in which any progressive action must be regarded as a stalking horse for the coming global takeover. Echoing the first generation of fundamentalists, Lindsey wrote that "God didn't send me to clean the fishbowl, he sent me to fish."

While earlier fundamentalists advocated separation from the temporal work of politics, Lindsey's belief in an impending One World Government fed a hawkish nationalism that aligned with politically engaged churchmen like Jerry Falwell. "The Bible," Lindsey asserted "supports building a powerful military force." Ronald Reagan was reportedly an enthusiastic reader of *Late Great*, and Lindsey claimed to have spoken regularly at the Pentagon.

One of the things that distinguishes a modern prophet like Lindsey from his counterparts in the fifteenth, seventeenth, or even nineteenth century, is that his catalog of portents is light on natural disasters. Instead, his focus is on political machinations. (Until the twentieth century, it would have been hard to align John's account of global domination and total war with existing technologies.) While Lindsey professed to "step aside and let the prophets speak," he demonstrated how endtimes prophecy can be made into a machine for generating reactionary politics or, at the very least, stamping those politics with the imprimatur of holy writ.

Other would-be revelators soon followed in Lindsey's footsteps. *Late Great*'s success unleashed a flood of prophecy, much of it shot through with right-wing conspiracism. In the 1970s and '80s, prophecy texts and TV shows became more accessible, more lurid, and much more widely consumed. The biggest titles sold in the millions. Along with new works, older tracts from the early days of Fundamentalism were revised and released as mass market paperbacks. Lindsey's most notable successor was Tim LaHaye, whose wildly popular *Left Behind* series (co-authored with Jerry B. Jenkins) debuted in 1995, expanding from a single novel to a series of books, films, and games. *Left Behind* imagines life on Earth during the years between the Rapture and the Second Coming. (Spoiler alert: the Antichrist is the smooth-talking UN secretary general.) The series hews closely to Lindsey's formula, wedding Darbyite dispensationalism to a gripping action-adventure plot, this time without even the pretense of nonfiction.

As endtimes prophecy became an object of mass entertainment, Lindsey's account, with its emphasis on turmoil in the Middle East and the emergence of a globalist cabal, became the commonplace, multigenerational faith of countless Americans, even when their churches preached a different vision of the End or neglected the subject altogether. By one conservative estimate, at least 40 million Americans can currently be classified as premillennial dispensationalists. Many more, having absorbed dispensational theology through Christian pop culture rather than denominational authority, expect the endtimes to look approximately like Lindsey or LaHaye described them. Hal Lindsey, with his popular reworking of Darby's dispensationalism, probably supplied more DNA to the contemporary American right than the likes of Edmund Burke or Leo Strauss.

———

The Late Great Planet Earth lit a fire under the Weavers, clarifying and sacralizing their foreboding sense of a world off kilter. "You've got to read this book," Vicki excitedly told her younger sister Julie, in the way she might previously have recommended a sci-fi page-turner.

After she read the book, Julie Jordison worried about the effect such a tale might have on her sister and brother-in-law, who already seemed to be getting more zealous and combative about their faith. The way that endtimes prophecy overlays the disorder of everyday life with an exciting narrative—a secret conspiracy to establish a One World Government! creeping Satanism! a shooting war between Good and Evil!—spoke to the mythic and literary tendencies of Vicki's imagination and to Randy's taste for anything combative or shocking.

Like iron filings before a magnet, every aspect of the Weavers' lives began turning to face the gathering End. Even more than the preaching they heard at Cedarloo Baptist, or from Jerry Falwell and *PTL*, the decisive push had come from a simple paperback. Despite several radical leaps to come, Vicki's beliefs about Armageddon— when and how it would arrive—never strayed far from the predictions laid down in Hal Lindsey's bestseller.

CHAPTER FIVE

GOING UNDER ON THE PLAINS

IT WAS VICKI who first started having visions. In one, she saw herself and Randy driving up a steep, densely forested mountain road. In the rearview mirror were three young kids, each with a biblical name. At the time, they only had baby Sara. And Iowa contained no such elevations. Other scenes followed: snatches of future vision accumulating into a story. She saw her family living on a mountaintop, safe and secure, as the world below unraveled. Whether or not she noticed it, these scenarios echoed some of the fiction she had read in her youth, notably Ayn Rand's *Atlas Shrugged* and H. G. Wells's *Dream of Armageddon*. It certainly fit with what Hal Lindsey had described. Before long, Randy said he could see it, too. Trouble was coming. Mass violence. Persecutions. They needed to be prepared.

Something about the vibrancy of these images, which came to Vicki in the tub or as dreams, made her interpret them the way someone from a previous century might have. Instead of taking them as amorphous transmissions from her own inner depths — for instance, a new mother's desire to shelter her brood from an uncertain world — she took them as direct instructions from God: Go, hurry, don't look back. There was something lightly messianic in Vicki's belief that she had been favored with a special warning—that she, like Noah or Lot, had been plucked out from the great, sleepy mass for special knowledge and special travails. Or maybe it was just that Vicki, a perfectionist in most matters, was suffused with the perfectionist's gnawing sense that nobody else was paying enough attention.

In 1978, the Weavers brought two-year-old Sara to a barbecue with some of Vicki's old high school friends. By then she was pregnant with child number two, Samuel. It had been a long twelve years since graduation. Amid the usual catching up about kids, houses, and jobs, Randy and Vicki announced that bad things were coming down the line. They were going to move out West, somewhere they would be safe when the trouble began.

———

From the outside, the slide into conspiracism looks like a descent: down the rabbit hole; off the deep end; deeper and deeper into the darkness of unreason. From within, it feels like the opposite, a journey upward into the clear light of truth, like the angel's-eye view of history offered by prophecy. In the Greek, *apokalypsis* means uncovering, laying bare—a revelation. John of Patmos, like the older Hebrew prophets he imitated, described rising up into the sky to see the full sweep of history, past and future. Inside their home on University Avenue, Randy and Vicki had begun thinking about higher truths and higher ground.

Convinced that events were "fast ripening," as fundamentalists sometimes say, the Weavers plunged into the growing body of literature devoted to a malevolent cabal that Americans would variously call ZOG, the New World Order, or the Deep State. Before the Internet, it took significant effort and time to pursue this at-home curriculum. The Weavers sent away for tracts, purchased cassettes, tuned in to prophecy broadcasts, drove to specialty bookshops, and combed the back pages of right-wing magazines for ads pointing to other, more extreme sources.

With Hal Lindsey's klaxon still ringing in their ears, they began to formulate a plan. Like many others of their era, Randy and Vicki had embraced the premillennial account of the coming End without the consoling promise of a pre-Tribulation Rapture. They would have to find more practical ways to ride out the coming crisis.

———————

By the late 1970s, Randy had developed the habit of walking down University Avenue after his shift at Deere & Company to Sambo's Restaurant. It was a Denny's-type chain, with cheerful young servers, lots of brightly lit linoleum, and a minstrel-style mascot called Little Black Sambo. (The last remaining outlet changed its name in 2020, during the season of protests after George Floyd's killing.) A loose, rotating crew of about ten men — Deere workers, shopkeepers, retirees, an off-duty cop — had begun meeting there in the evenings with their Bibles and cigarettes to parse scripture and pray.

Apocalyptic prophecy, with its evergreen account of social decay and creeping perversion, jibes easily with the crabby bullshitting that is native to small-town coffee shops at off-hours. As such groups often do, the men at Sambo's talked themselves toward increasingly radical notions. "We were crazy born-again legalists," recalled one regular at the Sambo's conclave. "We just fed off each other and got more and more out there." The writer Jess Walter, then a young reporter for the Spokane, Washington, newspaper *The Spokesman-Review*, would later interview several members of the Sambo's crew. They recalled Randy as a principal member of their scene, which Walter identified as "the center of the radical born-again movement in Cedar Falls."

As the '70s wound down, the guys at Sambo's had plenty to grouse about. While Randy and Vicki accumulated evidence that ancient prophecy was being fulfilled, a very real disaster touched down on the prairie. Stands of small white crosses began cropping up at town lines and on courthouse lawns across Iowa. They offered a grim public tally of a rolling economic crisis: each cross represented the foreclosure of a family farm. Some crosses memorialized specific farmers. Iowans had begun killing themselves at four times the national rate.

American farmers live on credit, borrowing in the spring to buy seed, fertilizer, and equipment, and then repaying their loans after the harvest. Following the Dust Bowl and the Depression, a series of federal programs were established to shelter farmers from the twin hazards of a volatile commodities market and bad weather. To stabilize the size of the harvest (and therefore prices), growers were offered price supports and low-interest federal loans if they agreed to limits on what they grew. In many cases, the government accepted repayment in the form of grain, establishing a network of government-operated storage depots. These programs ensured a steady food supply for the nation and protected small farms from the predations of the large grain companies, which benefit from the fact that most farmers need to sell at the same time of year, when prices are at their lowest.

Under Presidents Eisenhower and Nixon, and thanks to the lobbying efforts of companies like Cargill and Continental Grain, these federal programs were eroded in favor of a more laissez-faire approach that necessarily favored larger farms that benefited from economies of scale and had the capital to ride out price swings. At the same time, new technologies allowed fewer and fewer farms to produce more and more food. Besides cheaper grain and meat, the main consequence was steady consolidation: bigger farms, fewer farmers.

The Midwest was so fertile and the new machines and chemicals were so effective that it began to seem as though the only relevant limit on what farmers could grow was the market. During most of the '70s, with a world hungry for American crops and the Soviet Union buying up a large share of the harvest, sales kept expanding, with exports tripling over the course of the decade, keeping prices aloft despite rising yields. Old fears of overproduction came to seem like a relic of the past. Urged on by a bullish Department of Agriculture, Midwestern farmers invested in expensive new machinery, bought up land, and worked every arable acre—planting "hedgerow to hedgerow," as the secretary of agriculture urged.

To pay for all this expansion, small regional banks plied farmers with cheap credit. "They almost hauled you in and stuffed the money down your shirt," recalled one Iowa farmer. Things were booming in the heartland. Soaring inflation tripled the price of land, making many farmers rich, even if only on paper. At the same time, in the space of little more than a decade, the amount of debt held by American farmers increased tenfold. It was as if the entire Great Plains, that vast ocean of grassland bisecting the continent, had been mortgaged.

Then, in December of 1979, the Soviet Union invaded Afghanistan to prop up an unpopular left-wing regime at war with the American-supported Mujahideen. A month later, President Carter canceled contracts with the USSR for the purchase of American soy, corn, and other grains. Midwestern farmers were suddenly sitting on an enormous bumper crop. Prices tumbled. The next year, at the outset of Reagan's first term, the Federal Reserve took drastic measures to curb inflation, sharply raising interest rates and spiking the value of farmers' loan payments. First the market had shrunk, and now the cheap credit was gone, too.

When farmers rushed to sell off surplus acreage, the value of farmland cratered. Since that same acreage served as collateral on all those loans, the banks began to foreclose. Families were evicted from land they had owned and worked for generations. With so many farms being auctioned off at bargain prices, land values fell even further, leading to more defaults and more foreclosures. Then the banks themselves began to fail. Things were in freefall.

What came to be known as the farm crisis did little damage to the sprawling fruit and vegetable operations of the West and Southeast, let alone the rest of the national economy, which was emerging with apparent vigor from a long period of high inflation. Meanwhile, the small, family-owned beef, pork, and grain farms of the Midwest were devastated. Between 1981 and 1988, 625,000 family farms simply vanished.

An economic crisis in farm country is its own special sort of calamity. Since almost everyone is selling the same handful of commodities, the damage spreads very fast. When a farm is foreclosed, an entire family becomes homeless and unemployed in a single stroke. For farmers driven off land that their families had improved relentlessly for years, the shame and anger were acute. So-called deaths of despair surged in the Midwest. In a place where almost every aspect of the economy flowed, in one way or another, from agriculture, the crisis hit everyone. For every four farms that failed, at least one nonfarm business — a grocer, a feed and supply store, a bank, a barbershop, a restaurant — went under. "The sharp report of the auctioneer's gavel echoed across the prairie," wrote the North Dakota journalist James Corcoran. "It serves as the death knell to a way of life."

Even compared to its Midwestern neighbors, Iowa was truly a one-industry state. It became the epicenter of the crisis. By the early '80s, Iowa ranked forty-ninth in the nation for total employment growth. In 1983, the state held five hundred farm auctions each month.

In 1979, at the start of the crisis, Deere & Company employed almost a quarter of the population of the greater Waterloo area, Randy Weaver among them. As farmers made do with older machines or gave up farming altogether, the company laid off ten thousand workers. Eight years later, Deere would employ just 10 percent of the local population. Many people simply left. Over the course of a decade, Waterloo lost 14 percent of its population.

Small communities seemed to be vaporizing under the pressure of vague, distant forces. The fact that nothing more concrete than "the market" could be blamed — grain prices down, interest rates up — made the whole thing even more bewildering. The silos were overflowing. There hadn't even been a drought (although two would come later in the decade, compounding the situation). Postwar confidence slid into queasy paranoia. For people steeped in prophetic faith, the cruel, invisible hand of the market looked like the work of more sinister forces.

At Sambo's, talk of Jewish bankers, tyrannical usurpers, and currency manipulation mixed with the prayer and prophecy. Randy, who enjoyed holding forth in his frank, smoky voice, stood out for his command of scripture and his increasingly far-out ideas. He bristled with theories, waxing irate about the evil forces that had wrested control of the government, intent on destroying an entire way of life. He said that everyone's guns were going to be confiscated in advance of martial law. He said that the Federal Reserve was corrupt, and that the dollar was on the brink of collapse. Best put your money into silver. The communists might invade from Canada. He started sleeping with a pistol under his pillow.

There is no single explanation for the persistent undercurrent of conspiratorial thinking in the United States. Since well before the American Revolution, hysteria over fantastical secret plots (by enslaved African Americans, by Catholics, by Masons, by Jews) have been a recurring and destabilizing force. Recently, as conspiratorial politics have moved squarely into the mainstream, there has been much debate about why such thinking continues to exert such pressure. The usual explanations range from the brain-heating effects of social media, to economic despair, to white anxiety about racial displacement. Some point to the fact that American-style liberalism, with its insistence upon each citizen's command of their own destiny, fails to supply a satisfying secular theodicy — that is, an explanation for why bad things happen to good people.

The prevailing diagnoses give little consideration to the actual story at the center of most conspiracy theories, a narrative that has remained remarkably stable, despite dramatic changes in real world affairs. The sheer power of that tale and its manifest satisfactions — secret knowledge, martyrdom, community, a grand finale — might be reason enough for the stubborn persistence of conspiratorial thinking in American culture. For the Weavers, as with millions of other citizens, a conspiratorial interpretation of events emanated naturally from their faith. As the conservative theologian R. J. Rushdoony put it, "While the liberals may view belief in the conspiracy view of history as absurd, or even as a sign of membership in the 'lunatic fringe,' the orthodox Christian must assert it to be basic to the philosophy of history."

Since most critics and historians are not religious fundamentalists, they are disinclined to attribute social phenomena, no matter how baffling, to theological causes. On the contrary, they tend to look through the other end of the telescope, assuming that the faithful are propelled to their beliefs by material forces. The right-wing activist Andrew Breitbart famously declared that politics are downstream from culture. Whether or not that is true, for millions of Americans, religious convictions are at the headwaters of everything else. "No Western nation is as religion-soaked as ours," wrote the critic Harold Bloom, "where nine out of ten of us love God and are loved by him in return. The mutual passion centers our society and demands some understanding, if our doom-eager society is to be understood at all."

Of the various forces that contribute to the conspiracism that saturates American life, apocalyptic faith may be the most potent, the most widespread, and the least understood. One reason for this lack of understanding is that, given time, ideas imbibed at church — ideas, for instance, about where history is bound and how it gets there — tend to ramify, sprouting shoots and branches that wend in unexpected directions. Eventually, it is possible to lose track of the theological roots pumping life into what, up near the canopy, resemble political tendencies and cultural moods. In the case of apocalyptic Christianity, those roots plunge very deep, gripping the American soil like a fist.

In the same way that thermonuclear weapons lent newfound plausibility to ancient visions of a world-devouring fire, the globalization and systematization of the economy laid bare by the farm crisis echoed Revelation's description of a global empire that could use economic mechanisms (i.e., a "mark" required for buying and selling) to squelch resistance. Even before the Internet, the birth of the information age bred anxieties about a mathematized, dehumanized future. To some, it felt like they were being reduced to spindled punch cards in the cabinets of some sinister bureaucracy. In 1982, *Time*'s Person of the Year was the computer. For the first time in history, the specter of some all-seeing, all-controlling system seemed like a material possibility, especially in a place where Big Ag, monetary policy, and distant commodity markets bossed the prairie without mercy. Revelation's account of Babylon — evil made manifest as a system, rather than an individual — fit the moment.

Even the style and syntax of biblical prophecy, with its hidden codes, numerology, and tantalizing ellipses, prefigures modern conspiracism. Describing the birth pains of the End, the Book of Matthew warned not only of wars but of "rumors of wars."

Previous generations of American Christians found the Mark of the Beast lurking behind everything from the Stamp Act of the Revolutionary era, to social security numbers, to the blue eagle logo of FDR's National Recovery Administration, to a surge in "union made" labels. In the late 1970s, seated in his booth at Sambo's, Randy wondered aloud if credit cards would serve as the Mark. Subsequent generations would quail likewise at the arrival of barcodes, biometrics, COVID vaccines, 5G networks, and AI.

As the Weavers were drawn into a culture and communion organized around resistance to a global conspiracy, they betrayed signs of a more overtly local variety of paranoia. Again and again, people around them — "so-called friends," as Randy repeatedly put it — seemed to be scheming against them.

In 1984, a friend of Randy's named Woody contacted the IRS to report Randy for trying to foment "a tax protest," leading to a pro forma investigation and audit by the IRS. As Randy later told it,

Woody hoped that (falsely) accusing the Weavers of being involved with the growing and occasionally violent tax resistance movement in the farm belt would somehow get him off the hook for his own unpaid tax bill. Besides the fact that this certainly would not work, one reason to doubt Randy's precise version of events is that, just a few years later in Idaho, nearly the exact same thing happened again, when a different "so-called friend" reported Randy to the feds for plotting political violence.

The notion that unconnected individuals in two states sought to harm the Weaver family through the rather exotic method of lodging false accusations with the federal government seems farfetched. A more likely explanation — one that recalls the interminable "literally vs. seriously" discourse of the Trump era — is that Randy was a natural-born tirade artist, who, when he got up a full head of steam, reached for the most shocking possible provocation, occasionally frightening or angering his audience enough that they took him at his word. Once, during a living room debate about gun control with his father-in-law David (hardly a gun-shy progressive), Randy exclaimed that "someone ought to kill the Supreme Court justices," adding, for good measure and no apparent reason, that the Holocaust was a hoax. To his family, such statements were merely conversation enders — just Randy trying to get a rise. As Vicki's sister Julie put it, Randy "talked about a lot of crazy stuff. But he would have never done it." In 2023, Sara Weaver would use a more contemporary formulation when she said that her father simply "had no filter," as if politesse was the main thing keeping most people from Holocaust denial and assassination fantasies.

Paranoia has a way of generating its own content. If you walk around town fretting about how everyone is watching you, people might steal glances. "It is possible," observed Walter Lippman in 1914, "to work yourself into a state where the world seems a conspiracy and your daily going is beset with an alert and tingling sense of labyrinthine evil." Regardless of what motivated separate individuals in separate states to report Randy for (theoretical) threats against the state, both instances triggered contact from federal authorities (the IRS the first time, the Secret Service and FBI the second).

These visits heightened the Weavers' tingling sense that malign forces were keeping watch over them — even though the truth was that nobody was really paying much attention to Randy and Vicki Weaver in the early '80s. They had their kids and were halfway through paying off their mortgage. Even as the farm crisis battered the region and layoffs spread at Deere, Randy kept his job doing machine maintenance. Over in Coalville, the Jordison clan managed to hang on to the farm, with the land and operation eventually passing from Vicki's father David to her sturdy, hardworking brother Lanny.

Vicki's newly strident religious convictions brought her a confidence that she had lacked as a younger woman. She grew her hair long, got some tight bellbottoms, and bought an embroidered leather jacket. Although she could be quick to correct people on points of theology or child-rearing, the Weavers were friendly and openhanded. Randy, in a display of genuine gospel conviction, periodically brought home "strays" — hard-up young men — for a meal, a place to crash, and a strong dose of evangelism. Convinced of an impending financial crisis, he gave friends and family silver coins and ingots.

In the summer of 1981, Vicki gave birth to Rachel. The steep mountain road from her dreams was still just a vision, but now they had Sara, Samuel, and Rachel, three healthy children with biblical names.

CHAPTER SIX

UNCHURCHED

AS RANDY AND Vicki grew more certain about the coming Tribulation, they began to sour on their church. The gospel on offer at Cedarloo Baptist may have been dispensationalist and literalist, but nobody there seemed to be taking the implications very seriously. The Weavers were warm and gregarious neighbors, but fellowshipping over casserole was not what they craved. For the Weavers, the ceremony of innocence was over.

There are few notions as radicalizing as the belief that you are living in the final days of history. The restraining civic virtues — posterity, good manners, neighborly accord, tolerance — are rendered trivial in the face of looming apocalypse. If time is running short, who can bother with the warm opinion of others? It is the same logic that drives conspiratorialism. If people cringe and flinch, you must be on the right track. The more they say you're crazy, the closer you must be to the truth.

For reasons that remain vague, Randy and Vicki felt ridiculed or targeted by fellow congregants for the increasing urgency of their faith. To them, it seemed like everyone else was unwilling to accept the heavy burdens of prophecy. Even Hal Lindsey, who had more or less promised an imminent Armageddon, seemed oddly unmoved by his own predictions. "I have never taken to the hills with my possessions and loved ones to await Doomsday," he wrote in the introduction to *The Late Great Planet Earth*, as if speaking directly to Vicki Weaver. "I believe in hope for the future." Of course, most books don't require a preamble advising readers *not* to dash for the high country.

Countless people pull off the remarkable trick of a deeply religious life—keeping one foot in the grand cosmic drama and one in the skim of daily life. Vicki's father, for instance, studied prophecy on Sundays while devoting the rest of his week to the future-oriented business of farming. That balancing act eluded Randy and Vicki.

When they resolved to quit Cedarloo Baptist, the choice was not purely theological. Despite being quick to take up new theories and ideas, the Weavers were ill-suited for membership in any sort of organization, religious or otherwise. Randy in particular was a born gadfly. Like hundred-percenters of every sort, he and Vicki saw hypocrisy wherever they looked. Mike Roethler, a police officer friend who prayed and studied with the Weavers, claimed that the family left their church because Randy "felt all the organized churches [had] sold out." Even after the family moved to North Idaho, and found themselves surrounded by people who shared their apocalyptic beliefs, they never joined any organized group. Although Randy was later filmed worshipping inside the Aryan Nations chapel in Idaho, the Weavers would never again belong to any formal congregation.

Sara Weaver, who was a young child at that time, later recalled that there was "some kind of friction between my folks and the church, and soon afterwards, we stopped attending." At various times, she has alluded to some specific betrayal or slight, without revealing exactly what happened. Most likely, someone told Vicki she was wrong about something. Whatever the case, they left Cedarloo Baptist with a lingering distaste for professional preachers.

Years later, having been born again into a more conventional evangelical faith, Sara would describe her parents' exit from Cedarloo

Baptist as a turning point. "This was the first domino that fell. It was the domino that began triggering the chain of events that some ten years later would end in the unspeakable tragedy at Ruby Ridge."

Inside the ranch house on University Avenue, the Weavers were locked into their own miniature Reformation, descending downward through layers of received belief, communal tradition, and clerical authority, never quite finding bottom. Having rejected the familiar path to salvation, they became certain of their own route. "That was how and when it started," Sara wrote. "Everything changed."

Inevitably, Randy and Vicki's uncompromising zeal alienated friends and neighbors, hardening the couple's impression of a world arrayed against them. "Apparently some people were offended as our religious and political views changed," Randy later wrote. "We soon realized that people who seek and share what they have learned, are quickly out of the mainstream. Those that do share can pay a high price."

After Woody's letter to the IRS triggered a call from the authorities, Randy became convinced that their phone was tapped. At work, he was repeatedly scolded for preaching on the shop floor. "I know there are people who want to see me fired," he said at the time. "The ones who see the truth will accept us. The ones who do not want the truth will call us crazy. But that's fine. People can call us anything they want. I will speak the truth and they won't stop me."

Unchurched, the Weavers began hosting a regular Bible study, gathering with a group of like-minded seekers several evenings a week in their carpeted living room. In the 1970s and '80s, this sort of thing was happening all over the country. As mainline churches shrank and fundamentalist theology spread over the airwaves, small "Gospel tabernacles," "Bible fellowships," and at-home prayer groups proliferated, often blending practices from various denominations. This was the logical endpoint of the *sola scriptura* literalism upon which

Fundamentalism had taken its original stand. If the book contains everything, why not do away with the trimmings — the smells and bells, as Catholics sometimes say — of organized ritual and communion?

Abiding the conspiratorialist's first commandment, the Weavers did their own research. Hal Lindsey, who helped set them on this path, identified the first Christians as the original doers of their own research. Unbelievers in Christ's time, he wrote, "knew there was something unusual about this carpenter from Nazareth, but their religious leaders rejected Him and they took their opinions instead of searching for the truth themselves. It was because people will not do their own research that Jesus...showed simply and clearly how prophecies were being fulfilled by His life." Vicki delved into Christian apocrypha — texts excluded from the canonical Bible — seeking additional information about the Apocalypse and, in particular, evidence of their latest conviction, that the Jews would have a special role to play in what was to come.

Some of the people who joined the Bible study were members of the crew that had formerly gathered at Sambo's. Apparently, those evenings had grown too large and boisterous to be held in a public restaurant. One Sambo's regular who joined the Bible study was Shannon Brasher, a handsome young ex-marine and Vietnam veteran who worked security at Deere. Randy and Vicki had initially talked him into joining Cedarloo Baptist. When they left the church, he followed them out.

Vaughn Trueman, another Bible study regular, credited Randy with personally bringing him to the Lord. Trueman ran a gun shop in Cedar Falls called the Bullet Hole. One day Randy came in asking about which guns would be best for some sort of survivalist scenario. The two men became fast friends. Recalling the Weavers' Bible study, Trueman described faith healings, glossolalia, and a great deal of weeping. "Randy and I cried together many times. I saw healings and heard things you can't explain."

Over the course of the late 1970s and early '80s, the Bible study became a close-knit community, with Randy and Vicki naturally assuming positions of authority. She was the resident theologian; he was the ardent preacher. The gatherings sometimes went late into the night. People brought their children. While the adults discussed prophetic signs, Hebrew etymologies, and how best to prepare for what was coming, the kids would play downstairs. Some days, the group drove out of the city to run shooting drills.

Other preparations were more domestic. The more Vicki read and prayed, the more emphasis she placed on what is known as theological legalism. For most Christians, Jesus's gospel of salvation through grace rendered the elaborate rigmarole of Torah strictures obsolete, but Vicki, stirred by the majestically wroth divinity of the Old Testament, felt otherwise. Despite her own warm disposition, her God was not a gentle redeemer who takes your hand. He demanded purification and obedience, shouting: "I am!"

They started by giving up pork and shellfish. Next, Vicki adopted a highly literal reading of the Second Commandment, which forbids keeping or making images. While it is generally understood to regard idol worship, the text is plain: "Thou shalt not make unto thee any graven image, or any likeness of anything." Vicki went through the house, taking down art and photographs. The television, once an important source of theology, not to mention the kids' beloved *Scooby Doo*, was put away. Randy and Vicki asked Samuel and Sara whether they would be willing to give up any toys that could be regarded as images. The children consented. "Sam got rid of his stuff to please God," Sara later wrote. "I got rid of my stuff to please Mom and Dad." Vicki even went next door to trade plates with her friend Carolee Flynn. The Weavers' dishes were decorated with a hand-painted pattern of birds. The Flynns' were plain white.

As Vicki came to see it, the great mass of Americans were not just atheists or shaky half-believers, they were (perhaps unwitting) acolytes of a wholly different faith, an ancient polytheism that she identified with Babylon. Since the days when Puritans described the Indigenous population of North America as minions of the biblical

Satan, many of the most devout American Christians have regarded the unredeemed not merely as neutral on the matter of Christ, but as devotees of an equal and opposite creed. This shift may appear subtle, but it raises the stakes considerably. The struggle is not between faith and doubt, but between worshippers of Christ and followers of Satan. Randy felt the same. As one old friend said of him, "I guess you could say he thought the world was full of Satans and he was a godly man."

Taking seriously the proposition that evil and corruption will spread until Christ's return, Randy and Vicki racked up evidence of satanic influence all around them. They read Salem Kirban, a briefly popular fundamentalist author who wrote what he called "newspaper exegesis." His works include *Satan's Angels Exposed*, *A Guide to Survival*, *The New Age Secret Plan for World Conquest*, and *666*, a novelization of the endtimes that prefigured the *Left Behind* series. Kirban's books are like Hal Lindsey's, but pulpier in style and more paranoid in their conclusions. "Events in history are no accident," Kirban wrote. "They are a conspiracy orchestrated by Satan himself." In 1981, at the height of the doomsday craze, Kirban established a toll-free prophecy hotline. (Like many castoff prophets, he eventually drifted into health faddism, selling supplements and a book called *Unlocking Your Bowels for Better Health*.)

Bent on her own notions of spiritual hygiene, Vicki turned her attention to the place where civic life and conservative reaction most often clash in the United States: public school. In the 1920s, it had been a fight over the science curriculum in Tennessee that first revealed the existence of the Fundamentalist movement to most Americans. In the century since Scopes, public schools have been the battlefield for a series of moral panics, ranging from the rights of parents to their children's labor, to racial integration, public professions of faith, vaccinations, LGBTQ rights, and the nature of American history.

Vicki herself had thrived at Fort Dodge Senior High, earning top grades and involving herself in clubs, but she came to believe that

the public schools in Iowa were awash with drugs, sex, and Satanism. The true purpose of public education, she decided, was to groom
rising generations for submission to the coming One World Government. After Sara's first-grade class held a Halloween event—blatant
Satanism!—Randy and Vicki pulled her out of school. It wasn't just
Halloween that bothered the Weavers. Vicki concluded that most
Christian holidays were satanic or pagan in origin. No more Christmas tree. No more Easter bunny.

Vicki resolved to teach her kids herself. In the '70s, the chief
advocates of homeschooling had been free-thinking graduates of the
counterculture. By the '80s, the movement had grown dramatically
(and gained significant political clout) as fundamentalists took up the
cause, seeking to shield their children from the influence of liberal
teachers and administrators. Since homeschooling without a teaching
certificate would not be legalized in Iowa until 1991, Vicki researched
where it was allowed. Idaho was on that list.

Conspiracy theorists have a peculiar tendency to mimic the cabals they
seek to expose. The most ardent anti-communists formed secretive cells
much like those employed by the CPUSA. The Klan cooked up elaborate rituals, costumes, and secret handshakes that bore a strong resemblance to the rites of the Masons and Catholics they abhorred. As the
Weavers' conspiratorial faith grew more antisemitic, they lived more
and more like observant Jews, devoting their worship to the Old Testament, eating their own version of kosher, and keeping a twenty-four-
hour Sabbath that began Friday at sundown. In place of the usual cycle
of church holidays, they celebrated Torah-based holy days, albeit with
modifications. They marked the "Feast of the Trumpets," a Christianized Rosh Hashanah, as well as the "Feast of the Tabernacles," a messianic Sukhot. More generally, they began to speak of the United States
as a modern Babylon in which they lived as internal exiles, harried and
persecuted despite their special covenant with God.

While old Iowa friends like Shannon Brasher and Vaughn Trueman would later testify in court that Randy and Vicki's turn to hard-
core racism and antisemitism did not begin until the family reached
Idaho, the process had obviously begun in the Midwest. Mike Roethler, the Cedar Falls police officer who became a member of their
at-home Bible study, recalled an afternoon at Sambo's when Randy
leaned across the booth and explained that Jews were descended
from Satan. "How can you believe that?" Roethler recalls responding.
"Jesus was a Jew!" This sort of talk, along with the family's adoption
of the word *Yahweh*, and the fact that Randy had (rightly or wrongly)
been identified as a "tax protestor," strongly suggests that, even before
they moved west in 1983, the Weavers had begun to absorb a particular bundle of religious and political ideas that filtered into the Midwest at the start of the 1980s.

The modern militia movement, with its paramilitary trappings
and revolutionary rhetoric, is usually traced to the early '90s, and the
aftermath of Waco and Ruby Ridge. In fact, the movement's first rum-
blings were heard more than a decade earlier, in those places worst
scorched by the farm crisis.

At the start of the crisis, some Midwesterners directed their ire at
the small regional banks that were calling in loans and conducting
foreclosures. One Iowa banker was murdered by a ruined farmer. As
the crisis progressed, it became obvious that the lenders were doing
as poorly as the growers. In Iowa alone, twenty-eight banks failed —
more darkened storefronts along newly blighted Main Streets. So who
to blame?

In 1977, a group of farmers formed the American Agriculture
Movement to protest foreclosures and falling crop prices, directing
their appeals to the government. They organized strikes and "trac-
torcades" to demand federal assistance, creating a paradox whereby
farmers raged at Washington's meddling while calling for dramatic
support and intervention. The movement sought legally enforced
"parity," meaning price supports to balance the costs of running a

farm with what farmers could hope to earn. In the winter of 1979, a large convoy of trucks and tractors rolled into Washington, DC, threatening an all-out farm strike — no planting, no reaping, no food — if Congress did not backstop falling prices. Smaller satellite protests took place in state capitals across the country. For Americans beyond the Plains, these protests were the first indication that something was amiss in the heartland.

When Congress failed to address the farmers' demands and the crisis worsened with a spike in interest rates, the AAM was derailed by factionalism, most of it stoked by far-right activists who hijacked meetings and took over local chapters. They framed the crisis in conspiratorial rather than structural terms. Preaching armed resistance, antisemitic conspiracy theories, and bogus legal schemes, they sapped the grass-roots energy out of the AAM.

Iowa has a history of progressive organizing and agrarian populism that goes all the way back to the abolitionist movement. During the farm crisis, however, it was the radical right that made the most significant inroads in the region. After a decade of steep decline, Klan membership exploded in the Midwest, rising by 20 percent in 1979 alone, producing what some describe as a fourth wave for the "invisible empire." Likewise, the John Birch Society, already a decade past its demographic peak, expanded in the region, convincing farmers that their birthright was being stolen by international financiers intent on forming a socialist global order.

One of the era's most profuse and effective founts of far-right ideology was *The Spotlight*, a weekly newspaper published by the Liberty Lobby, a self-described "pressure group for patriotism" founded in the late 1950s by a former Bircher named Willis Carto. Along with supporting the presidential campaigns of nationalists like George Wallace and Pat Buchanan, *The Spotlight* focused on the influence of global organizations like the United Nations, the ever-looming specter of gun confiscation, and the malign doings of international Jewry. During the farm crisis, the magazine had 300,000 subscribers, the

Weavers among them. Its masthead included several staffers who had been pushed out of the John Birch Society for their overly explicit antisemitism. It paired stories about struggling farmers with polemics against the Federal Reserve, prepping tips, and a steady drumbeat of Holocaust denial. Its back pages were a hub for neo-Nazi and "Christian Patriot" organizing, as well as a clearing house for information about alternative medicines, survivalism, and guns. After his arrest, Timothy McVeigh would claim that much of his worldview had come directly from *The Spotlight*.

Even more than the white-robed Klansman or the "little old ladies in tennis shoes" of the Birch Society, it was a newer, more militant strain of right-wing activist that became the face of resistance in farm country. The Posse Comitatus was more of a movement than an organization — loosely organized and comprised of chartered branches, small study groups, and unaffiliated enthusiasts. The group's name, Latin for "power of the county," derives from the Posse Comitatus Act of 1878, passed after Reconstruction to prevent federal troops from interfering in state affairs — most specifically, to keep the feds from policing Southern elections.

Posse ideology was a syncretic hodgepodge of endtimes Fundamentalism, conspiratorial antisemitism, and paramilitarism — all wrapped up in arcane legal cant about common-law courts and the illegitimacy of pretty much every American institution beyond the county sheriff. The aesthetics of the movement were greatly influenced by the militarized culture that had boomeranged home from the war in Vietnam. In place of seed company hats, axe handles, and shotguns, Posse activists styled themselves as citizen soldiers, wearing fatigues and carrying light assault rifles (then still advertised as "military style"). While the Klan and earlier far-right organizations generally regarded themselves as a vigilante arm of state authority, the new activists — many of them radicalized by what they saw as their government's twin betrayals in Indochina and farm country — regarded the feds as their main antagonist. They claimed that paper money was illegitimate and urged citizens to invest in silver, guns, and dehydrated food.

Because one of the ways Posse adherents expressed their beliefs was by refusing to pay taxes, the group was often mischaracterized by the media, law enforcement, and even many adherents as little more than a collection of rambunctious tax resisters, which hardly captures the scope of the movement's beliefs or ambitions. The true animating force behind the Posse was religious, specifically a strain of racist, endtimes Fundamentalism known as Christian Identity. While most Posse adherents probably did not think of themselves as devotees of a religious sect, all of the movement's founders and leaders, along with its most celebrated martyrs, were members or ministers of Identity churches.

Within the Posse movement, politics and faith were inseparable. Along with a lot of talk about gun rights, sovereign citizenship, and tax laws, Posse charters routinely stated that "the chief executive of this government, now and forever, is Yahweh." The word *Yahweh*, known as the tetragrammaton, comes from four Hebrew consonants Romanized as YHWH. According to Exodus, this is the name the Lord supplied to Moses. In English translations of the Bible, the Hebrew is usually rendered "God" or "the Lord." When used by Christians, "Yahweh" often (but not always) implies some link to Christian Identity theology, which places special importance on God's "sacred name."

While the farm crisis greatly accelerated the spread of the Posse in the Midwest, the movement had been around for almost a decade. Its roots, like so much else on the modern right, lay in Southern California.

William Potter Gale, a retired lieutenant colonel in the US Army who had served on the staff of General Douglas MacArthur, dabbled in many of the far-right organizations active in Los Angeles County during the 1950s. After long sessions of Bible study with a Klansman friend, he converted to the fledgling Christian Identity faith, which tied together various far-right preoccupations with a single, if somewhat elaborate, theological bow. Along with a lot of peculiar notions about how to read the Bible, Christian Identity's animating idea was that international communism, "race-mixing," and pretty much everything else that was wrong with the world was the work of a demonic Jewish cabal that was orchestrating the global government described in Revelation. This funhouse mirror version of Fundamentalism represents one more turn in the long cult of Patmos, with its panting visions of Babylon aflame and Christ swinging an iron rod.

It was not until the early 1970s that Gale, then preaching at his own Identity church in the Sierra foothills, began formulating the ideas that would become known as Posse Comitatus, creating a sort of ideological Swiss Army knife of the far right, offering something for everyone from hardcore racists to endtimesers, anti-communists, antisemites, weekend commandos, tax resisters, and pissed-off farmers. In the same way that Hal Lindsey wrung boilerplate New Right conservatism from ancient prophecy, Gale scooped up the assorted fixations of the far right and welded them to the apocalyptic story told in Revelation, framing the coming Armageddon as a conflict between God's chosen people (white Anglo-Saxons) and the seed of Satan (the Jews). In Identity cosmology, people of color are regarded as less than human — mere weapons used by the Jews to diminish, dilute, and replace the righteous power of whiteness.

The Posse movement first spread up the West Coast into Oregon and Washington, mostly through a network of Identity churches. In Portland, Henry Lamont Beach, a former member of the American-Nazi Silver Shirts, founded an early Posse chapter and began issuing charters and paperwork to groups throughout Oregon. (Because Beach plagiarized some of Gale's writings and did a good job distributing them, he has often been misidentified as the Posse's founder.)

In North Idaho, not far from where the Weavers would soon settle, an aeronautics engineer turned neo-Nazi preacher named Richard Butler established the Kootenai County Christian Posse Comitatus, which would evolve into the Aryan Nations, a sort of ecumenical congress for the radical right.

When the farm crisis hit, Posse activism leapt from the West Coast to the farm belt, spreading like the proverbial prairie fire. Riding an upwelling of right-wing populism and organizing, Gale spread his movement with agitprop aimed squarely at distressed farmers. His pamphlets were passed hand to hand at churches and farm auctions. His blazing radio sermons were broadcast from a country music station in Dodge City, Kansas. In a raspy bark, Gale exhorted citizens to ignore the feds, form their own municipalities, and, when push comes to shove, take any "official who violated the law and the Constitution…to the most populated intersection of the township at noon and hang him by the neck." He left no ambiguity about who exactly those officials might be. "Arise and fight!" he yelled over the radio. "If a Jew comes near you, run a sword through him." Posse members took to calling the federal government ZOG—"Zionist Occupied Government." The term caught on. It would not be long before presidential hopeful Pat Buchanan winkingly referred to Congress as "Israeli Occupied Territory."

Posse activists told distressed farmers to ignore liens, stop paying their taxes, and reject the efforts of volunteer lawyers and activists who were working tirelessly to halt foreclosures and save family farms. Instead of sound legal advice, Posse spokesmen offered high-flown rhetoric and weapons training. Addressing distressed farmers from his pulpit in Idaho, Richard Butler explained that the crisis was the work of the Jewish Antichrist. "The farmers were the first victims of the Revolution of 1776, as they are the first victims of this revolution. He's been dispossessed of his land, he's been used and abused… He's going to get a lot more angry, and eventually he'll see that the only way to turn things around is to fight to win his country back for white Christians." Posse literature told farmers to rip up their birth certificates, drivers' licenses, and Social Security cards.

In 1982, William Gale co-led paramilitary training retreats in Kansas that featured classes in knife fighting, poisoning, bomb making, perimeter defense, booby traps, guerilla warfare, and, in the evenings, family Bible study. At a permanent base on a farm in Wisconsin, Posse activists held "survivalist" trainings. For Gale, as for others who would organize under the banner of the Posse, guns were always near the center of things. As they told it, the first objective of the One Worlders was going to be the forced disarmament of white Americans. By the mid-'80s, according to Daniel Levitas, an advocate for Iowan farmers turned scholar of the complex lineages of the radical right, the Posse had between twelve and fifteen thousand "hard-core activists," with ten times that many people supporting the movement in less formal ways. A surprising twist in all of this, as painstakingly documented by Levitas, is that William Potter Gale was Jewish, a fact known to him, if not his legions of followers. In the '80s, while Gale was leading the nation's most militant antisemitic movement, his first cousins were prominent members of the Jewish community in Portland, Oregon.

A 1986 advisory sent to federal law enforcement agents claimed that Posse members could be identified by the gold, noose-shaped lapel pins they sometimes wore. The hangman's rope, long a tool and emblem of racist terror, was now a symbol of resistance to the feds. As with everything related to the Posse, including the historical significance of its name, the line between antigovernment reaction and white supremacy was blurred to the point of invisibility. For many white radicals, "federal tyranny" seemed to mostly mean the enforcement of civil rights legislation or the imagined redistribution of white wealth to citizens of color. The unknown Trumpists who erected gallows during the Capitol insurrection probably did not intend to actually hang Mike Pence — their setup was too janky for a real execution — but they certainly got their message across.

While there is no clear evidence that the Weavers knew him, a Posse activist named Ed Murphy worked alongside Randy at the Deere foundry in Waterloo. Murphy had attended paramilitary training camps in Iowa and Missouri "to prepare," he explained, "for an invasion of the United States or the end of the world." Along with another Deere employee identified only as Charlie, Murphy, who was recruiting for the Idaho-based Aryan Nations, told student reporters from the University of Northern Iowa that Jews were descended from Lucifer, that they had orchestrated the farm crisis, and that the federal government was establishing concentration camps for white Christians in advance of the coming Tribulation.

Randy, being neither a farmer nor a joiner, does not seem to have been directly involved with any Posse organizing, but he and Vicki were plainly influenced by the movement's presence in Iowa at the start of the 1980s. They would soon be espousing their own version of Christian Identity theology, and, in the years to come, would come into contact with some of the movement's biggest names. Even late in his life, after Randy had given up all talk of Yahweh and Babylon, he continued to spout the Posse's eccentric reading of the Constitution, in particular the idea that county sheriffs are the sole legitimate source of civic authority — a notion that would be one of William Potter Gale's most lasting contributions to the American right.

CHAPTER SEVEN

THINGS UNSEEN

DURING WHAT TURNED out to be the Weavers' final two years in Iowa, events gathered speed. The weekly "Church Notices" section of the Waterloo *Courier* offers a nice glimpse into the busy spiritual lives of the hundred thousand souls residing in the greater Waterloo–Cedar Falls metro area. In the second week of March 1983, thirty-eight different churches (and exactly zero mosques, temples, or synagogues) announced events. It was midway through Lent, the season of abstinence inspired by Christ's forty-day fast at the outset of his ministry. Taken as a group portrait, the notices reveal the great multiplicity of ways that Christ's followers interpret their shared text and common traditions, even within the relatively homogenous confines of Central Iowa.

At St. John Lutheran, parishioners were gathering for a Lenten potluck, with a sermon provided by the aptly named Rev. Fish. Across town, at the Breath of Christ Fellowship, a charismatic revival was underway, calling down the healing gifts of the Holy Ghost with foot-stamping and tongues. Over at Sacred Heart, the Ancient Order of Hibernians, once the subject of lurid anti-Catholic conspiracy theories, had invited Bishop Dunn over from Dubuque to lead the annual St. Patrick's Day mass. At Faith Temple, one of just a few

African American churches in the area, a Seventh-Day Adventist was scheduled to address the Baptist congregation, suggesting the ways that racial affinity can trump denominational commitments within American Christendom. The Episcopalians had chosen to mark the season quietly, with a one-day meditation retreat (please bring a sack lunch). At Hagerman Baptist, where signs and portents were the order of the day, Dr. Manfred Kober, a German-born dispensationalist from the Dallas Theological Seminary (the Darbyite "Vatican" and Hal Lindsey's alma mater), was leading a prophecy conference. And for the eldest generation of Lutheran farmers, Trinity American was offering a German-language service, with coffee and delicacies to follow.

The shortest listing on the page announced a religious gathering within the temporal precincts of the Cedar Falls Holiday Inn. The notice did not mention any denomination, proclaiming only: "Todd to Speak." And beneath that: "John Todd will be teaching fundamental Bible… at 7:30 p.m. Monday, Tuesday, and Wednesday." The event's organizers, though unnamed in the notice, were Randy and Vicki Weaver.

Todd, a tall, slender man with blond hair, a mustache, and the shaggy good looks of an outlaw country singer, showed up at the Weaver house wearing a sidearm and accompanied by a neo-Nazi "bodyguard." Friend and neighbor Carolee Flynn, out of her element but trying to be supportive, baked rolls and brought them over. Vicki, who would later grow accustomed to the presence of neo-Nazis in Idaho, warned Carolee to keep her distance from Todd's companion.

On the first evening of Todd's three-night engagement, a disappointing crowd of twenty straggled into the Holiday Inn ballroom. Just a few years earlier, Todd had been drawing huge crowds, touring the country preaching to various fundamentalist and Pentecostal congregations. Like many popular Evangelicals, his ministry centered on a dramatic account of personal salvation. He claimed to have been born into the Collins family, a clan of Druid witches that had disguised themselves as Puritans to import Satanism to the New World, first coming to public notice during the Salem witch trials. Gradually they became "the most powerful witchcraft bloodline on the North American continent." Raised as a witch, Todd (who also went by John Wayne Collins, Kris Sarayan Kollyns, and other names) assumed that his family's faith, which goes all the way back to Lucifer himself and was the official state religion of ancient Babylon, was just like any other denomination.

As a young man, he explained, he had gone into the army to help spread witchcraft in the armed services. (Todd sometimes claimed to have been a Green Beret in Vietnam. Military records show he spent just twenty-five days overseas, at a desk job in Germany.) As he told it, one drunken night in Stuttgart he shot and killed his commanding officer. Awaiting trial for murder in a prison cell, Todd was surprised by the arrival of a US senator, a congressman, and several generals. They released him, handed him an honorable discharge, and destroyed all evidence of the murder. They even sent some of the witnesses to die in Vietnam. It was only then that Todd realized his family's real power, learning that they served as the in-house clergy for the political and financial cabal that rules the world: the Illuminati. (*Lucifer* means "light-bringer." So does *Illuminati*.)

Todd's standard sermon recounted how he rose through the ranks of the Illuminati, organized in the USA under the banner of the Council on Foreign Relations—a real organization, based in New York City, that has been a bugaboo of the conspiratorialist right since the early days of the John Birch Society. (It was a particular preoccupation of Hal Lindsey.) As Todd told it, he ascended to the rank of Grand Druid High Priest, earning a seat on the Council of Thirteen where, along with Freemasons, Rothschilds, and other influential individuals, he worked to advance the Illuminati's plans for the coming One World Government. This conspiracy involved the Rockefellers, the Kennedys, the World Council of Churches, the Anti-Defamation League, and the United Nations.

Todd's remit within the Illuminati was to distribute bribes to prominent politicians, religious leaders, and cultural figures, which is how he was able to learn exactly who had been corrupted by the cabal. Flattering his churchgoing audiences, Todd explained that

Bible-believing Christians, by virtue of their well-girded souls and natural distaste for change, represented the only impediment to the Illuminati's scheme of global domination.

In preparation for the rise of the Antichrist, whom Todd periodically identified as Jimmy Carter, the Illuminati planned to confiscate everyone's guns, round up all the Christians, and sow disorder with drugs, sex, crime, and rock and roll. Under the influence of Todd's preaching (and widespread belief in the novel theory of "brainwashing"), fundamentalists leaned into the notion that Satan was spreading his influence through popular music. As Todd told it, the Illuminati set him up with a job in the record industry, which is how he learned that the lyrics to most hit songs had been penned by professional witches and their melodies were lifted from ancient Druidic manuscripts. The Beatles; the Stones; Crosby, Stills, Nash & Young; and other stars of the era were all priests within various satanic orders. Among witches, he explained, the Beatles are commonly known as "the four prophets." The *White Album* contains Illuminati prophecy. KISS is an acronym for Kings in Satanic Service.

Todd dropped famous names with relish. David Crosby was once "his closest friend in the whole world." Carole King, a Satanist and a lesbian, was also a friend. Charlie Manson was a good buddy. Todd's recollections of his life in the Illuminati bring to mind the type of pastor whose testimony of rebirth shades into bragging. ("I was lost without Jesus, my friends. A different beautiful woman every night. Fast cars. A big fancy house.") Along with his undercover work in the music business, Todd claimed to have served as JFK's private warlock. Kennedy, he explained, had been shot because he had somehow become a real Christian, refusing to submit to the pope and the Illuminati.

For conspiracy hunters, there is no source more thrilling than the insider turned whistleblower, especially one who tells his tale at great personal risk. Todd said that his Illuminati career had come to an end in 1972, when he gave his life to Christ and resolved to blow the lid off the cabal. His story, which blended endtimes theology with an Illuminati-centered conspiracy theory that goes back to the

1790s, spread quickly within Baptist and Pentecostal churches. His matter-of-fact, oddly charming talks circulated widely as cassettes, which is where Randy and Vicki first heard them.

Todd's sermons, which ambled off in every possible direction, illustrate two of the abiding paradoxes of the conspiratorial interpretation of events. The true-believing conspiracist blends devouring skepticism (*consensus reality is all a lie*) with shocking credulity (*this weird thing I read must be true*). The fact that an idea is taboo is often sufficient to certify its veracity. The theories propounded by everyone from Todd to William Potter Gale, to the online community that collectively generates QAnon's protean cosmology, inevitably drift toward ever-increasing complexity—producing a feverish semiotics of signs, symbols, numerologies, and genealogies. The conspiracists' red string unspools into a wild tangle. The result is a chaotic scrum of images and ideas: adrenochrome and black helicopters; the Rothschilds and the Beatles; Comet Ping Pong and FEMA camps.

Beneath this inclination toward the byzantine, the conspiratorial worldview rests upon an assumption of childlike simplicity and optimism: bad things happens because of bad people. Poverty, injustice, crime, alienation: all the ills of the world are the work of some hidden villain. "As a framework for thought, this has its advantages," wrote the novelist Denis Johnson. "It's quicker to call a thing a crime and ask, *Who did it?* than to call it a failure and set about answering the question, *What happened?*"

The story at the heart of Todd's tale is nothing new. In his celebrated history of millenarian movements, Norman Cohn summarized "the central phantasy" of apocalyptic believers: "The world is dominated by an evil, tyrannous power of boundless destructiveness—a power moreover which is imagined not as simply human but as demonic. The tyranny of that power will become more and more outrageous, the sufferings of its victims more and more intolerable—until suddenly the hour will strike." In that instance, Cohn was writing about the Maccabean revolt of the second century BCE, but without changing a word he could be describing the beliefs of Todd, the Weavers, or, more recently, the adherents of QAnon.

In the 1970s, Evangelicals most often encountered Todd's revelations in the form of "Chick Tracts," a series of cheap, pocket-sized comics that were distributed in churches, passed out on street corners by youth groups, and scattered in places (bus stations, porn shops, bars) where sinners congregate. These comic books, which often involved the Illuminati, witchcraft, and scheming Jesuits, were drawn and written by Jack T. Chick, a reclusive Southern California illustrator. *Broken Cross*, one of Todd's collaborations with Chick, tells the story of an underground network devoted to ritual blood sacrifices, lightly updating an ancient libel about Jews that has precipitated countless episodes of non-make-believe violence. In this and other instances, Todd serves as a missing link between the antisemitic fantasies of the Middle Ages and contemporary conspiracies about liberal elites and their youthful victims.

A 1978 Chick Tract featuring John Todd.

Chick, an ardent fundamentalist and anti-communist, consciously modeled his comics on the brightly illustrated, pocket-sized booklets printed by the Chinese Communist Party to win over the rural peasantry. Chick Publications claims to have produced 900 million printings in 102 languages, which would make Chick Tracts the most widely distributed comic books in history.

For a time, popular ministers hosted Todd in their churches and vouched for his shocking story. He began to fall out of favor when he added prominent churchmen to his ever-growing list of Illuminati operatives, starting with leaders in the charismatic movement, whom he accused of introducing witchcraft into the liturgy, and eventually including Jerry Falwell and the broadcasters at *Praise the Lord* and the Christian Broadcasting Network. Even then, some preachers claimed that Todd's account of the Illuminati was basically true, but that, as a confessed Grand Druid, his specifics might not be reliable in every detail. His claims were taken seriously enough that Senator Strom Thurmond, a Freemason, was forced to give up his seat on the board of Bob Jones University.

In 1979, *Christianity Today*, the leading evangelical magazine, which had been founded by Billy Graham, set out to investigate "the Todd phenomenon." The resulting feature reported several instances in several states in which Todd had been caught trying to establish "covens" of teenage girls. The magazine also reported that Todd had "converted" to Christianity more than once (and in a variety of denominations) only to repeatedly backslide into a lifelong obsession with witchcraft. In 1974, long after his first ballyhooed conversion, Todd was employed at The Witch's Cauldron, an occult bookshop in Dayton, Ohio. There and elsewhere, he was caught recruiting young women into his occult ceremonies and forced to leave town.

Todd was quite obviously a delusional charlatan. What matters is not what he said, but how he was received. There will never be a shortage of raving paranoiacs with delusions of grandeur. Some portion will be charismatic enough to gather a crowd. What is remarkable about John Todd is that he was taken seriously by so many, including people in positions of real influence. Even skeptical fundamentalists regarded his claims as something in need of corroboration, rather than merely the ravings of a broken mind. *Christianity Today* framed its Todd exposé as a debate to be conducted within the family: "Is witch-turned-evangelist John Todd a prophet sent from God to warn America about an impending takeover by sinister forces, or a fraud? Fundamentalists across America disagree on the question." One book devoted to Todd's claims was titled, *The Todd Phenomenon: Fact or Phantasy?* (Answer: A little of both.)

By the time the Weavers invited him to Cedar Falls, Todd had been denounced by Jerry Falwell and other fundamentalist leaders. Even the John Birch Society had condemned him as a huckster. On the other side of street, so to speak, the national Church of Wicca, to whom Todd had turned for legal support when arrested for "contributing to the unruliness of a minor," revoked his coven charter.

Only his most hardcore followers remained. Along with Randy and Vicki, that group included the members of a Baptist church known as Zarephath-Horeb, which had relocated from Missouri to a large, wooded property in the Arkansas Ozarks. There, under the influence of Todd, the Posse Comitatus, and the Christian Identity movement, the church morphed into a commune-cum-paramilitary known as the Covenant, Sword, and Arm of the Lord (CSA). "Our group embraced everything Todd preached," explained one church leader. "He explained the source of our problems."

Rather than just talking and praying, members of the CSA were training to be the tip of the spear in the coming apocalyptic ground war. They were certainly well prepared. According to the historian Michael Barkun, the compound in Arkansas was "arguably the most heavily armed communal settlement in American history." Taking an accelerationist approach to the endtimes, they evolved from apocalyptic survivalism to overt acts of terror, intent on bringing the war to ZOG. In 1985, the FBI raided the Arkansas community, an event that would reverberate on the far right and greatly influence how federal law enforcement thought about well-armed apocalyptic Christians, including, eventually, the Weaver family.

Even as Todd's name drifted into obscurity, his insider's account of a secretive occult network grew, feeding into what came to be known as the Satanic Panic, in which many Evangelicals became convinced that their kids were being groomed by the devil with rock music, Ouija boards, and Dungeons and Dragons. Todd's preaching helped produce the panic's leading subplot: the belief that powerful people were trafficking children for "satanic ritualistic abuse." This

notion, stoked by the testimony and memoirs of alleged victims, contributed to a wave of misguided police investigations (often triggered
by recovered memories), many of which focused on daycare centers
and reflected a generalized anxiety about women entering the work-
force and leaving their children in the care of strangers.

Despite these lurid imaginings, child abuse generally originates in
the home. In 1984, two years after the Weavers hosted Todd in Cedar
Falls, he was arrested in Kentucky for molesting his own niece. He
received probation. Four years later, he was sentenced to thirty years
in prison for raping a University of South Carolina graduate student
at knifepoint. Released into a psychiatric facility in 2004, he brought
a civil suit against the government for denying his right to freely practice Wicca, to which he had evidently returned. He died in 2007.

Today, John Todd's influence lingers in conspiracy theories about
celebrities, Masons, the Illuminati, and a secret cabal that rules the
world. While such stories have always been a feature of American life,
Todd helped hitch those old stories to a prophetic vision that remains
highly influential among American Protestants. (Todd's narrative is
notable in that it did not arrive at the most common terminus for
such theories: the Jews.) Four decades after the height of his celebrity,
Todd can fairly be called the unheralded progenitor of QAnon.

As has become obvious in recent years, fringe panics of the sort Todd
kicked up are a politically potent force, especially when they are laun-
dered into more reasonable sounding concerns. It is just a few short steps
from shocking tales of ritual pedophilia—*à la* Pizzagate and QAnon,
which were plenty popular in their own right—to more mainstream
panics about librarians "grooming" children with rainbow flags and picture books about gay penguins. Always and forever, anxious parents like
Vicki Weaver represent a large, well-networked, and energetic constituency. Anything that lights them up will be an irresistible political tool.

By the time Todd came to visit the Weavers in the winter of 1983,
he had conflated his own "persecution" with the state of the world,
concluding that the awaited Tribulation was already underway. Along

with his family, he had moved to a ten-acre farm in Montana where, with his weapons and supplies, he intended to ride out the final days. It was precisely the type of retreat the Weavers were considering.

———

Randy and Vicki were no longer just the sort of people who sent away for conspiratorial cassettes and read *The Spotlight*. Despite having three kids under six, they were now something like grass-roots activists within a loosely defined movement — the sort of folks who took it upon themselves to track down Todd (no easy task), get him to Iowa, rent a ballroom, and submit a notice to the local paper. They had also landed on a shorthand for their worldview, a term that was just then coming into use by a subset of right-wing, well-armed Christians. When a reader of the Waterloo *Courier* wrote to the editor asking who was responsible for the Holiday Inn event, the paper replied that Todd's appearance had been arranged by "a number of individuals in Cedar Falls, characterizing themselves as Christian Survivalists." For the Weavers and many others who expected to experience the Tribulation here on Earth (i.e., without being taken up into the sky beforehand), "survivalism" became something like an earthbound Rapture: a way for those with their ears cocked for the final knell to ride out what was coming. Survivalism added a quixotic turn to the whole issue of the endtimes: you can make it, but you'll have to do it yourself, like an action hero.

At the Bible study on University Avenue, there was more and more talk of moving west. "I remember very clearly when they had their vision," Vaughn Trueman recalled. "Everything seemed to be pointing to leaving and going to the mountains." The members of the group started to plan a communal exodus. At the very least, Vaughn Trueman and Shannon Brasher, Randy's friend who worked security at Deere, were both planning to go.

Vicki found sanction for their plan in prophecy. In the Book of Matthew, when Jesus sketches out the endtimes for his apostles, He said: "When ye therefore shall see the abomination of desolation, spoken of by Daniel the prophet, stand in the holy place... Then let them which be in Judaea flee into the mountains... For then shall be great tribulation, such as was not since the beginning of the world to this time, no, nor ever shall be." Likewise, the Old Testament prophet Ezekiel, when describing the rise of the endtimes government known as Gog, wrote: "And I will call for a sword against him throughout all my mountains, saith the Lord God."

In a city as small as Cedar Falls, it did not take long for rumors to spread about the people on University Avenue arming themselves and talking about the Apocalypse. In 1982 and '83, Shannon Brasher sometimes lived at the Weaver home. People around town had begun to refer to the Bible study as "the group." At some point, Brasher brought his new girlfriend to the house. When she described the proceedings to her parents — the guns, the wall lined with canned food, talk about a coming holy war — their minds turned naturally to a cult. A decade since the Manson killings and five years after Jonestown, the United States was still experiencing a rolling panic about the dangerous potential of cults. The young woman's parents called the police. As it turned out, the Cedar Falls PD had been keeping an eye on "the group" for the previous two years. Whatever they had learned, they were not concerned enough to say anything to Mike Roethler, who was both a local police officer and a central member of the Bible study.

While no laws had been broken, local curiosity was sufficient for the Waterloo *Courier* to put a reporter on the story. Shannon Brasher, a man apparently given to passionate enthusiasms, had been a hang gliding fanatic before he got into survivalism. In the mid-'70s, a local journalist named Dan Dundon had profiled Brasher about his (then exotic) hobby. It was through Brasher that Dundon secured an invitation to the Weaver home sometime around Christmas of 1983.

Today, people like Randy and Vicki Weaver would likely generate a great heap of message-board comments and Facebook posts, allowing future historians to track their evolving beliefs with the precision of a geologist studying layers of sediment in a roadcut. As it happened, the Weavers did not leave much of a paper trail in the early '80s. In 1983, a full decade before they came under the searing limelight of the national media—at which point parties on every side had reason to hype, distort, or soft-pedal the family's beliefs—the profile that Dan Dundon wrote for *The Courier* offers a glimpse into what the Weavers were thinking, as recorded by a reporter with no way of knowing what was to come.

Dundon was greeted warmly by Randy, Vicki, and Brasher, all of whom seemed eager to dispel the cult rumors and accusations of "indoctrinating young people." Randy, always happy for an audience, seemed genuinely keen to get out "the truth to metro area residents." The Weavers speculated that the cult talk might have started because they had been passing out literature, books, and cassettes. They explained that they were just a group of friends who met to talk about religion. Unprompted, they denied any connection to a group called The Way International, a cultlike fundamentalist network that was organized around small, at-home Bible fellowships.

As they had with the John Todd event, the Weavers described themselves as "Christian survivalists" and said that the Tribulation was coming soon. "The Bible teaches," Randy patiently explained, "that somewhere near, during the reign of the one-world leader, God will remove his restraining hand from Satan, the destroyer, and let him wreak havoc with the inhabitants of the earth for a period of time known as the great tribulation." The way it would go down, he explained, was that the government would initiate some sort of chaos as an excuse to institute martial law. Blending Hal Lindsey's predictions with Posse-style legalese, Randy explained that certain obscure laws, combined with some sort of "computer technology," would soon be used to bring the populace under total control, paving "the way for the establishment of a one-world government with a one-world leader." They added, without any apparent context, that the Catholic Church was satanic.

Dundon's Sunday feature is a restrained and respectful account of the family, without much in the way of editorial commentary. Explaining the absence of a television or any photos on the wall, Randy is quoted as saying, "We reject idolatry. We do not bow down to, nor make, nor own idols or images." The Weavers declined to be photographed for the resulting Sunday feature, citing the Second Commandment. Instead, the piece was illustrated with a drawing of a Bible and two oversized bullets.

Randy, whom the article identified as a Green Beret, described his plans for a defensible mountain stronghold. Using a phrase that would become important during his trial a decade later, he said that he planned to establish a "300-yard 'kill zone' encircling [their future] compound." The concept of a "kill zone" surrounding one's home is not uncommon among survivalists. Years later, when Senator Arlen Specter asked Randy about the phrase, he grew heated. "That was a straight-up lie," Randy said. It is not clear why a local reporter, with no apparent axe to grind and no way of knowing what was to come, would fabricate such a specific lie. Dundon, who was flown to Idaho to testify at Randy's trial, stood by his reporting under oath.

Dundon's article about the Weavers underscores the way in which the family's circumstances and beliefs seemed so discordant to an outsider. Here were clean-cut, steadily employed, working-class Americans, with a mortgage, toys on the floor, and fresh-baked cookies in the kitchen. Warm and neighborly Midwesterners, they had a nice home on a safe street, in a safe town, in a relatively tranquil part of the country. And yet they were arming themselves to the teeth and warning about a demonic "one-world leader." Brasher, who had seen serious combat as a marine in Vietnam, slept with a flak jacket, a helmet, and a loaded pistol beside his bed. Randy did the same. They seemed to be living in relation to events that were invisible to an outsider like Dan Dundon—shadowboxing an apocalypse only they could see. Their minds were fixed, in the apostle Paul's famous phrase, "not on what is seen, but on what is unseen."

PART II
ACROSS THE GREAT DIVIDE

The sound of a shaken leaf shall chase them; and they shall flee, as fleeing from a sword; and they shall fall when none pursueth.

— *Leviticus 26:36*

CHAPTER EIGHT

AWAY!

AFTER MORE THAN a year spent turning in a gyre of expectation, the Weavers achieved escape velocity in the summer of 1983. It was time to cash in on the great centrifugal promise of being an American: upping and leaving. Through some mix of prophetic math and private revelation, Vicki now believed that the End would commence in about three and a half years, a timetable closely aligned with the one Hal Lindsey had laid out a decade earlier, but six years short of the private apocalypse that was actually coming for the family.

They put the house up for sale. Yahweh would let His will be known through the real estate market. A good offer would be the Go sign. "We're servants and what the lord tells us to do we will do," Vicki said. "He has told us we have to pull up our roots and leave. I don't want to leave my home, but if we are obedient then He will protect our children." At the start of the summer, the house sold for fifty thousand dollars. They cleared almost half of that.

By then, all talk of "the group" decamping *en masse* to establish what Mike Roethler once described as a "survivalist, fundamentalist retreat" had faded. God told Vaughn Trueman to stay put in Iowa. Shannon Brasher, who had definitely been planning to go the previous winter, had fallen out with the family. While he had been living with the Weavers, Randy caught him having sex with his girl-friend. If hand-painted dishes were forbidden under Vicki Weaver's roof, premarital sex was way over the line. Perhaps more significantly, the Weavers blamed Brasher for orchestrating the *Courier* profile, which had done little to quell local chatter about the family's radical-ism. More names were added to the roster of "so-called friends." The family would be striking out on its own.

———————

Although Vicki claimed that she did not want to leave, their departure seems to have been less in spite of suburban security than because of it. The Weavers had attained a version of the American dream and it left them cold.

It would be hard to find a pair of youngish Americans more overtly at odds with the cultural upheavals of the long 1960s, but the Weav-ers' disaffection with what Randy would call their "meaningless exis-tence" in the "rat race" of suburban Iowa echoed the counterculture's insistence that there was something hollow at the core of postwar prosperity, with its neat yards, ticky-tacky ranch houses, and nine-to-five shifts. "Vicki and I had come to the conclusion," Randy wrote, "that we wanted to raise our children away from the . . . ever-increasing intrusions of government. I could no longer envision spending the rest of my life working in a factory for forty or fifty hours a week and waiting all year for my three-week vacation." His elision of intrusive government and factory shifts is telling. It was all one big thing, and Randy wanted out from under it.

The idea of roving west for a harder, more authentic existence mirrored other seekers of their generation, many of whom had fled middle-class comfort to make their fate in the wilderness. There was certainly more room for apocalyptic heroism and drama out West in the mountains than in Cedar Falls, a town that proudly identifies itself as "the Lawn City."

No one family ought to stand in for an entire subculture, but the spirit that carried the Weavers west underscores one of the abiding misconceptions about the apocalyptic and conspiratorial right, namely that it is born of fear and precarity. The belief that you are living through the last days of history can fill life with vitality and adventurism. In the end, the Weavers were not direct victims of the economic disaster in the heartland. Despite making himself a nuisance with his evangelizing, Randy did not lose his job at Deere & Company. What made the difference was that the Weavers were on the ground when the farm crisis brought new ideas to town. It was proximity to those ideas — Posse Comitatus, Christian Identity, survivalism, John Todd's satanic conspiracy — that swept them up. And since those ideas were all, in one way or another, offshoots of the apocalyptic faith that had been reorienting American Protestantism for a century, it all seemed to fit together.

Rather than a retreat from gathering doom, the move west felt like the start of a Swiss Family Robinson–type escapade. "He was excited, and so were we," Sara recalled about her father. "This was going to be a *real* adventure." They would get horses. They would build their own home. They would eat big pots of venison chili. Load up the prairie schooner! Away to the mountains! *Away!*

Dragging their furniture and possessions onto the lawn, they held a series of yard sales to raise cash and unload the trappings of middle-class American life. Randy sold his Harley, which must have stung. To replace their suburban "luxuries," they collected new things — a cast-iron woodstove, kerosene lamps, garden tools, canning equipment. DeEtta Lisby, a Cedar Falls neighbor whom Randy used to annoy by wandering over to prattle on about Armageddon, sold them an old-fashioned toaster that worked on top of a woodstove. Vicki's conviction that the dollar was about to collapse lent their preparations a special urgency. "I prayed," she wrote, "that He would let me know so I could finish getting supplies before our money was useless."

Randy amassed a large collection of hunting knives, guns, and a great deal of inexpensive ammo. In 1982, looking upon what many twenty-first-century Americans would regard as a fairly ordinary domestic arsenal, the journalist Dan Dundon marveled at the family's collection of "military assault rifles," shotguns, handguns, and more than four thousand rounds of ammunition. Among the various impulses that fed into Christian survivalism (and the militia movement that was its direct descendent), the lure of the gear itself cannot be underestimated. Anyone who has flipped through the pages of *Soldier of Fortune* magazine or seen Oath Keeper types strolling suburban sidewalks laden to the point of comedy with tactical doodads can surmise that the equipment offers its own satisfactions: a soothing sense of invulnerability and a Cub Scout fascination with the accoutrements of war and wilderness. It is an impulse as old as the "arming of the hero" passages that recur in epic poetry and as reliable as the clickety lock-and-load montages in every action movie. Randy, who had fast cars, a Harley, and a snowmobile before he got serious about survivalism, was a confirmed gearhead.

Vicki, for her part, had no problem with guns and would eventually take to carrying one most of the time, but for her, "survivalism" mostly meant home-birthing, herbal medicines, and canning. In the run-up to their departure, she researched food-storage techniques, learning to dehydrate fruits and vegetables. The whole family took a field trip to a local Amish community to learn about living without electricity. Even before it became a matter of practical necessity, Vicki was known for her green thumb. Vaughn Trueman marveled over her huge homegrown "Jesus tomatoes." By the time they left Iowa, she had accumulated a year's worth of supplies: five-gallon buckets filled with flour, sugar, rice, beans, matches, spices, toilet paper.

Carolee Flynn watched in distress as Vicki ran herself ragged preparing for departure. Already slim, she lost fifteen pounds during the frenetic weeks before they hit the road. Randy traded the family station wagon for a one-ton moving truck and a trailer to pull behind his pickup. The day before they left, four-year-old Sam fell off the back of the new truck, breaking his foot.

———————

Then, on a humid August morning, with Sam's new cast propped up on pillows, they pulled out of Cedar Falls. Their first stop was the Jordison farm, where they said farewell to Vicki's siblings. Of all the family they left behind in the Midwest, Vicki's parents were the only ones they would see regularly during their Idaho years. No amount of distance or extremism would keep them from their grandkids. Randy's father Clarence visited once, but Wilma never made the trip.

On their first full day on the road, the Weavers stopped for breakfast at a restaurant in Clear Lake, not far from the Minnesota border. In the bathroom, Randy struck up a conversation with Fred Jess, who wrote a weekly column of folksy commentary for Iowa's *Jefferson Bee & Herald*. Randy excitedly told Jess that he had graduated from Jefferson High and the men chatted through breakfast. And so it was that the Weaver family's grand adventure made it into that week's paper. "Turned out to be Randy Weaver, son of the Clarence Weavers, and of course he knew practically everyone in Jefferson. He and his wife Vicki and three kids have lived in Cedar Falls for about 10 years, but at the time they were on their way to a new home in far northern Idaho." (Here, trapped in the amber of a small-town paper, is evidence that the Weavers were consciously aiming for North Idaho, a fact that Randy would later fudge in his statements and memoirs.) This parting shot of Midwestern familiarity fit the moment. In the tradition of lighting out for the territory, part of the deal is shrugging off generational weight for something lighter. Randy's name would appear in thousands of subsequent newspaper articles around the globe, but nobody would ever again identify him as "son of the Clarence Weavers." Nor would he retain much association with the Midwest. He would become a creature and icon of the West, like a smaller version of fellow Iowan Marion Morrison, who traveled in the same direction to become John Wayne.

Full of talk about persecution and freedom of conscience, the Weavers were recreating the journey that Vicki's forbears had opted out of a century earlier, when the men and women of the nascent RLDS church declined to join Brigham Young's exodus out of the United States. "Our goal and our dream," wrote Randy, "was to be free. Free to worship the Creator in our own way." In North Idaho, along with Mennonites, Identity Christians, and various other religious separatists, the Weavers would have quite a few Mormon neighbors, many of whom were animated by the same apocalyptic and survivalist impulses as the family. Vicki, who, in keeping with Deuteronomy, had let her hair grow long and traded her snug jeans for prairie skirts — "The woman shall not wear that which pertaineth unto a man" — already looked the part of a frontier pilgrim.

They made a road trip out of it, touring the Black Hills and stopping at roadside attractions like Reptile Gardens and the Corn Palace. All in all, they spent a week on the road.

On the first of September, 1983, the Weavers pulled into the small river and train town of Bonners Ferry, the seat of Idaho's Boundary County and its only sizable settlement. They got a room at a local motel with a small kitchenette. Vicki cooked hot dogs and mac and cheese for the kids while Randy went out to look for work and land.

Long after the frontier had been chased into the Pacific, Idaho still retained some of the romance of the Old West. While Montana has trademarked "Big Sky Country," the epithet applies just as well to the area south of Bonners Ferry, where the vast level floodplain of the Kootenai River is hemmed in by green, rearing slopes. On bright days, some optical effect renders the sky a towering dome, perhaps a product of the area's broad valleys, jagged horizons, and crystalline mountain air swimming with cumulus clouds. Even if you can technically see more atmosphere out on the prairie, the sky just looks bigger here. And while much of Iowa remains vacant and unplowed, North

Idaho, with its glacial lakes, coniferous density, and icy streams, is *wild*. Unlike Midwest corn country — a literal grid of roads and townships laid out at the fixed intervals once dictated by train and horse travel — this is a landscape of meandering roads and makeshift settlements. By the river bridge in Bonners Ferry, the air is filled with that most distinctive and reassuring noise of the West: the clangor and hoot of long, slow trains, laden with the fruit, fat, and quarry of the continent.

During the Senate judiciary hearings on Ruby Ridge that took place in 1995, Idaho Senator Larry Craig, with his wide Western stance, rhapsodized about his state's "deep clear lakes and tall green mountains," and proclaimed elegiacally that "Idaho is what America was."

While the Latter-day Saints had exited the geographic bounds of the United States to secure and grow their embattled faith, such a move was no longer an option for Randy and Vicki. However, they had pointed their two-truck convoy toward a region where American civic authority is hardly felt — a place that cleaves to the Thoreauvian maxim: "That government is best, which governs least." In Boundary County, you do not need to fill out any paperwork to build your house, cut your trees, shoot your dinner, educate your kids, or dig a shitter. You can even hunt inside the "wildlife refuge" on the edge of Bonners Ferry.

At the same time, in North Idaho as in much of the rural West, you cannot drive ten minutes in any direction without being reminded of the distant federal colossus. Given the proximity of the Canadian border and a great deal of publicly administered land, the roads around Bonners Ferry are busy with shiny new Silverados and F-250s — white for Border Patrol, mint green for the Forest Service, pale lemon for the Bureau of Land Management — all piloted by federal employees in crisp uniforms.

Idaho has long been a bastion of idiosyncratic politics — with lots of outsider candidates, split-ticket voting, and registered independents —

but much of the state's *don't-tread-on-me* ethos has been imported by transplants — people who, for whatever reason, felt stifled in (or priced out of) the Sunbelt, New England, or the Midwest. At some point, they all had the same romantic notion: Idaho! Just moving to the state can be a political act: a referendum on the insufficient Americanness of one's former home. In 2009, when Tucker Carlson was still playing the bow-tied avatar of country club Republicanism, he demonstrated how the word *Idaho* could semaphore an entire ideology. "I'm as conservative as any person in this room," he told a restive gathering in DC. "I'm literally in the process of stockpiling weapons and food and moving to Idaho." (He literally was not.) According to legend, Daniel Boone would pull up stakes whenever he could see the smoke from a neighbor's chimney; that same spirit animated many of the people who settled in the Panhandle. It is a place for those who require a little extra elbow room to secure the blessings of liberty. Tellingly, almost all the Idahoans mixed up in the Weaver saga came from someplace else.

By the time the Weavers arrived, the hills around Bonners Ferry were full of people like them — survivalists, homesteaders, back-to-the-landers, goldbugs, self-rusticators, and bulk-shoppers of every stripe. At the local market, Vicki and Sara, with their floor-length skirts and their long hair held back in bandannas, could pass for one more Mennonite family out buying supplies. Still feeling the sting of small-town gossip about "the group," the Weavers were delighted to immediately meet folks who saw the world as they did. "There are a lot of people here who say they're Christians and that the Lord sent them here," Vicki wrote her parents soon after arriving. "They just smile and don't think we're crazy at all!"

Whether or not Randy and Vicki realized it at the time, they were part of a general migration of like-minded Americans into the inland Northwest. With its affordable land and sparse, homogenous population, the region was rapidly becoming a haven for members of the far right, from separatists and fundamentalists to self-declared white supremacists. It was one of those seemingly spontaneous demographic shifts that periodically re-sorts the American populace. While such shifts are barely perceptible at the time, in retrospect they look almost like something planned.

Along with countless separatist families like the Weavers, the region was in the process of becoming a hub for far-right activism. While most Americans still associated the Old South with organized white supremacy, a 1989 study ranked Montana, Oregon, and Idaho as the top three states for far-right organizing. By the mid-'80s, the upper left-hand corner of the country was spangled with the rising stars of white power.

While some Iowans turned to conspiracy theories and tactical training during the farm crisis, the temper of the rural Midwest was still largely defined by a liberal, Gospel-inflected agrarianism — the sort of disposition associated with tight-knit farming communities and the works of Marilynne Robinson. Once the Weavers had departed Cedar Falls, the other members of "the group" drifted back to more conventional strains of evangelicalism.

In Idaho, it became possible for Randy and Vicki to surround themselves almost entirely with people who held beliefs like their own. The region's extremism was partly fired by an uncomfortable paradox: hating the federal government while depending so thoroughly upon it. At the time the Weavers lived there, a fifth of Boundary County citizens received public assistance. The main local industry — cutting softwood timber, milling it, and stacking it onto railcars — was (and remains) heavily subsidized by taxpayers elsewhere.

As the region became the de facto homeland of the far right, some tried to make it official. The Northwest Territorial Imperative, an idea championed by white separatists in the 1970s and '80s, aspired to establish a white, fundamentalist caliphate in the inland Northwest. In 1986, activists selected Kootenai County, just south of where the Weavers settled, as the "provisional capital" of this Aryan utopia.

In their motel room, Randy and Vicki got antsy as the days ticked by. The Lord had promised Randy that they would find their land by the "Feast of the Trumpets" (aka Rosh Hashanah), which, in 1983, fell on the seventh of September. That left them just six days to find their new home.

One day before the holiday, some new friends brought them to look at a tract near the village of Naples, seven miles south of Bonners Ferry. The settlement, named by Italian immigrants laying railroad track in the 1890s, comprises a bar, a mill, a school, and a general store with a post office and gas pump, all arrayed along one side of a shallow creek and a railroad siding. The parcel in question was a boulder-strewn woodlot along the spine of Caribou Ridge, which rises abruptly from Ruby Creek.

"When we drove up to see [the land]," Vicki wrote to Carolee Flynn, "Weaver couldn't believe it. It's just what the Lord had showed him it would look like." For five thousand dollars plus the moving truck, they were able to get twenty steep acres with a small, year-round spring and one of the grandest views in North America. The man who sold them the land bulldozed a rough, switchbacking driveway up from a small meadow where an old logging road terminated. There was another family — "tax protestors," in Sara's recollection — already homesteading nearby. From them, the Weavers rented a single-wide trailer. The family would winter in the trailer while Randy and Vicki built their cabin up on the ridge.

Deep in thrall to the front of the Bible, the Weavers had begun to regard themselves as members of the true Israel, inheritors of a special covenant between the Lord and "the seed of Isaac." The place in which they had landed was well matched to a faith that demanded separation, both geographically and through elaborate strictures about cloven hooves, graven images, and the cut of a woman's garments. *Wilderness* is practically a leading character in the Old Testament. The word appears 245 times in the Hebrew Bible, where it connotes an arid waste in which farming is impossible, herding is chancy, and permanent settlement is prohibitive. In the Old Testament, Evil is found down in the cities and towns, where the people pile up their wealth. In contrast, the wilderness enforces its own spiritual hygiene—a place of purifying hardship. Since the era of white settlement, the economy of the inland Northwest has centered on brief, transitory rushes—trapping, gold mining, timber cutting—none of which have left much of a mark on the place beyond the occasional tailings pile or stubbly clear-cut. In the Weavers' new home, contending with nature and weather would be the most consistent fact of daily life.

CHAPTER NINE

MIDNIGHT IN AMERICA

BY THE TIME Randy and Vicki were framing their little house above Ruby Creek, the theological sea change wrought by the Fundamentalist movement—from the sanguine postmillennialism of the old mainline denominations to a new, urgent premillennialism—was playing out at the fringes of American life, at the very center of national power, and at all points between. A Gallup poll from the early 1980s found that 62 percent of Americans had "no doubts" about the eventual, literal Second Coming of Christ. A 1982 cover story in *The Atlantic* trumpeted a surge of apocalyptic faith among American Protestants. Endtimes belief slipped into all the fissures that trace American life.

As the signal voice of the 1980s, Ronald Reagan is remembered for sunny rhetoric about "morning in America." In private, he put the hour much later. When he was still governor of California and, by several accounts, avidly reading Hal Lindsey, Reagan freely opined that "most of the prophecies that had to be fulfilled before Armageddon can come, have come to pass. Everything is falling into place. Ezekiel said that fire and brimstone will be rained upon enemies. That must mean that they'll be destroyed by nuclear weapons." During his first term as president, Reagan told *People* that "never, in the time between the ancient prophecies up until now, has there been a time in which so many of the prophecies are coming together. There have been times in the past when people thought the end of the world was coming, and so forth, but never anything like this."

This sort of thing was Eschatology 101 for conservative Evangelicals, but the reelection campaign worried that talk of Ezekiel and brimstone might jar the ears of some voters, especially at a moment when Star Wars and ICBMs dominated debates about the defense budget. Fortunately for Reagan, by the time of his second bid for the White House, a substantial and exceptionally well-organized voting bloc knew all about "the ancient prophecies."

As a demographic category, "Evangelical" — the "white" is usually silent — has so much electoral currency that, every four years, like swallows twittering back to Capistrano, American pundits instinctively take up the work of updating its definition. This rite was inaugurated with H. L. Mencken's snide coverage of the Scopes "monkey trial," when the key term was still *fundamentalist*. It did not become a proper seasonal ritual until the presidential campaigns of Carter and Reagan, when many newspaper readers needed to be informed (or at least reminded) that there was such a thing as an "Evangelical," and that this novel genus was terribly keen on voting. Over time, the waxing and waning of public interest has created the illusion of a rising and falling movement, when in fact Christian fundamentalists have always been a larger, more stable, and more influential group than secular observers tend to realize. "It seems careless," Garry Wills wrote, "to keep misplacing such a large body of people."

One reason that outsiders need constant reminding that Christian fundamentalists even exist is that everyone else vaguely expects them to fade away, burned off by the enlightening glare of modernity. "Ever since [Fundamentalism's] rise to notoriety in the 1920s, scholars have predicted the imminent demise of the movement," wrote Ernest Sandeen in his landmark history of the movement's origins.

"The Fundamentalists, to return the favor, have predicted the speedy end of the world."

In the final debate of the '84 campaign, one of the moderators asked Reagan about the eleven times he had spoken on the record about the imminence of "some kind of biblical Armageddon." Seated in the audience, Nancy was heard to gasp, "Oh no!" Reagan's response was deft. He began with a trademark look of bemused annoyance: a smiling intake of breath that created a shared moment between the candidate and the millions who knew what he knew. Okay friends, the Hollywood face said, let's handle this one gingerly for the egg-heads. "The biblical prophecies of what would portend the coming of Armageddon and so forth, and the fact that a number of theologians for the last decade or more have believed that this was true, that the prophecies are coming together that portend that," he said vaguely, before waving it all away. "No one knows whether those prophecies mean that Armageddon is a thousand years away or the day after tomorrow."

Reagan was hardly the only national figure endorsing an apocalyptic interpretation of events in the early 1980s. In the same way that nineteenth-century politicians and reformers drew upon widespread millenarian faith to hype everything from the metric system to costly infrastructure projects, conservative politicians of the late twentieth century spoke the language of endtimes prophecy to militate against social change and government action. To those who believe that earthly conditions are *supposed* to be growing worse, all the old hopeful schemes for sprucing things up come to resemble schemes of a more sinister nature. What's more, if time is truly running short, there is not much point in pursuing expensive improvements.

The Pentecostalist James Watt, whom Reagan appointed secretary of the interior, demonstrated the premillennialist attitude toward federal action when he told Congress that we should not worry too much about the natural resources he had been tasked with stewarding. "I do not know how many future generations we can count on before the Lord returns." Likewise, Defense Secretary Caspar Weinberger, the man Reagan placed in charge of the American nuclear arsenal, reassured precisely nobody when he said, "I have read the Book of Revelation, and, yes, I believe the world is going to end — by an act of God, I hope — but every day I think time is running out."

Much of this shift, at least insofar as it made the jump from the pulpit to the ballot box, can be attributed to Jerry Falwell, whose Moral Majority rallied the new Christian Right by devoting as much energy to registering voters as baptizing them. Falwell and his organizing efforts were key to Reagan's overwhelming support among white Evangelicals, even when the twice-married Californian movie star was running against a born-again Sunday school teacher from Georgia. Like Reagan, Falwell, an ardent dispensationalist who expected the Tribulation to commence in his lifetime, found a way to talk about prophecy that resolved the old Fundamentalist instinct for separatism — *this world is doomed, ours is not to fix it up* — with a savvy and engaged patriotism. Among other things, Falwell's energetic coalition-building helped erode the lingering distinction between the exclusionary term *fundamentalist* and the more capacious *evangelical*.

Apocalyptic theology lent the Christian Right a politics organized around fantasies of persecution and decline, and just beneath that, an inclination to more sinister premonitions. Wondrous Christians speak of the "blessed hope" of Christ's return, but the intervening darkness — including a world-devouring war — has a way of focusing the mind. In the contest between hope and fear, the latter wins every time, at least when it comes to mobilizing (or stifling) collective action.

From this perspective, the future itself becomes a sort of adversary. Another word for "fast ripening" is *rot*. Minimizing sin and winning souls are all the church can properly hope to accomplish. Everything

forward-facing or reform-oriented — "hope and change," as one campaign pithily put it — is vanity at best, anti-Christian hubris at worst.

In retrospect, the apocalyptic faith of Reagan and several of his
closest advisors is easier to square with his administration's policy
priorities than his happy talk of national renewal. Reagan cannily
plundered endtimes rhetoric, most famously when he framed the
Cold War as a Manichaean struggle against an "Evil Empire," a phrase
he first deployed in a speech to the National Association of Evangelicals, a crowd well primed by Hal Lindsey and others to regard the
USSR as the imperial Gog of ancient prophecy. Aside from Cold War
policy and Reagan's embrace of Christian Zionism, his vigorous
unweaving of the New Deal safety net, a longstanding fundamentalist bugbear, aligns with the *we're-not-here-to-fix-things-up* attitude that
partly defines dispensationalism. If nothing else, the approaching
End serves as a mandate for inaction. If the ship is going down, why
worry about repairing the mast or rationing provisions?

Other prominent conservatives were more overt in their efforts
to wed contemporary politics to endtimes prophecy and the conspiratorial vigilance it tends to generate. Pat Robertson founded both the
Christian Coalition and the immensely popular Christian Broadcasting Network, which the Weavers had faithfully watched before
junking their TV. In 1988, Robertson, who had worked in the Reagan administration, ran for the Republican presidential nomination
spouting dire warnings about the rise of a sinister global order. After
his loss, he wrote a bestseller titled *The New World Order*, ushering into
the mainstream a term that had mostly been confined to conspiracy
circles. Robertson's book tells the now-familiar story of a Luciferian
conspiracy working to usher in a One World Government. He identifies George H. W. Bush, who had just whipped him in the primary, as
a leading agent of that conspiracy. It did not help that Bush had run
the CIA and been a member of Skull and Bones at Yale, both longstanding loci of the conspiratorial imagination. Bush, who was no
savvier about the folkways of his base than he was about dairy prices,

casually dropped the phrase "new world order" into a speech about the post–Cold War landscape, a gaffe which was greeted in some circles like evidence that the schemers were finally, brazenly coming out of the shadows.

Like John Todd before him, Robertson blended the greatest hits of American conspiracism — the Freemasons, the Illuminati, the UN, the Council on Foreign Relations, the Trilateral Commission — with endtimes prophecy, adding to it the lively excitement of his own charismatic faith. *The New World Order* (the book) is especially vituperative about a Rothschild-dominated cabal of "international bankers" whom Robertson, like Todd, identifies as "the missing link between the occult and the world of high finance."

The barrier separating the apocalyptic fantasies of the conspiracist right from the prevailing moods of movement conservatism has always been more porous than some would like to imagine. A common story about the birth of the conservative movement begins with William F. Buckley purging the Birchers, cranks, and antisemites from the pages of *National Review* — the great "dekooking," one historian called it. As has been abundantly reported, that story was never really true. Barry Goldwater perfected and demonstrated the relevant political maneuver when he publicly repudiated John Birch Society leader Robert Welch while warmly gathering rank-and-file Birchers into his coalition.

In the nineteenth century, optimistic postmillennial theology had put a spring into the step of mainstream reformists while stoking utopian follies among the most hopeful. In much the same way, the rise of a more apocalyptic style of faith helped shape movement conservatism while simultaneously inspiring fanatics at the fringe: people who, like the Weavers, took endtimes prophecy so deeply to heart that they could hardly see anything else.

To wholeheartedly believe in Revelation, as literalized by Darby, popularized by Scofield, glossed-up by Lindsey, and politicized by Falwell and his successors, is to perceive a world deranged by dark forces intent on snuffing out Christianity. For some, it also means regarding violence as a necessary and occasionally sanctified force. In the special case of the USA, those feelings have often attached themselves to a vibrant civic religion that sets tyranny and personal firearms upon opposing pans of a never-quite-balanced scale, imbuing guns with such fetishistic power that they become not just a guarantor of safety, but the embodiment of liberty itself.

The Jesuit activist Daniel Berrigan called Revelation "The Nightmare of God." Sinclair Lewis called it "Alice in Wonderland wearing a dragon mask." Under the disquieting influence of John of Patmos, even some of history's most secure believers — men and women awash in the prerogatives of citizenship in the world's most powerful nation and membership in its dominant faith and race — can end up peering out through their blinds at ravening wolves. With almost metronomic regularity, this besieged outlook has generated literal sieges. During the summer of 1983, as Randy, Vicki, and the kids rolled west by northwest across the country, one such siege was unfolding in the Arkansas Ozarks, awakening American law enforcement to a new and baffling threat and paving the way for what was to come for the Weaver family.

CHAPTER TEN

GIVE ME DEATH

GORDON WENDELL KAHL grew up in North Dakota, on land his father homesteaded in 1906. He signed up for the army after Pearl Harbor and served as a gunner in a bomber over Europe and Asia, flying fifty-seven missions and earning a Silver Star, a Bronze Star, two Purple Hearts, and other commendations. He returned home, married his girlfriend, Joan Seil, planted a hundred acres of barley, and had six kids.

Kahl started out on Bircherism but soon hit the harder stuff. For a time, he converted to Mormonism, impressed by the LDS church's hard-line stance on communism. Kahl's gathering impression of a sinister hidden hand locked into focus when he read Henry Ford's *The International Jew: The World's Foremost Problem*. The book—really a collection of articles that began running in 1920 in the *Dearborn Independent*—would have an outsize influence not only on Kahl, but upon the entire course of American antisemitism. Hitler, who kept a portrait of Ford in his office, claimed that the automaker's modernized version of antisemitism was a key inspiration for the Third Reich.

Ford's book was based upon another, older document: *The Protocols of the Learned Elders of Zion*, the most influential conspiracy text in history (with the possible exception of Revelation, which is more conspiratorial in consequence than intent). *The Protocols*, which presents itself as the secret record of a Jewish plot to start wars, sow chaos, encourage Bolshevism, and undermine Christian civilization, was written (assembled, really) in Paris by czarist agents at the end of the nineteenth century. Many of its passages are lifted almost verbatim from a satirical dialogue between Montesquieu and Machiavelli written by a French attorney named Maurice Joly, in 1864. *The Protocols* was first printed in Russian, then English, and has since been translated into countless languages. Despite being revealed as an obvious forgery in the 1920s, it continues to circulate widely around the world, generating updated editions, films, and TV miniseries.

Considering *The Protocols'* overwhelming popularity, including among non-Christians—it is cited by name in the 1988 Hamas Covenant—it is often forgotten that the document was initially associated with Christian prophecy. The version that circulates today was first printed in 1905 as an appendix to a book about signs of the coming Antichrist. It proved especially popular among American fundamentalists of the 1920s and '30s, who slotted its story about a globalist cabal into the Revelation narrative. Arno Gaebelein, a prominent Methodist and dispensationalist, publicly certified that *The Protocols* were the work of a "believer in the Word of God, in prophecy." (Which, oddly, is an admission that the text is not actually the minutes of a secret gathering of Jews. As with other conspiratorial texts, readers can regard it as true-in-spirit, even after its authenticity has been debunked.)

For American populists and isolationists, Henry Ford's red, white, and blue rehashing of *The Protocols* offered up "the international Jew" as a sort of skeleton key, capable of unlocking scourges as divergent as global finance and global socialism. After reading Ford's book on his North Dakota farm, Gordon Kahl became convinced that the war in which he had served with such distinction had been orchestrated by a cabal of Jewish profiteers whispering in FDR's ear.

Struggling to make the farm pay, the Kahl family made seasonal trips back and forth between North Dakota and sunnier, more remunerative climes — first Southern California and later the West Texas oilfields. As with so many who would go on to shape the modern far right, it was in Los Angeles County that Kahl first encountered Christian Identity, the apocalyptic and racist strain of Fundamentalism that would become the bedrock of his beliefs.

In 1967, Kahl wrote to the IRS declaring that he would no longer pay his taxes, calling them "tithes to the synagogue of Satan," a phrase lifted from Revelation. Summoned to tax court, he refused even to respond to the government's letter. Since the family farm seldom earned enough to owe any income tax, the IRS ignored the matter.

As the first tremors of the farm crisis arrived in North Dakota, with crop prices plummeting and foreclosures on the rise, Kahl latched onto the Posse Comitatus. His zeal, charm, war record, and folksy manner made him an effective activist within the movement. He was gifted at that special trick of worshipping America's past to denounce its present: the man so patriotic he wanted to burn his country to the ground. He traveled to American Agriculture Movement events and farm auctions to preach against the Jewish–communist conspiracy that was subjugating the USA by undermining its most stalwart citizens: Christian farmers. "We are a conquered and occupied nation," he said, "conquered and occupied by the Jews and their hundreds, maybe thousands, of front organizations doing their un-Godly work."

In 1976, Kahl went on local TV in Texas to preach the Posse and beseech white Christians to stop paying taxes. The following year, he was charged with "willful failure" to file income taxes. In court, he was defiant. He had not "failed" to pay his taxes, he declared. He had "refused," on religious grounds. He would not enter a plea and told the judge that he did not recognize the authority of the court.

The court recognized its own authority and, starting in 1979, Kahl served eight months in Leavenworth, with five years of probation to follow. His mugshot shows a round-faced old man with thin, close-cropped hair, and a ruddy farmer's complexion. In horn-rimmed glasses and a work shirt buttoned to the neck, he looks more like a kindly grandpa rendered by Norman Rockwell than any sort of zealot.

Released from prison, Kahl went back to organizing for the Posse and refusing to pay taxes. He painted a sheriff's star on the side of his truck with the words "Posse Comitatus" below it, expressing the notion that the only legitimate legal authority derives directly from individual citizens. Despite the world-historical drama of Kahl's rhetoric—he claimed to be at war with an ancient, global despotism—his crusade focused on the minor tyranny of paperwork. Along with ignoring his tax bills, he refused to get a permit for his gun, his car, or even his small airplane. He and other Posse activists encouraged citizens to rip up their drivers' licenses and Social Security cards. Social Security and the income tax, he claimed, were devilish creations lifted directly from the "second plank" of the Communist Manifesto. (Marx and Engels did not write in planks, though they did propose a graduated income tax.)

When Kahl received a fresh summons from the IRS, he threw it in the trash. He also stopped filling out his probation forms. Eventually, a lien was put on his farm. Despite offers of money from his brother-in-law, Kahl refused to pay, raging at his wife when she tried. Although he became a hero to people battered by the farm crisis, when Kahl lost his land, it was not due to the one-two knockout of debt and foreclosure. The farm was seized to pay taxes that had been withheld for religious reasons. Meanwhile, Kahl went everywhere armed and told all listeners that he was ready to "engage in a struggle to the death."

The case of Kahl, like that of the Weavers, illuminates one of the defining features of the apocalyptic right and its periodic collisions with the wider world, namely, the ways in which a certain type of rhetoric can generate volatile misunderstandings. The style of speech in question — at once trite and melodramatic — can be heard wherever self-styled patriots gather to rattle their sabers, be they sage brush rebels in Stetsons, Oath Keepers in tactical vests, Anons in MAGA hats, or the torrent of anonymous Punisher skull avatars who cheer them on digitally. It is a language laced with anachronistic phrases that seem plucked, in equal parts, from the writings of Patrick Henry and the movies of Mel Gibson, with a romantic dash of the Saint Crispin's Day oration thrown in. Every ally is a brother in arms. The barricades forever need manning. Every day is Independence Day. "We the people" is the preferred pronoun. And the Tree of Liberty is never quenched with the blood of patriots. If this sort of talk were a font, it would be Timothy Matlack's swoopy calligraphy on the Declaration of Independence. If they could shout it all in Latin, they would.

The catharsis of a good rebel yell is easy enough to understand, and a propensity for flattening, hundred-proof rhetoric is not the sole province of the radical right. During the same years that Gordon Kahl was fulminating like John Wilkes Booth about his right not to file a 1040, members of the New Left whipped themselves into such a lather of Maoist sloganeering that they contributed, in Renata Adler's stinging phrase, "as much to serious national concern with the problems of war, racism, and poverty as a mean drunk to the workings of a fire brigade."

For men like Kahl and Weaver, steely talk of Liberty and Tyranny feels good in the mouth the same way that a gun feels good in the hand. "I'd rather die on my feet, than live on my knees," Randy said again and again. Fair enough, but for most of that time, nobody had suggested he kneel. In the years before the Ruby Ridge siege, Vicki, the family spokesperson, wrote repeatedly of her family's (kids included) willingness to die for their faith. You do not have to be a psychologist to detect a sharp pong of fatalism amid all this "give me death" talk.

This kind of rhetoric has a way of nudging even minor conflicts toward calamity. The ready analogy is Don Quixote, who delivered his florid orations about defending maidens and righting wrongs before sallying forth into a muddy ditch and waking up with broken bones. Quixote made his addled speeches while swinging an antique lance. This sort of patriotic chest-thumping sounds a bit different when the speaker is holding a gun.

There is no law against being a blowhard, but amid the interminable tootling of so many tin horns, it can be hard to hear the occasional note of genuine menace — to tease actionable threats from spluttery theater. With their hard talk and tilted berets, radicals of every persuasion look like they are playing dress-up, right up until the first bomb detonates. Unlike Randy Weaver, who spoke this way but is never known to have performed a single act of criminal (or even noncriminal) violence, Gordon Kahl was among that portion who apparently meant it.

In the winter of 1981, a federal bench warrant was issued for Kahl on the minor charge of misdemeanor probation violation. Whenever the US marshals assigned to the case asked after him in North Dakota, they were warned to stay clear. He told anyone who would listen that he would not be taken alive.

Theoretically a fugitive, Kahl went about his normal life, walking the streets of his hometown, traveling with his wife and kids to Arkansas, and attending Christian Patriot and Posse Comitatus meetings, protected from arrest by his guns and the air of menace he projected. For a time, the marshals let the warrant slide, unwilling to risk gunplay or waste too many man-hours on a probation violation that began with a tax issue.

A movement like the Posse Comitatus, being built upon fantasies of sinister tyranny and heroic resistance, demands martyrs. Kahl seemed intent on being the first. He spoke proudly about his legal situation and urged others to imitate his defiance. He publicly threatened the life of his probation officer. In a phone call with a US marshal trying to find a peaceful off-ramp, Kahl said, "I haven't shot anybody since World War II, but I haven't forgotten how."

On an unseasonably warm Sunday in February of 1983, Kahl, along with his wife Joan, his son Yorie, and a friend named Scott Faul, drove to a Posse meeting at a medical clinic in Median, North Dakota, that was run by a physician friend of Kahl's who was sympathetic to the Posse's constitutional arguments, although not its racist theology. The three men in Kahl's party all carried Mini-14 semi-automatic rifles.

The meeting had been called to discuss the incorporation of a Posse-organized "township" that could govern and defend itself without the meddling of state or federal authorities. For a brief time, such township schemes were popular on the far right. Like a premillennial inversion of the utopian colonies that sprang up during the millennium-drunk decades before the Civil War, Posse Comitatus townships were intended to serve as Christian strongholds during the coming social collapse. None of them ever really got beyond the paperwork phase. Despite an abhorrence for bureaucracy, the Posse movement was, in many ways, a revolution built for pencil pushers. Along with lots and lots of guns, it mostly expressed itself through charters, declarations, common-law liens, articles of incorporation, spurious lawsuits, and court-choking acts of "paper terrorism."

The meeting in Medina was attended by nineteen men, including an old friend of Kahl's named Len Martin, a writer for Willis Carto's *Spotlight*, who planned to serve as the future community's scribe. After some debate, the meeting descended into an argument about whether their theoretical township should formally bar Black and Jewish members (not that any were applying or even lived in the vicinity). Kahl, following a blueprint established by Posse Comitatus organizer and Aryan Nations founder Richard Butler in Idaho, was adamant that only white Christian "freemen" could join. He backed up his argument with citations from scripture.

As the meeting broke up, some of the men realized that they were being observed by a local police officer parked across the street in a green pickup. Bradley Kapp, the young deputy in the truck, knew there was an APB for Kahl's arrest and had noticed his car. Seeing Kahl amble out of the meeting, Kapp radioed the state police, who radioed the US Marshals' office in Bismarck, North Dakota. The deputy also called his boss, the local police chief, who happened to be a regular at local Posse meetings. The chief expressed no interest in making the arrest, saying that he "believed Kahl when he said he wouldn't be taken alive." As Kapp watched the Posse members mill about outside the clinic, two marshals hopped in their car in Bismarck and headed east for Medina. Another two marshals left Fargo, traveling west toward the clinic. They intended to finally arrest Gordon Kahl.

Before any of the marshals made it to Medina, Kahl and his crew, along with two other men from the meeting, left the clinic, driving out of town in a two-car caravan. To confuse the police, Yorie swapped jackets with his father. As evening descended, they saw the flashing lights of a small roadblock up ahead. Kahl tried to swing his car around but realized that they had been followed. The marshals had arrived and blocked the road behind them.

Yorie and his friend Scott Faul leapt from a station wagon and spread out on either side of the road, training their guns on the local police in front of them and the marshals behind. Joan Kahl lay down on the floorboards. Gordon, who was in the other car, stepped out and crouched behind his door. He aimed his rifle at the marshals.

The marshals announced themselves and told the men to drop their guns. "It's not worth getting killed over," one of them shouted.

Kahl yelled back, telling the agents to drop *their* guns.

"What do you guys want?" he asked.

"All we want is you," replied Marshal James Hopson. "Put down the guns. We'll talk about it."

Everyone remained silent for a minute. It was a standoff at twenty feet.

Yorie shot first, hitting Deputy Marshal Cheshire in the chest. In an instant, everyone was firing. Yorie shot at Deputy Kapp, but missed. Kapp returned fire with his shotgun, hitting Yorie in the stomach. Kahl aimed for Kapp, blowing the tip off the young deputy's finger and shattering the windshield of his cruiser. A piece of flying glass cut Kapp badly across the forehead. With just two more shots, Kahl hit a local Median policeman named Steve Schnabel in the leg and US Marshal Ken Muir in the chest.

After thirty seconds, everything went silent. Kahl surveyed the damage. He walked over to the injured Schnabel, who begged him not to shoot. Kahl obliged but relieved the officer of his gun and his cruiser, driving it over to where Yorie lay bleeding. Before attending to his son, Kahl went to where Deputy Marshal Cheshire was lying half inside his car. Yorie's shot had slipped through a seam in Cheshire's bullet proof vest and he could barely move. Kahl shot him point blank in the head, twice. He then went back for Yorie. Along with Scott Faul, the Kahls got into the police car and drove back to the medical clinic to get help with Yorie's wound.

In the final tally, Deputy US Marshals Kenneth Muir and Robert Cheshire were both killed. Deputy Marshal Hopson plus local police officers Bradley Kapp and Steve Schnabel were injured. Yorie survived his wound, but was arrested along with his mother. Kahl and Scott Faul slipped off into the woods and escaped. Faul later turned himself in. He and Yorie, both now in their sixties, are serving life sentences.

Kahl disappeared into a large underground network of supporters. As would later happen with the Weavers, the case — now dramatically escalated by bloodshed — was transferred from the US Marshals to the FBI, which commenced a nationwide manhunt. With two dead lawmen and three more in the hospital, the tax matter that had started all the trouble was basically irrelevant, at least from the perspective of law enforcement. The Marshals Service posted a $25,000 reward for information leading to Kahl's arrest — the largest sum they had ever offered.

As an obvious first step, the FBI raided Kahl's house. Nerves were running high. Maybe the house was rigged with explosives? Maybe

FBI wanted poster for Gordon Kahl, 1983.

Kahl was inside preparing an ambush? When the family Labrador gave away the position of an advancing tactical team, an agent shot the dog. Whatever Americans think about anti-government fanatics, everyone agrees on the fundamental innocence of Labradors. As with Samuel Weaver's dog Striker, the dead Lab instantly became part of the story, proving, as one Kahl supporter put it, the government's "satanic...contempt for life." Although there was nobody inside the farmhouse, the FBI pumped it full of bullets and teargas just to make sure.

As agents fanned out across the country looking for Kahl, they were startled to discover the scale of the subculture to which their fugitive belonged. Chasing various leads, agents visited survivalism expos, Klan meetings, gun clubs, Posse Comitatus gatherings, and tax protests. Almost by accident they stumbled into a few unrelated arrests, one for possession of explosives and another regarding a plot to rob a bank. Members of the Covenant, Sword, and Arm of the Lord were overheard in a diner plotting to smuggle Kahl into Canada.

Like a dose of radioactive liquid swallowed before a medical scan, the four-month hunt for Kahl illuminated an otherwise invisible nexus of people and organizations who regarded themselves as combatants in a real (if mostly cold) war against the federal government. At door after door, investigators were met by ordinary-seeming Americans—women with babies on their hips, men in dusty work shirts—who fulminated about ZOG, the Masons, the Illuminati, and the Federal Reserve. To them, Kahl was not a ruthless cop killer, but a heroic grandpa who just couldn't take it anymore. From their perspective, the vast manhunt for Kahl only demonstrated that the same government that was unwilling to provide price supports for their crops could fly sharp-dressed G-men all over creation looking for one old farmer in bib overalls. And what's more, the wily old coot was outwitting them.

Kahl kept on the move, traveling from North Dakota to Texas (where he burned his car), and then to Arkansas. The full details of his itinerary remain unknown. On the run, his legend grew. Like Randy Weaver after him, Kahl became what the historian Eric Hobsbawm called a "social bandit," an outlaw who becomes the face of a noble struggle against oppression.

"Run Gordon Run" signs went up in small towns. Someone sold "Gordon Kahl Is My Tax Consultant" T-shirts. He earned at least two ballads. "Prairie fog has chilled the trail / But it's known by one and all / Just what happens / When you mess with / Freedom fighter Gordon Kahl."

At the Aryan Nations in Idaho, Richard Butler read aloud from one of Kahl's dispatches from the underground. It described the Medina shootout as "a struggle to the death between the Kingdom of God and the Kingdom of Satan." "Let each of you who says that the Lord Jesus Christ is your personal Savior, sell his garment and buy a Sword if you don't already have one, and bring his enemies before him and slay them." He signed off: "Gordon Kahl, Christian Patriot." James Wickstrom, a leader within the Posse movement, held a press conference claiming that, with the attempt to arrest Kahl, the government has "declared war on the people of this country."

Finally, at the end of May, while Randy and Vicki were packing up the house in Cedar Falls, a woman named Karen Russell Robertson called the FBI from a payphone in Mountain Home, Arkansas. "I know where you can find Gordon Kahl," she said.

Kahl had been hiding out in the home of Robertson's father, where she and her two girls were staying in the aftermath of a divorce. Robertson liked Kahl. He was helpful around the house, more respectful of her than her own father, and sweet with her girls. In the evenings, he taught her how to interpret prophecy in light of current events. Still, while her father and his Christian Patriot buddies treated the old man like a hero, Robertson was uncomfortable having a confessed killer—who, incidentally, described plans to shoot the judge presiding over the trial of his wife and son—under the same roof as her daughters.

Robertson met an agent named Jack Knox at a restaurant inside a Ramada Inn. He bought a bucket of fried chicken and some sodas for the girls and they went to a park across the street. Having chased a few bad leads, Knox asked Robertson if she had anything that might carry one of Kahl's fingerprints. From her purse she produced Kahl's copy of *The One-Straw Revolution*. The fact that Kahl spent his time on the lam reading the Japanese philosopher Masanobu Fukuoka's spiritual treatise on low-intervention farming suggests how, in a different cultural context, his native loathing for the entangling systems of modernity might have taken a different form.

As Knox debriefed Robertson, she suddenly panicked. "You're one of them," she said. "You work for the Jews!" It took the agent a moment to realize that the frail, terrified young woman was staring at his Masonic signet ring. She said that Kahl had told her all about how the Masons are an instrument of global Jewry. He had even drawn her a picture of the Beast described in Revelation, showing how the monster represented the Jews, with the Masons forming one of its seven heads. Knox, having never heard any of this stuff, calmly explained that he was not Jewish and did not work for any Jews. He promised to look into it.

Kahl had moved on, but following Robertson's tip, the FBI surveilled the property of a Posse activist and Arkansas Christian Patriot Party member named Leonard Ginter from a rented airplane. The Ginters' passive-solar home was built into a hillside, with heavy concrete walls, a grass roof, and large air vents. The agent in the plane saw two men walking outside. One of them looked a lot like Gordon Kahl.

On June 3, 1983, FBI agents, US marshals, Arkansas state troopers, and local police encircled the property. Ginter, who had noticed the circling plane and seen unfamiliar cars in town, suspected that something was up. He tried driving out to take a look around but was immediately apprehended. He was instructed to call his wife Norma out of the house. When she stepped outside, they were both put in cuffs and hustled behind a barn.

The FBI's plan was to summon Kahl outside with a loudspeaker. If necessary, they would drive him out with teargas. For some reason, before any of that could happen, county sheriff Gene Matthews walked through the front door with his gun drawn, trailed by a US marshal and an Arkansas state police investigator. When Matthews walked into the kitchen, Kahl stepped out from behind the refrigerator and shot the sheriff with his Ruger Mini-14. Matthews returned fire with his revolver, hitting Kahl in the head and likely killing him. The other two officers dragged the bleeding sheriff from the house.

Unsure whether Kahl had even been hit, the SWAT team unloaded on the house with bullets and teargas. Apparently fearing that Kahl might be hiding inside with a gas mask, they took the dramatic (and clearly criminal) step of pouring diesel down one of the air vents. For two hours, the bunker-like house burned while the assembled peace officers unloaded a steady fusillade into the flaming building. In the afternoon, word came from the hospital that Sheriff Matthews was dead. As evening fell, it began to rain. The barrage slowly let up.

Kahl's charred body was found in the kitchen with a single bullet in his head, most likely from Sheriff Matthews's pistol. As word of his death spread through the networks of the far right, he was promoted from folk bandit to martyr. The fact that his body had been burned beyond recognition stoked an ongoing conspiracy theory, with the dead sheriff — the man who probably killed Kahl — counted as one more victim of federal perfidy. Gerald "Jack" McLamb, a former Phoenix policeman turned conspiracy theorist who would play a key role in negotiating with the Weavers during their own standoff, eventually exhumed Kahl's body on camera to prove that the feds had lied about every aspect of the siege. His investigation was inconclusive.

When Kahl's supporters (and a lot of reporters) packed into a small North Dakota church for his funeral, the minister roared Patrick Henry's famous ultimatum: "Give me liberty or give me death." *The Spotlight* proceeded to spend several years stoking the legend of Gordon Kahl, the kindhearted Christian farmer murdered in cold blood for his small-government beliefs. Kahl's old friend Len Martin eventually wrote a book called *Terror at Ruby Ridge* which cast the Weaver case as a direct consequence of what happened to Kahl. In Martin's telling, Randy and Gordon had both been hunted down by the US Marshals — "the main front group" for the Jews — simply because they knew too much.

The Kahl affair even generated a ripped-from-the-headlines TV movie starring Rod Steiger (the sheriff from *In the Heat of the Night*) as Kahl and Michael Gross (the hippie dad from *Family Ties*) as the agent on his trail. In the film, as with much of the coverage of the case, Joan Kahl was depicted as a long-suffering wife dragged into her husband's violent crusade. In reality, Joan was a true believer who went on to occupy a prominent position on the radical right, eventually marrying Neuman Britton, an old-school neo-Nazi whom Richard Butler would anoint as his successor at the Aryan Nations. Along the way, she became friendly with Randy and Vicki Weaver.

In death, Kahl, who was usually characterized as a farm crisis avenger, helped consolidate the far right, uniting factions that had once been separately preoccupied with guns, taxes, Armageddon, and white power. While race, class, and faith often look like distinct well-springs of political identity, the case of Gordon Kahl shows how thoroughly scrambled those categories can be. Kahl's martyrdom helped usher groups like the Posse Comitatus, the Aryan Nations, the Klan, the CSA, and various Christian survivalist and paramilitary outfits under the relatively unified banner of the Christian Patriot movement, which was the term Kahl himself had favored. In this way, he helped prepare the ground for the militia movement that blossomed after Ruby Ridge and Waco, and has continued to grow, in fits and starts, for the last three decades.

Just as the Weavers were arriving in North Idaho, their new neighbor Richard Butler used the publicity surrounding Kahl's death to graft the anti-tax movement onto his own white power crusade. "Since the name Gordon Kahl has caught the attention of the nation, it is important that we take this opportunity to awaken our Racial Nation," he said. "A speaking tour will be a catalyst for awakening the racially uninformed but tax-aware Aryan kinsmen as to the true nature of our Nation's plight."

CHAPTER ELEVEN

IDENTITY POLITICS

MARCH 16, 1984, was Sara Weaver's eighth birthday. The family celebrated by moving into their mostly finished home atop Caribou Ridge. Because the spring thaw rendered their steep driveway too muddy for Randy's truck, some new friends helped the Weavers carry their furniture and boxes up the road.

For two people who had never done more carpentry than the usual little-bit-of-everything work of farm life, the speed and ingenuity with which Randy and Vicki built their house during one (blessedly mild) winter is a testament to their energy and their sense of apocalyptic urgency. "I feel like...we had to get this house built quickly," Vicki wrote Carolee Flynn back in Cedar Falls. "I can't help but think things are shortly going to come to pass."

They built on the cheap. Pine and cedar mill scraps were free for the taking down at the railhead in Naples and they helped themselves. For girders and posts they used unmilled logs from their own land. The windows and doors were salvaged. For siding, they used unpainted plywood. Despite all this thrift, their savings had dwindled by the time the house was finished. Vicki insisted that they pawn her diamond engagement ring to buy a pallet of corrugated steel for the roof. Randy replaced the ring a few years later.

The upstairs loft was partitioned into three small bedrooms. Downstairs, there was a living room with a woodstove, a kitchen with wood and propane cook stoves, and a large pantry for preserves and herbs. One corner was set aside for Vicki's sewing, where she made curtains, bedding, and many of their clothes, often in blue, her favorite color.

With the rush of building behind them, a cryptic four-word phrase from the Old Testament began looping through Vicki's mind. As the Book of Daniel tells it, the Babylonian king Belshazzar throws a party for his courtiers and concubines at which, in an act of blasphemous ostentation, he serves food and wine in sacred vessels plundered from the temple in Jerusalem. Midway through the feast, a disembodied hand appears in the air, scrawling the words *mene, mene, tekel, upharsin* on the wall. The king's astrologers cannot make sense of the words, which have no clear meaning in Aramaic. Daniel, a Jewish prophet attached to the court, is summoned to interpret the spectral graffito: "You have been found wanting," Daniel translates. "Your days are numbered. Your kingdom will be divided." Belshazzar dies that night, throwing Babylon into a period of disorder.

In the same way that Vicki had interpreted her Iowan dreams as divine visitations, she took this scriptural earworm as a direct message from God. The days of her own private Babylon were numbered. "Jesus is telling me," she wrote, "that the USA is going to fall soon."

Given the way in which the Weavers viewed their private travails through the aggrandizing lens of prophecy—usually placing themselves near the center of the great drama—it seems notable that the scene immediately following Belshazzar's Feast closely prefigures what was soon to come for the Weavers, or at least how they would interpret it. After Belshazzar dies, a group of scheming bureaucrats resolve to set up the pious Daniel. They draft an arbitrary statute with an outrageous punishment, hoping that the unbending prophet will run afoul of the law. When Daniel flouts the rule, he receives the prescribed sentence: being sealed up in a lion's den. The next morning, as every Sunday schooler knows, the prophet emerges unscathed. This miracle convinces the new Babylonian king that Israel's Yahweh "is the living God." He tosses the scheming bureaucrats (and their families) into the den to be eaten — a happy ending, by Old Testament standards.

Vicki did not only listen within for portents. After a small earthquake hit the Northwest, she wrote her parents about the "birth pangs" mentioned in Matthew. When a new bridge for the highway that ran down from the Canadian border was being built in Bonners Ferry, she speculated about a planned Russian invasion from the North.

Beyond the ridge, more and more Americans were thinking similar thoughts. In 1981, Hal Lindsey had produced a follow-up to his 1970 bestseller titled *The 1980s: Countdown to Armageddon*, granting himself a short extension. The sequel was even more explicit than *Late Great* in its alignment of ancient prophecy with the Cold War. A 1984 poll showed that 39 percent of citizens believed that biblical prophecies about the Earth's destruction by fire foretold a nuclear conflagration.

What the 1980s actually counted down was the Cold War itself. As the central storyline of American apocalypticism petered out with the breakup of the USSR, prophetically minded Americans turned their gaze inward, focusing on the possibility that the real conspiracy was coming from within. A new breed of American conservatives — the self-described "paleocons" — turned their conspiratorial ire on the federal government, forging a combative populism that offered a more mainstream version of the worldview that animated people like the Kahls and the Weavers. As one historian summarized the far right's response to American victory in the Cold War, "One Evil Empire down, one to go."

While the paleocons talked about "repealing the twentieth century"—meaning the New Deal, the Great Society, and civil rights—Vicki Weaver, with Deuteronomy in hand, seemed intent on rolling back all two thousand years of the Common Era.

For a time, the work of staying dry and fed in the great north woods was so consuming that the specter of Armageddon lost some of its grip on the Weavers. The rhythms of life off the grid in North Idaho are straightforward: Summer is for getting ready for winter. Winter is for staying warm and sane. The family went long stretches without seeing anyone else, happily busy on their land. Just chopping wood for the stove and hauling water from the spring a quarter mile downhill could use up much of the day. (Randy had wanted to build below the spring, but Vicki's vision of a mountaintop aerie prevailed.) Vicki and Sara did laundry for five in big galvanized tubs with washboards and bar soap (more water, more firewood). They were acquiring skills lost over the course of generations and learning to depend on each other for everything. Of those first few years, Sara said that "basic survival was a full-time job." For a while the daily business of survival drowned out the theoretical drama of survivalism.

During the brief summers, Vicki and the kids picked buckets of huckleberries. Some they canned to lay up. The rest they traded downhill at the market for mesh bags of onions and potatoes or waxy cardboard lugs of peaches, bananas, tomatoes, and green beans. They preserved the bananas and veggies by drying them on old window screens.

Working from books, Vicki taught herself how to make plant remedies. She foraged herbs to dry—mint, chamomile, mullein, comfrey, and wild raspberry. Everything went into oversized jars and tins with neatly handwritten labels. According to Sara, nobody in the family visited a doctor during their decade living in Idaho.

Several hours each day were set aside for homeschooling: "readin', writin', arithmetic, and the Bible," as Vicki put it in a letter to Carolee Flynn. The promise of legal homeschooling had been one of the things that drew the Weavers to Idaho. "Everybody knows the government is not right," Vicki told a reporter. "We don't have the freedom to believe what we want. We moved here to remove our children from the trash being taught in public schools and to practice our faith...to keep Yahweh's laws." Even in those first few months, as she and Randy worked grueling days clearing their building site, piling up slash to burn, setting aside good logs for building, she taught the kids from old textbooks, the Bible, and a set of McGuffey Readers, a collection of nineteenth-century primers that were popular among twentieth-century homeschoolers for their emphasis on Christian values. It was later revealed when Sara and Rachel reentered public school that their mother was an excellent teacher.

As had been promised back in Iowa, they bought two horses and built a little corral by the cabin. Randy used one of the animals, Amigo, for skidding logs. Lightning, a dappled gray Arabian, was Sara's horse. She rode him bareback around the ridge and through the high grassy meadows. Rachel or Sam sometimes joined her, riding double, with the littler kid up front. The children had the run of the woods. They spent their free time building forts, chasing lizards, fishing for trout, and catching garter snakes. A hoop swing hung from a tall fir tree just outside the cabin. They were each other's best friends.

As they settled in, the work eased up. During one of the Jordisons' annual summer visits, Vicki's father rigged up a gas-powered laundry wringer with a kick start. Later, he and Randy installed a motorized pump to fill water tanks up on a scaffold behind the house, supplying them with clean, gravity-fed water, at least during that part of the year when the pipes were not frozen. (The soil was too rocky to bury them.)

With children and animals ranging around the cabin, the family enjoyed the potent satisfactions of near-total self-sufficiency — the warm smells of woodsmoke, fresh bread, chickens in a coop, and horses in a corral. They were kept dry by a house they had built and fed from a garden they had grown. They were educated, doctored, and entertained by themselves alone. And since this was not the life they had been born into — having rather suddenly been transplanted from a suburb flush with modern conveniences — they could marvel at the romantic sight of themselves living like frontier settlers. In the evening, when work was finished, they played Monopoly and Risk in the living room. From the foot of their back porch, endless miles of dramatic, faith-affirming beauty stretched away on three sides. Sara remembers the thrill of standing on the large overlook rock beneath the house and seeing thunderstorms rush across the valley. On calm days, they watched the turkey vultures and hawks sailing easy in the sky, both above and below their little mountain home.

They were no longer just stockpiling food and weapons for the coming collapse. They were living as if it had already arrived. Down the hill in Bonners Ferry and the rest of the United States, people were dropping off their kids at school, rushing to work with a big coffee, grabbing a roasted chicken on the way home, and falling asleep in front of Letterman while towels tumbled softly in the dryer. Up on their rocky knoll, the Weavers lived as if the whole precarious miracle of modern life had already come undone.

It is not difficult to imagine the exaltation, even occasional transcendence, that the family knew during those first years in Idaho, unbound from everything familiar and caught up in a heroic tale that stretched from the start of time to its ripening finale. To live intimately with prophecy is to live self-consciously within history — to feel its sweep as a single, cohesive story, as if personally hitched to the driving telos of the universe. On clear nights, with the cold air hanging in the pines and the heavens undimmed by the electric haze of human settlement, the sky in North Idaho teems with vivid, ancient stars. Caught up in the drama of God's special plan for their family, the Weavers must have considered that those same lights had vaulted over Adam and Eve at the foundation of the world, over Daniel in the wicked court of Babylon, and over John on his Aegean island. It was those very stars that would, before long, come crashing down, when time winked over into eternity.

————————

As happens out in the country, little outbuildings sprang up around the cabin as necessity and materials came along. There was a two-seater outhouse (dug a bit too close to the house, according to one visitor), a chicken coop, a woodshed, a root cellar, and a pump house. Besides the cabin, the largest structure on the land was a small gambrel-roofed shed, well insulated and fitted out with shelves and a bed, where Vicki (and eventually Sara) sequestered themselves each month during their period, according to strictures laid down in the days of Moses.

Their unlikely frontier dream was working, but they still needed cash. Randy took short-term jobs — selling firewood, logging, doing carpentry, working for spells on a tree farm and a sheep ranch. For a year he operated equipment and did chores at the Paradise Dairy in Bonners Ferry. But even compared to Iowa during the farm crisis, wages in North Idaho were low. With plenty of work to be done up on the property, Randy was happier staying at home until the need for cash became acute. In the notes of a US marshal tasked with cobbling together a clear picture of the Weavers, there was a line, credited to some unnamed relative, calling Randy "as lazy as they come." It seems more accurate to say that he did not like working for anyone else. He certainly did whatever he could to avoid a steady gig.

Vicki, on the other hand, had deep, almost manic stores of energy. As well as keeping house along the lines of a nineteenth-century wilderness settlement and educating the children, she refurbished old furniture for a local shop — sanding, varnishing, and cleaning out crannies with a solvent-soaked Q-tip. She was a master economizer. Sara recalls the family of five going a whole year on five thousand dollars. During the snowbound winters, Vicki and the girls wove rugs on a home-built loom to sell in town.

It was not long before another set of helpful hands arrived on the scene. When the Weavers had first arrived in Idaho and were still half living in the trailer down in the meadow, a quiet, somewhat lost young man named Kevin Harris drifted into their lives. Harris's father had died when he was two and he'd had a series of stepfathers. At nine, he started running away from his mother's home in Washington. At times, he lived in foster care. At times, on the streets of Spokane.

At sixteen, he was staying with friends of his mother on a piece of land above Naples. In exchange for long hours of cutting firewood to sell, the family fed him on a meager diet of squash, tomatoes, and cigarettes. Tall and baby-faced, Harris spoke with a guileless, aw-shucks manner. He had apple cheeks and big dark eyes that the state-trooper mustache he mustered did little to harden. After a chance meeting with Vicki and the kids on the road, he began coming by the Weaver cabin for proper meals.

Back in Iowa, Randy and Vicki had occasionally brought home wayward young men for brief stints. Kevin was different. On the day he was leaving his wood-splitting job to return to Spokane, Randy called to him from across a field, inviting him to come back anytime. Next spring, there he was. Harris gradually became something like a member of the family, acting as a big brother to the three Weaver kids, who all adored him, and as a sidekick to Randy, who taught him to shoot. At the time, Randy referred to Kevin and Sam as "the boys." Years later, Randy would publicly refer to Kevin and Sam as "my sons."

Harris would stay with the Weavers off and on for nine years, periodically drifting to the city, or taking seasonal work on logging crews, picking apples, or cutting hay. In 1984, he lived with the family for a full nine months. At other times, he might go more than a year without seeing them. But if he sometimes strayed from the ridge, the ideas the Weavers imparted went with him.

Randy and Vicki taught Kevin about ZOG and the importance of addressing God as "Yahweh." They also explained their newfound conviction that scripture, read properly, commands separation of the races. Kevin had not been raised with strong religion and had never shown any overt signs of racial animus. Even so, he took the Weavers' beliefs in stride. For a young man coming from a turbulent homelife, it was hard to argue with the fact that this generous, hard-working, tight-knit family had something figured out. When asked later how he responded to Randy's racist beliefs, Harris shrugged and said, "Weaver likes to talk." Those who had known the family before their embrace of ardent, unembarrassed racism had a harder time adapting to a set of beliefs that were gradually coming to occupy a position at the center of their faith.

In letters and occasional phone calls to old friends like Carolee Flynn and Vaughn Trueman, Randy and Vicki laid out their new racial convictions. They had once called themselves Christian survivalists. Now they also identified as "white separatists." Later, Randy would take umbrage whenever he was described as a "white supremacist," as if the distinction was of great importance. In a similar vein, the neo-Nazis of North Idaho regularly carped to reporters about how they performed cross "lightings," not cross "burnings." To be clear, Randy and Vicki's own words leave little doubt that they regarded Jews and people of color as inferior to white Anglo-Saxons.

Vicki's sister Julie and her husband Keith were ardent liberals by the standards of Fort Dodge. In the early 1970s, when Randy was coming out of the army, getting married, and getting serious about the Bible, Keith was protesting the war in Vietnam, wearing his hair long, and playing lead guitar in a successful Midwestern band called Locust. (They put out one LP on a national label. The sound was prog-ish hard rock, a bit like Foreigner.) Despite the political gulf between the two Jordison sisters and their husbands, everyone generally managed to get along, arguing peaceably around the dinner table at the Jordison farm in Coalville. While Julie and Keith had made peace with the Weavers' stringent and conspiratorial faith, the turn to flagrant, Bible-based racism was harder to swallow. After the move to Idaho, communication between the sisters was sparse.

Once they were well settled in their new home, Randy and Vicki resumed hosting a regular Bible study, meeting on Friday evenings with friends who shared their apocalyptic expectations, conspiratorial beliefs, and the notion that God commands separation between the races.

Vicki's RLDS roots, which played only a minor role in the Weavers' embrace of endtimes Fundamentalism, apparently increased her receptivity to Bible-based racism. "You can't tell me," she wrote a cousin back in Iowa, "that Joseph Smith advocated race mixing. There were no black RLDS elders until our generation." In fact, it was Brigham Young, not Smith, who codified racism into Mormon theology, prohibiting the "descendants of Cain" from receiving the priesthood. That ban remained in effect until 1978.

Whatever the Weavers may have believed when they pulled out of Cedar Falls — and it is impossible to say for sure — their elaborate, theological racism took full flower in North Idaho, a place where non-whites and Jews were almost an entirely theoretical proposition. When the family arrived in 1983, Boundary County had a population of just 8,332 people, with a minority population of twenty-six Asian Americans and three African Americans. The population has since swelled to 13,000, but the racial breakdown has not changed much. In the mid-'80s, after a string of bombings by white power activists, the *Chicago Tribune* speculated that North Idaho must hold a national record for "number of crosses burned per black resident." (The overwhelmingly white population of Boundary County underscores one of the stranger aspects of the entire Ruby Ridge affair — namely, that it is a saga in large part about racism and antisemitism in which nary a person of color or a Jew makes more than a passing appearance.)

To be a conspiracy-minded fundamentalist amid the restraining influence of people who knew you pre-awakening is one thing. But drop that same person into a community of like-minded zealots and things inevitably accelerate. Vicki, by inclination, was always going to be the most ardent, best-informed person in any group, whether the subject was child-rearing, gardening, or biblical exegesis. Surrounded by people who spoke freely about prophetic signs and the coming One World Government, she grew several degrees more radical. At the same time, Randy's brash talk about resisting federal tyranny got several decibels louder. In an era before the echo chamber effect of online community became obvious, the family's move across the country allowed them to step through a sort of geographic Overton window.

———

Something peculiar was happening on the far right in the 1970s and '80s. From Reconstruction until the middle of the twentieth century, organized white supremacism — meaning activism by people who do not mind being called racists — was dominated by vigilante groups like the Klan or pro-Nazi organizations like the Silver Shirts, who dreamt of remaking America along fascist lines. While fundamentalist ministers were often at the fore of these organizations — working out biblical justifications for everything from the extermination of Indigenous people to slavery and segregation — the racism and the theology generally operated on parallel tracks.

By the time Randy and Vicki got involved in the movement, things had taken an emphatically theological, even mystical, turn. The early 1980s saw a proliferation of groups that the Idaho-based scholar James Aho called "paramilitary political-religious cults." Outfits like the Covenant, Sword, and Arm of the Lord, the Christian Patriots Defense League, and the Aryan Nations blended white supremacy, paramilitarism, and an apocalyptic strain of Fundamentalism that placed race at the very center of God's prophetic plan. The creed that united these assorted outfits was Christian Identity—the same faith that underpinned Gordon Kahl's crusade and inspired William Potter Gale to organize the Posse Comitatus.

Like John Nelson Darby's dispensationalism, Christian Identity sprang from the teeming theological soil of Victorian England. The theory, originally known as British Israelism, holds that modern Anglo-Saxons are descended from a lost tribe of ancient Israelites. While countless sects and churches, the New England Puritans among them, have claimed to be the spiritual inheritors of Israel's special covenant, proponents of British Israelism claimed that white Britons are the literal, lineal descendants of ancient Hebrews. This theory was buttressed with complex genealogies, migration maps, and a story about a group of Israelites who settled the British Isles. From there, with God's countenance shining upon them, they proceeded to colonize the globe. (This tale of far-wandering Jews has some parallels with the story contained in the Book of Mormon.)

In England, the obvious draw of such a theory was that it consecrated the "Rule, Britannia" chauvinism that undergirded the empire, which was, in the late Victorian era, approaching its highest heights. Not only, as William Blake put it, would New Jerusalem be built upon England's green and pleasant hills. Modern Britons were, in their very blood, the rightful heirs of the old Jerusalem, along with all the swell promises made to God's elect.

While the notion that Anglo-Saxons are descended from a lost tribe of Israel might have been implicitly antisemitic, British Israelism did not necessarily hold that modern Jews are uniquely evil. In the movement's original cosmology, modern Jews were just a different, *un*lost tribe. It was only after British Israelism began to spread into the Western United States in the 1930s, that it was picked up by a smattering of ardent antisemites and Christian nationalists. Retrofitting the theory for American purposes, they claimed that the founders of the United States had brought God's special covenant with them when they risked the Atlantic. In the USA, the movement became especially focused on the idea that modern Jews are demonic pretenders to the role of God's "chosen," and therefore guilty of all the sins Christians have long laid at their feet, along with several dramatic new crimes. (William J. Cameron, the Canadian-born editor of the *Dearborn Independent*, which printed the articles that Henry Ford compiled as *The International Jew*, was an early exponent of British Israelism in North America.) Among other things, this small fundamentalist offshoot—which combined biblical literalism, endtimes prophecy, sanctified racism, and a conspiratorial hatred for the federal government—has had an uncanny tendency to generate political violence.

If the basic premise of racism is that there are immutable, biological differences among various races, Identity theology goes a step further, claiming that white people are descended from Adam and Eve (i.e., are human) while non-whites are the product of a separate and earlier act of creation. As for the Jews, they are the offspring of a tryst between Eve and Satan who have, over millennia, come to secretly control life on Earth, mostly through the instrument of international finance and secretive organizations like the Masons and the Illuminati.

Reading the Bible through the lens of race, Identity Christians plucked out verses that supposedly describe an eternal, Manichaean struggle between the descendants of Adam and the descendants of Lucifer (the Jews), who have used people of color ("mud people," in Identity's hateful parlance) to dilute Aryan purity and divide humanity from the Creator. In essence, this is a scriptural version of an old and still-popular story—known recently as "white genocide" or "the great replacement"—in which Jews weaponize people of color to diminish the dominion of whites.

Like Randy and Vicki, most people who arrived at Christian Identity beliefs got there by way of ordinary fundamentalism. On an old pickup bed welded into a trailer, the Weavers mounted a large spray-painted sign proclaiming the merger of their religious and racial beliefs: "Yahweh is White Power!" The confluence of two of the strongest currents of American consciousness — millenarian faith and white supremacy — was perhaps inevitable, but one reason that Identity's bizarre cosmology found traction among fundamentalists is that most of them had already placed the Jews, in one way or another, at the very center of their prophetic story.

Among a majority of Evangelicals, the special role of the Jews in the endtimes has long generated a somewhat fetishistic philosemitism, with a special emphasis on the state of Israel. In a striking collision of the mythic and the practical, the widespread belief that Christ can only return after the Jewish diaspora has been restored to the Holy Land has directly shaped American foreign policy. Jerry Falwell, a key figure in rallying evangelical support for Israel — and shaking off the overt antisemitism that pervaded early Fundamentalism — explained the importance of the Jewish state to American Christians with a simple formula: "God deals with nations as they deal with Israel."

With Christian Identity, the centrality of Jewish people in endtimes prophecy took a turn, linking up with history's most enduring conspiracy theory: the idea that the Jews secretly control everything. In particular, Identity believers became preoccupied with the idea that the United States government has been seized by a demonic cabal of Jews (ZOG) at work to shore up the global order described in Revelation.

By the mid-1980s, Identity beliefs suffused every branch of the white power movement. Among other things, its peculiar theology solved an enduring riddle for the American far right — namely, how do you build a *völkisch* blood-and-soil nationalism in a place where only Indigenous people can claim any sort of ancient link between their blood and this soil? By identifying white Americans as the true Israel,

Identity theology recasts the American experiment as a sanctified racial project, subverted only by the contagion of Jews and non-whites.

Because Christian Identity is a decentralized and mostly leader-less faith, its teachings are an unstable clutter of theology, history, and conspiracy, which believers are free to assemble in their own ratios. By the mid-'80s, the Weaver family could fairly be described as its own tiny Identity congregation. Their devotion was sufficiently strong that, for a time, they stopped referring to themselves as Christians altogether. "We are Identity, but we are not Christians," a teen-age Sara told reporters in 1992.

———————

Psychoanalyzing historical figures can make for shoddy history, but it seems fair to say that there was something at work in the private dynamics of Randy and Vicki's relationship that propelled them toward ever-more-extreme beliefs. Perhaps it was some combustible mixture of Randy's extreme stubbornness (what he proudly called his "stiff neck") and Vicki's scourging perfectionism. Maybe it was the collision of her mythic cast of mind with Randy's self-conception as a warrior deprived of a war. One Iowa friend speculated that strong religion was Vicki's way of shaking off youthful insecurity and gain-ing authority in her marriage. Julie Jordison saw her big sister's evolv-ing fundamentalism as a way to tighten the bond between her and Randy. It is impossible to say what they might have become without each other, but together Randy and Vicki created a story that placed their nuclear family at the center of world events — the Weavers *contra mundum*. Perhaps there was even something romantic in their slide into radicalism. Like a fundamentalist Bonnie and Clyde, each step away from Midwestern respectability tied them closer together. *Will you follow me here? What about here? Would you be an outlaw for my love?*

It certainly did not hurt that Vicki's theological questing led toward a faith that matched Randy's predilections, especially given the prevailing culture of evangelicalism in the 1970s and '80s. The

Jesus Movement ebbed along with the rest of the counterculture, but not before leaving its mark on the style and culture of many evangelical churches, where men with neatly trimmed beards spoke about Jesus as their best friend. There would be no pressed chinos or weepy altar calls for Randy Weaver. He got to worship his God in the fresh air, with salty language, a cigarette, and plenty of gear.

For her part, Vicki clearly craved something more mysterious and potent than what was on offer at a church like Cedarloo Baptist. While many American Protestants reached for updated, colloquial translations of the Bible, she was activated by the resonant, lapidary phrases of the King James Version, which, by virtue of being composed in the early 1600s, and having infused spoken English ever since, hits the modern ear as majestically poetic yet fully comprehensible—strange yet familiar. Her inclination toward a faith that stands consciously apart from the dominant culture prefigured the recent trend of conservative Protestants turning to Roman Catholicism and Eastern Orthodoxy, drawn by antiquity and incense instead of soft rock praise music and a comparably soft liturgy.

While the Weavers delved deeper into apocrypha and prophecy, keeping their eyes on the horizon for signs of the End, the real trouble started on their own hill. It was at the start of 1985, just two years after their arrival in Idaho, that the name "Weaver, Randall Claude," became stubbornly lodged in the files of federal law enforcement, vindicating the family's conspiratorial faith and triggering a sequence of events that would ratchet forward like a bureaucratic Rube Goldberg machine, gathering fear and mistrust as it advanced.

CHAPTER TWELVE

SMALL-TOWN TALK

WHEN THE WEAVERS first arrived in Bonners Ferry and Vicki wrote excitedly to her parents about meeting like-minded Christians, it was probably the Kinnison family she had in mind. Terry Kinnison was an Indiana-born truck driver, who, along with his wife and two sons, drifted around a lot. The two families became fast friends. When the Weavers moved into their cabin on Sara's birthday and the road was too muddy for Randy's truck to make the climb, it was Terry and his boys who helped carry the Weavers' boxes up the hill. It was also Terry Kinnison who sold them Sara's beloved horse, Lightning.

Late in the fall of 1984, Randy invited the Kinnisons to park their camper on a low spot on the Weavers' land. In exchange for three thousand dollars, Randy let the Kinnisons commence building what Sara called "a huge slapstick barn" down below the spring. The whole deal was done off the books and somehow Terry Kinnison came to believe that he had purchased a half-interest in the property.

By the end of that winter, things had grown tense between the two families. It is not clear what precisely happened. Neither family ever told their full side of the story. Based on some of the harsh things Terry Kinnison later told the FBI about Vicki—specifically, that she was a dangerous zealot who would kill her own kids rather than let them fall into the hands of the government — the conflict might have begun between Vicki and Terry. It could have been something as mundane as the fact that, by Sara's account, the Kinnisons were extremely messy while Vicki ran a tight household. Sara would later recall the Kinnisons as villains of Dickensian proportions, with Mrs. Kinnison beating their dogs, her boys torturing the local wildlife, and one of them exposing himself to her when she was just nine.

After things almost came to hammer blows between Randy and Terry down by the half-built barn, Randy evicted the newcomers. Terry went to court and filed a lien on the Weavers' property, claiming that his three thousand dollars and the work he had put into his barn entitled him to a half share of the twenty acres — specifically, the half with the spring on it. The Weavers countersued, hiring as their lawyer Everett Hoffmeister, who was counsel to the Aryan Nations. By the time the case came to court, the Kinnisons had moved to Alaska and the court sided with the Weavers, awarding them a small payout for lawyers' fees. Terry Kinnison gave up the fight, writing to the court, "May the God of Abraham rebuke them for what they have done." Unfortunately for the Weavers, Kinnison did not leave matters entirely up to the God of Abraham.

As a parting shot, Kinnison called the county sheriff to report that Randy had been talking about assassinating President Reagan, the governor of Idaho, and various law enforcement officials. What seems most likely is that Randy, so often given to outlandish provocations (including earlier talk of assassinations), had said something crazy that Terry Kinnison, departing bitterly for Alaska, decided to take literally.

Whatever truth there might have been in the original accusation, the sheriff called the FBI, which passed the case to the Secret Service, which initiated a default procedure to gauge the threat. That process mostly consists of canvassing people who know the accused. As it turned out, several of the Weavers' neighbors had alarming things to say about the family.

Kinnison himself reported that Randy believed that the federal government was under the control of the Illuminati and that the Weavers were ready and willing to fight the usurpers. He testified that they would kill any government officials who came on to their property and provided a list of thirteen firearms he claimed to have personally seen at the Weaver home, including an automatic rifle.

When the Secret Service questioned the Weavers' other neighbors, they almost uniformly explained that Randy and Vicki believed that the world was soon to end and that Armageddon would commence "when [their] home will be under siege and assaulted." One Bonners Ferry resident speculated to investigators that the Weavers' driveway might be rigged with bombs — an absurd bit of conjecture that only took on the glimmer of possibility because of Randy's demolition training in the army. Pretty much everyone the Secret Service interviewed agreed that driving up to the Weaver place without an invitation would be dangerous.

Whether or not any of this was accurate, it was the impression that people living near the Weavers had acquired. While it is theoretically possible that a group of Boundary County residents conspired to smear the Weavers, it seems unlikely. What's more plausible is that the Weavers had slowly frightened or otherwise alienated many of those around them.

The guns certainly played a role. In Idaho you can "open carry" pretty much everywhere except bars and courthouses. Plenty of people do, especially that far north in the Panhandle. Everyone in the Weaver family, kids included, seemed to be permanently armed. (Randy told an FBI investigator that his policy was that each kid got a BB gun at eight and a .22 at ten. From there, the caliber and variety of weapons rose with age.) Even if, as Randy and Sara later insisted, they were vigilant about gun safety and merely carried to protect themselves against moose and cougars, the combination of the Weavers' apocalyptic rhetoric and the spectacle of so much firepower had put genuine fear into their closest neighbors, all of whom, it bears noting, were North Idahoans with their own guns and strong politics. Even if it was all just the gossip of an unusually gothic mountain village, that fear, once set down on paper, would become a matter of great consequence.

During the Secret Service investigation, Randy and Vicki became convinced that Terry Kinnison had not only filed a false report, but also forged a death threat in Randy's name and mailed it directly to President Reagan.

———

On a cold winter day in 1985, Randy and Vicki sat down with an FBI agent named Ken Weiss, a Secret Service investigator, and a local sheriff's deputy. Randy insisted that he had never threatened Reagan. Heck, he had voted for the guy! The whole mess was just a campaign by Terry Kinnison and other neighbors to get him into trouble and steal his land.

Someone had told the investigators that Randy was a member of the Aryan Nations, which he denied, saying that he did not care for their preaching. He explained that he and Vicki lived strictly by the Bible, which gave them the right to kill in self-defense. He added, however, that law enforcement officials could safely come onto their property.

Satisfied that Randall Weaver was just a big talker with a lot of guns and a propensity for pissing off his neighbors, the Secret Service dropped the matter.

The Weavers, however, remained spooked. On February 28, 1985, two weeks after their meeting with the investigators, Randy and Vicki drove to the courthouse in Bonners Ferry to submit a notarized affidavit.

> We hereby make a public notice on this date, that we... believe our lives to be in jeopardy. We are the parents of three small children whose lives are also in danger. We are the victims of a smear campaign of our character and false accusations made against us to the Federal Bureau of Investigations and the United States Secret Service... They accused me of saying I was going to assassinate the President of the United States and the Pope. Very possibly, a threatening letter was sent to the president with

my name or initials forged. My accusers hoped that the FBI
would rush my home with armed agents hoping I would feel the
need to defend myself and thus be killed or arrested for "assault
on a federal official." There is evidence of my innocence but they
continue to try to build an illegal case… because they don't like
my political beliefs or religious faith.

Three years after describing a less specific version of this scenario
to a reporter in their Cedar Falls living room and seven years before
an FBI tactical team encircled the Weavers' cabin following an "assault
on an officer," the affidavit is either evidence of Vicki's oracular gifts
or a testament to how prophecies of persecution can self-fulfill.

Still brooding about the whole affair three months after the case
had been dropped, Vicki sat down at the kitchen table and wrote two
letters. The first she sent to President Reagan. "Please," she wrote, "let
me apologize for their evil in using you to get at [Randy]." The second, which she mailed to the Secret Service field office in Spokane,
demanded an apology for the whole ordeal and requested a copy of
the (probably nonexistent) assassination threat. There is no record of
either letter receiving an answer.

———

When the Secret Service had made their initial canvass of Randy and
Vicki's neighbors, they interviewed a Naples local named Samuel
Strongblood Wohali. Wohali, a navy vet who served as a Kootenai
tribal judge for the Bureau of Indian Affairs, was a large, muscular
man who wore his hair in two long, dark braids. A year earlier, he had
hired Randy to help build a fence at his place, a bit downhill from
the Weavers' land. After three weeks, things soured between the two
men. Randy had become increasingly outspoken about his racial
theories and, according to Wohali, the Weavers had taken to firing
automatic weapons at night, stressing out their neighbors. A forest
ranger friend of the Wohalis testified that he had heard the distinctive

chatter of automatic gunfire coming from a spot in the woods where he had just seen Randy.

The Naples General Store, with its coffee pot and post office, is where people from the surrounding hills meet up to gossip and visit. One afternoon, Wohali came upon Randy talking with some of his local Identity buddies. (A friend described these men as Randy's "sidekicks.") They tended to wear a lot of camo and went everywhere armed, even if it was just to spend the day hanging around rolling cigarettes.

Wohali, an ordained Christian minister, who said he was half native, half Jewish, strode up to Randy and told him to cool it with the gunfire. Randy, talking tough for his buddies, asked Wohali what he might do about it.

As Wohali himself later recounted in court, he told Randy that if and when the great endtimes race war kicks off, the Weavers better steer clear of the Wohali home. "Whatever God you serve, when you come off that mountain, turn left, don't turn right. If you come to my house, I'll tie you up by your two big toes and I'll cut off your fingertips and I'll drip you dry. I'll not send you to heaven or hell."

That is about where things stood between the two men when investigators asked Wohali if Randy posed a genuine threat. Wohali told the same story others had. The Weavers have a lot of guns; they think the government is run by an evil cabal; and they believe that Armageddon is nigh. Most ominously, he said that anyone who goes up to the Weaver place without an invitation would "have three weapons brought to bear on them, Weaver's, his wife's, and his son's." He added that Sam, who was seven, was constantly armed and that Vicki was a "crack shot."

Fatefully, Wohali also mentioned a man named Frank Kumnick, with whom Randy had been spending a lot of time. Unlike Randy, Kumnick was already on the federal government's radar. The link between the two men went into the file.

CHAPTER THIRTEEN

THE ORDER

FRANK KUMNICK, WHO lived in Bonners Ferry with his wife Mary Lou, was, by Randy's own assessment, "a bit on the goofy side." An enthusiastic Aryan Nations supporter, he liked to spin outlandish, half-cocked schemes for fighting ZOG. Some of his ideas were genuinely alarming (kidnappings, arson, shooting IRS agents). Others sounded like demented hijinks (putting superglue into the locks of banks, stripping IRS agents naked and sending them into the woods, hammering shit-smeared nails into boards hidden where government employees would likely walk).

In July of 1986, Kumnick invited Randy to spend the weekend at Hayden Lake, an hour and a half south of Naples, for the Aryan Nations' annual World Congress. Randy went, he claimed, because he was "interested in learning more about religious beliefs." He evidently enjoyed the experience, returning for subsequent summer congresses with Vicki and the kids, and proudly sporting an Aryan Nations belt buckle for years.

The compound at Hayden Lake, just outside the idyllic lakeside city of Coeur d'Alene, covered twenty acres of woods, meadows, and waterfront campgrounds. At the entrance there was a Checkpoint

Charlie–style guard station with a big sign reading, "Welcome Kindred Only." Within the grounds, there was a bunkhouse, a watchtower, a "hall of flags," and assorted oversized, whitewashed buildings. It looked like a cross between a rundown Bible camp and a prison.

The perimeter of the compound was encircled by barbed wire and patrolled by armed young men in elaborate uniforms. As a rule, far-right activists devote great energy to their regalia, with the results often resembling the kit of some make-believe European autocracy. At the Aryan Nations, the main uniform consisted of black pants, powder-blue shirts with epaulets, black neckties, arm bands, little black caps, and lots of badges and patches.

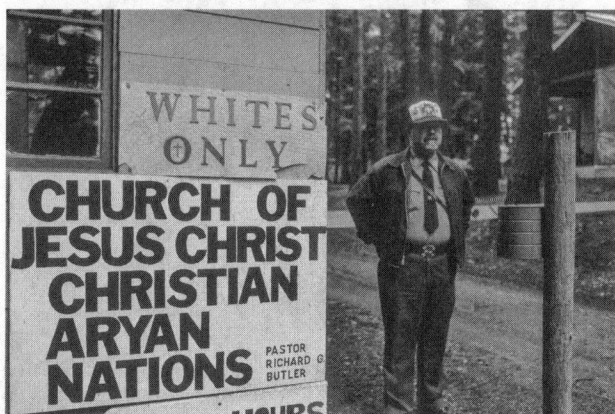

Entrance to the Aryan Nations compound, Hayden Lake, Idaho, April 1992.

The heart of the compound was the Church of Jesus Christ Christian, a white clapboard chapel with wooden pews, swastika banners, Confederate flags, and stained-glass windows depicting the Aryans' logo: a blue shield decorated with the "wolf's hook" arms used by some SS units and topped by a golden crown. The church's oddly repetitive name is meant to underscore the Identity proposition that the rabbi from Nazareth was somehow not a Jew.

The church and surrounding compound had been established in 1973 by Richard Butler, the Identity preacher who also founded the Kootenai County Christian Posse Comitatus. Butler had chosen North Idaho for its natural beauty, low taxes, and overwhelmingly white population. A strong believer in the Northwest Territorial Imperative, he hoped that his property on Hayden Lake would form the spiritual and organizational hub of the coming white utopia.

Rev. Richard Butler posing inside his church at the Aryan
Nations compound, 1985.

A jowly, dyspeptic man with liver spots and a Hitler Youth haircut, Butler was not particularly charismatic, but he was possessed of a grand vision. He aimed to unite the diverse sects of the far right into a coalition large enough to wield genuine political power. This ecumenical approach was the animating spirit behind the plural name "Aryan Nations" and his annual World Congresses, which hosted Klansmen in starched robes; skinheads from Portland, San Diego, and Vegas; neo-Confederates from the Southeast; Aryan activists from across Canada; uniformed neo-Nazis from the Midwest; northwestern

Christian survivalists; ex-cons tied to white prison gangs; teetotaling Identity fundamentalists; and speed-addled bikers.

The Aryan Nations effectively had two branches. On the religious side, there was the church, where Butler and various other pastors preached Christian Identity sermons while parishioners held up their hands in the familiar pose of worship—one arm aloft, palm wide, eyes closed—but with the important distinction that in Butler's church, the outstretched arms were dropped down to a forty-five-degree angle creating rows of static, prayerful *Sieg Heil*s.

On the political side, they held marches and demonstrations, ran paramilitary trainings, accumulated and organized white power literature, and maintained ties with like-minded groups in Missouri, Michigan, and Southern California. To propagandize the masses, Butler ran a large printing operation, staffed by ex-cons who lived in the bunkhouse at Hayden Lake. Like other white power activists, Butler proceeded from the assumption that once things got bad enough, some portion of hitherto blinkered white moderates would experience a racial awakening and join the crusade.

For years, the citizens of Coeur d'Alene dealt with the brunt of the Aryan Nations' parades and leaflets, not to mention the civic embarrassment of the media attention the group eagerly courted. Despite the live-and-let-live politics of the region, Kootenai County citizens overwhelmingly rejected the group and did plenty of counter-protesting and counter-organizing. (In the year 2000, with legal support from the Southern Poverty Law Center, a local woman and her son who had been run off the road and badly beaten by security guards from the compound would sue the Aryan Nations, driving the organization into bankruptcy and leading to the compound's sale and demolition.)

Back when Butler had started the Aryan Nations in the mid 1970s, the white power movement was approaching something like its zenith, driven by a rolling backlash to civil rights and the farm crisis. It is difficult to get reliable numbers for an underground, decentralized movement, but in her study of white power's post–Vietnam War ascent, the scholar Kathleen Belew estimates that by the early '80s, there were about 25,000 committed activists within the wider movement, with another 150,000–175,000 people buying books and T-shirts, going to rallies, and donating money to the cause. Almost half a million Americans at the time regularly read white power literature. By way of comparison, Belew notes, the John Birch Society maxed out at 100,000 members at its 1965 peak.

The shadow of Vietnam greatly shaped the movement. At Hayden Lake, the legacy and surplus of the war — jungle camo and M16s — were everywhere. While most conservatives blamed the American defeat in Indochina on anti-war activists, squeamish politicians, and a lack of national spine, the far right claimed that the United States failed due to deliberate internal sabotage and a secret deal between American leaders and the communists. For some, this perceived betrayal of American fighters by their own government produced great depths of rage and a deranging loss of faith in the state. Vietnam veterans made up an outsize part of the emerging white power movement. Visitors to Butler's summertime gatherings spoke the language of insurgency, oiling their weapons and running tactical drills as if the real war had yet to begin. Like the most ardent members of the New Left had done a decade earlier, activists like the Klansman Louis Beam urged Christian patriots to "bring the war home" through acts of violent resistance that would awaken white America to the real threat.

To the men and women who gathered each summer to barbecue, commiserate, and pray by the shore of Hayden Lake, America had truly gone off the rails. In one great simplifying sweep, every perceived social ill — crime, feminism, homosexuality, rural immiseration, racial integration — was taken as evidence of a rolling war between white Christians and the Jewish-controlled government.

When Randy Weaver and Frank Kumnick showed up at Hayden Lake in the summer of '86, some of the biggest names in the movement were present. Among them was a gangly middle-aged man with white hair, bushy eyebrows, and large, thick glasses. Among the summertime crowd of beer-drinking bikers and feral skinheads, he resembled a disheveled physics professor, which is precisely what he once had been. Everyone addressed him as Dr. Pierce.

After leaving a post at the University of Oregon in 1965, William Luther Pierce had devoted himself full-time to the coming white utopia. He moved to Washington, DC, to work for George Lincoln Rockwell, founder of the American Nazi Party. Rockwell would be shot dead two years later by an ex–party member, but Pierce carried on the work.

In 1974, the same year that Butler purchased the Hayden Lake compound, Pierce took control of the National Alliance, a West Virginia–based organization that had begun as a youth group supporting George Wallace's presidential campaign. Pierce cannily built the National Alliance into an organization that the FBI would eventually call the best-financed and best-organized white power outfit in the country. It published a magazine and books and produced a radio show. Imitating Rockwell, who had used Hatenanny Records to spread his views with racist folk songs, Pierce acquired Resistance Records, which released albums from the burgeoning subgenre of punk known as "hatecore," drawing young skinheads from the suburbs into a movement that had long been dominated by stodgy old preachers.

Despite his prolific organizing, Pierce's most significant contribution came in 1978 with the publication of *The Turner Diaries*, a dystopian novel that would become perhaps the most influential text on the anti-government far right. The book presents itself as the private diary of a man named Earl Turner, which has been found amid the rubble of what was once Washington, DC. The fictional historian who unearthed the journal writes to us from the Year 100 of the New

Era. In basic outline, Turner's diary tells a lightly updated version of the millenarian sequence laid down in Revelation: decline > cabal > bloodfest > paradise. The book's ideological pronouncements and hackneyed world-building are carried along by a sequence of commando fantasies — an extra-gory version of the *Rambo*-type material that became so popular in the post-Vietnam era.

The action begins in a near-future USA, which is under the thumb of an oppressive government known simply as "The System." The System, basically a cabal of Jews who run the media, the banks, and the government, has disarmed the citizenry and turned the country into a liberal hellscape. Civil rights has progressed to the point where it is illegal for white people to defend themselves against physical assault by minorities. Early in the book, a group of deputized Black thugs burst into Turner's home looking for any guns that have not been submitted to the state following passage of the "Cohen Act." Throughout the book, the heroes are derided as "racists" and "fascists" by other characters because they will not go along with The System. In one scene, white bystanders are beaten for failing to participate in an anti-racism parade as a violent mob brays "equality forever."

Turner and his comrades in a group called "The Organization" refuse to submit to the gun grabbers, and form an insurgency to fight back. They commit petty crimes and armed robberies to fund an uprising that kicks into high gear when they place a fertilizer-based truck bomb (the manufacture of which is described in cookbook-like detail) in a garage beneath FBI headquarters in Washington. The tremendous loss of innocent life (i.e., white people who are themselves victims of The System) is justified over and over by the world-historical nature of The Organization's holy war.

Eventually Earl Turner is admitted into a secret brotherhood of race-conscious guerillas known as "The Order." These men wage a merciless and bloody insurgency against The System, as complacent whites slowly awaken to their cause. The fighting reaches a turning point on August 3, 1993, a date thereafter known as "the Day of the

Rope." In a big offensive against The System, vast numbers of bureaucrats, Jews, reporters, minorities, race traitors, and white women who have slept with Black men are hung from "tens of thousands of lampposts, power poles, and trees." Turner, who is in Southern California at the time, sees the faculty of UCLA dangling in their academic robes. The amount of gore in Pierce's novel — including cannibalism and countless beheadings — is astonishing.

Turner consecrates his life to The Order and flies a crop duster loaded with a nuclear bomb into the Pentagon. From a stronghold in Southern California, the insurgents then nuke New York City and Tel Aviv. The war goes global as other countries launch their own nuclear attacks and, after a Revelation-scale conflagration, the Earth is cleansed of all Jews and non-whites. Starting in the year 1999, the Aryan millennium, called the New Era, commences with Year Zero.

By the time that William Luther Pierce and Randy Weaver found themselves mingling at Hayden Lake, Pierce's novel was already a canonical text on the far right, sold mostly at gun shows and by mail order from the National Alliance. In popular magazines like *Soldier of Fortune* it was advertised under the tagline "What will you do if the govt comes for your guns?" "The Day of the Rope" remains popular shorthand on the far right, affixed to countless Pepe the Frog memes.

Many actual crimes — murders, acts of racial terror, bank robberies, and even petty thefts — have been directly inspired by the *Diaries*, and not just in the United States. One tally puts the novel's real-world body count at two hundred. As one scholar told *Rolling Stone*, "William Pierce doesn't build bombs. He builds bombers." Timothy McVeigh, who sold red-jacketed copies of the *Diaries* from a folding table on the gun show circuit, was carrying a photocopy of certain passages when he detonated a fertilizer bomb in a truck parked at the base of the Federal Building in Oklahoma City, killing 168 people.

———

Besides McVeigh, the individual who went furthest to make Pierce's fantasy into reality was Robert Jay Mathews. In 1986, the year Randy first showed up at Hayden Lake, Mathews was on everybody's mind, even though he had died two years earlier, at the age of thirty-one. Handsome and charismatic, Mathews had long been a fixture at Butler's summer gatherings. He had lived nearby, in Metaline Falls, Washington, a small town in the Selkirks, not far from the Weavers' home. Rev. Butler had personally baptized his adopted son in 1982.

Mathews was born in Marfa, Texas. As with so many on the apocalyptic far right, he began his political journey with the ardent anti-communism of the John Birch Society, supposedly buying Robert Welch's *Blue Book* at age eleven. He became involved with Posse-style tax resistance and was charged with fraud. (As an unmarried nineteen-year-old, he claimed ten dependents on his W-4.) For a time, he led the Sons of Liberty, an anti-communist paramilitary group composed mostly of LDS survivalists. From there, he became a regional coordinator for William Pierce's National Alliance. During the farm crisis, he tirelessly spread antisemitism and racism to bankrupted farmers — working, as he put it in typically grandiloquent language, to "radicalize American yeomanry."

The virtue of deed over word is a big theme in *The Turner Diaries*. It was a notion that mapped perfectly onto a generational divide forming at the Aryan Nations. Under the *Diaries'* influence, Mathews and other young men in the movement grew restive with Butler's sermonizing, coalition-building, and goose-stepping along the banks of Hayden Lake. While most Identity believers, the Weavers among them, preached separatism in the runup to Armageddon, Mathews took a different approach, hoping to force the hand of history. As an old slogan put it, he and his friends would "immanentize the eschaton."

In a small tin barn in Metaline Falls, Mathews formed a paramilitary cadre of nine young men, most of them connected in some way with the Aryan Nations, the National Alliance, or the Klan. The group called itself the *Brüder Schweigen* (Silent Brotherhood), but, in a nod to the fictional guerillas in *The Turner Diaries*, most people called them "the Order."

With solemn oaths and a pseudo-mystical ceremony involving a lot of candles and a white newborn, the men in the barn pledged their lives to triggering the apocalyptic race war described in Pierce's novel. Having talked themselves into the belief that they lived beneath the thumb of a barely endurable tyranny, they decided that, if war was inevitable, it would be best to make the first move. As every insurrectionist knows, the surest way to start a revolution is to shoot at the state and wait for it to shoot back.

The group swiftly grew to a few dozen, with recruits coming from across the nation and the far-right vanguard. They trained on Mathews's farm and amassed a large stockpile of weapons, including a lot of illegally modified automatics. Small teams fanned out, committing a series of minor but escalating robberies, much like those described in the opening scenes of the *Diaries*. They robbed an armored car in Seattle and bombed a Boise synagogue.

In June of 1984, two years before Randy first came to Hayden Lake, Mathews and other members of the Order traveled to Denver to assassinate a popular radio personality named Alan Berg. Berg, a liberal Jew, had sparked the ire of white power activists by sparring on air with right-wingers, survivalists, and Identity believers, dropping their calls mid-rant and mocking them. Order members surveilled Berg for days before confronting him as he carried groceries from his VW Beetle to his townhouse. An Order member named Bruce Pierce shot Berg twelve times with an automatic MAC-10, while Mathews and a former Klansman named David Lane likely acted as lookouts. (The gun jammed on the thirteenth shot, which the assassins, full of millenarian hocus pocus, interpreted as God's blessing for their plan to return America to a time when it was just thirteen states.) In prison for his part in the murder, Lane would compose the so-called fourteen words that still serve as the credo of the white power movement: "We must secure the existence of our people and a future for white children."

A month after Berg's murder, a dozen members of the Order, armed with automatic weapons and wearing bandannas over their faces, forced a Brinks truck off the highway in Ukiah, California. It was an impressively planned attack, organized over weeks of scouting locations, planning escape routes, and arranging switch vehicles. The men made off with $3.6 million in cash and managed not to shoot anyone.

From this robbery and others, the Order poured millions into the white power movement, making large donations to a number of different groups. They also bought land on which to train and accumulated more high-end military gear for the coming war against ZOG. Along the way, they murdered one of their own, whom they regarded as a potential snitch. The cash and the ruthlessness both served a greater cause: the Order's long-range plans included bombing government offices and blowing up the LA power grid in hopes of sparking race riots.

It took the FBI a while to realize that these spread-out crimes were the work of one organization — an outfit whose crusade was more theological than criminal. But after an Order member was caught in Pennsylvania with counterfeit cash and turned informant, the Bureau tracked Bob Mathews to a motel in Oregon. After a brief shootout, he escaped, making his way to a safe house on Whidbey Island in Puget Sound. From there, Mathews issued a formal "Declaration of War" against ZOG, quoting directly from *The Turner Diaries*.

On December 7, 1984, the house was surrounded by more than a hundred FBI agents. Everyone else inside came out and was arrested, but Mathews refused to surrender. For a day and a half, he held off a small army of federal agents. He used a gas mask against a barrage of smoke grenades and fired a machine gun at agents who approached the house and at a helicopter hovering overhead. On the night of December 8, the FBI helicopter dropped flares into the house, igniting a stash of grenades and ammo. Mathews, unlike his co-religionist Gordon Kahl, did in fact burn to death.

Over the next few months, the rest of the Order was tracked down and arrested in ones and twos. One fugitive shot and killed a Missouri highway patrolman before fleeing into the woods. When it was learned that an Order member might be hiding in the Ozarks at "the Farm," the training camp and compound of the Covenant, Sword, and Arm of the Lord, the FBI raided the property, arresting four fugitives and several other CSA members. They also seized hundreds of guns, landmines, grenade launchers, and a large supply of cyanide, likely intended to poison a municipal water supply to trigger civil unrest.

In the spring of '85, twenty-four men associated with the Order were indicted. Charges included racketeering, conspiracy, arson, murder, counterfeiting, weapons violations, and armed robbery of more than four million dollars. The prosecution, which took place across several trials in several jurisdictions, represented a novel effort to use RICO laws against a terrorist organization. In all, it was a bit of a mess, with the government bringing sixty-seven separate charges against members of the Order. Half of those indicted supplied evidence against each other, raising doubts about the strength of oaths taken by candlelight over a white infant. From the prosecution, the Order's successors on the radical right learned the hazards of informants, excessive organization, and committing nonpolitical felonies (like robbery and counterfeiting) in service of their cause.

Hoping to crack down on the larger movement from which these young ultras had arisen, the government attempted to prosecute thirteen white power leaders, including Richard Butler, for seditious conspiracy. The blockbuster trial in Fort Smith, Arkansas, was a fiasco for the over-reaching prosecution. All thirteen men were acquitted.

Dead at thirty-one, Robert Jay Mathews, like Gordon Kahl before him, became a hero to the cause. His widow Debbie, like Joan Kahl, came to occupy something like a sainted position within the movement. Both women were at Hayden Lake in the summer of 1986, when Randy made his first trip to the Aryan Nations. At the merch table, visitors could purchase a seven-dollar medallion honoring the martyrs of the Order. It was inscribed with the words: "Should you fall, my friend, another friend will emerge from the shadows to take your place." Fearing precisely that, and hoping to stop the next terror spree before it got started, federal law enforcement was keeping a close eye on things.

For those gathered at Hayden Lake that July, the surge in federal attention was obvious. Like the "don't eat the brown acid" warnings issued over the PA at Woodstock, the loudspeakers at the Aryan Nations periodically reminded visitors that undercover feds walked among them. For people who styled themselves dissident revolutionaries, there might have been an affirming tinge of menace to glancing across the campfire and wondering if that unfamiliar man nursing a beer might be a snitch. Or maybe it was that guy with New Balances and a four-day beard, the one holding forth a bit too loudly about the fallen heroes? The uniformed Aryans at the guardhouse beefed up security, running background checks on new members and writing down license plate numbers. Paranoia struck deep on all sides.

Enter Randall Weaver, trailing along behind his chatterbox friend, Frank Kumnick. Aside from the fact that nobody was likely to invite Kumnick into their terror cell, he was an informant's dream: talkative, self-aggrandizing, and eager to make back-slapping introductions.

CHAPTER FOURTEEN

SO MUCH FOR THE STUD FINDER

DURING THEIR FIRST World Congress together, Kumnick introduced Randy to a man he had just met named Gus Magisono, a stocky, balding biker in his mid-forties from New Jersey. Outlaw bikers have long been a key constituency within the white power scene in the Northwest. Gus, who wore full leathers and a shaggy gray beard, claimed to be a gunrunner who supplied unregistered and illegally modified weapons to urban gangs. He was not steeped in the arcana of Christian Identity or endtimes Fundamentalism, but he was friendly and Randy liked talking guns just as much as religion. When they parted ways, Randy invited Gus to come meet the family sometime.

"Gus," whose real name was Kenneth Fadeley, was neither a biker nor a gunrunner. He was a Spokane security consultant and private investigator who mostly did industrial security work. In the wake of the Order's crime spree, he had signed on with the Bureau of Alcohol, Tobacco and Firearms (ATF) as a paid informant, with a mandate to insinuate himself into the Christian Identity movement, where a lot of illegal weapons seemed to be changing hands.

In the dense thicket of mythology that has grown up around the Ruby Ridge affair, Fadeley is generally cast as the classic snitch — a shady character, playing both sides of the law, trying to get himself out of legal trouble, or make an easy buck. In other words, as someone with a personal stake in Randy Weaver getting indicted. At trial, Randy's defense, led by the brilliant, theatrical Gerry Spence, would repeatedly describe Fadeley as a confessed liar, which is technically true insofar as undercover work is predicated on falsity. Fadeley had no criminal record. For several years of dangerous undercover work, the ATF paid him a total of five thousand dollars, plus gas and mileage on his Nissan Sentra.

Two years after the Ruby Ridge siege, Fadeley would be called to testify about his role in the case before the US Senate. By then he had been pilloried by far-right conspiracists and mainstream conservatives, both busily framing the case as a story about big government run amok. To preserve Fadeley's anonymity, his testimony was shielded from the audience and the C-SPAN cameras by a folding screen. A machine pitched his voice upward several octaves. In a chipmunk-like register, he explained how he got into freelance undercover work after a friend of his, a Spokane police officer, was killed by outlaw bikers. It was the Spokane PD who recommended him to Herb Byerly, the ATF special agent who was trying to keep tabs on where things might be heading next in the white power scene following the successful prosecution of the Order.

Fadeley, posing as Gus, befriended Frank Kumnick at the Aryan Nations, and the two men kept in touch. Kumnick was thrilled by the success of the Order, although critical of what he saw as their sloppiness. He spoke openly about starting up some sort of successor group. One of the schemes he laid out for Gus revolved around Kumnick's job as a janitor at Rocky Mountain Academy, a pricey private school in Naples that was part of a network of so-called CEDU schools. These schools, now shuttered, catered to the parents of "troubled teens" and had their roots in the harsh psychological methods of Synanon, an offshoot of Alcoholics Anonymous that, under the charismatic tyranny of a man named Charles E. Dietrich, devolved into a violent cult on a remote Northern California property overlooking Tomales Bay.

In Boundary County, where a lot of people talk about the elites who run the country from their coastal fleshpots, the Rocky Mountain Academy, which had graduated heirs to the Dupont and Hughes fortunes, was one of the few places where one might encounter a real-life Jew or a member of "the elite" — or at least one of their wayward offspring. Kumnick said that he could use his position as janitor to snatch the children of several wealthy Jews, hide them in a remote cave on a mountain near the Montana border, and then ransom them for millions to buy weapons and recruit troops for the war against ZOG. He specifically talked about nabbing Barbara Walters's daughter, Jacqueline Guber, who was then enrolled at the campus in Naples.

Kumnick laid this all out for Gus, and even brought him on a reconnaissance trip to the cave, where they scouted places to bury weapons and supplies. Rather than burn their informant over this half-baked scheme, the ATF reached out to the FBI, which contacted the school. Kumnick was fired under the pretense that his car had been spotted at the Aryan Nations, which gave him another feather of persecution for his cap and extra time on his hands. After his firing, Kumnick told the informant, "Of course, it's funny. I got the keys. And I got the layout of the place."

Kumnick's cracked Hardy Boys pipe dream about hiding rich kids in a cave was of far less concern to federal law enforcement than several other new developments in the region. A few weeks after Randy returned home from his first trip to Hayden Lake, a group of men in and around the Aryan Nations decided to make good on their commemorative medallions and pick up where Bob Mathews and his comrades had left off. Calling themselves the Order II, they carried out a series of bombings in and around Coeur d'Alene in September of 1986. A few small bombs went off at local businesses, as well as at the home of a Catholic priest who had organized a task force to push back against the Aryan Nations. The rest of the targets were local facilities associated in one way or another with the federal government. Despite significant property damage, nobody was hurt, which seems to have been by design.

The FBI's sedate, one-man field office in Coeur d'Alene suddenly became a hive of activity. Agents gathered tips and compiled lists of associates and associates of associates.

From the perspective of the FBI and the ATF, there was no way of knowing if all this violence — the first wave ominously disciplined and effective, the second more amateurish, but all clearly of a piece — was a flash in the pan, or, as its perpetrators loudly insisted, the start of a revolution. The fact that the Order II existed at all was proof that the wave of prosecutions following Mathews's death had not snuffed out the ambitions of far-right radicals to launch some sort of violent insurrection. The alarming prospect of a diffuse, heavily armed movement stoked by apocalyptic racism left law enforcement officials eager for any information about what might be coming next.

Unlike the FBI, which is a general law enforcement agency, the ATF has its roots in the Treasury Department's Prohibition-era war against the moonshine trade and the violent crime that went with it. By the time the ATF became an independent agency in the early '70s, its officers were more interested in explosives and illegal weapons than backwoods stills and unstamped cigarettes.

Because of the bombings and gun crimes linked to members of the Aryan Nations, the ATF had been keeping an eye on Hayden Lake since the early '80s, especially after Richard Butler began recruiting ex-convicts to live in the bunkhouse and operate his press. Butler's Nazi summer camp suddenly looked a lot more like a training ground for terrorists than a place where racists gathered to show off their guns and burn a few crosses (always with a county-issued burn permit). The big question was: Where, precisely, would the next threat come from?

And so, the informant Kenneth Fadeley, posing as the gunrunner Gus, was told to keep in touch with a minor wannabe like Frank Kumnick. The ATF later justified the operation by claiming that Kumnick was under suspicion for "significant arms trafficking." In reality, that was probably just a pretense for extending investigative contact with the man in hopes of stumbling onto something of substance.

On an icy day in January of 1987, Kumnick picked up Randy in his Jeep Wagoneer for an outing to Sandpoint, Idaho, to meet up with Gus. Kumnick, who had already met repeatedly with the informant, had enough sense to be worried about undercover agents. He wanted Randy, who had only met Gus the one time at Hayden Lake, to come along and get a read on the guy. Randy, who had been cooped up on the ridge for months, went along, he later testified, out of sheer boredom.

While Sandpoint is just twenty-five minutes south of Naples, the presence of two natural attractions—Lake Pend Oreille and the Schweitzer Mountain ski area—brings seasonal tourists and second-home owners, lending the town a far more prosperous aspect than Naples. In their differences and proximity, the two towns exemplify the diverging cultures of the Mountain West. In Naples there are tumbledown mills, shaggy rail sidings, lots of hand-painted "no trespassing" signs, and a single bar where a California license plate invites hard stares. In Sandpoint there are brew pubs, yoga studios, art galleries, and outdoorsy boutiques. While Naples is, at the time of this writing, plastered with fading "Stop the Steal" signage, Sandpoint has posters for ski clinics and a local production of *Fiddler on the Roof*. In the short drive from one town to the other, the ratio of Subarus to generously lifted pickups inverts perfectly.

The ostensible purpose for the meetup in Sandpoint was for Gus and Kumnick to discuss forming some sort of Order-like organization. After the Wagoneer pulled into a parking lot by the lake, Frank hopped into the back and invited Gus to take the front passenger seat. When he climbed in, Fadeley was surprised to see Randy Weaver at the wheel. The informant remembered meeting Randy the previous summer, but he had not been expecting to see him that day.

The three men greeted each other with some racist small talk about the previous day's "Martin Luther Coon Day." To general chuckling, Randy lamented his country's priorities. "Celebrate a communist, sex-pervert n****r. Son of a bitch." None of the three seemed in a hurry and the conversation meandered. It was Kumnick who eventually raised the possibility of organizing some sort of group. He said that he knew a few trustworthy former army guys he might ask to join. After a bit, the men drove around town looking for somewhere warm to talk privately. They ended up parked outside a coffee shop near the lakefront. When Kumnick went in to use the bathroom, Randy, who had not said much so far, started in with his usual preaching, talking about Yahweh, the evils of public education, and the coming End of Days.

After Kumnick returned to the Wagoneer, they drove to an abandoned park. There followed some edgy back and forth about how many people in the movement seemed to be going to jail. (It had only been a year since the big spate of trials.) At that point, Kumnick, still in the backseat, pulled out a little derringer and a small black device. Pointing the gun at the informant, Kumnick announced that he was going to "scan" Fadeley for a wire. He ran the device over the man's left arm, which was draped over the front bench seat.

Fadeley, who had a mic taped to the right side of his chest, snatched the device from Kumnick's hand. Turning it over, he saw that it was an ordinary electronic stud finder. Buying time and wondering if the gizmo even worked, he turned it upon Kumnick, leaning over the seat and wanding the other man's chest. When it beeped, Kumnick triumphantly pulled a set of Christian Patriot Defense Party dog tags up through his collar.

Fadeley filibustered, using the classic movie snitch maneuver of accusing Kumnick of being an informant himself. Cowed, but not fully deterred, Kumnick once again pointed the little gun at Fadeley's head and haphazardly scanned his left arm and the left half of his chest. The machine did not detect the wire or the transmitter that was sending their conversation to a tape recorder in the nearby car of ATF agent Herb Byerly.

With all three men still on edge, Randy took a more old-fashioned approach to snitch detection. He quizzed Gus a bit about where exactly he was from back East, as if the Iowa farm boy knew one New Jersey township from another. This interrogation devolved into chummy talk about who was worse, the Mexican Americans whom Randy had known in the army or the Puerto Ricans whom Gus claimed to have fought with during his childhood outside Philadelphia.

As would later become clear, Randy seemed to think that his best defense against legal trouble was his wholesome, tight-knit family. He repeatedly brought up the notion of introducing Gus to Vicki and the kids, as if such an introduction would eliminate all legal risk.

As nerves cooled, the men resumed bullshitting about how they might take the fight to the feds. Kumnick did almost all the talking, excitably suggesting that they could be "new leaders in the new age" of the revolution. He spun his various schemes, from the kidnapping plot to burning fields of hops where undocumented immigrants worked. In his harebrained way, he seemed to think that the three of them huddled in the Wagoneer might form the vanguard of the war against ZOG. He repeatedly looped back to the matter of snitches, praising the Order for having the steel to execute one of their own. When Randy did pipe up, it was to talk about the Bible and the importance of keeping your kids out of public school.

At some point, Kumnick ran into a store to meet his wife, once again leaving Randy alone with the informant. Away from his blustery friend, Randy explained that he wasn't particularly interested in joining the revolution. The End was coming soon — "according to the Bible, things are goin' down the tubes" — and nothing could stop it. He admitted to Gus that Kumnick had brought him along to help figure out if the gunrunner could be trusted.

Eventually they all retired to a pizzeria where Vicki and Mary Lou Kumnick were waiting. Vicki had spent the afternoon shopping and showed off a new biblical dictionary she had found. In total, the three men had spent more than four hours together, sussing each other out and talking in circles that never seemed to lead anywhere. At times, they sounded like old pals. At other moments, they were all sufficiently nervous that both Kumnick and Fadeley had quietly laid hands on their concealed pistols. The informant, keen to get something coherent on tape, had tried in vain to steer Frank toward saying something specific about his plans. But despite Kumnick's obvious desire for action, his skittering mind never landed on any one idea. As for Randy, he was now on record as saying that he was not interested in being part of any sort of terror cell or insurgency. The most damning comment he made was when they were talking about the IRS coming to evict a neighbor of his. "I hope he kills half of them," he said.

It would be five years before Randy learned that everything said that day was on tape. "So much for the stud finder," he'd quip.

———

After that, Randy did not see Gus until the following summer, when all five Weavers attended the Aryans' 1987 World Congress. Of her first trip to Hayden Lake, Sara, who was nine, recalled eating a lot of watermelon, making crafts in a big room with other kids, and attending a cross burning. Her father introduced her to Rev. Butler. "I remember getting the impression from him," Sara wrote, "that if you were cool and wanted to fit in, you had a shaved head, and wore black boots and black jackets with patches." (One such young man was a Vegas skinhead named David, who was nine years Sara's senior. They would eventually marry, have a son, and get divorced. Sara later remarried.)

At the '87 Congress, it was Randy who took Gus around, introducing him to a few Klansmen and Posse friends. The reunion between the two men was brief, but when they parted Randy mentioned that times were lean up on the mountain.

Fadeley still did not regard Weaver as a fruitful source of information. The man was clearly more interested in the Apocalypse than revolution. Still, the informant made a mental note: *Weaver knows a lot of these people — and he's broke.*

CHAPTER FIFTEEN

TWO CHAINSAWS

AFTER FIVE YEARS in Idaho and two past Vicki's predicted date for the start of the Tribulation, the Weavers wanted a break from life off the grid. Toward the end of 1987, they sold one of their horses and pulled together the rent for a house in Deep Creek, not far from the base of the ridge. The red house, as they called it, was just six miles from their land, but much closer to Naples, Bonners Ferry, and the highway. It sat along a deep, fast-flowing creek where the children could swim and fish for trout right out of the back door. The house belonged to the father of Jackie Brown, a local woman with dark eyes, a commanding manner, and a resonant smoker's voice. At the time, she worked as a waitress at the ski area in Sandpoint. Along with her husband, Tony, and their teenage daughter Maria, Jackie would grow close to the Weavers, especially Vicki. In 1992, she would play a decisive role in negotiating an end to the siege, after which she and Tony co-wrote a thoughtful, up-close account of the Ruby Ridge incident titled *The First Canary*.

The year and a half that the Weavers spent living in the red house was, by all accounts, a welcome change of pace. For the first time in five years, Sara recalled, "all of our time wasn't spent just trying to survive." Living down in town, the grip of Vicki's religious convictions seemed to loosen a bit. Some of the things that she had previously classed as grievous sins — having their pictures taken, watching television — drifted back into their lives. The kids collected cans from the roadside and sold nightcrawlers to fishermen for pocket money. They were still homeschooled, but they could bike to the Naples store to meet up with friends or buy chips and ice cream. Vicki still had a shed of her own out back, but it was for refurbishing furniture, not isolating during her monthly uncleanness.

The Weavers had become part of a small circle of folks living around Bonners Ferry who shared their survivalist and Identity beliefs. Jackie and Tony Brown, who were not among this group, noticed how Randy and Vicki naturally drifted toward the center of things. Aside from their native charisma — a mix of eloquence, competence, and profound certainty — the Weavers set a compelling example. A lot of people talk about fending for themselves in the wilderness, but here were people who had really done it, all while homeschooling three polite and clever kids.

One family felt so inspired by the Weavers' example that, following a chance meeting with Randy and Sam while fishing the Kootenai River, they moved several hours north from Moscow, Idaho, to Naples, just to be closer to the Weavers. Bill Grider was a tall, muscular iron worker from Detroit with a thick Fu Manchu mustache. His wife Judy shared Vicki's fierce religiosity. Like the Weavers, the Griders had fled the Midwest for Idaho, hoping to escape a world awash in liberal decadence and corruption. The families quickly became close. Under Vicki's tutelage, the Griders devoted themselves to Identity theology. (The conspiratorial racism, they apparently already had.)

Life down in town came with increased scrutiny. Around the same time that the Weavers raised the funds to move from their bare-bones cabin to the relative comfort of the red house, Randy began driving a new Ford pickup. In a tiny town where many people live near the poverty line, the Weavers' mysterious windfall became a subject of local speculation.

Steve Tanner, one of the Weavers' oldest and best friends in the area, provided an answer, telling people that Randy had ripped him off to the tune of thirty thousand dollars. The Tanners owed a lot in back taxes but also held title on some land they did not need. To raise cash without the IRS garnishing the proceeds, Steve signed over the land to Randy, asking him to sell it on the Tanners' behalf. For his part in this minor bit of fraud, Randy would earn a small fee. According to what Tanner told people around Naples, Randy sold the land and simply pocketed the proceeds. Since the deal was off the books — as far as the law was concerned, it was Randy's to sell — the Tanners had no recourse other than to go around saying that the Weavers were thieves.

Faith thrives in the wilderness, but politics do better in town. While Vicki's Old Testament fervor cooled off a bit down by the creek, the Weavers' conspiratorial, far-right politics seemed to grow more strident. Vicki might have been naturally suited to the isolation of pioneer life, but Randy liked to mix it up. (After the '92 siege, he would spend many of his remaining years as a one-man roadshow, speaking to Patriot groups, turning up at other standoffs, and posing for photos at gun expos.) Living down in Deep Creek, Randy's acetylene rhetoric found a wider audience. At a community meeting about the local bear population, he exploded over what he regarded as his neighbors' muzzy-headed conservationism. "If a grizzly bear comes and hurts my kids," he yelled, "I'm not going to hunt the grizzly. I'm going to come and hunt you."

The most persistent refrain of those who regard Ruby Ridge as a tale about the federal behemoth hounding lowly separatists is that the Weavers "just wanted to be left alone." While it is true that the family spoke a lot about separatism, it is not quite right that they simply wanted isolation. For one thing, people who truly want to be left alone seldom run for public office. And now, at age forty, that is what Randy Weaver did.

In 1988, after years spent fulminating against the US government, Randy decided he should be sheriff of Boundary County.

As Sara remembers it, the campaign was the reason they came off the mountain in the first place. You can't run for office without a telephone. As for the decision to run in the first place, Randy readily admitted that he did it in part because he needed a job.

To be sure, he also had a lot of strong opinions about law enforcement. In the Republican primary (in which Randy positioned himself all the way to the right), he expounded the theory of American jurisprudence that had first been articulated by William Potter Gale of the Posse Comitatus, in which directly elected county sheriffs represent the sole legitimate source of legal authority in the lives of citizens. They are empowered to interpret the Constitution and federal laws as they see fit, superseding the courts and remote federal and state agencies. (It is worth noting that sheriffs are not mentioned in the Constitution. The ideas Gale propounded derive, at least in part, from English Common Law, which designated the "shire reeve" as the sovereign's local proxy.) By the late 1980s, these ideas — currently thriving under the banner of the "Constitutional Sheriff" movement — had become popular on the far right.

The upshot of this theory is that the sheriff's authority works in two directions. They police the population under their jurisdiction, but they also protect their communities against threats from above — in the form of, say, gun-control legislation, public health mandates, or election laws they do not like — thereby placing themselves between the citizenry and a government embodied by far-off legislators and unelected judges.

The sheriff has always been among the most mythologized of American characters. Following the Vietnam War, as American police departments absorbed military surplus, spending, and tactics — i.e., bureaucratized and militarized — local sheriffs came to be seen, by some, as uniquely unsullied by compromising entanglements. On the far right, the archetypical sheriff, with his low-slung pistol and hat of many gallons, represented an uncorrupted version of the "good guy with a gun." Closely tied to the passions of the local populace, the sheriff was just one step removed from the heroic vigilantes of Old West lore and the racial enforcers of the Jim Crow South. It is not a coincidence that this hyperlocal conception of law enforcement was a total inversion of the one embraced by the civil rights movement, which reached beyond local police for the support of federal agencies and courts. (Randy would ultimately co-author a book with Richard Mack, the founder of the far-right Constitutional Sheriffs and Peace Officers Association and a board member of the Oath Keepers militia.)

In his 1988 run, Randy pledged not to enforce any laws his constituents did not like. As a campaign gimmick, he printed business cards with "Vote Randy Weaver for Sheriff" on one side and "Get Out of Jail Free" on the other. Asked by a reporter if he would permit drunk driving, he said yes. Asked whether he would enforce seatbelt and motorcycle helmet laws, he said, "I question whether they should pass any laws to protect the individual from themselves." The "most important thing," Randy said, "was not to let federal agents come into the county and mess with people wrongfully... especially the IRS."

Even within the context of Idaho's northernmost county, Randy's campaign was sufficiently controversial to garner coverage in the *Spokesman-Review*, which is based in Spokane but is essentially the paper of record for the inland Northwest. As with the 1983 newspaper profile of the Weavers back in Cedar Falls, the brief flutter of reporting occasioned by Randy's run for sheriff offers a meager but valuable public record of his thinking prior to the '92 siege, after which point it was all but impossible for anyone to clearly recall what came before.

The main reason the election got covered at all, is that it served as a proxy for a broader debate about the radical right in North Idaho. While Randy's two opponents in the Republican primary kept their focus on a local scourge of "teen keg parties," the biggest headline to come out of the Weaver campaign was "Boundary County Sheriff

Candidate Opposed to Mixed Marriages." Robert E. Miles, a KKK grand wizard turned Identity preacher had recently announced plans to relocate his large Michigan-based church to Bonners Ferry. To oppose this plan, a group of local citizens formed the Boundary County Task Force on Human Relations, modeled on a similar out-fit in nearby Kootenai County, where the Aryan Nations was based. While the other candidates for sheriff went on record supporting the task force, Randy spoke out against interracial marriage and asked why nobody was worried about "the Indian racists in this county."

When the task force screened a documentary about the Aryan Nations, Randy attended. During the Q & A, he rose to defend the Aryans. According to one attendee quoted in the newspaper, Randy took the opportunity to preach about "the Jews running the world economic system." Asked by a reporter if the US Constitution reflects the views of the Aryan Nations, Randy said that it did, pointing out that the country had been founded by white slave owners. "I don't believe in slavery," he clarified, "but, religiously speaking, I don't believe in mixing the races."

The whole family pitched in with the campaign, printing bumper stickers and painting huge red-white-and-blue signs saying, "Vote Randy Weaver for Boundary County Sheriff." Apart from that, Ran-dy's strategy mostly consisted of hanging around the nearby Deep Creek Resort, talking up his candidacy in the bar and restaurant.

Randy lost the primary, earning only one hundred and two votes. He partly blamed the media, which he regarded as just one more head of the ZOG hydra. The election ultimately went to a Democrat, who won with 800 votes. Afterward, one voter told the *Spokesman-Review* that Randy's vote tally basically matched the number of Aryan Nations members living in the county. Since noth-ing about the Weavers would remain untouched by conspiracism, one theory, promulgated by a far-right newsletter, held that Randy actually won the race "but was kept from entering the office by the rigging of election results."

———————

A month after the election, the Weavers loaded up the truck with camping gear and drove south for yet another Aryan World Congress. Nineteen eighty-nine was supposed to be a banner year for the Aryans, with special events marking the hundredth birthday of the man whose large silver bust stood beside Rev. Butler's pulpit and whom *The Turner Diaries* referred to simply as "the Great One": Adolf Hitler. Butler, then seventy, was trying to energize his movement with outreach to young skinheads, some of whom lived full-time at his compound as part of a disciplined "youth wing," complete with ranks and uniforms. Along with a special celebration on April 20 to honor Hitler's centenary, Butler traveled to Whidbey Island for a skinhead meet-up to mark the fifth anniversary of Bob Mathews's immolation.

By the summer of '89, the Weavers knew their way around Hayden Lake and had plenty of friends with whom to catch up and grill hotdogs. Randy once again ran into Kenneth Fadeley, aka Gus Magisono, who was now sufficiently embedded in the movement for Butler to have deputized him as private security for Joan Kahl, who, in her stoical widowhood, was a walking emblem of federal tyranny. Randy and Vicki introduced Gus to a crew of young skinheads they had taken a vaguely parental interest in. The informant would later testify to hearing Randy invite the skins up to Naples for some weapons training, although that never seems to have happened. Randy also introduced Gus to an (unnamed) old friend from Waterloo, a fact that undermines the notion that the Weavers did not encounter organized racism until their arrival in Idaho.

Despite all the youth outreach, Butler's organization was somewhat adrift. The Order and the Order II had been broken up, with most members in jail (although millions in unrecovered stolen cash continued to circulate within the movement). With Hayden Lake awash in informants and undercovers, it hardly seemed like the place to kick off the next American revolution. A more general cultural rift was forming, too. As the hoopla over Hitler's birthday suggests, the elders of white power were still looking backward, fixated on the symbols and fantasies of European fascism. By the late '80s, the real energy on the far right was moving on, trending away from neo-Nazism and the KKK and toward a militant Identity-tinged Christian nationalism.

The movement still revolved around the same race war eschatology, but its aesthetics, tactics, and goals were changing. The new guard did not want to bedeck themselves in swastikas and Sam Browne belts to play Nazi Ren faire or, as Butler once hoped, run for the US Senate—although some portion of the radical right did begin to flirt with electoral politics. (The same year that Randy stood for sheriff, David Duke, once the grand wizard of the KKK, exchanged his robes for a plaid sportscoat and ran for president on the ticket of the Populist Party, a creation of *Spotlight* founder Willis Carto.)

Rather than storm trooper uniforms and hooded robes, the new radicals styled themselves like American commandos. Instead of denaturalizing into some Aryan redoubt, they seized the mantle of American patriotism, even as they trained for a war against the USA. When they invoked a glorious past, it was 1776, not 1942.

Observing this shift from the ATF office in Boise, Herb Byerly turned his attention to several men who seemed to be drifting away from the Aryan Nations and accumulating an alarming amount of firepower. These men were not preaching the Northwest Territorial Imperative. They wanted to take their whole country back.

In particular, Byerly hoped to get his informant close to two men living not far from Naples, in northwest Montana. Chuck Howarth was a former Klansman who had been convicted on federal explosives charges and was suspected of ongoing illegal weapons dealing. David Trochmann was a conspiracy theorist and Identity Christian who, along with his brother John, would later form the Militia of

Montana. MOM, as it was known, would become the template, organizing hub, and clearing house for the network of militias that emerged in the early '90s, uniting and expanding the far right to a degree that Richard Butler had only dreamt of.

As it happened, the Weavers were good friends of the Trochmanns and, at the '89 Congress, Fadeley saw Randy having a long chat with Chuck Howarth. Weaver was still obviously a small fry — more focused on preparing for Armageddon than starting a war of his own — but maybe he could be turned into what the ATF called an "unwitting informant," making introductions to the men in Montana and vouching for Gus. When Randy and Gus parted at the end of that summer's gathering, Randy once again invited the informant to swing by if he was ever up near Naples.

At the end of August, not long after the Weavers returned to the red house, Gus came calling. When he walked up to the front door, he was surprised to discover Frank Kumnick in the living room. The last time they had spoken, Randy told the informant that he and Kumnick were on the outs. As Fadeley looked on, Randy and Kumnick got into a heated argument, with the latter accusing Randy of ripping off the Tanners and also insinuating that Randy was involved in a much more serious crime: a recent (and still unsolved) double homicide at a nearby marijuana grow, where a stash of guns was discovered amid the ashes of an apparently intentional fire. Randy angrily denied it all, saying that people were just trying to smear his name. When Vicki began to cry, Kumnick took off, followed a bit later by Fadeley.

A month later, Randy and Gus met up at Connie's Café in Sandpoint. Still rattled by the stud finder incident and not expecting any crimes to be discussed, Fadeley was not wearing a wire. What he wanted was for Randy to take him to Montana to introduce him to Chuck Howarth. Randy explained that he couldn't go that day, but promised to make the trip soon.

According to notes Fadeley wrote after the meeting, Randy then brought up the idea of selling Gus some weapons. Whether Weaver was invited to sell guns or made the offer on his own is still contested. Fadeley claimed Randy brought it up. Randy claimed that the informant tempted him into doing a one-time sale at a weak moment.

What nobody disputes is that the informant, still posing as a gun-runner, told Randy that business was brisk and he was low on product. Randy asked what kind of weapons sold best. Gus told him that sawed-off shotguns were a popular item — "the shorter the better." By scouring local shops and the classifieds for unregistered guns and modifying them himself, Randy calculated that he could double his money on each weapon.

After paying for their coffees, the two men walked out to Randy's truck. Randy took a Remington 870 pump-action shotgun out of a case. According to Randy, Fadeley pointed to a spot on the barrel, just at the end of the magazine tube, where he wanted the gun cut. Fadeley claimed it was Randy who pointed to the spot.

None of that was on tape, and so, two days later, with Herb Byerly on the line and a tape recorder spinning, Fadeley dialed the number for the red house. Vicki answered and, after a friendly exchange, passed the phone to Randy.

Randy and Fadeley discussed their plan to go to Montana. Randy said he was ready to go. This time, it was Fadeley who begged off, explaining that his mom had suffered a stroke and he needed to go visit her. In truth, the ATF wanted to delay the outing until they could arrange for air surveillance.

The two men then discussed the terms of their business deal, referring to the shotguns as "chainsaws." Randy asked where the finished product would end up. Gus said that the guns would not be sold locally. Randy said he hoped they ended up with "street gangs."

Nine days later, on October 24, 1989, Randy and Fadeley met up again by Connie's Café and drove to the park that runs along the shore of Lake Pend Oreille. This time the informant wore a wire. Randy handed over a cardboard box with two guns wrapped in bath towels, the Remington pump-action from the previous week and an older single-shot, both with newly modified stocks and barrels, cut well below the legal limit. ("I cut 'em as short as you could cut 'em without ruining the guns," Randy later explained.) Randy wanted $450 for the pair, but Fadeley had only been given $300 to make the buy. Fadeley handed over a stack of twenties and promised another $150 when they made the trip to Montana, which was still the ATF's real object. "We talked about other things," Randy later recalled, "but [Fadeley] kept coming back to Chuck [Howarth]."

It was only once the actual crime was concluded, that Randy grew cautious. He told Gus that his wife didn't know about the gun deal and said that he would be more comfortable if they could get their two families together for a meal. "Other than that, we don't have to be real buddy-buddy." If the Weavers and the (fictional) Magisonos could break bread, Randy explained, Vicki would be okay with them getting into business together. "She's, you know, uptight."

The sale finished, they went back into the café. Fadeley ordered buttermilk pancakes and Randy got a cup of coffee. He explained how he had modified the guns under a shade tree with nothing but a hacksaw, a file, and a vice. He said that he intended to set up a workshop where he could easily produce more weapons of higher quality.

"Four or five a week?" asked Fadeley.

"Or more," said Randy.

They agreed to meet up in a month to drive to Montana so that Randy could introduce Gus to Chuck Howarth. But in the meantime, winter was coming and the Weavers were low on cash. It was time to head back up the mountain.

PART III

TRIBULATION

. . . then the Last Judgment begins, & its Vision is seen by the Imaginative Eye of Every one according to the situation he holds.

— William Blake, "A Vision of the Last Judgment" (1810)

CHAPTER SIXTEEN

GO TO HELL

AFTER A YEAR and a half in the red house, the Weavers returned to the cabin in the fall of 1989 with a renewed sense of discipline. Having slackened a bit down in the valley, Vicki's premonitions of doom surged back with all their old force. No more bike rides to the store for the kids. No more rock music. Sara resumed wearing floor-length skirts. She was fourteen now and, like her mom, she started moving out to the "guest shed" for a week out of each month during her period.

Amid all this busy forsaking, there were other changes, too. When the Weavers returned to their cabin, their friends Bill and Judy Grider, along with their son Eric, followed them, moving onto a foreclosed property just downhill from the Weaver tract. The Griders, who had relocated to Naples in large part to be near the Weavers, were now fully committed to the Identity faith that Randy and Vicki had taught them.

Up on the ridge, the two households combined to resemble a loose version of the "survivalist, fundamentalist retreat" that members of the Cedar Falls Bible study had once discussed. They shared meals, flew Confederate and Aryan Nations flags, parsed scripture, prayed together, and did a lot of target shooting, mostly up at the Weaver place. At some point, the men and boys—Randy and Sam, Bill and Eric—all shaved their heads, in keeping with the skinhead fashion and the prophet Jeremiah's commandment: "Cut off thine hair, O Jerusalem, and cast it away, and take up a lamentation on high places."

———————

On November 30, 1989, the day Randy and Gus had agreed to make their trip to Montana to see Chuck Howarth, Randy drove down to Sandpoint to meet the informant. The ATF was all ready, with tail cars gassed up and a spotter plane standing by on a Spokane runway. After the Bob Mathews fiasco, the feds were not skimping on resources.

When Randy arrived, he immediately announced that he could not make the trip to Montana. In the month since selling the two guns, a friend from the Aryan Nations had given Randy an ominous, if belated, warning. "Don't be doing any business with that Magisono, he's a snitch." In a panic, Randy had come clean to Vicki about selling the guns.

Sitting in Fadeley's Nissan, Randy told the informant what he'd been told. Fadeley hotly denied it, demanding Randy's source. "If you want to believe someone else that is walking around paranoid that I'm a...fuckin' pig, it's been nice doing business with you." Randy softened a bit. The two men joked nervously about how Weaver himself had just run for sheriff. "If I was a badge," Fadeley offered, "then I suppose I'd be wired, and you're welcome to check me for a wire." By then, the ATF had moved their microphone from his chest to the dashboard of his sedan.

Randy was placated. He was also still broke. He said the Montana trip was still off the table, but he had more sawed-offs to sell. Fadeley had not come planning to make a buy. In fact, he only had a hundred of the hundred and fifty dollars that he still owed Randy. The informant handed over the cash and the men parted.

They would not see each other again until Randy's trial. Randy never forgave or forgot. More than three decades later, at the age of seventy, with his hair gone white and his voice a thin rasp, Randy told an interviewer that, if he ever comes across Fadeley, "I will kill him. I *will* kill him."

Meanwhile, the United States government still owed Randy Weaver fifty bucks.

———

That should have been that. The ATF, trawling for bigger fish, had little interest in Randy's piddling violation — technically the manufacture, possession, and sale of two illegal firearms. The gun deal had just been a device to keep Randy and Fadeley in contact and to burnish the informant's cover story about being a gunrunner.

Unfortunately for Randy, Fadeley's cover would not remain intact for much longer. And when it came apart, Randy Weaver would once again become a person of interest at the ATF.

That spring, a group of Aryans approached Gus at Hayden Lake. One of them carried a camcorder. They asked Gus why his VIN didn't match his plate, if he knew anyone by the name of Kenneth Fadeley, or if he was a cop or a member of the Jewish Defense League. His cover obviously blown, Fadeley was escorted through the gates of the compound and told never to return. He counted himself lucky to have been ejected without incident.

In a stark illustration of how poorly various law enforcement agencies were coordinated in the days before shared databases were used to "deconflict" sources, Fadeley came to believe (and Randy later confirmed) that he had been compromised by an FBI informant. Rico Valentino was a three-hundred-pound professional wrestler who had performed in the '60s under the name Beatnik Rick. At some point, he started doing undercover work on the drug beat — the wrestling circuit apparently being a hotbed of narcotics — before helping investigate the radical right. A splashy figure at Hayden Lake, he taught martial arts to the Aryan Youth Wing, performed feats of strength, wore dramatic outfits, and served as Richard Butler's personal bodyguard. He always seemed to have plenty of cash, once purchasing a book signed by Hitler, presumably on the dime of the American taxpayer.

In 1990, several Aryans were charged with plotting to bomb Neighbours Disco, a gay dance club in Seattle. Valentino had been present for the planning meetings. When the others were arrested en route to plant the bomb, the wrestler walked free and testified against the plotters. One of the men convicted was a friend of the Weavers, whom Randy and Vicki believed to be innocent: another victim of ZOG treachery.

The exposure of both Gus and Valentino as federal informants deepened Randy and Vicki's conviction that the government was systematically setting up and persecuting Identity Christians. It was certainly true that a lot of attention was being devoted to the radical right in the aftermath of the Order's spree. As evidence that the feds could not organize a cabal even if they wanted to, Fadeley later testified about a secretive meeting he had attended in Spokane. It was three men: himself (on behalf of the ATF), Valentino (playing for the FBI), and just a single genuine Klansman.

Meanwhile, with Fadeley out of circulation and ominous noises still coming from the Christian Patriots in Montana, the ATF wanted a new informant. It had taken Fadeley years to build up his profile in the movement. What the bureau needed now was someone who knew the players but was not a total fanatic. Under a bit of pressure, someone like that might be willing to keep tabs on what was coming down the line. One name came to mind.

———

At the end of May 1990, Herb Byerly of the ATF submitted a report to the US Attorney in Boise recommending that Randy Weaver be charged with possessing and selling two illegally modified shotguns.

It was an open-and-shut case. They had the actual guns and a recording of the sale. Byerly hoped to use the charge as leverage to turn Randy into an informant. On paper, he looked like a good candidate: a pious family man with only loose connections to the movement—the kind of guy who might believe in the white power cause, but not to the point of violent criminality. As a proud veteran and a recent candidate for sheriff, they figured he might be inclined to help law enforcement.

Three weeks after Byerly submitted his report to the US Attorney, but before any charges against Randy were filed, Byerly and his colleague Steve Gunderson borrowed a green Forest Service truck and drove up the steep road to the Weaver cabin. When they pulled up, their way was blocked by Sara, who was wearing a holstered pistol over her denim skirt. Sam stood beside her holding a large hunting knife. The agents, dressed in their office clothes, claimed to be looking for a lost hiker. The Weaver kids were too savvy to believe that.

Seeing that Randy's pickup was absent and feeling spooked by the kids, the men turned around and drove down the mountain. On their way out of town, at about six in the evening, they noticed Randy's truck in the driveway of a house in Deep Creek, where Kevin Harris was staying with his girlfriend Danielle.

Pulling in behind Randy's rig they asked Danielle, who was outside smoking, to send Weaver out for a word. Randy emerged wearing his Aryan Nations belt buckle and a leather jacket with SS lightning bolts on the lapel. Vicki followed him out, but hung back.

Byerly, a mild-mannered civil servant with a soft Georgia accent, was the opposite of the swaggering Western lawman that Randy had aspired to be. Randy later said that he looked like "one of those kids in school everyone kicked in the lunch line." The two agents identified themselves and handed over business cards. From a folder they produced pictures of the shotguns and explained that they had him dead to rights on the gun sale. If Randy would provide them with some information, they explained, they would put in a good word with the US Attorney.

Randy flushed with anger and told the men to "go to hell." Snitching, he said, was against his religion. Rather than stick around for the sermon they sensed coming, the two ATF agents climbed back into the truck. They figured Weaver just needed to cool off and think it over. They asked Randy to come to room 380 in the Spokane federal building the next day at 11:00 a.m. to talk. Maybe his wife could calm him down in the meantime.

From Byerly's perspective, the stakes were low. If Weaver cooperated, he could avoid the hassle of going to court, and the ATF would get some useful information about what might be happening with the radicals in Montana. If Weaver refused, it would not be such a big deal. The man had knowingly committed a misdemeanor. As a first-time offender facing a gun-friendly North Idaho jury, he would probably get probation or work release.

To Randy and Vicki, however, things looked very different. For a decade, they had been saying that the Tribulation would commence with a battle between their family and the One World Government described in Revelation. Five years earlier, they had been so concerned that something like this would happen that Randy had filed his affidavit warning that "the FBI would rush my home with armed agents hoping I would feel the need to defend myself and thus be killed or arrested for 'assault on a federal official.'" Verily, it was all coming to pass. They had been tricked by a man whom they treated like a friend (Gus) and now the Beast had arrived at their doorstep in the form of two bureaucrats in khakis.

The couple jumped in Randy's truck and tore up the mountain. Once there, Sam and Sara told them about the visit from men posing as forest rangers. The fact that their kids had been alone with those liars only heightened their impression of ZOG treachery. At ten that night, the whole family gathered in the living room where Vicki drafted a letter in her neat cursive. It was addressed to "Aryan Nations & all our brethren of the Anglo-Saxon Race" and warned that the feds were trying to infiltrate the movement. The Weaver family, the letter declared, would not "make deals with the enemy."

"This is a war against the white sons of Isaac," Vicki wrote. "The decree (genocide treaty) has gone out to destroy Israel our people. If we are not free to obey the laws of Yahweh, we may as well be dead." After a decade steeped in endtimes prophecy, Vicki interpreted an invitation to talk at the courthouse as a "genocide treaty."

"We have decided to stay on this mountain. You could not drag our children away from us with chains. They are hard core & love the truth...So [Randy is] going to stay with them and let the Edomites bring on the war!" (This latter flourish might relate to the fact that Herod the Great, that famous Jewish pawn of Roman imperialism, was from the kingdom of Edom.) "If it is our time, we'll go home. If it is not, we will praise his Separated name! Halleluyah!"

The next morning, instead of Randy driving to Spokane, Vicki drove to Bonners Ferry to photocopy her letter. She tacked copies to the doors of friends and dispatched Bill Grider to Hayden Lake with one for Richard Butler.

———

Herb Byerly, with a pile of other cases to pursue, was in no rush. He did nothing for six months. Randy never called. But the bureaucratic wheel, indifferent to the white sons of Isaac or the hardcore-ness of the Weaver children, began to turn.

On December 13, 1990, the US Attorney in Boise put Weaver's gun charge before a federal grand jury, which returned an indictment for "manufacturing and possessing an unregistered firearm." A warrant was issued for Randy's arrest.

Byerly and his colleagues met to discuss what to do next. When they had gathered all the paper they could find on Randy Weaver, they were confronted with a surprisingly thick stack, especially for a guy with no criminal record. It included complaints from neighbors to the local police, the testimony generated by the Secret Service investigation in '85, and the Weavers' own affidavit. It all seemed to say different versions of the same thing: the Weavers have long been preparing for some sort of violent showdown, and they will feel compelled, as a matter of faith, to defend themselves rather than submit.

Byerly called Boundary County sheriff Bruce Whittaker to discuss the safest way to arrest Randy. Whittaker, the man elected to the job Randy had wanted, knew the Weavers pretty well. He had personally sat through several of Randy's stemwinders about the Jews and the Apocalypse. He had also taken several heated reports from neighbors about Randy's threatening behavior and the persistent racket of gunfire coming from the family's property.

Byerly, who had only met Randy once, could not shake the sight of Sara with that big pistol riding on her hip. He worried that if he simply drove up the hill in a squad car, armed kids would be in the mix. "Ambush City," was the phrase he used. Everyone agreed that they would have to arrest Randy away from his home and children.

On a freezing day in January of 1991, with the ridge under heavy snow, Randy and Vicki made one of their rare winter trips to town to get supplies. This involved leaving the kids in the cabin, hiking through deep snow to their snowmobile, riding down to the plowed road where their truck was parked, and then taking the highway into Bonners Ferry. Coming home, they would do the whole thing in reverse, their packs loaded with milk and canned goods.

At the bottom of Caribou Ridge, past the large, flat expanse known as Homicide Meadow, the road turns to blacktop and passes over a short, two-lane bridge that spans Ruby Creek. Crossing the bridge, with Randy at the wheel, they came upon a young couple whose camper truck appeared to have broken down in the middle of road.

As was always their way, Randy and Vicki hopped out to lend a hand. Randy ambled over to the front of the camper asking what the trouble was. The longhaired, surfer-looking guy leaning into the engine came up with a pistol. He identified himself as a federal agent and told Randy to put his hands up.

Randy turned to run, but was wrestled to the ground. Herb Byerly, Sheriff Whittaker, and two other agents jumped out of the back of the camper. Vicki ran and was tackled by a female agent, pinned face down into a snowbank, and cuffed. The agent who subdued Randy later claimed that Weaver tried to grab his gun, although he was not charged with resisting arrest.

"Nice trick," Randy said to Byerly while sitting handcuffed in the snow. "You'll never do that again."

A small .22 pistol was taken from Randy's pocket and a .38 revolver was found in Vicki's purse. Randy was taken into custody. Vicki was released. They even gave her back her pistol, minus its five rounds.

Randy was booked at the courthouse in Coeur d'Alene, where he stood for a seething mugshot. The next morning, after a long night in jail, he was led into a courtroom in an orange jumpsuit, handcuffs, and shackles.

As was often the case in such a sleepy jurisdiction, there was no judge on hand for the arraignment—usually a fairly rote piece of business—and the matter fell to a part-time magistrate. The proceeding was a fast, somewhat confused affair. Randy had no counsel. Vicki showed up with a security guard from the Aryan Nations to serve as a character witness, although there would be no testimony.

Having put so much effort into safely arresting Weaver away from his home and kids, the ATF worried that if the court released him on bail, he would never return for trial. Byerly had asked the

Mugshot of Randy Weaver in Kootenai County, Idaho, January 17, 1991.

US Attorney to send a lawyer up from Boise to make that case to the magistrate, but nobody showed up. Over the phone, the US Attorney explained that even if they sent a prosecutor, there were no legal grounds for holding Weaver. The man was hardly a flight risk. He had a family, a house, and no criminal record. Plus, the charge was a minor one.

The magistrate released Randy on an unsecured $10,000 bond, meaning that he did not have to pay anything up front, so long as he turned up for his trial and abided by routine bail conditions, like trying to get a job, sticking around North Idaho, and staying away from guns. Even if he was found guilty, Randy would only be liable for the cost of the bond if he failed to show up for his court date.

Due to the confusing and misleading explanation given by the magistrate—an error the government later acknowledged—Randy misunderstood this. He somehow thought that if he lost his case, he would have to pay the full ten thousand. Since he and Vicki were certain that the trial would be rigged against them, they had no doubt that he would be found guilty. And since the only thing they had that was worth ten thousand dollars was their land, the Weavers became convinced that ZOG intended to take their home and break up the family. In actuality, the bond's sole purpose was to get Randy to show up for his trial.

Before letting him go, the magistrate explained that it would be a new and separate crime not to return to court on the appointed day. Randy signed a document saying that he understood and confirming his mailing address at a PO box in Naples. He was told to call his pretrial officer in four days for further details. The magistrate then asked if he had any preference for his court-appointed attorney. Randy said that he would like Everett Hofmeister, who had formerly helped the Weavers with the Kinnison dispute. Hofmeister was a Brooklyn-born lawyer who had a successful record defending Richard Butler, members of the Order, and himself (after he was charged with murdering his wife). The magistrate said that he would try to get the lawyer appointed.

Randy and Vicki returned to their mountain in a grim mood. ZOG had vindicated their darkest suspicions. Vicki had not been charged with anything, but they tossed her into the snow like a criminal. The feds had used Sheriff Whittaker, who ought to have been the final legal authority in the county, like an errand boy. Randy was especially galled about the confiscation of his .22 and the fact that, as a condition of his release, he was not supposed to carry weapons. Like many Americans, he regarded his home arsenal as something like a fourth branch of government—a final, balancing check on the power of the state. Despite owning many other weapons and suffering far, far worse at federal hands, the confiscation of that little pistol stuck in his craw for years, perhaps because it aligned with decades of overheated rhetoric about emasculating gun grabbers.

Back home, the Weavers gathered to pray. According to Randy and Sara's later recollection, the kids (aged fifteen, thirteen, and nine) were full and equal participants in the subsequent decision-making.

After a long family meeting, they resolved that Randy would stay put on the mountain. As Randy later told the story, the final decision really came from Vicki and Sam — the two people who, along with William Degan, would pay the highest price for what followed. Randy claimed that he was inclined to go to court, but his wife and boy would not hear it. "You ain't going anywhere, Weaver," Vicki supposedly said. "Screw 'em, Dad," Sam added. As far as the family was concerned, American civic authority was a dead letter — a flimsy sham before the revealed truths of Yahweh. American law, as Randy put it, having consulted his own inner plebiscite, was "null and void in my mind." So they would simply opt out.

Before going to bed, Vicki wrote to her mother back in Fort Dodge. She explained that Randy had been set up and that the family had no intention of following the court's orders. Instead, they would further separate themselves and put out the warning about the approaching Tribulation. "I'll keep writing as long as someone can come up [to collect letters]. We have the peace that passeth understanding."

————

Along with Randy's confusion about the nature of his bond, there was also a clerical mix-up about his court date that would later assume great significance, even if it ultimately changed nothing about what was to follow. The trial had initially been set for February 19, 1991, before being pushed to the 20th, on account of President's Day. When Randy's pretrial officer sent him a letter, he mistakenly gave the date as *March* 20th. When someone noticed the error, the court tried to contact Randy through every available channel, including Everett Hofmeister, the lawyer Randy had requested and whom the court had successfully assigned to the case.

From the court's perspective, the error made no practical difference. After Randy did not show for the real court date, the judge, made aware of the typo, issued a bench warrant for Randy, but told the US Marshals not to attempt an arrest until the second, erroneous date had passed. That way, if Randy turned up ready for trial in March, his charge for "failure to appear" could simply be dismissed.

A feature of conspiratorial logic is a false assumption of balance between cause and effect — the belief that events of great consequence must be born of great forethought or planning. The man who mixed up the dates was named Richins, and "the Richins letter" became something like a Zapruder film within the Ruby Ridge cosmology — a bit of murk for the truthers to slide beneath the microscope. Some people, the Weavers included, interpreted the mix-up as evidence that the government wanted to trick or confuse the Weavers, rather than proof that "the government" is mostly just clerks sitting at desks filling out forms. Sometimes, especially in those IBM Selectric days of yore, they type March when they mean February. To this day, commentators talk as if the whole affair hinges upon Richins's typo. ("They intentionally gave him the wrong court date!")

In reality, the judge's instruction to the Marshals — to defer any action until the later date passed — rendered the whole thing moot. Making it even moot-er was the fact that the Weavers had already made it abundantly clear that Randy was not coming to court. On February 7, 1991, weeks before either the real or the mistaken court date had fallen from the calendar, Maurice Ellsworth, the US Attorney for Idaho, received two letters in a single envelope. Both were written in the neat, curving hand of the onetime vice president of the Future Business Leaders of America at Fort Dodge High.

The first letter came with a note instructing Ellsworth to "pass the attached message up the line of your chain of command," to a person whom Vicki addressed as "the Queen of Babylon." This, Ellsworth surmised, was a reference to the scarlet woman of Revelation, who personifies the Antichrist government that will dominate the globe in the latter days. The fact that Vicki, never one to bandy scripture, wrote "Queen" rather than "Whore" — the latter being how the KJV styles it (more decorous translations use "prostitute") — suggests that there was still something deep and Midwestern within her that could not write "Whore" to a stranger, even as she promised bloodshed.

"A man cannot have two masters," Vicki told the Queen. "Yahweh Yahshua Messiah, the anointed One of Saxon Israel is our law giver and our King. We will obey Him and no others." Vicki then included an excerpt from Jeremiah and an ominous paragraph attributed to "Mathews": "A long forgotten wind is starting to blow. Do you hear the approaching thunder? It is that of the awakened Saxon. War is upon the land. The tyrant's blood will flow."

In the second, shorter note, Vicki addressed US Attorney Ellsworth directly. She wrote, "The stink of your lawless government has reached Heaven, the abode of Yahweh our Yahshua… Whether we live or whether we die, we will not bow to your evil commandments."

Vicki's letter to the Queen of Babylon was dated January 22, 1991, which was the very day that Randy had been instructed to call his pretrial officer for details about his upcoming court date. On that day, Randy had done as instructed and driven down to the pay phone at the Naples store. Unfortunately, whoever picked up the phone at the courthouse told him that his file had not yet arrived — he would have to try back later. Randy left no number (he had none to leave) and never called back. The fact that Vicki wrote her fiery "Queen of Babylon" letter that day suggests that it was only then, after the phone call, that the Weavers fully decided, as Randy put it, "to stay home." (If he was already certain that he would not be going, why call in for pretrial instructions?)

It is not hard to imagine a world in which his paperwork *was* ready and Randy begrudgingly went to court a month later, gave the obligatory sermon about tyranny, got probation for the shotguns, and the words *Ruby Ridge* never entered the lexicon of American violence.

Instead, Randy hung up the pay phone, probably did a little finger sweep to check for a dropped quarter, and drove back up the mountain brimming with his usual vexation, along with the added cussedness known to anyone who has been kept on hold too long only to receive a curt bureaucratic brush-off. By that evening the Weavers had moved on to "the tyrant's blood will flow . . . "

———————

At his desk in Boise, Maurice Ellsworth pondered these strange letters. He had never heard of "Mrs. Vicki Weaver," but he did not care for the sound of "war upon the land." The US Marshals, whose remit includes protecting federal prosecutors, investigated. Turned out, the author was the wife of a Naples man who was loosely attached to the Aryan Nations and awaiting trial on a minor gun charge. Given all the scripture on the page, Ellsworth assumed that the "approaching thunder" stuff came from the Gospel of Matthew. It was a colleague who recognized the words from Bob Mathews's "Declaration of War," issued by the Order commander just before he burned to death during the siege on Whidbey Island.

Once Randy failed to appear on either the original date of February 20, or the mistaken date of March 20, his file effectively moved to the US Marshals, who, in addition to safeguarding federal prosecutors, enforce court appearances and pursue fugitives. The ATF's Herb Byerly had hoped to make Randy an "unwitting informant" by getting him to introduce Kenneth Fadeley to the radicals in Montana. When that gambit failed, Byerly had tried to make him a witting informant, creating a (mostly unforeseeable) mess in the process. Now, the ATF was relegated to the sidelines, out of the game except in an advisory capacity.

For the Marshals, Randy's "failure to appear" was the operative crime, albeit with the unusual twist that they knew precisely where their fugitive was. The question was: How do you arrest a man who has surrounded himself with armed children and pledged not to be taken alive?

Job one for the Marshals was a threat assessment. They interviewed Herb Byerly, Sheriff Whittaker, and more than fifteen people in the community. Byerly, who knew the Weaver case better than anyone else in law enforcement, contributed the opinion that Randy "believes that this charge by the federal government against him is the beginning of Armageddon. The religious war is about to begin. The end of the world is coming, and he is ready to make his stand in the final battle. I would urge utmost caution and care in his arrest. I believe his children are going to be armed." Based on everything Byerly knew, this summary was plainly accurate. The Marshals office in Idaho sent a heads-up to DC: they might have another Bob Mathews or Gordon Kahl on their hands, albeit one who had not committed any violence.

Dave Hunt, a Boise-based deputy US marshal, took the lead. A beefy, crewcut guy with an emphatic manner and a raspy voice, Hunt gave the impression of a no-nonsense high school football coach. He had done two tours as a marine in Vietnam before going into law enforcement. By the time he took over the Weaver file, he'd been a marshal for fifteen years, most of that time spent in Idaho. As a rule, Hunt took things slowly, using what he called a "wait-and-see attitude." He had brought in hundreds of fugitives that way, never having fired a shot in the line of duty.

Of the various branches of law enforcement, the US Marshals spend more than their share of time chasing fugitives with an ideological, anti-government bent. The reason is simple. They often come onto a case when somebody has been charged, but refused to submit to trial. Most criminals rationally presume that, once caught, jumping bail will not improve things.

While that pattern is true for marshals everywhere, Dave Hunt did his marshaling in Idaho. He knew about zealots. Even so, there was something about the Weaver case—the armed kids, those letters quoting scripture and Bob Mathews—that made him uneasy. His boss, Ron Evans, felt the same. Evans had been the top marshal in North Dakota during the Gordon Kahl debacle, when a simple tax protest spiraled until two marshals, a local sheriff, and Kahl himself were dead. With the Weavers, everything was just so heightened, so, for lack of another word, *religious*.

Since Randy had no phone and was no longer coming into town, Hunt knew he would need help from the family's friends and relations. His first step was to hang around Naples, getting to know people and building trust. He interviewed dozens of locals who knew the Weavers — people he met at the Naples store, the local sheriff, the family's nearest neighbors. He also reached out to Vicki's parents in Iowa, who were growing increasingly anxious.

So, too, were the Weavers themselves. When news that Randy was officially a fugitive reached the family over local radio — KBFI out of Bonners Ferry, which Randy called "K-FBI" — it heightened their long-held feeling of being hounded by malign, inexorable forces. Complicating matters, they had a new reason to feel protective of home and hearth: in February, soon after Randy was due in court, Vicki discovered she was pregnant. At forty-one, she had not been anticipating a fourth child. However, despite their precarious legal situation and a rough first trimester, she and Randy were thrilled.

On March 5, 1991, Dave Hunt approached Bill Grider outside the Naples store. What would happen, the marshal asked Randy's closest friend and neighbor, if he were to just walk up to the cabin, knock on the door, and arrest Weaver? "I wouldn't do that," Grider said. He summarized Randy's attitude thus: "If a man enters my property with a gun to do me harm, you can bet that I'm going to shoot him to protect myself."

Hunt asked Grider to tell the Weavers that nobody wanted any sort of confrontation. Randy could surrender to the sheriff, to Hunt, or to the court. He could bring his lawyer and do it "in any other manner which was convenient to him."

The next day, Grider came down the hill with a letter for Hunt. This one was signed by Randy, Vicki, Sara, Samuel, and Rachel.

> *We, the Weaver family, have been shown by our Savior and King Yahshua the Messiah of Saxon Israel, that we are to stay separate on this mountain and not leave... You are servants of lawlessness and enforce lawlessness. You are on the side of the One World Beastly Government. Repent for the Kingdom (government) of Yahweh is near at hand... Whether we live or whether we die, we will not obey your lawless government.*

For Hunt, a father himself, it was the kids' signatures that shocked him. "I was astounded. Rather than shielding his children from any involvement with the bench warrant, [Weaver] actually was placing them right smack in the middle of the process."

The notion that federal officials were overly concerned with the safety of the Weaver kids would become hard for many people to credit after Samuel was shot. But at the time, the Marshals regarded the Weaver children as "hostages," being leveraged by their parents to protect their dad. The way Randy and Vicki saw it, everything they did was to preserve the safety of their family. When Hunt eventually suggested, through Bill Grider, that Randy and Vicki send the kids to stay somewhere else, Grider returned with a message from Vicki: "If the kids can't live in peace on the mountain, they don't want to live."

CHAPTER SEVENTEEN

A TIME OF GREAT DECEPTION

SO BEGAN A year and a half of self-imposed house arrest during which the Weavers hardly left their property. The apocalyptic survivalism that had driven them from Iowa eight years earlier, their trucks low on the springs with furniture, ammo, and supplies, came back in full force. The long-awaited trouble had arrived. They would finally dip into those white buckets of freeze-dried food.

For a family that had long conflated separation with holiness, it was, for a while, a surprisingly fulfilling time. With their world reduced to the cabin, their knoll, and a small patch of surrounding forest, the Weavers played games, studied their Bibles, ran tactical drills, raised chickens, hunted, and tended the garden. For news of the outside world, they had their radio and a little twelve-volt black-and-white TV. Vicki continued to weave rugs and mend their clothes. A steady procession of supporters and friends came to visit. A few tried to talk them down. Most steeled their spines and cheered their heroism.

The case dragged on for so long that that Dave Hunt tried, unsuccessfully, to get the initial charges dismissed. Maurice Ellsworth grimly joked that they should build a fence around the ridge and have it designated a federal prison.

While Hunt tried in vain to talk Randy down from his hill, the Marshals' tactical arm, the Special Operations Group, gamed out plans for more "dynamic" ways to make an arrest. The SOG is not a standing force. It is made up of ordinary deputy US marshals with special training in tactical situations. They convene for specific, difficult assignments and then disperse back to their usual posts. In Ron Evans's initial request for SOG's analysis of the Weaver case, he compared the quagmire to the Gordon Kahl situation, which had famously left two marshals dead. It was not an auspicious precedent.

———

Adding to the general volatility of things up on the ridge, there was a Hatfield-McCoy-type situation unfolding between the Weavers and the family who lived near the bottom of the ridge, in what was known as Homicide Meadow.

The trouble had begun before Randy's arrest. Wayne and Ruth Rau, along with their three kids, had moved to Idaho just a year before the Weavers. In many ways the two families were similar. Like the Weavers, the Raus wanted to live in the wilderness and home-school their kids. They built themselves a log home and started a small tree farm.

The two families were close at the outset, with the kids all playing together. As Ruth Rau later explained in a round of emotional testimony before the Senate Judiciary Committee in 1995, things soured between the two families when the Weavers returned to the cabin after their stint in the red house. The Raus had heard about Randy allegedly ripping off their mutual friends the Tanners, and evidently believed the story. As a result, there was no warm reunion when the Weavers came back up to the ridge. Randy and Vicki had let the Raus run a long line of pipe downhill from their spring while they were away. When they came home, the Weavers cut off the water without warning and stole the pipe.

Ruth Rau, already put off by Randy's racist diatribes, decided that she did not want her three kids playing with Sam, Rachel, and Sara. That was a slight that Vicki Weaver could not abide. "That is when they started treating us like enemies," Ruth recalled. "It was a nightmare and I literally feared for our lives at that time." Making matters worse, the Griders, living on the abandoned property between the Raus and the Weavers, joined the feud on the side of the Weavers.

Things escalated in the spring of 1990 when the Raus, not wanting to live beneath what was starting to feel like a white power shooting gallery, bought the foreclosed land where the Griders were squatting. When some deputy sheriffs and a bailiff came out in a couple of patrol cars to evict the Griders, Randy, Vicki, and Bill Grider, all armed, stepped outside and fanned out in a way that the lawmen regarded as threatening. While Randy shouted about ZOG, the bailiff nervously handed the eviction papers to Vicki before beating a hasty retreat. To the bailiff, it felt as if a routine, if unfortunate, bit of county business—evicting squatters after a land auction—had nearly turned into some sort of religious O.K. Corral.

That night Randy stood outside the Rau home with his rifle. "Come on out and fight like a man, Wayne," he screamed, before firing a volley into the air while the Rau kids, according to Ruth Rau's later testimony, cowered inside. "Fucking n****r," shouted Randy, "we're going to cut your fucking head off." (Wayne Rau is white.)

A few days later, Samuel, Sara, the Griders' son Eric, and another local boy staged a miniature protest in front of the Rau home. They donned swastika armbands, shouldered their rifles, and goose-stepped back and forth in the Rau's driveway shouting white power slogans and doing stiff-armed salutes. Asked about this incident in the US Senate three years later, Randy flashed an unmistakable look of pride, explaining that his children were not the sort to be pushed around. He compared the episode to "soaping the windows" of a grumpy neighbor on Halloween. The word *trolling* did not have its current definition in the early '90s, but the Weavers' use of racist symbols to menace their white neighbors anticipates the joking/not-joking discourse that would accompany the rise of online extremism in the early twenty-first century.

The feud between the Weavers and the Raus may have begun as a classic rural drama—a fight over water, petty theft, late-night noise, and gas siphoned from the Raus' tractor for Kevin's motorcycle—but, once Randy became a fugitive, it would prove consequential. Every complaint the Raus lodged with the local sheriff added to the government's portrait of the Weavers as volatile, permanently armed radicals.

Living at the base of the Weavers' road, the Raus had a front-row seat to the long and complex effort to arrest Randy. (The Marshals asked Ruth and Wayne to keep them informed about anyone coming or going from the Weaver place and used the family's shed to conceal surveillance equipment.) While many of the Weavers' neighbors—including some who had no affinity for the Weavers' radical politics—later excoriated the feds for bringing such force to bear on a lowly family, Ruth Rau told a very different story. From her perspective, everything that went wrong on Caribou Ridge was directly caused by Randy and Vicki's reckless disregard for reality and, in particular, Randy's long-simmering fantasies of some sort of confrontation. She later testified about how, for most of a decade, she had listened to Randy idolize Gordon Kahl and talk about the possibility that he, too, might end up in a shootout with the feds. Inverting the prevailing line on Ruby Ridge, she claimed that, "Randy Weaver set the Marshals up."

Other neighbors would also testify that Randy seemed oddly intent on some sort of showdown. Ed and Beverly Torrance were a quiet, middle-aged couple whose family owned property near the Weavers. One day during Randy's year and a half as a homebound fugitive, Ed drove up to look over some land he was planning to sell. Passing beneath the Weavers' overlook rock, he was surprised to find Sam holding a rifle and manning a cable strung across the road. A moment later, Kevin and Randy appeared on the rock above his truck, both armed. Randy approached Torrance's vehicle with a short scat-tergun in hand. Torrance, a laconic man with a clipped Idaho accent, did not know that Randy was a wanted man. Unfazed but curious, he asked what all the firepower was for. Randy, his head freshly shaved, explained that they were on the lookout for federal agents and that, as Torrance later testified, he "was set to stand them off."

When the two men retired to the Weaver cabin to discuss their property lines, Randy started talking about the coming Tribulation and the notion that—as a somewhat baffled Torrance later recalled—"the people that called themselves Jews are impostors." According to Torrance, Randy explained that his cabin would someday come under attack and that, if the "feds came after him, they were not going to take him alive, he was going to die fighting, and that he would take out as many of them as he could with him." Randy denied saying anything of the sort, insisting, "I was just waiting for someone to come up and show me a warrant and arrest me."

"If you look at the history of America," Ed Torrance testified, "you see there's been a lot of problems caused by people trying to prophecy the future and the end of the world... I believed it was a dangerous type of religious conviction, where people feel they are being persecuted, it's a paranoia."

There it was, the inescapable word: *paranoia*. It made Randy bristle. When, during the long runup to the siege, he offered Dave Hunt preconditions for his surrender, among them was an apology, in writing, from Sheriff Whittaker for having called him paranoid. The historian Richard Hofstadter, whose essay "The Paranoid Style in American Politics" was delivered as a lecture one day before JFK was shot, did more than anyone to shape the way that Americans think about the role of conspiracism in our national life. By affixing a clinical term (*paranoia*) to an ideological phenomenon, Hofstadter knowingly muddied the waters a bit. "I call it the paranoid style," he half-apologized, "because no other word adequately evokes the qualities of heated exaggeration, suspiciousness, and conspiratorial fantasy that I have in mind." Hofstadter knew that the matter he sought to illuminate was not the result of some widespread mental illness, writing that the phenomenon is interesting precisely because it causes "more or less normal people" to end up sounding like paranoiacs.

Hofstadter cannot be faulted for the common misuse of his memorable term, but his postwar faith that American civic life sits atop a great aquifer of clearheaded liberalism allowed him to shunt the paranoid style off to the side. The thorough mainstreaming of conspiratorial politics that has taken place over the intervening half century suggests that there is something altogether different sloshing around down there. Rather than a fringe phenomenon, conspiracism now looks like a core condition of American politics.

While there are plenty of left-of-center conspiracy theorists — especially as relates to matters of bodily health — the tendency has historically had a steep rightward tilt. One general reason is that conspiracy theories are usually reactionary — an allergic response to social change. A more immediate explanation is that American conspiracism is often rooted (directly or indirectly) in Fundamentalist faith, which, by definition, recoils from modernity and holds that there no accidents. The proposition that there is a supernatural struggle playing out behind the veil of current events is core to prophetic Christianity, especially the Darby-style dispensationalism that launched and molded the Fundamentalist movement. The notion that evil elites are pulling the strings in the runup to Armageddon is built into the eschatology of millions of American Protestants. It hardly makes sense to call them "paranoid" for taking seriously the precepts of their faith.

The main reason that Hofstadter's formulation remains so influential is that the metaphor of paranoia feels right. When the mind's wondrous capacity to sort the incoming torrent of sense data into a coherent story runs amok, the paranoiac sees links where none exist, assigns agency where there isn't any, and exaggerates the importance of the self at the center of things, producing an anxious feeling of persecution. In his notes about Randy, Marshal Dave Hunt was careful to tease apart the medical and political implications of the term. "[Randy] was paranoid," he observed, "maybe not clinically, but in practice."

The Weavers may have been deluded about their central role in the coming Apocalypse, but during the year and a half that they spent sequestered on the ridge, their existence really did come to resemble a version of every paranoiac's most outlandish nightmares. Unseen snoops orbited the family, dispatching reports to powerful people in distant cities. Video cameras hidden in the trees recorded their banal comings and goings. "Paranoids are not paranoid because they're paranoid," observed Thomas Pynchon, the hands-down laureate of American paranoia, "but because they keep putting themselves... into paranoid situations."

As the months rolled past, Dave Hunt kept sending messages up to the Weavers through friends. Everyone returned with versions of the same message: *Stay away.* Alarmed by the phone calls that they had received from the Marshals and the sheriff, David and Jeane Jordison came early for their annual summer trip, driving out in April. They brought books for the kids, a load of ground beef for canning, two hundred pounds of potatoes, and parts to rig up a gas-powered pump from the spring to tanks above the house. Vicki, just exiting the first trimester of her pregnancy, was visibly exhausted from the long, isolated winter. Her parents begged her to come down so Randy could turn himself in and she could have the baby in a hospital. She would not hear of it. Vicki believed that her well-meaning parents had been duped by government men who sounded friendly on the phone but were actually trying to destroy her family. With the End so close, now was not the time to let her guard down. "I wish the Master would not tarry," she wrote in a note to Judy Grider.

When the Jordisons made the drive back to Iowa, they could at least take comfort in knowing that their grandkids were happy and healthy. A spring garden was planted and the root cellar was stocked. In a chipper letter to their old Iowa neighbor Carolee Flynn, Sara listed the family's animals: three dogs, a few parakeets, and twenty-six laying hens — so, no chance of running out of eggs.

Kevin Harris came and went from the land during this time, helping with chores and bringing up cases of mac and cheese, sugar, and flour. The Griders, evicted from the adjoining land but still living nearby, visited often, too. The Trochmanns came from Montana, no doubt aware that Randy's predicament stemmed, at least in part, from his refusal to introduce a snitch into their midst. They brought milk, bags of groceries, and M&Ms for the kids. Carolyn Trochmann, an experienced homebirth midwife, talked Vicki through her birth plan.

As word spread of Randy's refusal to surrender, the Weavers became minor celebrities on the far right. People they had never even met wrote to them, explaining how their case related to wider conspiracies involving George H. W. Bush and his plans for a New World Order. Well-wishers from the Aryan Nations brought toys for the kids. Richard Butler, who had beaten his own indictment for sedition in a federal trial, but whose organization was still hobbled by its association with the Order, sent a letter and an emissary encouraging Randy to come down and go to court.

True to form, Randy became convinced that some of the people who came to "sit in our home and chat, as Vicki served them coffee and cookies," were in fact "snitches and federal agents who were lying and deceiving us." He was almost certainly correct on that score. As Joseph Heller famously put it, "Just because you're paranoid, doesn't mean they aren't after you."

———

While the snow thawed, the weakness and nausea that had afflicted Vicki early in her pregnancy subsided. In a letter to Carolee Flynn, she reported that "we are all fine, happy on our little mountain and in good health." In June, they had a party for Vicki's forty-second birthday, with a chocolate cake baked by Sara.

For a time, the Griders were the Weavers' main line to the outside world. But eventually, following a familiar pattern, the two families fell out. The reasons are vague. Maybe it was just the natural combustibility of a tense situation peopled exclusively by hotheads. Bill Grider had been passing messages back and forth between Randy and Marshal Hunt. At some point, Randy got it into his head that Bill was "a traitor." In response to the accusation, Grider threatened to kill Randy. Vicki wrote her mother in Iowa, saying that she could no longer trust Judy with their correspondence. "I have no way of knowing for sure who is a friend and who is not. We live in a time of great deception." It was a phrase she would use repeatedly during that year.

Allen Jeppeson, a Naples man whose politics aligned with the Weavers' — he was a John Birch Society member and spoke freely to reporters about the New World Order — took over where Bill and Judy Grider left off, bringing up groceries and the mail, and acting as an occasional go-between with Marshal Hunt. Hunt asked Jeppeson what sort of assurances Randy needed before he would talk. Jeppeson returned with another maddening letter about the One World Government and the Beast.

The story the Weavers told themselves gradually grew more dramatic and more clear-cut. The fix had been in from the start. Frank Kumnick, who had introduced Randy to Gus, was a snitch all along. The mix-up over the court date was a deliberate ploy to confuse them. Even Marshal Hunt's patient approach came to seem nefarious. "Dave Hunt was just playing a waiting game," wrote Randy. "I believe he was hoping that I would tire of staying home on the mountain."

At the same time, the consequences of surrender also seemed to grow more dramatic. Because of the confusion about his bond — confusion that was undeniably the fault of a careless magistrate—the Weavers remained convinced that if Randy were convicted, they would lose the land. Vicki believed that ZOG's plan was to tear her family apart. Randy would be murdered in prison and the kids would be forced into drug- and AIDS-infested schools. It was religious persecution. "Our situation is not about shotguns," she insisted, "it's about our beliefs. They want to shut our mouths."

Beyond the ridge, Vicki saw her family's situation within the context of larger prophetic events. "Things aren't looking good in this country or the world," she wrote Carolee back in Iowa. "What do you think of Geo. Bush's New World Order? Keep your eyes open. It's what we've talked about for years. This is a time of great deception. Deception is what the people of the world are being fed by the news media." (Her final letter to Carolee arrived wrapped in tinfoil—a safeguard against ZOG snoops.)

Vicki was not alone. With American troops mobilizing in the Middle East following the Iraqi invasion of Kuwait in August of 1990, talk of endtimes prophecy was, once again, everywhere. Sales of *The Late Great Planet Earth*, almost two decades old, shot up. That September, Bantam Books released *Armageddon: Appointment with Destiny*, which tied the situation in Kuwait to Revelation. A few months later, the influential dispensationalist John F. Walvoord reissued his popular *Armageddon, Oil, and the Middle East Crisis*. Walvoord, a former president of the Dallas Theological Seminary, used scripture to show how the war in Iraq (i.e., Babylon) was foretold in prophecy. The End was close. Another popular title released that year was William T. Still's *New World: The Ancient Plan of Secret Societies*, chronicling the rise of the Illuminati, the Rothschilds, the Masons, and the Council on Foreign Relations. A front-page story in the *New York Times* proclaimed that American interest in prophecy was reaching a "fever pitch."

In early October 1991 — ten months after Randy's arrest at Ruby Creek bridge — the Jordisons returned to see their grandkids and take another go at talking Vicki into coming down off the mountain to deliver her baby. It did not put them at ease to hear that Vicki, whose first three kids had been born at a hospital in Iowa, suspected that she was carrying twins.

Two weeks after her parents departed, Vicki went into labor. After thirty-six difficult hours in the shed, with only Randy to help, she gave birth to a healthy baby girl, whom they named Elisheba. She was followed out of the womb by an enormous blood clot, which probably accounted for Vicki's expectation of twins. In her Bible, she recorded the birth in terms that suggest the fortifying romance with which Vicki regarded her family's life in the magnificent sanctuary of the northern Rockies: "Elisheba Anne Weaver, Born Oct. 24, 1991, Roman. 11:15, 7th month, 15th day Hebrew, Feast of Tabernacles, On a mountain, Ruby Creek Canyon, Naples, Idaho."

In keeping with Old Testament guidelines about the "uncleanness" associated with childbirth, Vicki and the baby spent a few weeks out in the shed, which had been made cozy with a little kitchen area, quilts, and potted plants. Ten-year-old Rachel helped her mom with the baby, while Sara, just fifteen, took on the considerable work of cooking, cleaning, and doing the laundry. When Sara got her period, she kept it a secret, not wanting to stay out in the shed with her mom and the baby.

While Vicki nursed Elisheba, Randy cut and split firewood. It was getting chilly up in the Panhandle, and preparing for the winter — almost a full-time job, under normal circumstances — took on extra urgency. Once the snows came, it would be harder for friends to resupply the family. Fortunately, the root cellar was well stocked.

Down in the valley, Dave Hunt hoped that a second winter would do the trick. Through Allen Jeppeson, he assured Randy and Vicki that, no matter what happened in court, they would not lose their land or custody of their children. Vicki responded with a fresh round of fire-eating cant. "Your lawless One World Beast Courts are doomed," she wrote. "We will stay here separated from you & your lawless evil in obedience to Yahshua the Messiah." She also demanded that Hunt answer for a string of conspiracy theories loosely related to Randy's case. Why were Green Berets being "set up" for arrest or murder? (They were not.) Why are "constitutional sheriffs" disappearing? (They were growing more common.) Hunt responded as best he could, but Randy told Jeppeson to cut off contact.

Ironically, Dave Hunt was getting the same message from his superiors. Although Randy was not communicating with his lawyer, technically he had been assigned one — Everett Hofmeister, whom Randy had requested during his arraignment. Since it is generally illegal to negotiate directly with someone who has retained counsel, the Marshals worried that they might be accused of violating Randy's rights by sending notes through intermediaries. (The Justice Department later deemed this to be a mistake, since the relevant statute allows for exceptions in unusual circumstances.)

For his part, Randy insisted that only the county sheriff could legally negotiate with him. Three years later, addressing the Senate Judiciary Committee — a collection of heavyweights including Arlen Specter, Dianne Feinstein, Strom Thurmond, Larry Craig, Fred Thompson, and Patrick Leahy — Randy made it all sound like a simple matter of manly forthrightness, a quality he found lacking in Sheriff Whittaker. "I respect courage and would have trusted that man," he said, somewhat implausibly. Echoing this, Allen Jeppeson told the committee that Sheriff Whittaker was not "man enough" to arrest Randy. When Senator Spencer Abraham (R-MI) asked directly how the situation might have been resolved, Randy was at a loss. "I was looking for Jesus Christ to walk in and solve the situation."

When the snows came, there was no plausible way to communicate with the Weavers or even surveil them. The case was put on hold for a second winter.

CHAPTER EIGHTEEN

TIME HAS TURNED AGAINST US

WHEN WINTER LOOSENED its grip on Caribou Ridge and the roads became passable in the spring of 1992, the Marshals took a final stab at the sort of direct approach Randy later claimed he had been waiting for. Wearing plain clothes and driving an unmarked vehicle, two marshals drove up to the cabin to talk. They had just driven past the Weavers' big sign about Yahweh being White Power when Striker, Sam's big yellow Lab, ran barking toward the vehicle. Randy, Sam, and Sara, all carrying long guns, stepped onto the overlook rock that loomed above the driveway. Randy shouted that the men were trespassing. Unprepared for any sort of violent confrontation, especially with armed kids involved, the two officers turned and drove back down the mountain.

Around that same time, in the somewhat accidental way that small but lurid incidents can become national news, the media got ahold of the story. It started in March, with a *Spokesman-Review* article that ran under the headline: "Feds Have Fugitive 'Under Our Nose.'" The reporter, Bill Morlin, had done a lot of work on the local Aryan beat and would become one of the most astute and dogged chroniclers of the Weaver affair. His colleague Jess Walter, then also on staff at the *Spokesman-Review* and now a celebrated novelist, covered the case from every possible angle, later extending his frontline reporting and far-ranging interviews into an exhaustively researched book called *Every Knee Shall Bow.* Walter's work in particular has provided essential, event-defining source material for everything subsequently written about the Ruby Ridge affair, especially since many of his interviewees subsequently clammed up. (In 1996, his book, rereleased as *Ruby Ridge,* was turned into a two-part TV movie starring Laura Dern as a wild-eyed Vicki, Randy Quaid as a lumbering, slightly dim-witted Randy, and Kirsten Dunst as a frightening yet sympathetic Sara.)

Morlin's initial article triggered a flood of coverage. It was a compelling item. Even just aerial photos of the Weaver homestead, teetering up on that high ridge, stirred something romantic in the American imagination. The *Chicago Tribune* ran a long, well-reported story, describing Randy as a local "folk hero" for standing up to the feds. Allen Jeppeson was quoted as saying, "He's sitting up there with plenty of firearms and a strong faith and belief in Yahweh. They will not take him off that mountain peaceably." That piece, like others, made the inevitable comparisons to Gordon Kahl and Robert Mathews. After the AP picked up the story, articles ran in the *New York Times* ("Marshals Know He's There But Leave Fugitive Alone"), the *San Francisco Chronicle* ("U.S. Slow to Nab White Supremacist"), and elsewhere.

According to Sara, the racket of helicopters coming to photograph the family became a stressful regular occurrence. One magazine ran a picture of her taken from above, flipping the bird. The case received so much publicity that the marshals snooping around the area decided that, if they were confronted by locals, they would pretend to be reporters.

The upshot of almost everything written about the Weavers during the spring and summer of 1992 was that the feds were too scared to make an arrest and were, thereby, setting a dangerous precedent. "It is the duty of the Marshals to bring him in, but the agency is holding back," declared an AP story that ran nationally. One head-line, printed over a picture of the cabin, read: "Holed Up on a Moun-taintop and Armed to the Teeth: The Desperado Even the Feds Are Scared to Arrest." Sheriff Whittaker complained to a reporter that "the Marshal Service is sending a message to people all over this coun-try that, if you are a fugitive from the law, all you have to do is move to northern Idaho and build a cabin and strap on a pistol." Speaking to the *Chicago Tribune* and clearly alluding to the Philadelphia PD's 1985 bombing of the headquarters of the Black liberation organiza-tion MOVE, an incident that killed eleven, Whittaker said, "I have to wonder what the feds would do if this was a case involving Black Panthers in Philadelphia instead of white supremacists in Idaho." For their part, the Marshals insisted that they were not giving Randy a pass, merely exercising caution on account of the children. Besides, as Ron Evans told reporters, "[Randy's] kind of under house arrest up there."

Geraldo Rivera, with his preternatural ear for the American media appetite, wanted in. By '92, he had already had his nose broken before a studio audience by a rowdy group of young Aryans. He had also received (unrelated) cosmetic surgery live on air. His then show *Now It Can Be Told* had done pieces on Jeffrey Dahmer and the time John Lennon saw a UFO. For someone with Geraldo's sensibilities, the Weaver situation—A wily Green Beret! Armageddon! Gun-toting children! Cowardly feds! — was perfect.

According to Randy, Geraldo's producers offered a truckload of food and supplies in exchange for an interview. The Weavers refused. The news clippings they had already seen proved to them that ZOG intended to try Randy in the court of public opinion, possibly to soften up the populace for his eventual murder. Why would "Jew-raldo," as they called him, be any exception?

Failing to secure an interview, Geraldo hired a helicopter to hover low over the cabin, with his crew pointlessly shouting questions over the thwap of the rotor. Randy and the kids obligingly waved their guns and middle fingers. When producers later reviewed the tape, they claimed to hear gunshots, presumably fired in their direction. On April 18, the Marshals Service received word that the TV crew "may have been shot at while flying over the Weaver property." The Weavers later proclaimed their innocence, and no charges were filed. Even though it seems clear in retrospect that no shots were fired, the notion that the family *might* have shot at a helicopter became one more alarming detail in the Weaver dossier. It would prove a consequential scrap of misinformation.

For the Marshals, the Geraldo (non)incident offered one more reason to end things before somebody got hurt. After so much press, anything that went wrong in Naples would surely be blamed on their hesitancy to arrest Randy.

———————

That spring, Henry Hudson, a hard-charging prosecutor sometimes known as "Hang 'em High Henry," was appointed director of the US Marshals Service by George H. W. Bush. Still awaiting confirmation, Hudson was chagrined to have inherited this minor but vexing stand-off. In late March, he called a meeting at Marshals headquarters in Virginia to discuss the case. The meeting included the marshal in charge of Idaho, a surveillance expert, various SOG leaders, and a public relations specialist. All hope of talking Randy into handcuffs seemed lost. The Weavers appeared to be digging in with each passing month, growing more dismissive of the government's entreaties. "While time may have initially been on our side," Ron Evans, the chief deputy marshal in Idaho, wrote in a memo, "it has now turned against us."

Halfway through the meeting, Hudson stepped out of the room. Trying for a Hail Mary, he called Maurice Ellsworth, the US Attorney in Idaho (and "Servant of the Queen of Babylon"). Hudson asked Ellsworth if there was any way he could simply drop the charges or, failing that, re-indict Randy "under seal" (i.e., secretly). Ellsworth explained that it would be unethical to toss a grand jury's indictment just because the accused did not want to be arrested. A judge would never go for it. As for re-indicting Randy under seal, Ellsworth believed that such a move would look shady to any future jury, and besides, Randy would never fall for such a simple ruse. Also, there was a public safety issue. Suppose, Ellsworth later explained, the indictment was dropped or reissued under seal and Randy, by some miracle, believed that he was no longer a wanted man. What would happen if he were to get pulled over for a broken tail light? Might he not assume that he was being captured and start shooting? A Missouri state trooper had been killed and another injured when two Order members were pulled over for a routine traffic violation. As it was, the Weavers seemed to regard every passing logger as a potential agent of ZOG. Even if Ellsworth and the Marshals all believed that the ATF had screwed up by trying to recruit a zealot like Randy as an informant, the wheel was in motion.

Hudson hung up the phone and returned to the meeting. With the only paperwork-based solution off the table, the group ran through various plans to storm the property with nonlethal weapons. These were all rejected as too dangerous for Vicki, the kids, and any SOG members involved. The presence of a newborn in the cabin was not lost on anyone. Neither was all that talk about the "tyrant's blood" or Vicki's pledge that "whether we live or whether we die, we will not bow."

Everyone agreed that the safest option was to get Weaver alone. The previous spring, the Marshals had commissioned a Texas psychologist to write a profile of Randy. The report, a single-page document that misidentifies its subject as one "Mr. Randall," neatly encapsulates the scrim of misunderstanding and fear that hung between the Weavers and their government. In the opinion of Dr. Walter Stenning, "Mr. Randall has indoctrinated his family into a belief system that the end of the world is near and that his family must fight the fences [sic] for evil that want to take over the world. I believe his family might fight to the death." Stenning further speculated that Randy may have "defensively fortified [the property] to repel assault," and warned of the potential that "Mr. Randall and family will resist and have the means to resist all but a military-type assault." This, the psychologist concluded, was definitely *not* the way to go. The best way to resolve the standoff, Stenning wrote, was "to wait until Mr. Randall leaves his house and is alone to make the arrest on the Federal Warrant."

The job of concocting a plan to do just that fell to Deputy Marshal Arthur Roderick. Despite what many would later regard as overkill, the complexity and expense of what he came up with—dubbed "Operation Northern Exposure," for the then-popular TV show—is mostly a testament to the Marshals' eagerness to wrap things up without risking any gunplay.

Phase One of the operation—study the Weavers and the area around the cabin—was technically already under way. Phase Two involved installing hidden cameras in the woods, and scouting the ridge for good places to hide and watch. Phase Three, which never happened, was to purchase land on the ridge and have a deputy marshal named Mark Jurgensen pose as a homesteading logger. The Weavers let people they knew pass through their improvised road block. Jurgensen, who was a competent carpenter and had a bushy mountain-man beard, would not have much trouble passing as a local. The hope was that the Weavers would become inured to his comings and goings. At some point, Randy, still a gregarious and helpful Midwesterner, would step outside to chat or offer to help with a bit of fencing. When that happened, an arrest could be made before anyone got a chance to start shooting.

While this sounded safer than any of the other options, nobody liked the idea of Jurgensen trying to subdue Randy all by himself. Consequently, SOG tacticians planned to establish a couple of hidden observation posts—little spots in the woods above the cabin where armed, two-man teams could watch with binoculars and, if need be, rush in to provide backup.

The sheer slowness of this plan was part of its appeal. Everyone still vaguely hoped that Randy would come to his senses and surrender. As it was, the Marshals were spending about $30,000 a month on the case, mostly on gas, salaries, and surveillance gear.

In April, Roderick, a former policeman and commercial fisherman from Provincetown, Massachusetts, flew to Idaho to get acquainted with the ridge and learn about the case from Dave Hunt. The two men set up shop in a ski condo in Sandpoint, not far from where Randy had sold the two shotguns. They filled the condo with high-tech video gear, night vision goggles, and first-aid equipment. Carrying equipment into the woods at night for a week straight, a SOG team installed motion-activated cameras in the trees around the cabin. Footage of the Weavers going about their lives — usually with guns in hand — began streaming directly to recording equipment hidden inside a shed on the Raus' property.

Watching the family that spring and summer, the Marshals noted that every time a car was heard coming up the road, Randy and the kids, along with Kevin Harris when he was around, would grab their weapons and run to the big rock overlooking the road. To the Weavers it might have felt like some sort of preparedness exercise. To the Marshals, it looked like a crack military maneuver.

———————

The Weavers knew they were being watched, and not just from all the overflights. It only took a month for Sara to stumble upon one of the cameras. Kevin and Sam took it apart and stuffed the pieces in a box inside a shed. Another time, Kevin came up the road on his motorcycle while Arthur Roderick was working in the woods. Roderick thought that Harris might have seen him and, when he returned to his truck a bit later, someone had let the air out of the tires.

Sensing that things were coming to a head, the Weavers decided to get their side of the story out. Through mutual friends, they invited a journalist named Mike Weland up to the cabin to talk. Weland, a charming and dogged local reporter who still lives in Bonners Ferry, was asked to wait at the bottom of the hill for two hours while the family debated and prayed over the wisdom of letting in an outsider. During that time, Weland later learned, Harris and Sam had watched him from the trees.

Once inside the cabin, Randy asked Weland to pledge that he was not a Freemason before giving the reporter a five-hour interview. Randy did most of the talking. Vicki, who was in the kitchen making a pizza for everyone, occasionally chimed in to clarify some matter of theology. Weland's personal impression was that Vicki ran the show, even if she did less of the talking. It was little Samuel, glaring at the reporter with a big pistol strapped to his waist, who made Weland the most nervous. "He scared the shit out of me," the reporter recalled. As for Randy, he came across as a "weak reed," without much violence or certainty within him. Others who visited the family during this time made similar observations. Carolyn Trochmann, whose husband John would later found the Militia of Montana, said that "Vicki was the strength of that family. Randy was the weaker one." Another neighbor told a reporter that "everyone thought of Vicki as the head of the household." Even Randy himself boasted that Vicki was the brains of the operation. "You really ought to interview my wife," he told James Aho, a scholar of the far right. "She's really intelligent."

During the interview with Mike Weland in May of '92, Randy explained the family's conviction that the government could not let him go free because they were afraid of what he might say. "Right now the only thing they can take away from us is our life. Even if we die, we win. We will die believing in Yahweh."

———

At the start of the summer, Operation Northern Exposure was temporarily put on hold. Henry Hudson would be sitting for confirmation hearings in the Senate and did not want any unexpected publicity. By mid-August, Hudson was confirmed and the operation resumed.

After that two-month hiatus, the SOG team wanted one last

round of fresh surveillance before sending in the undercover agent to pose as a new neighbor. One concern was that the feud between the Weavers and the Raus seemed to be heating up again. If there was violence on the ridge before Randy was arrested, the US Marshals would obviously take the blame for letting an armed fugitive walk around freely.

On Monday, August 17, six marshals—Art Roderick and Dave Hunt, along with Frank Norris, Joseph Thomas, Larry Cooper, and William Degan—convened at the condo in Sandpoint. Degan had flown in from Boston, where he led the Marshals' Northeast task force. He was a longtime SOG member with useful experience getting fugitives out of the backcountry. He was an old friend of both Cooper and Roderick, and they were all happy to be working together in such beautiful country. Degan—usually Bill or Billy—was an earnest New Englander from Quincy, Massachusetts, with a trim mustache, aviator frames, and a dry sense of humor. He was one of the Marshals' most decorated agents and a commander and instructor within the Special Operations Group. At forty-two, he was tall, blue-eyed, and athletic. He had been a football star at the University of New Hampshire before enlisting in the Marines and going to Vietnam. He joined the Marshals right out of the service, remaining a member of the Marine Corps Reserve. He played hockey in the winter and took his two sons fishing off Cape Cod in the summer. When the call came to fly to North Idaho, he and his wife Karen were getting ready to take their son Bill, himself an eventual US marshal, to college.

As with Dave Hunt, there was something about this minor case in Idaho that gave Degan a bad feeling—some combination of the kids, the guns, and all that religious rhetoric about not being taken alive. At a party in Boston the night before he flew west, Degan told his wife that Weaver, despite having no record of violence, was the most dangerous guy he had ever been sent to retrieve.

At the condo, the six marshals went over their gear. Each man had his own service weapon, and they borrowed a few M16s from the field office in Spokane. In addition, Roderick, who was in charge of planning, asked Degan to arrange for some submachine guns and suppressors to be sent out from Boston. On Thursday, the six marshals, along with some local sheriff's deputies, drove to a shooting range to test and re-sight the weapons. "Zeroing" guns after shipping is standard procedure, but in the years to come, as people strip-mined a mountain of public information for incriminating facts, this trip to the range looked like proof that the marshals went up the mountain looking for a fight.

CHAPTER NINETEEN

AMBUSH

AT 2:30 THE next morning—Friday, August 21, 1992—the six marshals laced up their boots, double-checked their gear, and left the condo in a van and a white jeep. It was a cold, cloudless night. They drove to Sheriff Whittaker's house in Bonners Ferry, parked the van, and squeezed into the jeep. By 4:30 a.m., they were pulling into the Raus' driveway. They got out, adjusted their night vision gear, tested their radios, and started uphill on foot, with Hunt and Roderick leading the way up the steep logging road. The mission for the day was to do some surveillance and give the new arrivals the lay of the land.

They had already made several trips up the ridge that week. The pre-briefing was always the same: *Do not confront anyone. If detected, retreat.* Instead of raid jackets (blue windbreakers emblazoned "U.S. MARSHAL"), they were dressed for stealth: jungle camo, gloves, black mesh masks. There was a sniper rifle among their supplies, but they left it in Sandpoint. Dave Hunt, already laden down with cameras, batteries, and assorted surveillance gear, carried no rifle at all. Because scrambling up and down the ridge was hot, athletic work, they also left their bulletproof vests back at the condo. They did not expect to see any of the Weavers except through binoculars or Hunt's telephoto lens.

When they reached the place known as the Y, where the road from Homicide Meadow forked into a rough logging track and an overgrown trail, they split up into two three-man teams, maintaining contact by radio and using coded language that would make them sound like loggers in case someone stumbled onto their frequency. The "observation team" went left, climbing to a spot they had already selected, high on the ridge to the north of the cabin, almost a thousand feet above the Weaver home and a half mile away.

The "reconnaissance team" — Degan, Roderick, and Cooper — turned right, proceeding up the road that led to the cabin. A few hundred yards from the rock outcropping that overlooked the road, they hid in the woods. Roderick, who had made this trip several times, wanted to show the others the area and explain how the Weavers responded to the sound of approaching vehicles. As the sun crested the eastern ridge, the men turned and headed back for the Y.

Meanwhile, the "observation team," looking down from above, watched the Weavers and Harris start their day. They emerged one at a time from the cabin, eating breakfast, taking turns in the outhouse, playing with the dogs. Nothing appeared out of the ordinary. Hunt took photos: Randy and Harris standing with their guns and cigarettes; the kids with their guns, trailing behind the dogs.

Harris had spent much of that spring and summer with the family, serving as one of their last reliable connections to the world beyond the knoll. By mid-August, he was already supposed to be off baling hay on a farm in Washington. Because the hay was still too damp to bale, he had lingered a few extra days on the ridge. The day before, he had taken the Weaver kids (minus the baby) to swim and fish at a nearby creek, catching a bunch of small trout and frying them for dinner.

From high up on the facing ridge, Hunt looked through the lens of his camera at Vicki, briefly alone in the yard. He released the shutter. In the resulting photograph, her arms are crossed, her head is down, and her dark curls hang low. She is wearing a long white nightgown.

Through the blurred grain of the telephoto lens — a sinister, prurient texture — she looks vestal, almost angelic.

Dave Hunt's surveillance photo of Vicki Weaver, taken on the morning of August 21, 1992.

By 9:00 a.m., the sun was getting hot. All six marshals convened at the upper observation post. Watching the Weavers through binoculars, they discussed the case and that morning's findings. As they watched, Striker started barking at some unseen object of interest. Various family members responded by running out to the rock. Randy, Sam, and Kevin all carried rifles. Sara had a pistol.

Roderick wanted to get a better look at a spot where he planned to position a sniper to provide backup during Randy's eventual arrest. He led Degan and Cooper downhill to a cluster of birch trees and large rocks, about three hundred yards from the cabin. The dogs were a source of concern, not because they might attack, but because the element of surprise was essential if the marshals were going to get Randy into handcuffs before Vicki or any of the kids came running with guns.

From across the valley, Caribou Ridge looks like an abrupt, wooded fin. Up close, it is a jumble of gullies and ravines, interspersed with cliffs, meadows, and steep washouts. Hiking from place to place is tricky. Loud noises bounce around confusingly. To test whether or not the Weaver dogs would respond to sounds from his chosen position, Roderick tossed rocks down a cliff in the direction of the cabin. No barking. No response.

After waiting about half an hour, Roderick, Cooper, and Degan moved a bit closer to the cabin, down near the lower garden and the spring house. With the sun fully up, it was a somewhat reckless move if they did not want to be detected. But with the observation team watching the family from on high and communicating by radio, they could count on plenty of warning if the Weavers appeared to detect their presence.

———————

Having gotten closer to the cabin than on any of their other trips up the ridge, the three men turned to go back downhill toward the Y. Just then, the observation team radioed to report the sound of an approaching car. No car ever appeared; the noise was probably just someone starting up a vehicle in the meadow.

The Weavers appeared to hear the sound, too. As usual, they ran to the overlook rock with their guns. Again, Striker started barking.

As the marshals below the house made their way downhill, the barking seemed to grow louder and more insistent. Rather than performing what the marshals called a "typical vehicle response," Randy, Sam, and Kevin started jogging down the slope in the direction of the withdrawing reconnaissance team.

Sam and Kevin followed Striker, dipping down into the woods and out of sight of the uphill observers. Randy began walking down the logging road. The observation team watched as ten-year-old Rachel went back into the cabin and reemerged with her Mini-14 rifle.

Over his radio, Roderick dropped the pretense of logger code, telling his team to pull back. "The dogs are on us." The three men started running downhill through the brushy woods, periodically stopping to listen for Striker. As they cut through a field of ferns, they hunched low, feeling exposed in the open sunlight. The barking only got louder.

Arriving back at the Y, the men startled Randy, who was trotting downhill with his shotgun. One of them yelled, "Freeze, Randy!" (Roderick and Cooper claim to have identified themselves as US marshals. Randy says they did not.) Randy shouted, "Fuck you!," spun around, and took off uphill, firing his shotgun into the air and calling for Sam and Kevin to hurry home. When he jammed the shotgun trying to reload, he took out his pistol and squeezed a few rounds into the air. Sam, who was a bit lower down the hill, where the other trail terminated at the Y, shouted back, "I'm coming, Dad!"

Striker was now directly in front of Roderick, jumping from side to side in the road. Roderick, who could hear the approach of Sam and Harris, shot the dog with his suppressed submachine gun, still hoping to conceal their position and make an escape. All of a sudden, there was the boy, raising up his light assault rifle and screaming, "You shot my dog, you sonofabitch." Sam fired in the direction of the marshals, hitting nobody (although Roderick would later find a bullet hole in his outer jacket and a streak of lead across his undershirt). One of the marshals—the exact officer has long been disputed, but all signs indicate that it was Larry Cooper—returned fire, hitting Sam as the boy turned to run.

Kevin Harris, shooting from the hip in Cooper's recollection, fired into the woods toward where he saw the glint of cartridges and little puffs of smoke. A single shot from his large-caliber hunting rifle hit Bill Degan square in the chest. Cooper fired a short burst at Harris, who fell to the ground, unharmed, before scrambling to his feet and heading up the hill.

The woods went silent, gunsmoke thinning in the light breeze. Sam and Striker both lay dead in the road, while William Degan bled out behind a stump just inside the forest.

It is impossible to say with certainty how many shots were fired in total. Unlike the Weavers, the marshals had a standard practice of counting bullets before and after any outing. When they later checked their magazines, it was revealed that Roderick had fired a single shot, the one that killed Striker. Cooper had fired six bullets (in two three-shot bursts). In a testament to the general confusion of the firefight, Degan's magazine was short seven bullets, even though his comrades did not think he had gotten off a single shot.

Cooper testified under oath that he had not shot Sam and had seen him running up the hill. A ballistics expert would determine that the shot that killed the boy likely came from a 9mm, which only Randy and Cooper were carrying that morning. A subsequent investigation by the local sheriff, which involved gridding out the whole area and going at it with metal detectors, unearthed the 9mm slug that apparently killed Sam. (It had not been found at the time of the main trial.) Another ballistics expert claimed that it had come from Cooper's 9mm Colt submachine gun.

In the coming days, the two marshals who survived the shootout said that they did not know that Sam had been hit, which sounded like a preposterous lie to the Weavers, but seems possible given the chaos of those brief moments in the sieved light of the forest, especially since, right after the shooting stopped, both Cooper and Roderick raced to help Degan while simultaneously trying to find cover for themselves. Cooper thought he might have hit Harris but he had not.

Despite an immense amount of investigation and analysis—by the FBI, the local sheriff, the Department of Justice, freelance investigators, journalists—the full and precise truth about what happened at the Y is still disputed. Even those present at the time probably never knew the order of all the shots fired. They could agree on one thing, however: both the marshals and the Weavers insisted that the other side shot first.

When, two days later, the marshals learned—cynics would say "claimed to have learned"—that Sam was dead, they openly speculated that Randy might have accidentally shot his own son, which never made any sense given where everyone was standing. In a similar fashion, Randy would later suggest that it was Cooper who actually killed Degan, even though Kevin Harris never denied having shot at the man.

The bulk of the bullets fired at the Y were never recovered, which makes sense given the vertiginous topography and all the tall trees in the area. Among the Weavers' many supporters, the general perception was that the marshals were trigger-happy assassins willing to gun down dogs and children without hesitation. The fact that they had all previously effected hundreds of arrests, including of heavily armed drug traffickers, without ever discharging their weapons implies otherwise. Regardless of what precisely happened, the situation took on its own grim momentum.

———

Up at the observation post, Dave Hunt heard all the gunfire, estimating about twenty shots, from various calibers. His team raced toward the Y, scrambling down steep and rocky terrain. As they ran, Roderick came over the radio to report that Degan had been shot. Passing through the fern meadow, they heard a nearby volley of gunfire and dove for cover. When they realized that none of them had been hit, they got up and resumed running.

When the observation team arrived at the Y, Cooper waved them over to the spot behind a stump where Degan lay bleeding. Norris, the medic, tried CPR, but Degan's lungs were full of blood. He pulled off Degan's shirt, looking for the wound. When he felt for a pulse, there was none. As the other marshals explained it, Harris had shot Degan on sight, without provocation, before the dog had even been killed.

Sitting over their dead friend with their guns at the ready, the surviving marshals continued to hear gunfire from up the hill. It was probably just Randy firing his weapons into the air to summon Sam and Kevin home, but the marshals had no way of knowing that.

Once Kevin made it back to the overlook rock, he reported that Sam was dead. In his grief, Randy emptied a magazine into the air, reloaded, and did it again. Huddled in the woods around Degan's body, the marshals interpreted those shots as an ongoing assault. They also heard Vicki screaming, "Yahweh! Yahweh!," and someone else shouting, "Stay the fuck off our land!"

Marshals Hunt and Thomas took off through the woods, heading for the Raus' place, where there was a phone. Worried about being shot in the back, the two men kept off the road, thrashing downhill through thick brush. When they arrived panting at the Raus' porch, Hunt told Ruth to take her kids and leave. He called 911 and was patched through to the local sheriff. Badly winded, he said, "I have one officer dead. I need help quick. We've had an incident with Randall Weaver. I want the State Police. I want all the help here I can get."

Meanwhile, Vicki changed into jeans. She and Randy left the girls at the house and walked down the logging road to collect Sam's body. They half-expected to be shot by the ZOG assassins whom they assumed were hiding nearby. Finding their son face down in the road, just uphill from the Y, they scooped him up out of the loose dirt and wept over his body. After screaming curses into the silent trees all around them, they carried Sam uphill, laid him out on the mattress in Vicki's shed, cleaned his body, and wrapped him in a sheet.

The three marshals still crouching by the stump around Degan were similarly determined not to leave their colleague's body behind. They feared that if they tried to carry him off the hill, they might be shot from above. Late in the afternoon, a cold rain began to fall. They attempted to drag Degan's body downhill, but he was a big man and the brush was thick. As the sun sank, fog and rain covered the ridge. Their night vision gear became useless. The batteries in their radios were slowly dying. After trying various ways of carrying and dragging their friend, they gave up and went back to hiding in the trees just off the logging road. The temperature kept falling. The rain turned to wet snow. The three men, who had been out in the woods since 4:30 that morning, shared a single granola bar.

At the Raus' house, Hunt hung up with the 911 dispatcher and called US Marshals headquarters in DC to report that William Degan had died from a gunshot wound in his chest during an operation near Randy Weaver's cabin. Hunt explained that three other agents were trapped in the woods with Degan's body. He reported that a dog had been shot and that Kevin Harris might have been hit. There was no mention of the dead boy.

In the rush to set up a crisis response center and to brief the FBI, which has jurisdiction over all assaults on federal officers, a false belief took hold that the marshals who were hiding in the woods with Degan's body were still under fire. On the phone, Hunt's exact words had been that they were "pinned down." The precise meaning of that phrase would be debated at the trial. Hunt evidently meant that his fellow marshals did not believe that they could safely leave their posi-tion — which was clearly true — but the notion of an ongoing firefight spread. Whatever was really happening in the woods, nobody can deny that the remaining marshals were sufficiently worried to stay huddled in the freezing rain for hours without food.

Concerned about another "ambush" — for that is what everyone on the federal side seemed to think had occurred — the authorities in DC elected to hold off on a rescue mission until full dark and the arrival of a local SWAT team. Just before midnight, an Idaho State Police tactical unit went up the road and helped carry Degan's body off the ridge on a stretcher. They made it to the meadow a little after 1:00 a.m.

The five surviving marshals were taken to the hospital in Bon-ners Ferry in the back of a prisoner van, the only vehicle on hand that could fit them all. Rumors about armed supporters of the Weavers descending on the property had begun to spread. A knot of angry locals was already gathering along the far side of Ruby Creek bridge, where the police had established a roadblock, effectively cutting off the ridge from the village of Naples and the highway that went north to Bonners Ferry and south to Sandpoint. Unable to find a light switch in the back of the van and not wanting to be seen by the crowd, one of the marshals knocked out the bulb with the butt of his gun. The exhausted officers brought their weapons with them to the hospital, worried that someone might be waiting to attack them. By dawn, more than a full day after setting out for their surveillance operation on the ridge, the five men were back at the condo in Sandpoint.

———————

The Weaver file, which had already moved from the ATF to the US Marshals, now passed to the FBI. Even if it had not been a clear-cut matter of jurisdiction, there was some concern that if the Marshals maintained control of the case, whatever happened next might look like retaliation for a fallen comrade. While Randy continued to believe that only the county sheriff had legal authority to deal with him, the case had belonged to Washington from the start. It was a federal investigation, a federal gun crime, a federal charge. And now there was a dead federal officer.

The FBI called up SWAT units from Salt Lake City, Seattle, and Portland. The Hostage Rescue Team (HRT), an elite tactical unit based out of Quantico, Virginia, was put on alert.

Two realities diverged. What Randy described as "a ZOG/New World Order ambush," looked, to the FBI, like the murder of a US marshal who was in possession of a warrant, fleeing the area, and not even on the Weavers' land. Roderick, who experienced the incident through the eyes of a seasoned tactical commander, recalled how Randy and Harris "performed a good pincer move on us… It was a perfect movement." Larry Cooper agreed, saying it was "like someone hunting rabbits." For the Weavers, the only reason it might have felt like a rabbit hunt was that they thought they were pursuing late-summer game. Still, while the Weavers were obviously not out hunting feds, there is no doubt that they were aware that officers were snooping around the ridge that August. They had been watching overflights, manning an improvised checkpoint across the road, and running their "vehicle response" drills. Sara had found that camera. Harris had let the air out of Roderick's tires.

As a game of bureaucratic telephone played out on the other side of the continent, reports about the Weavers seemed to grow more ominous the farther they got from the source. The FBI learned, for instance, that the Weavers had repeatedly vowed — in letters to the authorities, in conversations with neighbors, and in the press — that Randy would not be taken alive. The FBI noted that Randy had special forces training, including with explosives. They were told that he was an associate of the Aryan Nations, and a member of the same Christian Identity movement that had produced Gordon Kahl and the Order. They were also told that, based on months of surveillance, the family, kids and all, were almost constantly armed.

All of the above was technically true, but it did not add up to an accurate picture of the situation. The Weavers did not want to kill anyone and they believed that they had been ambushed out of the clear blue. Looking over the Weaver file in an office three thousand miles from Naples, the FBI failed to see the nuances of the yearslong escalation that had led to this moment, and took Randy and Vicki at their (overdramatic) word. Set alongside the indisputable fact of a dead marshal, all of their apocalyptic saber-rattling sounded both literal and serious.

Making matters worse, these true yet misleading facts were supplemented with a lot of shoddy speculation. There was talk of hidden explosives, a "bunker network," hand grenades, secret tunnels, automatic weapons, and Aryan cadres itching to join the fray. The almost certainly false story about the Weavers shooting at Geraldo's helicopter recirculated.

As briefing begat briefing on either side of the Potomac, it started to sound as though the Weavers had stalked William Degan and murdered him in cold blood. Later, amid a flood of baseless theories about why the government responded with such overwhelming force, it would be suggested that William Degan had been old Boston friends with an assistant attorney general named Robert Mueller. As it happened, Mueller had been out of town at the time and took no part in the mobilization.

And so it was that the FBI set to work under the impression that the Weaver family was trying to start some sort of holy war, or at least launch a minor insurrection against their own government. The federal image of Randy swelled until he resembled a Revelation-addled Rambo who was, in the government's assessment, "clearly...willing to shoot at federal officers." Nobody seemed to mention that the man had not been seen even pointing a gun at anyone. Once Harris and the family retreated into the cabin, none of them fired another shot.

By 9:30 p.m., Gene Glenn, the FBI special agent in charge of the bureau's Salt Lake City division, had arrived to establish a makeshift command center near the Rau home in Homicide Meadow. Glenn assumed formal leadership of the operation. His first move was to establish a perimeter around the entire ridge, ensuring that nobody could get in or out.

Earlier that afternoon, a mile up the hill, Randy, Kevin, Sara, Rachel, and Vicki, with Elisheba in her arms, had gathered out on the overlook rock, crying and praying. Randy, whose shotgun was still jammed, went inside for a fresh weapon. Sara changed out of her shorts, putting on camo pants. They brought blankets outside and sat waiting.

When it started to rain, they went inside, tying Sara's dog Buddy to a tree by the chicken coop to raise the alarm if anyone approached. As the sun went down, the family listened to the low purr of diesels accumulating down in Homicide Meadow. A seemingly endless stream of sirens came pouring off the highway and over Ruby Creek bridge — Idaho State Police SWAT teams, local sheriff's deputies, Border Patrol agents — all responding to Hunt's 911 call. "It sounded like every patrol car in the state had pulled into the valley," Kevin recalled.

Inside the cabin, the Weavers drew the heavy denim curtains that Vicki had sewn herself and waited, certain that another attack was coming. Huddled together in the living room, they prayed and mourned Sam. Between bouts of crying, they raged against the evil forces that had finally brought the Great Tribulation to their mountain. In the dark, Kevin and Randy slipped outside to bring up food from the root cellar. Vicki went to the kitchen sink to clean their breakfast dishes. The dirty plates must have looked left over from some other lifetime. On the local radio they heard a report about how white supremacist zealots had murdered a US marshal. There was no mention of their dead son.

The Weavers had no doubt that the marshals knew they had killed Sam, and his omission from the radio report confirmed everything they already believed. If ZOG's agents, with their black masks and submachine guns, were willing to shoot an eighty-pound kid in the back, then surely they would not hesitate to kill everyone else in the house. What's more, as the Weavers saw it, Randy had already been set up once. Why would the same people hesitate to kill them all to cover their tracks? Thanks to the radio, they were able to confirm what Kevin had already speculated: he had hit one of the marshals. There was no way Randy and Vicki were going to let their faithful young friend get railroaded in a Babylon court.

For a decade, since even before they left Iowa, Randy and Vicki had been talking about something like this happening. Over that time, the circle in which they dwelled had, in fits and starts, closed tighter and tighter. Now, with the death of Sam, the Final Things were truly at hand. The mountaintop fastness that Vicki had seen so long ago in her visions was crowded with books, board games, guns, quilts, toys, hand-painted tins of herbs, and furniture worn soft by nine years of intimate family life. They would have to stay put and stay firm, keep their guns at the ready, and let Yahweh's perfect will be done.

Late in the evening, Vicki carried Elisheba and her Bible upstairs to bed. The girls, unable to go near Sam's empty room, slept downstairs. Randy, racked with rage and guilt, stepped onto the porch and went through the dark fog to Vicki's shed. He needed one more look at his son. When he came back inside, he silently mounted the stairs to join Vicki and the baby.

CHAPTER TWENTY

LAMENTATION ON HIGH PLACES

SETTING ASIDE RANDY and Vicki's determination to remain "separated" at any cost, perhaps the single most fateful choice made during the long chain of bad decisions that came to be known as "Ruby Ridge" was made five hours after the shootout, on board an FBI jet flying from Washington, DC, to Spokane.

A few hours before that flight left, Larry Potts, head of the FBI's criminal division, spoke with Hostage Rescue Team commander Richard Rogers about how to proceed. Potts, laboring under the false impression that William Degan had died without discharging his weapon, was convinced that Degan was dead because the Marshals Service had underestimated how dangerous their fugitive was. Neither Potts nor Rogers wanted their men making the same mistake. Within hours of the shootout, Potts received preliminary approval from the Bureau's legal advisor to revise the FBI's standard rules of engagement, with the stipulation that the final decision would have to be made on the ground, once a better assessment was available.

By 6:30 p.m., an advance team that included Rogers of the Hostage Rescue Team and Wayne "Duke" Smith, deputy director of the

Marshals Service, was cruising westward above the clouds. On the jet, Smith briefed Rogers about the situation. Neither man knew the case intimately, but their tray tables were piled with files and reports chronicling the situation all the way back to the gun sale. Everything they read implied that the Weavers had grown more paranoid and more militant during their eighteen months of wilderness exile.

Along with speculation about landmines, booby traps, under-ground tunnels, and Aryan confederates hiding in the woods, the men on the plane noted that the Weavers had the advantage of a high, "fortified" position.

The FBI's standard rules of engagement dictate that agents can only use deadly force if they perceive mortal danger (to themselves or someone else) and a verbal warning has been issued. At the time, Rog-ers thought that the Weavers might be creeping around the woods, waiting to pick off feds. More importantly, it was not clear how the standard rules applied if their guys were entering what the planners mistakenly took to be an active gun battle. Once shooting has begun and an officer has been killed, it would seem that the "mortal danger" and "verbal warning" thresholds have been cleared.

On the plane, Rogers wrote a rough draft of new rules stating that any armed adult in the vicinity of the cabin "could be the subject of deadly force" once a surrender announcement had been made. The Weaver children, whom the FBI classified as hostages, would remain under the standard rules of engagement, meaning that they could only be shot if they directly threatened a life. (Rogers did not know that one of the children was already dead.) From the plane, Rogers called Potts at the FBI and read through what he had written. He received preliminary approval for the new language, although formal approval was still pending a written version.

By the next morning, the advance team was at the command post in the meadow, joining an ever-swelling crowd of law enforce-ment officers — Idaho State Police, local SWAT teams, sheriff's depu-ties, Border Patrol agents, SOG members — all technically under the command of Gene Glenn of the FBI. Dick Rogers would more or less be in charge of the tactical side of things.

Over the coming days, the federal encampment in Homicide Meadow grew exponentially. As if by some twitch of institutional muscle memory, the expanding outpost of mess tents, mobile command centers, porta-johns, and camo-painted convoys looked a lot more like Khe Sanh than any sort of domestic police operation. Officers in jungle camo and face paint wandered around with their M16s. Jeeps, Humvees, and armored personnel carriers churned the grass to mud, then dust, then mud again. A minor exaltation of Hueys flocked in and out of the meadow, spraying pine needles.

Maurice Ellsworth, the US Attorney, installed himself at the encampment as an on-site legal affairs office, drafting charges for when the whole thing came to an end. On Saturday, the day after the shootout at the Y, charges were filed against Randy and Kevin Harris for the murder of William Degan. Idaho governor Cecil Andrus declared a state of emergency in Boundary County, placing the Idaho National Guard at the disposal of the FBI. In Bonners Ferry, the first day of the school year was postponed; the gymnasium had been converted into a barracks.

With the FBI in charge, all the other agencies fell into supporting roles, helping with logistics, establishing a perimeter around the mountain, and holding back the crowd of protestors that was gathering on the far side of the small bridge that spanned Ruby Creek. A single strip of yellow police tape was strung across the bridge, separating the citizens from the law.

Amid all this bustle, the handful of marshals who had been dealing with the Weavers for over a year were sidelined. Dave Hunt was summoned before the FBI, asked a few basic questions, and told he could go. He watched in distress as two years' worth of carefully compiled notes were taken apart and distributed. He had learned that the real challenge of dealing with the Weavers was sorting their apocalyptic bluster from their actual intentions, a task that required a level of sensitivity that literal-minded tacticians fresh off a plane from Virginia were unlikely to possess. As the FBI guys saw it, they had been called in to clean up a mess created by the US Marshals.

Back at the ski condo on Saturday, the five SOG members who had been on the hill when Degan was killed were given a cursory debriefing. They would visit the command center in Homicide Meadow over the next two days, but the matter was clearly out of their hands. A few days later, they left Idaho, flying to Boston for William Degan's funeral. The service, held at a church in Quincy, was a massive gathering of police, marshals, marines, friends, and family. The mayor of Boston and the governor of Massachusetts were both in attendance.

———

With the Weavers uphill and a growing rabblement of angry citizens across the creek, the people at work in the meadow felt somewhat besieged themselves. Something akin to the conspiratorial logic and motivated reasoning that animated the Weavers took hold among the federal tacticians. Scraps of information—Randy's experience with explosives in the army, the family's intention to ambush and kill as many feds as possible, a wild-eyed matriarch panting for the Apocalypse—were lifted from their context and reassembled into an ominous new story. Because Kevin Harris was technically not part of the family, the government referred to the people up the hill as the "Weaver/Harris group," rather than "the Weavers" or "the Weaver family." It was small thing, but it helped make the people in the cabin sound more like a criminal outfit—the Naples Seven—than a family. Opposing facts found little purchase.

Federal power mobilized amid a cascade of questionable choices. The first was the decision to activate the HRT, a force that specialized in taking down criminals with rapid and overwhelming force. The next, and most overtly illegal, was the decision to revise the FBI's rules of engagement before anyone had communicated anything more than a single "Freeze, Randy!" Of course, as the feds saw it, they had been demanding Weaver's surrender for a year and a half, only to be met with Bible verses and professions of a willingness to die fighting.

Of all the information the government still did *not* have, the most important was that Samuel Weaver's body was lying wrapped in a white sheet on the mattress in Vicki's shed. Ironically, as faxes trilled back and forth between Naples and Quantico, one of the FBI's biggest worries was that the Weaver kids were "well trained and capable of firing at law enforcement," whereas federal officers would be reluctant to shoot at children. To the FBI, this asymmetry, when combined with the fact that the Weavers knew the land intimately and had been readying themselves for this battle for over a year, presented special dangers.

To anyone looking in from the outside (or after the fact), the spectacle of an army descending upon a ramshackle cabin looked like a very different sort of asymmetry. From the very outset, reasonable observers wondered how this immense mobilization was remotely proportionate to the crime of cutting a few inches off two shotguns? For better or worse, the answer was that nobody in the meadow was thinking about those shotguns, or even Randy's failure to appear. Those infractions were mere prologue now that William Degan was dead. His killing was the crime that summoned an army to Homicide Meadow.

———

Saturday, the day after the shootout at the Y, dawned wet and chill, with the ridge shrouded in fog. Nobody inside the cabin had slept much. When Vicki descended from the loft she was still crying. The waiting and the silence were maddening. Sam was dead. Kevin had killed a US marshal. Why had nobody come up the hill with a bullhorn to demand his surrender?

Rachel and Sara, their eyes red and puffy from a night of tears, ran to use the outhouse before hurrying back inside. Randy and Kevin went out to check on the chickens and move the dogs. They could hear noises drifting up from the meadow — humming generators, slamming car doors — but they could not see anyone. The judder of low-flying helicopters, just out of sight, was becoming constant. Because the Weaver file included that (likely false) story about someone firing on Geraldo's helicopter, the FBI was extra cautious about exposing their aircraft to gunfire. Many of the officers on the scene had fought in Vietnam and probably carried some residual feelings about the vulnerable underbelly of a Huey. They tried to remain at least two hundred yards above the cabin, but the wet, windy weather made that difficult.

Assuming that they might be settling in for some sort of siege, Vicki and Sara dashed to the root cellar and returned with cans of fish and jars of fruit. They filled jugs at the spring and brought them inside. The night before, they had set buckets under the eaves to catch rainwater. Vicki was determined that her family, Kevin included, would not split up. Everyone but the baby checked and loaded their weapons. They placed boxes of ammo near each window.

———————

By 10:30 that morning, the HRT had a rough plan. The most important thing was to establish communication. Because the government was convinced that anyone who approached the cabin was in mortal danger, they would not go up the hill until teams of sniper-observers were in position on the ridges around the cabin. Once the snipers were in place, the plan was for a pair of armored personnel carriers (APCs), essentially tanks without turrets, to drive up to the cabin. From there, they would call for Randy's surrender over a loudspeaker, drop off a siege phone (fitted with a hidden mic) and retreat. The Weavers could then pick up the phone and start negotiating. One of the two APCs would contain the FBI negotiator. The other would carry a small assault team, ready to make an arrest in case Randy and Harris came out with their hands up. If there was no response, they would try again the next day. If nothing changed after that, they would return with the APCs and start knocking down outbuildings, water lines, and the generator. If that did not do the trick, they would fire tear gas into the cabin.

By noon, the sniper-observer teams were ready to head up the hill, but the HRT was still waiting on formal approval of their plan and the arrival of a special APC fitted with loudspeakers. At 2:40 p.m., a draft of the plan was faxed to Quantico. Appended to the fax was a version of the revised rules of engagement. The new rules, which would soon be distributed to all HRT members, stated:

> 1.) *If any adult in the compound is observed with a weapon after the surrender announcement, deadly force can and should be employed to neutralize this individual. 2.) If any adult male is observed with a weapon prior to the announcement, deadly force can and should be employed, if the shot can be taken without endangering any children.*

After some back and forth about how negotiations would be conducted — the Bureau wanted more details — the plan (with the new rules of engagement still attached to the document) was approved.

Due to criminally poor record-keeping by the FBI, the question of who (if anyone) actually approved the revised rules became almost as muddled as the matter of who shot first at the Y. The question would generate years of blame-shifting up and down the FBI's chain of command. All of this recrimination would be amplified by the disaster in Waco, where the FBI once again took over for the ATF and Dick Rogers was once again in command of the Hostage Rescue Team. In the aftermath of the Weaver siege there would be a few suspensions and censures, but they would mostly pertain to the Bureau's attempts to cover up its mistakes, rather than its agents' conduct during the siege. Larry Potts, who had risen to the number-two position at the Bureau, was demoted. One veteran agent, Michael Kahoe, former chief of the FBI's violent crimes division, was fined and sentenced to eighteen months in prison for shredding an internal "after action" report that was critical of the Bureau's conduct. When the DOJ finally took up the matter in 1995, the revised rules were deemed to contain "serious constitutional infirmities" — which is a roundabout way of saying they were illegal. Those illegal rules would become the hook upon which every one of the government's compounding errors would be hung.

On that damp Saturday, however, all that really mattered was how the members of the Hostage Rescue Team interpreted the rules. Did they constitute an order to shoot any adult holding a weapon? Or was their function, as Larry Potts put it, "to assist HRT personnel in making a determination regarding what constituted a threat to them in this extraordinary circumstance"? From the FBI's perspective, the Weavers had already proved willing to shoot and kill federal officers. Gene Glenn, who was technically running the show in Homicide Meadow, later argued that the phrase "can and should" was merely intended to let the agents on the ridge know that they were *authorized* to use deadly force against the Weavers "if appropriate." Whatever the intention of the new guidelines, at least one sharpshooter on the scene told Congress that he understood the revised rules to mean: "If you see 'em, shoot 'em."

In the early afternoon, nine members of the HRT were briefed about what awaited them up the hill. They were given the revised rules of engagement and a detailed (if one-sided) account of the shootout at the Y. They were told about what sorts of weapons the Weavers had. They learned that the family usually responded to vehicle noise by coming out to the overlook rock with their guns. They were told about the Weavers' stated intention to resist arrest, even to the point of death, and that, for years, the family had been preparing for some sort of confrontation. The possibility that they had previously fired on a helicopter was mentioned.

The special APC rigged with speakers still had not arrived, but around 3:30 p.m., the sniper-observer teams started uphill on foot to establish their outposts around the cabin. As they hiked into the woods, they did not know for certain whether the person or persons who had killed Bill Degan were inside the cabin or if they might be hiding somewhere nearby. The HRT teams had been instructed to set up concealed positions around the "crisis site" (i.e., the Weavers' cabin and surrounding outbuildings). From there, they could radio updates about any activity and, if need be, deliver "long-range precision fire." Members of the ATF's SOG team were assigned to cover the HRT guys from behind, in case of attack by Weaver sympathizers or unknown confederates.

Between 5:00 and 6:00 p.m., four heavily camouflaged sniper teams settled into their hidden positions in the woods around the knoll. The first team to get set up was the one closest to the cabin, exactly 646 feet due north of the Weavers' front door, across a small ravine. It consisted of two men, Dale Monroe and Lon Horiuchi. Horiuchi, a Hawaiian-born West Point grad who had been an infantry officer before joining the FBI, was known as one of the Bureau's best snipers. He and Monroe had a clear view down the length of the Weavers' porch. From that angle, they could see if the cabin door swung open, but they could not see through it, even if it were wide open.

———————

Sometime before 6:00 p.m., the dogs started barking. Sara went outside to check on them and take a look around. All seemed quiet. Randy and Kevin tentatively stepped outside with their guns. The three of them walked to the overlook rock and peered down the road. Nothing. Kevin took the opportunity to grab some batteries for his flashlight. Then they all started back toward the porch. At the last moment, Randy turned and started walking toward Vicki's shed. "I wanted to go see my boy one more time," he later explained.

At 5:57 p.m., a helicopter carrying Duke Smith of the Marshals, Dick Rogers of the HRT, and several other officers took off from the meadow. It was the sixth such flight that day. As Horiuchi later told it, he heard the helicopter rise up from the meadow, behind and below his position. On account of the poor visibility, the chopper flew low, moving in a zig-zagging pattern to avoid making an easy target.

Just as he registered the sound of the helicopter, Horiuchi, peering through the scope of his camo-painted, large-caliber sniper rifle, watched two armed men and an unarmed ponytailed girl go to the overlook rock. Just as they turned to go back to the cabin, he saw one of the men peel off and start for the shed. It was Randy going to take his last look at Sam, although Horiuchi thought it might be Kevin Harris.

Through his scope, Horiuchi watched the man hurry around the far side of the shed. To the sniper, the man seemed to be looking up in the direction of the rising chopper. According to his later testimony, Horiuchi believed that the man was scanning the horizon and readying his gun, as if preparing to shoot at the helicopter. Other snipers in the area also saw Randy over by the shed and thought (or at least claimed to think) that he might be getting ready to take a shot.

At 5:58, Randy switched his rifle from his right hand to his left. With his right arm, he reached up to turn a small scrap of wood on a nail that served as a latch on the door of Vicki's shed. Just as he touched the wood, a sharp pain jolted his arm. A moment later, a deep boom echoed off the rocks.

Horiuchi's bullet pierced Randy's arm just below the shoulder and exited through his armpit. It felt, he said, like being kicked by a mule. Assuming that his attacker was standing directly behind him, Randy spun around, hoping "to spit in the coward's face." There was nobody there. Randy scrambled around to the other side of the shed and crouched down. Sara jogged over to ask what had happened. "I've been shot," Randy told her.

Hearing the boom, Vicki stepped onto the porch with Elisheba in her arms and a pistol on her hip. "What happened?" she shouted across the knoll.

"I've been shot, Ma!" Randy responded.

Vicki began screaming into the woods, "You bastards! You bastards!"

Randy and Sara turned to run, with Sara pushing her father from behind and protectively covering his back with her own body. Kevin fell in behind them as they sprinted across the stony path that led back to the cabin.

Horiuchi chambered another round. He had obviously not killed the man. The sniper reasoned—if a split-second choice can be called reasoning—that if the running men got back inside, they would be free to shoot at the helicopter or anyone else. Since there were "hostages" in the cabin, nobody could return fire. Settling his barrel onto a tree branch, he led Kevin Harris with his scope, aiming a few feet ahead to account for speed and distance.

Vicki stood at the threshold of the cabin, holding open the door so that it was between her and the sniper across the ravine. She yelled for her husband, daughter, and friend to get inside. As they got close, she stepped aside, scrunching up against the inside of the open door, so the runners could pile through without breaking stride. While the door concealed her body from the sniper's view, the top of her head may have been visible through the glass windows in the upper portion of the door, depending on whether or not the small denim valance that hung behind the glass was drawn closed or not. Just as the man in Horiuchi's scope reached the narrow porch, the sniper squeezed.

Randy got inside first, followed by Sara and Kevin. As they tumbled across the threshold, there came another booming crack. A hard, wet spray hit Sara's cheek. She almost tripped over Kevin, who had suddenly dropped to the floor. Confused, Randy spun around to see his wife kneel then sprawl face down on the floor. "Like a washrag," he said later. Kevin lay still, looking at a piece of Vicki's head lying by his feet. After a moment of stunned silence, Sara and Rachel began wailing.

Hunkered down in the woods just over a tenth of a mile away, Horiuchi looked up from his scope. All three of the runners had made it inside the cabin, but the screaming suggested that he had hit the armed man whom he'd been leading with his gun. What he did not realize was that his bullet had gone through one of the glass panes near the top of the open door, passed through Vicki's skull, and come to a rib-smashing halt in Kevin Harris's upper arm.

Inside, Randy and the girls looked at each other and suddenly yelled, "The baby!" Randy scrabbled under his dead wife for Elisheba, who was still stuck in her mother's hands. The baby was covered in blood and bits of bone, but physically unharmed. She was not even crying. Nearby, ten-year-old Rachel, like her big sister, was covered in a mist of her mother's blood. She had seen it all.

It took a few seconds for everyone to register that Kevin was also hit.

As blood pooled around Vicki, Randy dragged her body out of the doorway and into the kitchen. He knelt over her. They were two months away from their twenty-first wedding anniversary. For the benefit of his daughters, he arranged Vicki's long black hair as best he could to conceal the large void on the side of her head.

Kevin groaned in agony, writhing on the floor, certain that he was bleeding out. He begged for water. After placing a blanket over her mother, Sara brought him a glass.

Randy eventually remembered that he, too, had been shot. Sara removed his shirt and inspected the wound. She could not figure out where the bullet had exited, but she bandaged him up anyway. His arm was numb, but he seemed okay. Randy and Sara helped Kevin out of his blood-soaked leather jacket and got him up into a recliner.

So this is how it ends, Sara thought. There would be no invitation to surrender, no arrests. ZOG would pick them off one at a time. First Striker, then Sam, and now her father, Kevin, and her mom. "They were shooting at us from unknown hiding places. They could see us, but we couldn't see them. It was obvious they weren't interested in talking," Sara later wrote. During the week ahead, it would prove almost impossible to disenthrall her from the notion that they would be shot if they showed themselves. It was a conviction forged amid the most extreme possible trauma. It also happened to match everything her parents had ever told her about the government.

"After dad put his shirt and jacket back on," she later wrote, "he and the three of us girls crouched down on the living room floor and waited to die."

CHAPTER TWENTY-ONE

SIEGE

IT WAS THE hard hammerfall of prophecy fulfilled. Everything they
had ever predicted was coming true. The seals were breaking and the
bowls of wrath were spilling forth. For Victoria Weaver, the end of the
world had truly arrived. But for those left behind to breathe the close,
coppery air inside the cabin, it was all so much more intimate than
the forty-thousand-foot vantage of John's Apocalypse.

And now came a terrifying new sound. At 6:30 that evening, half
an hour after Randy, Kevin, and Vicki had all been shot, an armored
personnel carrier on steel tracks groaned its way up the hill and into
the Weavers' rocky yard.

Learning that two shots had been taken and that Kevin was
likely hit, the FBI decided to go up the hill in the APCs, even though
the speakers were not yet rigged up. Their plan was proceeding in
reverse—first the shooting, then the order to surrender and invitation to negotiate.

Inside the APC were HRT commander Dick Rogers and a hostage
negotiator named Fred Lanceley. Stopping about thirty feet from the
cabin, they lowered a telephone down onto the ground. Lanceley
came up out of a hatch and, using a bullhorn, announced the warrant

for Randy and Kevin's arrest, then asked to commence negotiations for surrender.

"Vicki," Lanceley called out, "maybe one of the children could run out and grab the phone."

There was silence from inside the cabin, where Vicki lay in a pool of blood and everyone else was waiting to be shot, bombed, or burned to death. After a few more tries by Lanceley, the APC slowly retreated on its heavy tracks, paying out a mile of telephone line along the road back to the meadow.

Night fell. The temperature dropped. Some of the snipers, crouched in the woods since midday, were on the brink of hypothermia. The cold and damp caused their scopes and night vision to fog up. They were called back to the meadow.

Up on the ridge, the survivors were left alone. Inside the cabin, with both men wounded and Vicki — their strength and prophet — lying dead beneath a blanket, sixteen-year-old Sara took command of the situation. Absolutely certain that they would be killed if they showed themselves, she refused any talk of surrender. Her faith was undimmed. Speaking to a reporter just one month later, she said that "the world is nothing compared to everlasting life."

Kevin was pale and coughing up a lot of blood. Sara cut off his shirt. The large-caliber bullet, slowed by its long flight across the ravine and its passage through Vicki's head, had lodged in his left arm, near the shoulder. The arm was swollen to twice its normal size and the entry wound was a raised, angry-looking crater the circumference of a tennis ball. A few of his ribs were broken and his chest was peppered with human shrapnel, fragments of Vicki's jaw. Sara doused the area in peroxide and, following her mother's recipe for infection and inflammation, put Kevin on a heavy regimen of cayenne pepper and other herbs.

Starting a little after 9:00 p.m., the telephone lying out in the yard began to ring every half hour. Randy locked the front door. Clutching her gun, Sara prayed to Yahweh for the feds to simply firebomb the house, as they had with Bob Mathews. At least they could all die together.

During the endless night that followed, Kevin begged Randy to shoot him. "Can't do it, buddy," Randy recalled saying. He offered his young friend a revolver, saying, "You got one good arm." This exchange started the girls screaming all over again. Kevin gave up the idea of suicide.

———

The next morning was Sunday. Kevin had soaked the recliner in blood, so they moved him to the couch. Rachel took over care of Elisheba, shushing her to sleep and feeding her dry cereal and the syrup from cans of fruit. The baby kept calling for her mother. Randy piled furniture by the front door and moved a large chair to the middle of the room. They could all crouch behind it when the shooting resumed.

Around 10:00 a.m., the sniper-observer teams were back in their concealed positions encircling the cabin. Two APCs rolled into the yard. Dick Rogers spent about half an hour trying to convince the Weavers to negotiate. Over and over, a voice from a loudspeaker beseeched one of them to come outside, pick up the phone, and carry it into the cabin.

Sara wondered how the feds could imagine they were so stupid. It was clear that anyone who ventured onto the porch would instantly be shot. "We kept our silence and our heads down," she recalled. Rogers announced that if negotiations did not commence soon, they would begin knocking down outbuildings.

Realizing the obvious—that the family was far too scared to come out to the yard to retrieve the phone—the FBI brought up a remote-control robot, a bomb disposal unit retrofitted with cameras, lights, and a microphone. It drove right up to the porch with the phone dangling from a hook. Peeking through the curtains at the machine, Randy saw that, among its many bells and whistles, there was a single barrel shotgun pointed directly forward, right beside the phone they were being instructed to pick up. "Whoever grabbed that telephone was dead meat," he concluded.

In the afternoon, the APCs returned, driving around the property and crushing outbuildings and belongings: the generator, the water tanks, Rachel's bicycle. Nobody inside had fired a shot since Friday, but the FBI still feared some sort of ambush. What looked to the Weavers like wanton destruction was, to the HRT tacticians, an effort to hurry things along and simplify the "siege environment," making room for their vehicles and eliminating hiding places. It was the raze-and-defoliate impulse of a real war.

Just prior to knocking down Vicki's shed, several FBI agents, weapons drawn, opened the door and looked inside. There, they discovered Sam on the bed, his body stripped, cleaned, and wrapped in a sheet. While the Weavers were certain that the government already knew about Sam's death, all evidence indicates that this was the moment — two days after the chaotic shootout at the Y — that anyone from the FBI learned that Sam was dead. One indication of just how badly the FBI misunderstood the Weavers is that, upon finding the boy's body, their first thought was that Randy and Vicki, acting on some sort of deranged Jonestown-type impulse, had started killing off their own children.

The discovery changed things. The FBI immediately stopped destroying outbuildings and made another attempt at communication. They assumed that the pious people inside the cabin might have something to say about the disposition of their son's corpse. When their questions were met with silence, the body was carried downhill to be inspected by the coroner.

At a press conference by the creek the next morning, Gene Glenn announced the discovery of Sam's body, remaining vague about how the boy died. For the crowd of protestors gathered at the bridge, the news landed like a spray of gasoline. People who had been hanging back from the police tape, praying or silently holding signs, surged forward, screaming "Animals!" and "I'm gonna get you!" directly into the faces of individual Idaho State Policemen. One man approached the phalanx of officers, pounding his chest and shouting, "Fucking kill me, you bastards!"

———————

Inside the cabin, the next eight days passed in a miserable gloom. Day and night ran together, with the quicklime glare of floodlights seeping in around the curtains. Randy and Kevin, both in considerable pain, lay smoking in the dim light while the girls muttered curses and prayers. Rachel shushed the baby. The radio prattled quietly, occasionally giving news of the siege, still without any mention of Vicki's death. Gradually, the metallic scent of fresh blood turned to the sick, heavy fetor of Kevin's rotting wound and Vicki's decomposing body. When they had to go to the bathroom, they used a small portable toilet. Sara, in a state of perpetual fear, believed that any noise or light — the flick of a lighter or a whispered conversation — might give away their precise positions, drawing sniper fire. Beneath the floorboards, they could hear the shuffling murmurs of men creeping around under the cabin. (Agents were installing listening devices, which turned out not to be very effective. While the FBI could hear the chirping of the Weavers' parakeets, they mistook Sara's voice for Vicki's.)

Randy crawled into the pantry for food, staying below the window that faced the northern slope, where the shot that killed his wife had originated. Terrified for her father's life, Sara insisted on taking over this duty. "I stayed close to my rifle," she wrote. "I had made peace with death — it was not a matter of if, but only a matter of when."

Because everything the FBI knew about the Weavers suggested that Vicki was the dominant voice in the family, negotiator Fred Lanceley spent several days attempting to negotiate with a dead woman. He pled with Vicki to come out and talk. He offered food, water, medicine, and help with the baby. One morning, he suggested that Vicki send the children out to eat pancakes with the army mustered in Homicide Meadow.

As they had with Sam's death, the Weavers made the entirely reasonable assumption that the FBI knew that Vicki was dead. As a result, Lanceley's efforts to engage her in dialogue felt like some sick ZOG mind game — "psychological warfare," Sara called it.

Because none of them would go near the telephone dangling from the robot, the FBI's only way of addressing the family was by shouting through a bullhorn from a distance of thirty yards, or by speaking over the APC's loudspeaker. For his part, Randy could only yell hoarsely through the walls of the cabin, making communication grievously one-sided. "You killed my fucking wife!," Randy shouted again and again, with mounting frustration. Nobody seemed to hear him. The Weavers came to believe that the agents could hear Randy just fine, and that they simply pretended otherwise so as not to have to admit that they had killed Vicki.

Down in the meadow, at the sprawling encampment that some were now calling "Federal Way," Lanceley was advocating patience, while others were inclined toward a fast, "tactical" solution. Inside the cabin, however, it was the negotiator's voice that became the most immediate object of the Weavers' rage. His constant invocation of Vicki's name drove the family mad. "By this time," Randy later said, "I didn't want to negotiate with anybody." Using the only means of defiance still available to them, the Weavers went almost completely silent.

The FBI started to worry that if they got too close to the cabin, the Weavers might attempt suicide, either by shooting themselves or by coming out with guns blazing. After the loudspeaker announced that the robot was going to roll up onto the porch and push the phone through a window (breaking it in the process), Randy screamed back, "Get the fuck out of here!" The FBI evidently heard that. The window smashing was tabled.

———

At the first word of trouble, David and Jeane Jordison had driven straight from Iowa. Vicki's siblings came, too. Unnerved by the rowdy protestors congregating at the bridge, they told the FBI that they were willing to help in any way they could and then went to a motel in Sandpoint. There, they got most of their information from the radio and television. At the request of the FBI, they recorded an audio message for their daughter and Randy, begging them to pick up the siege phone. The message was played over the loudspeaker. "Sensing some sort of trick," as Sara put it, the Weavers refused.

By midweek, with nothing but silence or the occasional defiant scream from the cabin, the FBI started sobering up to the reality that the "Weaver/Harris group" might not be the murderous gang they had imagined in the immediate aftermath of William Degan's death. Instead, they were starting to look more like a terrified family whose conspiratorial and apocalyptic faith rendered reasonable choices all but impossible. The aggressive rules of engagement put into effect on Saturday were quietly scotched, replaced by the FBI's standard rules. Later, this change would look a lot like an admission that the "can and should" guidelines had been a mistake.

On Wednesday afternoon, Randy could be heard shouting that he wanted to talk to his sister Marnis. The next day, Marnis was flown from Iowa and driven up the hill with Lanceley. Rather than being allowed to enter the house or go near the porch, the HRT gave her a microphone. Randy once again shouted that Vicki was dead, but Marnis did not seem to hear him. (Although her hearing was not good, this lends some credence to the FBI's claim not to have heard this fact, either.) Instead of responding to what Randy was yelling about Vicki, Marnis just kept pleading for her brother to pick up the phone or surrender. Growing frustrated, Randy yelled for Marnis and Lanceley to "back off!"

The following day Marnis was brought back up the hill with a parabolic microphone, to help her hear. Again, she pleaded with Randy to surrender or at least pick up the phone. This time, there was only silence from inside the cabin.

—————

After four days of listening to what they regarded as lies and propaganda on the radio (still no mention that Vicki had been killed!), the Weavers resolved to record their own version of events, for posterity if nothing else. With Kevin and Randy dictating, Sara wrote their account on a yellow legal pad. They described the "ZOG/NEW WORLD ORDER ambush" at the Y, with Kevin admitting, "I shot one of the sons of bitches." They also described the two shots taken on Saturday that injured Randy and Kevin and killed Vicki. They drew an explicit connection to the "covered up murder" of Gordon Kahl, citing it as a reason that they did not trust the FBI. "If they think we are going to trust them (we didn't trust them before they shot us) they're crazy!" They pledged to take "the offensive" if the feds attempted to starve them out. "If they even so much as crack a window pane on this house with a robot, telephone, gas grenades, etc. it's all over with."

The six-page document concluded on a defiant, Vicki-ish note: "We do not fear the ONE WORLD BEAST Government. They can only take our lives. Only Yahweh can destroy our souls. Samuel Hanson Weaver and Vicki Jean Weaver are martyrs for Yah-Yahshua and the White Race. Even if the rest of us die, we win. Hallelu-Yah!" Randy, Kevin, Sara, and Rachel all signed the letter. Sara added baby Elisheba's name in all caps.

The day after they recorded this testimonial, the people inside the cabin learned that their private nightmare had become national news. For tens of millions of Americans, the smooth, tickertape voice of Paul Harvey—"*Hello Americans, this is Paul Harvey. Stand by for the news.*"—served as daily background noise inside countless bars, banks, grocery stores, construction sites, and auto shops. During Harvey's midday broadcast on Thursday, he broke the radio equivalent of the fourth wall, addressing himself directly to Randy, whom he had been told was a regular listener.

In sympathetic terms, Harvey urged Randy to pick up the phone attached to the robot. Only by surrendering, Harvey said, could the Weavers get their side of the story before a jury of "understanding home folks." He also offered to help fund Randy's defense. Randy heard the broadcast but was unpersuaded. No way was ZOG going to let him and Kevin walk out of there and into a courtroom.

———

With scant new facts to relay, the reports coming over the Weavers' small radio talked more and more about the crowd gathered two miles downhill from the cabin, just on the far side of Ruby Creek bridge.

The first people to show up had been locals, drawn by the racket of helicopters and sirens. Jackie and Tony Brown, the Weavers' close friends since the red house days, arrived early on Saturday, offering to walk up the hill to collect the kids. The FBI, still terrified that the siege might metastasize into a wider conflict, turned them away.

After the locals, the next people to show up were those plugged into the surprisingly effective network of survivalists, separatists, and far-right activists. John Trochmann, who would harness the upwelling of anger over the deaths of Sam and Vicki to found the Militia of Montana, left for Naples as soon as he heard about the siege. His wife Carolyn followed close behind, stopping only to prepare huge batches of spaghetti and coleslaw for the protestors. Near the bridge, she and other women set up an outdoor kitchen under blue tarps. Even though it was still August, the nights were cold enough that snow dusted the nearby peaks. People gathered around barrel stoves to stay warm in the intermittent rain. Grills and stoves burned night and day.

Tom Metzger, a former grand dragon of the Klan, who was then leading a California-based Identity organization known as White Aryan Resistance, put out a call for his followers to head for Naples.

Metzger, who had his own radio broadcast and hotline—likely funded by cash from the Order's armored car robbery—claimed that Randy was a "subscriber associate" of WAR's newsletter.

In Colorado, an Identity pastor named Pete Peters used his "Scriptures for America" Bible camp, which happened to commence on August 22, to initiate a phone tree directing the faithful north. Willis Carto's *Spotlight* reported tirelessly on the siege, calling it a "Harbinger for America."

All week, while the Weavers languished inside their increasingly hellish cabin, the crowd kept growing. People parked haphazardly along the shoulder of Old Highway 95 and walked to the bridge. There were skinhead crews from Portland and Las Vegas. There were anti-tax protestors, bikers with POW/MIA patches, self-described Christian Patriots, survivalists, and assorted freelance preachers quoting Revelation and calling down brimstone upon wicked Babylon. Members of the Aryan Nations, many of whom knew the Weavers personally, came from Hayden Lake, Montana, and Canada, identifying themselves with special armbands. Someone handed out photocopies of the letter Vicki had addressed to her "brethren of the Anglo-Saxon Race," the one in which she quoted from Bob Mathews's "Declaration of War" against ZOG.

Richard Butler, who had encouraged Randy to surrender a year earlier, turned up in a rumpled suit, flanked by his uniformed security detail. He strolled through the crowd shaking hands. To underscore the continuity of the Weaver case with earlier white power martyrdoms, Butler was accompanied by the wife of imprisoned Order member Gary Yarborough and by Debbie Mathews, Bob's widow. Debbie's young son Clint carried a sign that read, "Baby Killers!"

Inevitably, the story of what was happening to the Weavers was embellished as it spread. In *Educated*, Tara Westover's memoir of growing up in (and away from) Idaho, she recounts the evening her father called a family meeting to explain the situation up by Bonners Ferry. "'There's a family not far from here,' Dad said. 'They're freedom fighters. They wouldn't let the government brainwash their kids in them public schools, so the Feds came after them... The Feds surrounded the family's cabin, kept them locked in there for weeks, and when a hungry child, a little boy, snuck out to go hunting, the Feds shot him dead... They're still in the cabin... They keep the lights off, and they crawl on the floor, away from the doors and windows. I don't know how much food they got. Might be they'll starve before the Feds give up.'" Westover's recollection can stand in for countless similar conversations that took place in households that did not, by the accident of a far-wandering prodigy, generate celebrated memoirs.

Like many others, young Tara Westover believed that it was only people like her family who even knew about what was happening to the Weavers — one more piece of secret knowledge for those with their eyes open. In fact, it is likely that by the time her father gave that speech, the name Randall Weaver had been spoken on every network news broadcast.

Over the course of the week, the creekside protest came to resemble something like a camp meeting of the nineteenth century, with tailgates and bullhorns replacing the buckboards and cupped hands of the frontier evangelists. As with a wilderness camp meeting, the sheer novelty of encountering so many fellow believers out in the middle of nowhere charged the air and reified the faith. But unlike at the revivals of the Second Great Awakening, the enemy — in this case the feds, rather than sin and perdition more generally — was on hand, too, making a big ugly display of itself. All day, every day, troops, trucks, and heavy military gear rolled off the highway and clattered over the little bridge. Each new truck was greeted with a chorus of angry jeers. When local contractors arrived with bulldozers and loads of gravel to smooth the road up to the cabin, protestors mounted the running boards, urging the drivers to reject the federal "blood money" and stand up against the tyrants.

Since information was scarce and the gathering at the bridge was, in large part, a congress of conspiracy theorists, rumors raced through the crowd. Some said that the Weavers were already dead and that the feds were just busy assembling a frame-up. Others suggested that the FBI had killed Degan themselves, as a false flag to justify mass gun confiscations or a crackdown on patriot groups. The protestors even looked upon each other with suspicion. Some believed that Bill Grider, perhaps the most vociferous demonstrator at the bridge, must be an agent provocateur, sent to trigger mayhem. (The previous winter's conflict between the Griders and the Weavers was forgotten. Bill, Judy, and their son Eric were leading participants at the protest.) Others speculated that the feds were using the Weaver case to draw New World Order resisters out into the open, to be cataloged for future arrest.

In the language of a different counterculture, the gathering became a scene of great consciousness-raising, with various half-formed strains of discontent uniting against a monolithic enemy: the federal government. Along the grassy bank of Ruby Creek, something like a new American subculture was being born, or, more precisely, discovering its own existence. It was something much bigger and more influential than the insular white power scene of the inland Northwest. While the crowd never grew past about three hundred people, the volume of organizing that came out of those days of grief and rage would be difficult to overstate. Nothing clarifies and accelerates a political movement like martyrdom. Mailing lists were compiled. Connections were made. Future meetings were planned. Several entirely new organizations sprang to life. One canny promoter wandered the crowd handing out flyers for the Preparedness Expo '92, an event to be held in Seattle, with a roster of far-right speakers.

Within a week of the initial shootout, the Weavers were transformed into something more than a family suffering a terrible tragedy. They had become irrefutable evidence of a notion many people already believed: that a vindictive federal government intended to wipe out even the smallest pockets of resistance. Such persecution would no longer be reserved for radicals like Gordon Kahl and Bob Mathews. ZOG had now come for a quiet family of Christian homeschoolers.

As the days dragged on miserably up in the cabin, radio reports about the scene at the bridge brought a tiny measure of solace. "Knowing that there were people pulling for us," Sara recalled, "was a small ray of comfort in the black hole of despair we seemed to be drowning in."

———————

To keep watch over the federal officers in full battle rattle and the young men in bomber jackets screaming about the Jews, a battalion of satellite trucks rolled onto the scene, telescoping their spindly antennae into the air. TV reporters, fresh from the airport in Spokane, delivered standups in the rain while convoys of heavy equipment splashed down the road behind them. None of the reporters could quite explain what was going on: a standoff, a siege, something to do with shotguns and the end of the world. Their only real sources were the tight-lipped FBI and the angry protesters, many of whom regarded the media as part of the usurping tyranny that had rigged America against people like them. But since nobody knew how it would end, it made for good TV.

The story quickly went international. "White Supremacy Fights On in the Rockies," ran the headline in a British daily on Monday, just two days after Vicki had been killed. Some of the first reports can best be described as unwitting propaganda, basically FBI press releases containing obsolete and misleading facts. On that same Monday, not long before the FBI announced the discovery of Sam's body, the *Washington Post* reported that "no one was injured in the shooting Saturday," which was the day Vicki had died, and Kevin and Randy were both shot. The Friday night canard about marshals being pinned down in the woods circulated several days past its expiration date. The cabin, sided in three-quarter-inch plywood, was described as a "fortress" or "fortress-like."

For the media, the announcement of Sam's killing, three days after the shootout at the Y, was the first indication that the situation might be more complicated than it seemed. The death of a child also greatly increased the reach of the story, bringing people to the protest who were neither locals nor attached in any way to the organized far right. By the end of the week, there were a lot of people by the creek who would never consider visiting Hayden Lake or subscribing to *The Spotlight.*

Since the FBI was stingy with its updates and the press was not allowed across the bridge, reporters turned their cameras onto the colorful throng all around them. Along with the surreal sights of American boys wearing Nazi armbands and camo-painted APCs rumbling through a sleepy mountain town, there were plenty of ordinary-looking white folks holding up hastily drawn cardboard signs. With a single pan of the camera, the signage hinted at a worldview unfamiliar to most Americans. "Death to ZOG," "FBI Rot in Hell," "Government Lies/Patriot Dies," "Zionist Murder," "Thank you Jews," "30.06 Go Thru Your Vest Easy Fed Dogs." (The author of that last sign had no way of knowing that it had been Kevin's thirty-aught-six that felled William Degan.)

A group of men from Portland, dressed all in black, unfurled a huge banner: "Whites Must Arm, American Revolution, American Front." A wholesome-looking teenage girl stood by the roadblock holding a placard that read, "Flexing Your New World Order." Another sign summarized Vicki's interpretation of things: "religious persecution pure and simple." A pudgy boy wore an orange T-shirt emblazoned with the words "Hail the Order." His sign read, "Your house is next!" Another had the words "FBI — BATF — U.S. Marshals" over a large Star of David. A few signs made reference to Bob Mathews and Gordon Kahl, household names for some by the bridge, but mysterious characters to the viewers at home. On the other hand, many signs could have been left over from any vaguely conservative demonstration: "Our Tax Dollars at Work" or "Tell the Truth Media!"

Rightly or wrongly, the people at the protest believed that their presence restrained the feds. In *Ruby Creek Massacre*, a VHS documentary filmed at the bridge and sold through the Militia of Montana's catalog, the camera lingers on a helicopter hovering near the ridge. With the chopper in the frame, the cameraman speculates that the FBI is preparing to firebomb the house. When the aircraft changes course, the voice concludes that the pilot must have realized he was being filmed. Later, the surviving Weavers would be among those who believed that the protestors had helped keep them alive. "We are truly convinced," Sara and Randy wrote to the people who stood by the creek, "[that] your presence had a lot to do with the reason our lives were spared."

Agents of the Bureau of Alcohol, Tobacco and Firearms and the Idaho State Police search the vehicle of five skinheads near the Weavers' property, August 25, 1992.

One reason for the massive deployment of law enforcement officers to Naples was that it takes a lot of manpower to secure a perimeter around an entire mountain, especially one traced with overgrown trails and old logging roads. The FBI's concern was twofold. They worried that their fugitives — meaning Randy and Kevin; everybody else was a "hostage" — might sneak out through the wilderness. A more alarming possibility was that outsiders might sneak in to join the fray.

On Wednesday, four days after Vicki was killed, a police helicopter noticed a black Jeep Cherokee on a back road. The vehicle had been spotted earlier at a local gun shop. A group of ATF agents and Idaho State Policemen pulled the SUV over. Five young skinheads were ordered out at gunpoint and made to lie face down on the road. They had been looking for a back way up the hill, seeking to reinforce the Weavers with seven assault rifles, several pistols, boxes of ammo, a bayonet, and (in a very '90s touch) a pair of studded nunchucks.

Many of the older lawmen standing around Homicide Meadow — playing horseshoes, doing pushups, cleaning their weapons, waiting in the chow line — were veterans of the war in Vietnam. The same was true on the other side of the cordon, where a lot of signage made reference to a war that had ended two decades earlier. One local vet kept a stern vigil at the foot of the bridge, silently holding a POW/MIA flag, as if Randy Weaver, who had never deployed to Vietnam, was up the road in a bamboo cage.

CHAPTER TWENTY-TWO

A WHIMPER, NOT A BANG

INTO THE COMBUSTIBLE scene at Ruby Creek Bridge strode the blustering, barrel-chested figure of retired US Army Colonel James "Bo" Gritz. If the long, destabilizing fallout of the war in Vietnam could be made manifest as a single individual, it would be hard to find a better candidate. Gritz — "rhymes with whites," he told reporters with a little smile — was a heavily decorated Green Beret and the self-proclaimed inspiration for *Rambo*, or at least the sequel, *Rambo: First Blood Part II*, in which the titular Green Beret returns to Asia to recover captured soldiers and lost valor.

Gritz had come to fame hyping conspiracy theories about the US government's knowing abandonment of POWs and a related theory that a New World Order was being orchestrated from within the United Nations. For a time, Gritz was a leading character in the immensely influential POW/MIA movement, which made electoral hay (and raised a lot of money) out of the grief surrounding American soldiers who never came back from Vietnam. Elected officials harnessed that pain and the spectacle of grieving families for their own ends by suggesting, without any evidence, that their lost boys might still be alive. Ross Perot, whose first foray into American politics centered on the POW issue, bankrolled Gritz's (unsuccessful) trips to hunt for service members who, according to one theory, were being held for slave labor in the heroin trade with the full knowledge of the Pentagon.

By the early 1990s, Gritz was a cult hero on the far right. Like so many others, he had taken up Christian Identity and begun advocating for the formation of survivalist militias, wrapping his endtimes faith in antisemitic conspiracism. "Do you see the sign, scent, stain, and mark of the beast on America today?" he asked in his newsletter. "The number of the antichrist system is 666, a six within a six, within a six. Six sides, six angles, six points." In other words, the Star of David.

When Gritz learned about the siege in Naples, he was in Arizona, campaigning for president on the ticket of the Populist Party—which, rather than competing with Bush, Clinton, or his old patron Perot, had him running against the incipient New World Order. (The Populist Party had been represented by David Duke in '88, but by the '92 election their slogan was "God, Guns, and Gritz.") Apparently, Gritz's presence at the Weaver siege made so much sense that multiple people simultaneously contacted him, all urging him to intervene. Among them was Randy's friend Tony Brown, who knew that there was a "Bo for President" poster in the cabin. At the same time, Kirby Ferris, the owner of a Stinson Beach, California, surf shop, who had taken a strong interest in the Weaver case and would later publish a book about the siege, began making phone calls to the US Marshals and an Identity Church in Sandpoint, suggesting that someone reach out to Gritz as a possible mediator.

On Wednesday evening, five days after the shootout at the Y, Gritz arrived in Naples. He was accompanied by Jack McLamb, the retired Phoenix police officer who would, a year later, disinter Gordon Kahl's body on camera, in an effort to prove that the official account of his death was a lie.

At the protest by the creek, Gritz, wearing a black safari shirt and aviators, walked around inside a scrum of cameras and supporters, giving speeches, hugging vets, and saying "welcome home" to baffled men who had returned from Vietnam twenty years earlier. His commanding presence gave both the protestors and the press something to organize themselves around. A few "Gritz for President" signs went up by the creek, but were soon taken down, possibly at the behest of Vicki's family.

Bo Gritz talks to reporters and supporters alongside Ruby Creek, Monday, August 31, 1992.

Gritz demanded to speak with special agent in charge Gene Glenn, offering his services as an intermediary. For two days he got no response. Then, on Friday — a full week since the shootout at the Y — Gritz told the assembled reporters and protestors that he was going to make an announcement. Standing on the bridge, he read aloud from a "citizen's arrest warrant," charging Glenn, along with the governor of Idaho, the head of the Marshals Service, and the director of the FBI, with the murder of Samuel Weaver. Since nobody was there to accept his warrant, Gritz, sweating in the hot sun, placed it on the bridge under a rock. "Consider yourself served," he bellowed, to applause and whooping from the crowd.

————————

Randy, who had been quiet since the frustrating encounter with Marnis on Thursday, heard about the citizen's arrest over the radio. Early Friday evening, he yelled, "I want to talk to Bo Gritz in person!" This time the authorities heard him, and his demand fell on receptive ears. By then, the FBI's behavioral scientist had written a memo proposing the use of a "third party" negotiator — someone without any connection to the government that the Weavers regarded as an instrument of the Antichrist.

Glenn ushered Gritz under the yellow police tape and up to the command post in Homicide Meadow. Gritz quickly convinced Glenn that he could talk to Randy, Green Beret to Green Beret.

At dusk, Gritz was driven up to the cabin. After unsuccessfully trying to communicate through a bullhorn, he climbed down from the APC and approached the Weavers' home on foot. Stopping a few yards short of the porch, he asked if everyone inside was okay. Randy shouted back that Vicki had been dead since Saturday, and that he and Kevin were both shot. Randy also explained how he and the girls had come to hate and distrust the voice of the negotiator Fred Lanceley, who had continued to direct his appeals to Vicki, unwittingly hardening the family's resolve to neither communicate nor surrender.

Shocked by the news about Vicki, Gritz offered to remove her body, but Randy and the girls refused to let him inside. They also refused his suggestion that they pick up the siege phone. They told him they needed to pray on it.

Gritz returned to the meadow to debrief the FBI commanders. According to the FBI, this was the first time that anyone in the meadow learned of Vicki's death. A subsequent review of notes and interviews with scores of personnel on the scene turned up no evidence that anyone outside the cabin knew that Vicki had been shot six days earlier. If the feds engaged in a conspiracy of silence about Vicki's death, they did a remarkable job covering it up.

Having briefed the FBI, Gritz and Glenn went together to break the news about Vicki to the Jordison family. They were devastated and baffled. How had the FBI not known that one of its snipers had killed someone? Gritz then walked across the bridge to address the protestors and the press.

The crowd, visibly relieved to have one of their own appearing to take charge, pressed in close. Behind Gritz, the police at the roadblock seemed to brace for something, perking up and spreading out across the width of the bridge.

Gritz told the crowd that negotiations would continue "at first light" and that a resolution was in sight. He went on, saying, "There's some bad news." By then, it was dark out and getting cold. Standing in the glare of floodlights and news cameras, Gritz told everyone to huddle together and hold hands, adding, "That's an order." He explained that Kevin had been badly wounded on Saturday, but that Randy and the girls were all right. "Yahweh is taking care of him," he said. Then, telling everyone to "get a grip on yourself," he said, "Vicki was killed."

The reporters, clustered around Gritz with notebooks and microphones, gasped in shock. The crowd behind them unraveled. Several people began to wail. Judy Grider, trembling with some combination of grief and rage, corralled a group of women into a line facing the police on the bridge. The women linked arms. In her hoarse smoker's voice, Judy, wearing a black beret, screamed, "We are women of Yah! We are the virtuous women!" Glaring at the police, she added, "You are His enemies!" From further back in the crowd, someone screamed, "We're going to war!" Judy's towering husband, Bill, paced back and forth in front of the bewildered phalanx of officers, as if about to lose the struggle to contain himself. "You're fucking nothing!" he screamed into the faces of the state troopers.

John Bangerter, a Utah skinhead who had been at the bridge all week, walked over to a reporter for the *Los Angeles Times* to offer a sentiment that was becoming general. "I'm ready to get my gun and my clips and take off my safety and pull my trigger with my finger. I don't care anymore. This is the beginning of a revolution, a war." Standing at the edge of the crowd, Vicki's grieving sister Julie was stunned to overhear a friend of Vicki's explain that Vicki, now a martyr to the cause, would want Rachel and Sara to also die for the white race.

During the long night that followed, a local pastor led a prayer circle. He started with talk of peace but wound up shouting: "Arise, O Israel! It is time for war!"

———

The next morning, one week since the day Vicki was shot, Gritz returned to the cabin. This time, he was joined by Vicki's friend Jackie Brown, his associate Jack McLamb, and a local Baptist preacher named Chuck Sandelin. Crossing over to the federally occupied side of the creek for the first time after a week spent keeping vigil at the bridge, Jackie Brown marveled at the scale of the encampment — helicopters, jeeps, ranks of men and women in full uniform, some coming off surveillance shifts with their faces painted and their guns at the ready. *Who*, she wondered, *were they at war with?*

On her way up the hill, Dick Rogers, the hardnosed HRT commander who, for many, had become the face of federal excess, offered Jackie a flak jacket. "Only if I can wear it backwards," she responded.

As the little delegation approached the cabin, Randy shouted for Sandelin to back off, and the preacher parted from the group. Sara, who did not trust Gritz as much as her father did, refused to let him inside the cabin. Instead, Gritz and Randy spoke through a window for several hours, mostly talking politics and religion. Gritz told Randy that Gerry Spence, among the most famous trial lawyers in the country, had made a provisional offer to defend him in court. Gritz explained that Spence, a theatrical attorney who lived in Wyoming and dressed for court like a dry-cleaned Buffalo Bill, had recently gotten Imelda Marcos, the former first lady of the Philippines, off the hook for embezzlement. The promise of such high-end legal assistance seemed to soften Randy up a bit.

Although Sara would not let Gritz or McLamb inside the cabin, she happily opened the door for Jackie Brown. The sight of a familiar and friendly face, a woman who had been so close with Vicki, unleashed a torrent of grief in Sara and Rachel. Jackie handed them a box of fresh fruit and milk. Kevin, who had been smoking Randy's dry Top tobacco all week, asked Jackie for some of her Camels. Gritz and Jackie offered to remove Vicki's body from the cabin, but the girls would not allow it. It was Saturday, their Sabbath. It would not be right. They needed more time to pray.

Whispering for fear of listening devices, Sara slipped Jackie the testimonial they had written four days earlier. Worried that Jackie would be searched on her way off the mountain, Sara folded the sheets of yellow legal paper into a maxipad, which Jackie put in her underwear.

When it was time for the small delegation to return down the hill, Sara asked Jackie to stop in the lower garden and pick a bunch of cabbages she knew to be ready for harvest. She asked Jackie to share them with the people at the bridge. Borrowing a knife from a skeptical FBI agent, Jackie cut as many heads as she could carry. As if imparting a sacrament, she passed out the cabbages to the protestors and announced that the Weavers wanted the whole crowd "to partake." Once she was finally alone with her husband, Jackie removed Sara's hidden note and told him to make photocopies for distribution to the crowd and the press.

The next morning, Gritz, McLamb, and Jackie returned to the cabin. Speaking through a window, Gritz explained that Kevin, who was still coughing up blood, was the only witness to the original shootout besides the marshals. They needed him to survive to tell his story in court. Gritz further explained that if the twenty-four-year-old were to die now, for lack of basic medical care, Randy might be held liable. Sara, still convinced that anyone who stepped outside would be shot, pleaded with Kevin not to leave. At this, Gritz lost his cool, ordering "Randall," as he called him, to be a man and get control of his family.

Gritz stepped away to consult with an FBI medic about Harris's condition. Jaundiced and weakened by a raging infection, the man was in obvious need of a hospital. Gritz also dispatched McLamb to get assurances from the FBI that they would back off a bit if Kevin were to come out.

By late morning, everyone inside the cabin agreed that Kevin should surrender. Rising shakily from the couch, he stepped outside. After sitting for a bit on the porch to catch his breath, Gritz and McLamb helped him onto a stretcher, which they carried to a medic tent at the FBI's forward command post. There, he was given an IV and fresh dressings on his arm and chest. A few minutes later, he was on a helicopter bound for the hospital in Spokane.

With Kevin gone, Randy and the girls finally agreed to the removal of Vicki's body, which had been lying in the kitchen for a week. Around six that evening, Gritz and Jackie came to the cabin with a soft, navy-blue body bag. With Randy's help, they eased Vicki into the bag and Gritz set it on a cot on the porch. Promising not to let the body touch the ground, Gritz and Jackie carried Vicki down the steps while Rachel and Sara wept and shouted goodbyes to their mother. Gritz slung the bag over his shoulder and carried it to a waiting Humvee.

Jackie then returned to the cabin with buckets of water, rags, and paper towels to clean up the mess where her friend had lain. Refusing to let the girls help, she scooped up chunks of skull and brain, tossing them outside. Then she mopped up a puddle of congealed blood, and scrubbed the floor with lemon-scented ammonia. Jackie later claimed that, so long as it was still inside the cabin, Vicki's body gave off no odor, a fact she attributes to divine intervention. (Agents on the scene reported otherwise.) Jackie joined Vicki's body in the waiting Humvee for the ride down the hill, simultaneously evacuating the Weavers' parakeets on her lap.

With Kevin and Vicki out of the cabin and the door open to the fresh air for the first time since the previous Saturday, the FBI and Gritz hoped to capitalize on the newfound sense of momentum. Randy, however, said that they needed more time. Sara remained confident that they would be killed if they stepped outside. She had spent most of her life steeped in her parents' ideas about ZOG and the Tribulation. The nightmarish, traumatizing week in the cabin had only hardened those beliefs. Besides, the departure of Kevin and the removal of her mother's body lent a new degree of finality to everything that had already been lost. Sara and Rachel spent another night in prayer and tears.

———————

Late Monday morning, ten days after the shootout at the Y, Gritz and McLamb set off again for the cabin. They both wore FBI wires, a fact that, if discovered, would have scandalized the crowd by the creek and destroyed their credibility with the surviving Weavers.

Now that some progress had been made, the Hostage Rescue Team was getting impatient with the Weavers' refusal to take the next step. The family kept insisting that they needed more time, but nobody could understand to what end. Plus, there were still a lot of loaded guns lying around the cabin, not to mention an infant and a man with a warrant for murder.

In case Randy still refused to budge, the HRT, along with Gritz and McLamb, had concocted a plan. Gritz would say the word "Alaska" into the mic hidden behind the sunglasses in his breast pocket and then tackle Randy. At the same moment, McLamb would grab Rachel and Sara, restraining them before they could raise their guns. Armed agents would then storm the cabin.

Naturally, Gritz hoped he could simply talk Randy and his daughters into coming outside. As the two negotiators approached the cabin, Randy shouted through the window that he and the girls had decided not to surrender. They had spent the night in prayer and Yahweh wanted them to remain in the cabin until the Feast of the Trumpets, which was weeks away. "We're going to stay here," Sara shouted. Randy added, "They can kill us if they have to."

Unlike the day before, they refused to even open the door for Gritz and McLamb, which ruled out the "Alaska" plan. Having already glimpsed their own martyrdom, maybe Randy and the girls could not envision any other way forward. Perhaps the idea of surrendering had come to seem like a betrayal of Sam and Vicki. After years of expectation, they had been dealt a sort of half apocalypse. It was not clear what should come next. If they surrendered now, what had any of it been for?

In his conversations with the FBI the previous evening, Gritz had gotten the impression that, failing a surrender that day, a raid was likely. The operation was costing a lot of money — a million dollars a day, by one estimate. More significantly, three people, including a federal agent, were dead. There was evidence to collect, arrests to make, and an investigation to commence. The FBI was losing faith that a negotiated outcome was even possible. For ten days — most of it spent in confounding silence — the Weavers had made no demands or given any indication that they would ever come out.

Gritz and McLamb stepped onto the back porch. Inflamed by the family's reckless course of action, Gritz hectored Randy, although he was now convinced that it was Sara who, in Vicki's absence, was calling the shots.

The day before, down by the creek, McLamb had approached a group of Las Vegas skinheads whom the Weavers knew and liked. McLamb asked them to sign a letter he had written encouraging Randy to surrender. (Many of the skinheads wanted Randy to fight on, and

McLamb may have forged a few names.) Now, with Randy insisting that they were not coming out, Gritz slid the letter under the door.

A group of skinhead protestors near Ruby Creek Bridge on August 28, 1992.

Randy read the note, and his mood seemed to shift. He opened the door a crack. Of all the messages that had been carried up to the cabin from family and friends, it is not obvious why this letter from the skinheads had such an effect. Perhaps the encouragement of such true believers felt like permission. By urging Randy to take his fight to court, the letter managed to put a heroic spin on surrender. Maybe Randy was just ready to give himself up and needed a nudge. Or maybe it had something to do with the fact that one of the letter's signatories was David Cooper, the skinhead from Las Vegas who would become Sara's closest confidant after the siege and her eventual husband.

Standing on the porch, Gritz and McLamb offered a fresh batch of assurances. They would personally keep the Weavers safe until they were off the mountain. They would all walk down arm in arm. There would be no handcuffs. Gritz pledged to stand with the family during their coming legal ordeal. (As it turned out, Gerry Spence's defense strategy would depend on keeping characters like Bo Gritz as far from the courthouse as possible.)

Randy retreated inside for a whispered family meeting. Just after noon on Monday, August 31, 1992, Randy, Sara, and Rachel all agreed to come out. They put Elisheba in a fresh diaper and a white romper. For the first time in over a week, Rachel and Sara unbuckled their gun belts. Randy set down Sam's rifle, which he had been carrying since the previous Saturday. They gathered up a few keepsakes. Randy, who was wearing faded jeans and a black T-shirt, slipped Gritz his Aryan Nations belt buckle for safekeeping. They tidied up the cabin a bit and took a last look around.

Randy stepped outside first, holding Elisheba in his good arm. (Cynical HRT officers figured that the baby was meant to serve as a shield.) With his other hand, Randy clutched Bo Gritz. After a week spent lying in the darkened cabin with a bullet wound, he looked gaunt and pale, his normally clean-shaven head and face both showing ten days' growth of stubble.

Sara and Rachel came out next, each holding one of Jack McLamb's hands. Sara, in a black leather jacket, had pulled her hair into a tight ponytail. Her mother's ruby wedding ring hung on a chain around her neck. Stepping onto the porch and blinking in the sunlight, she stiffened, awaiting the inevitable gunfire. "Unbelievably," she later recalled, "I heard nothing."

Randy was led to a medical tent and put on a stretcher. His wound was cleaned and his fingertips swabbed for evidence.

Rachel, Sara, and Elisheba climbed into a jeep that took them to the bottom of the ridge for the first time in a year and a half. In the familiar quiet meadow where they had often played, they saw the vast force that had piled up at the foot of their mountain. "It looked like a scene out of an army movie," Sara marveled. "There were guys walking around in their shorts like they had just been on a camping trip. And all for us. It made no sense."

Federal agents and members of the media outside the Weaver cabin in the aftermath of the standoff, September 1, 1992.

The sisters were escorted to a waiting helicopter so they could say goodbye to their dad, who would be flown first to Sandpoint, and then loaded onto a jet for Boise, to visit a hospital on his way to booking at the Ada County Jail, where he would await trial.

Once Randy was in the air, the girls climbed into a van with their grandparents, David and Jeane Jordison. They drove out of the meadow and down to the blacktop by the bridge. Passing through the crowd of protestors, they saw a lot of familiar faces.

As they drove away, investigators swarmed up the ridge, documenting the cabin, the Y, and the surrounding woods. Reporters followed close behind. The Weavers' mountaintop cabin, the realization of a vision that had come to Vicki a decade earlier back in Iowa, was now a crime scene. The Weavers' guns were laid out in the sun on a tarp for the news photographers.

In a motel room in Sandpoint, the girls and their grandparents, as well as Vicki's younger siblings Julie and Lanny, ordered a pizza and watched footage of Randy being taken into custody on the TV.

The next day—despite intense resistance from Sara, who wanted to remain in the place where her mother and brother had died, and among people who saw the world the way she did—the three Weaver girls boarded their first airplane and flew back to Iowa.

SLIPPING INTO THE FUTURE

AFTER THE SIEGE came the words: a great, ceaseless cataract of language. There were poems and ballads, sermons and slogans, apologetics, pamphlets, newsletters, and editorials by the yard. There were a few nakedly conspiratorial books, some excellent newspaper journalism, and one deeply reported account of the whole affair (Jess Walter's *Every Knee Shall Bow*). Some of the most influential words were of the official variety: depositions, opening statements, affidavits, cross-examinations, sworn testimony. With each retelling, the confused, many-sided muddle clarified and hardened, as if under the geological weight of myth and narrative. The participants were rendered characters, the events made parable. It is a special misfortune to become a stand-in — for your private suffering to become a metonym for some larger phenomenon. That is precisely what happened to the Weavers. (The preceding pages are one more contribution to that misfortune.)

———————

The first to have his say was Bo Gritz. Randy was still airborne on a gurney and the girls had not yet reached their pizza when Gritz ambled to the bridge and inclined his sweaty brow toward a bouquet of waiting microphones. For the protestors assembled before him, relief mixed with an edgy mood of unspent fury. Neither apocalypse nor civil war had broken out. Some diehards would linger by the creek for days, as if unable to resume doing whatever they had been doing before they came to the place that some were calling Weaver Mountain.

Addressing the crowd, Col. Gritz graciously shared his laurels with the Almighty, claiming that God had shown him a vision of things ending exactly as they had. From there he drifted into something like a campaign speech, talking about federal perfidy and commonsense governance, setting a pattern by which the tragedy would become fodder for a newly energized brand of conspiratorial, anti-federal populism. Glancing up at the skinheads whose letter had helped nudge Randy toward surrender, Gritz interrupted himself to offer a coy *Sieg Heil*. "[Randy] told me to give you guys a salute, and said that you knew what that is."

In the years to come, Gritz would use his rising profile on the far right to tend the thicket of conspiracism that grew up around the Weaver affair. Among many other things, he alleged that HRT sniper Lon Horiuchi intentionally killed Vicki because the FBI knew that she was the strength of the family. Wanted posters bearing Horiuchi's image began popping up on telephone poles around the country. To this day, his name sometimes appears online as a cryptic two-word comment, the implied message being: "Need we say any more about the government of these United States?"

In its exhaustive analysis of the case, the DOJ concluded that Horiuchi's first shot was "reasonable," given the confusing (and legally indefensible) rules of engagement he had been given. The second shot, however, was taken when the armed people in his scope were obviously retreating. That shot, according to the DOJ review, did not meet the legal standard of "objective reasonableness."

In a separate, deeply flawed internal investigation performed by the FBI itself, the Bureau claimed that Horiuchi was not even acting under the novel "can and should" rules of engagement when he took his two shots. Both shots (taken in theoretical defense of the helicopter) were, according to the FBI, justified under the normal guidelines. Five years later, a Boundary County prosecutor sought unsuccessfully to try Horiuchi for manslaughter.

In the meantime, just two months after the surrender, Pete Peters, the Identity preacher who had been among those who first encouraged Gritz to intervene, called an emergency meeting of far-right leaders at a YMCA in Estes Park, Colorado. William Pierce, of *Turner Diaries* fame, was there, as were Richard Butler, the Trochmanns, Jim Wickstrom of the Posse Comitatus, and Louis Beam of the Klan. Their stated purpose was to channel the public's outrage about Ruby Ridge into their vision of a new American revolution. Like Gritz's speech at the bridge, the meeting helped codify a politically useful version of what had happened that August. Erstwhile heroes like Gordon Kahl and Bob Mathews could be consigned to a dusty shelf. The needless deaths of a beautiful white woman and her little boy were far more compelling. As Beam put it, Sam and Vicki were victims of "the tender mercies of a government gone mad." In the flurry of organizing that followed, Beam — a longtime Klansman, Identity believer, and far-right leader — cast himself in the role of an ordinary citizen who had been shaken from his slumber by the events in North Idaho.

In their martyrdom, the Weavers were transformed from vigilant watchers for a global conspiracy into hard evidence of its existence — saints of circumstance, beatified by the calamity that had landed upon their heads. "The blood of these innocent ones, like a prism, makes everything clear," proclaimed Beam. "Someday, without a signal from anyone — yet, as if a signal had come from everyone — [men] will walk quickly out their front doors with a look of grim determination on their faces... It will happen nationwide. Ten thousand Randy Weavers are spread out from one coast to another."

The meeting in Estes Park, which became known as the Rocky Mountain Rendezvous, generated a report charging the federal government with "genocide," and calling for diffuse paramilitarism and "leaderless resistance." The Colorado gathering is commonly cited as the founding conclave of the modern militia movement, which would, by the mid-1990s, swell to include five million Americans. It is easy to overstate the importance of the meeting, which was more representative than historical—but it was another pang of something new being born.

While the far right made energetic use of the Weaver story, mainstream conservatives adapted it for their own purposes. For starters, the religious and racial elements of the tragedy would be played down. Through sheer repetition, it became canonical that the Weavers' connection to the white power movement was just a slander cooked up by the press. Ruby Ridge would gradually become a story about gun rights, the evils of big government, and the outer limits of free speech.

———

Next came the trial, which commenced on April 13, 1993. Along with several lesser crimes, Randy and Kevin were charged with the murder of Deputy Marshal William Degan. What followed in the US District Court in Boise was like a bloodless version of the siege: it went on forever, the feds overreached badly, and Randy and Kevin kept their silence. Over the course of more than two months, the government called fifty-four witnesses. Practically everyone even remotely connected to the case took a turn in the dock.

Randy and Kevin each had their own lawyer, but their fates and their defense were effectively united. As Gritz had promised during the siege, Randy was represented by the celebrity litigator Gerry Spence. With his fringe jackets and ten-gallon Stetson, Spence was like a cowboy Johnnie Cochran, laying on the down-home panache and placing himself—rather than his less than lovable client—at the center of things. He tried the case simultaneously in the courtroom and the press, giving frequent statements on the courthouse steps. Kevin was represented by the less-experienced but equally effective David Nevin, who took the case for the opportunity to work alongside Spence. (Nevin would go on to an illustrious career, representing, among other notables, Khalid Sheik Mohammed, the chief planner of the 9/11 attacks.)

Randy and Vicki had spent two decades spinning conspiracy out of prophecy. In Boise, the US Attorney tried to do the same. The government accused Weaver of a long-range criminal conspiracy to trigger a confrontation with the government. The family's well-documented history of violent prophecies — telling a reporter in Cedar Falls in '83 about the need to establish a "kill zone" against future attack; the affidavit from '85 alleging that Randy was going to be forced into an "assault on a federal official" — were marshaled as evidence that this was where the Weavers had been aiming all along. "If there was no persecution," prosecutor Kim Lindquist told the jury, "the core of their religion would have been false, a fallacy." By this logic, Randy and Kevin were not just responsible for the death of William Degan, but also for the deaths of Sam and Vicki, too.

While the government tried to keep the jurors focused on the family's reckless provocations, Spence and Nevin found a more compelling story — less a defense of Randy and Kevin than an indictment of the feds, most specifically for revising the standard rules of engagement outside of any established process. Given the fact that Ruby Ridge would become a rallying cry for those who talk about shrinking the government until it can be drowned in a bathtub, it is a sad irony that a few extra layers of red tape, a bit more going by the book, might have averted much of the fiasco.

By expanding the case in every possible direction, the government's conspiracy charge allowed the defense to talk about whatever they wanted. Spence found endless opportunities to sow doubt in the prosecution's version of the initial gun sale, the shootout at the Y, and the two shots on Saturday that killed Vicki and wounded the men. As Spence told it, the government had entrapped Randy to make him a snitch and then, when that failed, they murdered three people to cover it all up. (Entrapment is a defense, not a verdict. No court could rule that Randy had been entrapped, but that was Spence's main argument regarding the gun sale and the jury found Randy not guilty on that charge.) Mostly, Spence talked about a dead boy and his mother, a lovely, god-fearing woman shot through the jaw with a baby in her arms. He also spent a surprising amount of time on Striker, referring to the yellow Lab as "Old Yeller," and badgering Deputy Marshal Larry Cooper about whether or not the dog had done anything illegal before being shot. Randy, who had not been accused of shooting anyone and was now left alone with his grief and three traumatized daughters, looked far more like a victim than a reckless hothead.

Apparently confident that the death of a US marshal at the hands of heavily armed racist zealots would yield a guilty verdict, the FBI hamstrung the prosecution with a high-handed reluctance to turn over evidence, including a post-operation sketch done by Lon Horiuchi that seemed to indicate that he knew someone was standing behind the cabin door when he fired at Harris. The late appearance of the sketch and various other documents made it clear to the jury that the government was not acting in good faith.

In the backwash of such an inflammatory disaster, the federal government reverted to its default position of operating like the opposite of an all-seeing cabal, with the relevant agencies working at cross purposes, refusing to share information with each other, and commencing a yearslong effort to dodge accountability. As the jury looked on, judge Edward Lodge repeatedly reprimanded the prosecution for being stingy with evidence, although the fault was mostly with the FBI, not the US Attorney. For their part, Spence and Nevin did such a good job cross-examining the government's endless parade of witnesses that the two defense attorneys took a bold gamble: resting their case without presenting any evidence, putting their clients in the dock, or calling a single witness.

For all the theatrics and conspiratorial insinuations offered by the defense, the most important fact was that Randy, despite his obvious role in generating the situation, had not shot anyone. As for Kevin, nobody could reasonably blame him for creating the volatile standoff, and it was obvious that he only fired his gun in self-defense and to protect Sam.

Given the ravenous media scrutiny surrounding the case, the jury was heavily sequestered. Their conclusion was hardly foregone. Deliberations stretched on longer than the siege itself. Opposing factions formed, collapsed, and reformed.

When the twelve jurors finally emerged, Randy and Kevin were acquitted of everything except Randy's original failure to appear. The time he had already served while awaiting trial (fourteen months) accounted for most of that penalty. A supporter paid his fine.

On July 8, 1993, four months after the trial began (and three and a half years since the day Randy and Vicki vowed to "remain separated"), Randy and Kevin were free men. The surviving Weavers then sued the federal government, settling for $3.1 million in damages (with no admission of wrongdoing on the part of the feds). Kevin received a separate $380,000 settlement. Between the cost of surveillance, the siege, the trial, and the settlements, the whole affair cost American taxpayers about five and a half million dollars — plus the four hundred bucks that the ATF gave Randy for the two shotguns.

———

Perhaps the most significant event of the trial occurred sixteen hundred miles to the south of the Boise courthouse, just outside of Waco, Texas. News of a deadly conflagration at Mount Carmel, the compound of a religious group known as the Branch Davidians, broke on day five of the Weaver and Harris trial, right after a long round of testimony from the informant Kenneth Fadeley. The parallels between the two cases are startling. Once again, people who believed that the prophecies in Revelation were being fulfilled in their own time caught the attention of the ATF by illegally modifying guns. Like the Weavers, the Davidians dabbled in Hebraic customs and regarded the US government as the Babylon of prophecy. (Notably, there was no racial or antisemitic element to the Davidians' faith. Their church, which can be traced all the way back to the Millerite movement of the nineteenth century, was quite diverse.) While the Davidians disagreed with the Weavers on various theological matters, their leader, who called himself David Koresh, told his flock that Ruby Ridge might be a dress rehearsal for what was coming for them.

As with the Weaver standoff, the fifty-one-day siege in Waco seemed—to those on the inside—like the obvious fulfillment of prophecy. Whereas Vicki claimed prophetic vision, Vernon Howell, the man who anointed himself Koresh, said that he was the lamb foretold in Revelation, the one who will break the seals on the book of history, triggering Armageddon. Once again, federal tacticians failed to understand the ways in which apocalyptic faith drove the siege. In both cases, the only way the feds could have better performed their assigned role was if they had Sharpie'd "666" onto their helmets. At Waco, one FBI negotiator thought that the "seven seals" Koresh kept talking about had to do with amphibious mammals.

If, as many would later claim, the ATF's aggressive approach at Waco—attempting to raid the compound in search of automatic weapons, rather than just arresting Koresh on one of his occasional jogs—was an effort to save face after the fiasco in Idaho, it backfired badly. The Davidians were tipped off about the impending raid. When agents arrived to serve their warrant and search the property, a gunfight broke out. Four ATF agents and five Davidians were killed. Once again, the FBI, in the form of Dick Rogers and the HRT, was called in.

Because both sieges centered upon guns and apocalyptic faith, they were instantly connected, especially since, by the time of Waco and the Ruby Ridge trial, a Democrat with modest gun-control ambitions (Bill Clinton) was in the White House. As with the gathering by Ruby Creek, the area outside the FBI's cordon in Waco became a Temporary Autonomous Zone for the far right—a scene of protest, organizing, consciousness-raising, and fellowship. Somewhere in the crowd, a skinny Gulf War vet named Timothy McVeigh sat on the hood of his Chevy sedan, selling bumper stickers and copies of *The Turner Diaries*.

On April 19, 1993, in an effort to drive out the Davidians still inside Mount Carmel, the Hostage Rescue Team pumped the main building full of tear gas, most likely starting the fire that killed seventy-six people, twenty of them children.

Two years later, on the morning of April 19, 1995 — the second anniversary of the Mount Carmel fire and the tenth anniversary of the FBI's raid on the Covenant, Sword, and Arm of the Lord — Timothy McVeigh detonated his fertilizer and diesel bomb in front of the Alfred P. Murrah Federal Building in Oklahoma City. The blast killed 168, including nineteen children. (McVeigh, who had been drifting around on a circuit of gun shows, Christian Patriot gatherings, and Identity communities, was aided in his plan by Terry Nichols and Michael Fortier, like-minded army buddies.) Inspired by *The Turner Diaries*, McVeigh hoped that his bomb would set off a civil war, leading to the overthrow of ZOG and the New World Order.

McVeigh was obsessed with both Ruby Ridge and Waco. For a time, he considered killing Lon Horiuchi. After his arrest, he described the bombing as vengeance for both the Weavers and the Davidians, thereby permanently yoking the two sieges together in the public imagination.

Randy Weaver in Montana in 1996.

After McVeigh's execution, Randy expressed esteem for the bomber, calling him "a soldier's soldier." In 1998, Randy traveled to Waco, where he was greeted by a contingent of militia men and Alex Jones, who was just starting his career as one of America's most successful and pugnacious conspiracy theorists. Walking the grounds with a camera crew, Randy came upon a marker for the ATF agents killed during the initial shoot-out. "I tell you what, boys," he said, "I wouldn't put that one at my place. I have no regrets about them. They was looking for trouble and they found it."

Old age did little to dim Randy's defiance. In a 2018 interview, he was asked if, given the chance, he would do it all over again? "Absolutely," came the reply. "If my wife and son was here today, they would do it again. You know why? Because they are as stiff-necked as I am." He added, apropos of little, "I'd have probably made one hell of a Nazi." The interviewer, an ascendant Montana politician named John Lamb, tried to steer things back to a more palatable version of the Ruby Ridge story, adding, with a nervous chuckle, "This is about freedom for everyone."

After the siege, Sara, Rachel, and Elisheba moved back to Iowa, living first with Vicki's parents in Coalville, then with their aunt Julie and her family. When Randy was released from prison, the younger girls went to live with their dad in Grand Junction, Iowa, while Sara finished up high school. Eventually, they all made their way back to the inland Northwest, settling around Kalispell, Montana. Randy's politics never changed much, but, without Vicki, his faith ebbed. In his later years, he identified as an atheist. Sara, meanwhile, had a son, got divorced, and remarried. Along the way she had a powerful born-again experience and now speaks publicly about her faith. While the younger two girls have guarded their privacy closely, Sara and Randy have both written and spoken extensively about what happened in 1992, collaborating on a book about Ruby Ridge and, in Sara's case, writing a thoughtful memoir. Randy spent much of the decade following the siege out on a circuit of gun shows and patriot gatherings, posing for photographs, giving speeches, and selling books. Occasionally, he even turned up at other standoffs. He died in 2022, at seventy-four.

———————

The tragedy at Ruby Ridge took place in the historical doldrums between the collapse of the Soviet Union and 9/11. It was an era, not unlike our own, when a wave of reactionary populism and the absence of a compelling foreign antagonist turned the conspiratorial gaze inward. In the aftermath of the siege, the line on the American right was that the Weavers were canaries in the coal mine. The New World Order had shown its face. Worse tyranny would surely follow.

As of this writing, three decades have passed since the siege. The federal government has not gone on hunting white fundamentalists. The FEMA camps, black helicopters, and Mark of the Beast tattoos have not yet been activated. The guns and Bibles remain unconfiscated.

On the contrary, in the aftermath of Ruby Ridge and Waco, federal authorities have become far more circumspect in their dealings with white anti-government types. The various agencies involved in Ruby Ridge were all publicly excoriated (with no small amount of bipartisan grandstanding), although the resulting sanctions were minor. At the most basic level, the system worked. Facts were aired, blame was apportioned, and a jury of twelve citizens (plus several committees of voter-beholden representatives) made their judgments. A free press covered every minute of it.

In the twenty-first century, if you want a showdown with the feds, you must bring your long guns to them. And even if you occupy a statehouse or a piece of federal land—as some of those most influenced by Ruby Ridge have done—the government will likely wait you out. LaVoy Finicum, who served as a spokesman for the large gathering of militia types who occupied Oregon's Malheur National Wildlife Refuge in 2016, seemed so intent on some kind of Weaver-like encounter that, in the end, his death looked a lot more like suicide by police than patriotic martyrdom. Finicum had pledged not to be taken alive, and his final words, spoken while grappling for his Ruger after he'd almost run over an FBI agent, were: "Go ahead and shoot me. You're going to have to shoot me!"

In another small, grim aftershock of the Weaver case, something similar happened to Bill and Judy Grider's son Eric. Eric, the childhood playmate of the Weaver kids, had been part of the junior neo-Nazi rally outside the Rau home. He had delivered food to the Weavers during their long period of "separation," and been a big presence at the protest by the bridge. In 2020, after serving a decade in prison for shooting his gun during a tussle with the police in Colorado, Eric was forty-three, living near Detroit, running a dog-training business, and expecting a child with his new wife. When the FBI, monitoring a spike in far-right threats associated with COVID lockdowns in Michigan, tried to serve Eric a warrant for possession of illegal weapons (including a machine gun he had with him in his truck), Eric, who may have been involved in the accelerationist "boogaloo" movement, pulled out a pistol and started firing, wounding one FBI agent before being shot seven times and killed.

———————

Rather than galloping tyranny, what Ruby Ridge portended was a slow-moving ontological crackup—the fracturing of American reality itself. A steadily expanding portion of citizens have come to inhabit a world built upon the same apocalyptic story that sent Randy and Vicki up their mountain. As it becomes increasingly obvious that some measure of shared reality is a civic necessity, Ruby Ridge illustrates what can happen when a group of people live within myths that cannot be reconciled with life in an ever-changing society or the slow, hard work of democratic governance. Apocalyptic faith and the cynical conspiracism it generates can only undermine the high-flown civic promises that stream so gallantly above the republic—producing instead a completely starved sense of possibility. Even if those old promises are merely aspirational, they help knit the whole unwieldy business together. The galvanizing postmillennial notion of a long, triumphal march toward perfection may have been a fiction, but it was a vital one.

In recent years, the distinction between fringe and center has never been blurrier, with prominent officeholders openly talking about a Deep State conspiracy to rig elections, satanic pedophilia rings, a covert war against Christianity, and the galloping approach of some final Storm. In 2023, Sara Weaver said, "I almost feel [that my parents] were thirty years or forty years ahead of their time." While nakedly conspiratorial politics may not have become respectable, something more significant occurred. Respectability became moot.

When, in 2024, the time rolled around for the quadrennial updating of the term *evangelical*, pollsters discovered something that would have seemed nonsensical just one or two cycles earlier. Apparently, for some portion of American Protestants, the self-applied designation *evangelical* no longer connoted baseline attributes like being anti-abortion, revival-focused, or even regularly attending church. *Evangelical* was now being used (most notably by the 80-plus percent of Evangelicals who voted for Donald Trump in 2016, 2020, and 2024) to signify an identity organized around the battle against nebulous forces: secular humanism, wokeism, the Deep State. The reactionary, "battle royale" militancy that endtimes theology began pumping into American churches at the end of the nineteenth century has burned so hot, for so long, that, for some portion of believers, it has scorched out almost everything but a collection of irascible mental gestures which seek to resemble a theology.

In lieu of denominational ministers, many of whom have tried to corral their wandering flocks back into the pews and behind more overtly pious political leaders, a sizable portion of believers today get their theology from social media prophets whose freewheeling, pan-denominational approach echoes the camp meetings and revivals that defined the first and second Great Awakenings, albeit digitally. Many of these prophets blend scripture with conspiratorial politics in ratios that would make Hal Lindsey blush. Tension over whether the Christian faith ought to be led by prophets or bishops goes all the way back to the first century. John of Patmos was firmly in the prophetic camp, revelating freely while some of his contemporaries in the early church insisted that the "prophetic age" had come to a close and that a new "apostolic era" had begun.

Even as premillennial, Darbyite eschatology began to decline in the late twentieth century, with evangelical churches removing the word *dispensationalist* from their creedal statements and websites, the embattled conspiracism and militancy that it ushered into American faith has only seemed to grow stronger. "As a formal school of theology, dispensationalism has sharply declined," wrote *Christianity Today* editor Bonnie Kristan in 2023. "But as a cultural and political force, its influence is stronger than ever... In that sense, we're all dispensationalists now." Just months before his death in 1930, D. H. Lawrence observed the early stages of a process by which the Apocalypse might eclipse the Gospel. "And we realize, to our horror, that this is what we are up against today: not Jesus nor Paul, but John of Patmos."

One last flash of prophecy, this one still pending: In 1838, a twenty-eight-year-old Abraham Lincoln addressed the Young Men's Lyceum in Springfield, Illinois. He spoke in response to an uptick in mob violence, mentioning in particular the brutal lynching of a Black Saint Louis man named Francis McIntosh. The speech is famous for Lincoln's heartening assertion that all the armies of the world, with unlimited funds, and a brilliant commander, could not, in a campaign of a thousand years, "take a drink from the Ohio or make a track on the Blue Ridge." His point being, that if American democracy is to perish from the earth, it must die "by suicide."

Squinting into the distant future, Lincoln imagined a time when a significant portion of Americans would come to regard the government "as their deadliest bane... [and] make a jubilee of the suspension of its operations; and pray for nothing so much, as its total annihilation." It will be at *that* moment, Lincoln speculated, that some American Caesar or Napoleon — a figure whose slouching arrival upon the scene the young lawyer regarded as inevitable — will be able, for no reason loftier than the satisfaction of his own vainglory, to swallow the American experiment whole.

ACKNOWLEDGMENTS

ALEX LITTLEFIELD PROVIDED a degree of hands-on editing that I had always been told no longer existed in book publishing. Without his free-flowing, collaborative intelligence, this would be a very different book.

I am grateful to Ben George for acquiring the book for Little, Brown in the first place. Ben was the first person who thought that my notion of merging the story of Ruby Ridge with a larger narrative about apocalyptic faith might actually work as a book. I am eternally grateful for his help.

Amanda Urban made this entire enterprise possible. She is the reader I strive to keep in mind while at my desk, which is daunting but effective.

Since the research for this book came in large part from contemporaneous newspaper journalism, I am particularly indebted to the reporters and writers who have taken up this subject before me. Head and shoulders above the rest is Jess Walter — a rare combination of deep researcher, sensitive thinker, and graceful writer. Very often, while digging through this material, I imagined that I had finally found something new and illuminating, only to discover that Walter had been there first. His interviews and reporting were absolutely essential to this book.

Much credit belongs to the unnamed and uncredited employees of the US Department of Justice who typed out the massive trove

ACKNOWLEDGMENTS

of dry, imperfect documents that made my research possible. It's an unglamorous business—and they got plenty wrong—but there is something to be said for a government that piles up great heaps of public records. Praise be to the pencil pushers.

I am grateful to Mike Weland for his reporting in 1992, his hospitality in Bonners Ferry, and his example of what a local reporter ought to be. Every town in America needs a Mike Weland.

I learned most of what I know about the bigger ideas in this book from a handful of scholars who have written about fundamentalism, conspiracy culture, white power, and apocalyptic theology—in particular Michael Barkun, Ernest Sandeen, George Marsden, Elaine Pagels, Matthew Avery Sutton, Leo Ribuffo, Gary Wills, Norman Cohn, James Aho, Paul Boyer, Leonard Zeskind, and Daniel Levitas.

Larissa MacFarquhar and Jonah Stern were my first readers, and they provided excellent edits and insights. Alex Blasdel took a fine-toothed editorial comb to the final version of the manuscript, saving me from countless typos, repetitions, and clunky sentences.

Sara Morosi made acquiring images a breeze. Michael Fleming heroically copyedited his way through my idiosyncratic usages. June Park absolutely nailed the cover design. I am grateful to Michael Noon and everyone else at Little, Brown for shepherding my manuscript through production.

An informal guild of artists and musicians helped take care of our kids during the years it took to write this book. No childcare, no book. Thanks and love to Kaitlyn Fitzpatrick, Eva Parr, Jerome Porter, Monique Mouton, Sophie Wood Brinker, Jessica Dean Harrison, Rachel Fäth, and, first among equals, the incomparable Kimberly Hett.

As for those kids, thank you to Ilona and Tijs Jennings for "quietly" eating bunny crackers on the floor while I "did my computer stuff."

I am eternally grateful for the intelligence, editorial acumen, and boon companionship of my wife, Corrine Fitzpatrick. To say I could not have written this book without her would be an absurd understatement.

ILLUSTRATION CREDITS

The Beast with Two Horns Like a Lamb, from "The Apocalypse"
Albrecht Dürer, 1498, from National Gallery of Art

John Nelson Darby
Remember Your Leaders; 1935; Bibles and Christian Treatises

The Late Great Planet Earth
THE LATE GREAT PLANET EARTH, poster art, 1979/Everett Collection

Hal Lindsey in *The Late Great Planet Earth*
"The Late Great Planet Earth," 1978; Robert Amram, Rolf Forsberg; Robert Amram,
    Alan Belkin

John Todd
Spellbound? — Comic #10 (C10)
Art by Fred Carter — © 1978 Chick Publications
Copyright © 1978 by Jack T. Chick

Gordon Kahl, FBI Wanted ad
Old State House Museum Collection

Church of Jesus Christ-Christian Aryan Nation compound
William F. Campbell/Getty Images

Reverend Richard Butler
Bettmann/Getty Contributor

Randy Weaver mugshot
Kootenai County Sheriff's Office

ILLUSTRATION CREDITS

Vicki Weaver surveillance photo
Court Files, *U.S. v. Weaver* in Walter, *Ruby Ridge*, 2002

Arrests in Naples, Idaho
AP Photo/Mason Marsh

Bo Gritz
AP Photo/Gary Stewart

Neo-Nazi protest, August 28, 1992
AP Photo/Gary Stewart

Outside Randy Weaver's home, September 1, 1992
AP Photo/Gary Stewart

Randy Weaver
AP Photo/Jim Mone

BIBLIOGRAPHY

Aho, James. *Far-Right Fantasy: A Sociology of American Religion and Politics.* New York: Routledge, 2016.

———. *The Politics of Righteousness: Idaho Christian Patriotism.* Seattle, WA: University of Washington Press, 1990.

———. *This Thing of Darkness.* Seattle, WA: University of Washington Press, 1994.

Akenson, Donald Harman. *Exporting the Rapture: John Nelson Darby and the Victorian Conquest of North-American Evangelicalism.* Oxford, UK: Oxford University Press, 2018.

Allen, Gary. *None Dare Call It Conspiracy.* Rossmoor, CA: Concord Press, 1971.

Arbanas, Michael. "Friend: Weaver Became Racist." *Idaho Statesman* (Boise), May 15, 1993.

"Aryan Leader Will Still Meet Skinheads Despite Objections by Idaho Mayors." *Deseret News (Salt Lake City, UT)*, January 7, 1989.

Associated Press. "FBI Agent Gets Prison Term for Destroying Ruby Ridge Report," October 11, 1997. "Fugitive Showed No Racism in Iowa High School," August 25, 1992.

———. "Marshals Know He's There But Leave Fugitive Alone," March 12, 1992.

———. "Marshal Slain at Remote Idaho Cabin," August 22, 1992.

———. "Weaver Turned Racist in the West, Friend Says," May 16, 1993.

Barkun, Michael. "Conspiracy Theories and the Occult." In *The Occult World*, ed. Christopher Partridge. London and New York: Routledge, 2015.

———. *A Culture of Conspiracy: Apocalyptic Visions in Contemporary America.* Berkeley, CA: University of California Press, 2013.

———. *Disaster and the Millennium.* New Haven, CT: Yale University Press, 1974.

———. "Divided Apocalypse." *Soundings* 66, no. 3 (Fall 1983).

———. *Religion and the Racist Right: The Origins of the Christian Identity Movement.* Chapel Hill, NC: University of North Carolina Press, 1997.

Belew, Kathleen. *Bring the War Home: The White Power Movement and Paramilitary America*. Cambridge, MA: Harvard University Press, 2018.

Berger, J. M. "Alt History." *The Atlantic*, September 16, 2016.

Berrigan, *The Nightmare of God: The Book of Revelation*. Eugene, OR: Wipf and Stock, 2009.

Blake, William. "A Vision of the Last Judgment." In *The Complete Poetry & Prose of William Blake*, ed. David V. Erdman. New York: Penguin Random House, 1997.

Bloom, Harold. *The American Religion: The Emergence of the Post-Christian Nation*. New York: Simon & Schuster, 1992.

Blythe, William. "The Guru of White Hate." *Rolling Stone*, June 8, 2000.

Bock, Alan W. *Ambush at Ruby Ridge*. New York: Berkley Books, 1996.

Bowman, Matthew. "Everybody Loves Star Wars. But Here Is Why Mormons Especially Love Star Wars." *Washington Post*, December 21, 2015.

Boyer, Paul. *When Time Shall Be No More: Prophecy Belief in Modern American Culture*. Cambridge, MA: Harvard University Press, 1992.

Braun, Karen. "China's U.S. Grain Haul Sparks Backlash to 1972 'Grain Robbery.'" Reuters, January 21, 2021.

Brown, Tony, and Jackie Brown. *The First Canary: The Inside Story of Ruby Ridge and a Decade of Coverup*. Colburn, ID: Big Pine Publishing, 2000.

Burgmaier, Laurel. *The Farm Crisis*. Iowa PBS documentary, 2013.

Burkett, Elinor. *The Right Women: A Journey Through the Heart of Conservative America*. New York: Scribner, 1998.

"Call the Courier." *The (Waterloo, IA) Courier*, March 22, 1983.

"Cedarloo Baptist Church Dedication Set." *The (Waterloo, IA) Courier*, September 8, 1965.

Chambers, Whittaker. "Big Sister Is Watching You." *National Review*, December 28, 1957.

Chandler, Russell. *Doomsday: The End of the World—A View Through Time*. Ann Arbor, MI: Servant Publications, 1993.

"Church Events." *The (Waterloo, IA) Courier*, March 11, 1983.

Coates, James. *Armed and Dangerous: The Rise of the Survivalist Right*. New York: Farrar, Straus and Giroux, 1987.

———. "Standoff with Police Enters Second Year." *Chicago Tribune*, March 15, 1992.

Cohn, Norman. *The Pursuit of the Millennium*. Oxford, UK: Oxford University Press, 1970.

Cole, Michelle. "Weaver Isn't on a Crusade." *Idaho Statesman* (Boise), September 4, 1995.

Conley, Cort. *Idaho Loners: Hermits, Solitaires, and Individualists*. Cambridge, ID: Backeddy Books, 1984.

Corcoran, James. *Bitter Harvest: Gordon Kahl and the Posse Comitatus: Murder in the Heartland*. New York: Viking, 1990.

Crothers, Lane. *Rage on the Right*. Lanham, MD: Rowan & Littlefield, 2019.

Cummins, Cathy. "Fugitive Won't Budge, Friends Say." *The (Waterloo, IA) Courier*, August 27, 1992.

Davis, Mike. *City of Quartz: Excavating the Future in Los Angeles.* London, New York: Verso, 2018.

Day, Meagan. "Welcome to Hayden Lake, Where White Supremacists Tried to Build Their Homeland." *Medium*, November 4, 2016.

Dickey, Colin. *Under the Eye of Power: How Fear of Secret Societies Shapes American Democracy.* New York: Viking, 2023.

Didion, Joan. *The White Album.* New York: Farrar, Straus and Giroux, 1979.

Dundon, Dan. "Hang Gliding Man Fulfills Quest to Fly." *The (Waterloo, IA) Courier*, March 27, 1977.

———. "Survivalists Make Plans for Time of 'Great Tribulation.'" *The (Waterloo, IA) Courier*, January 9, 1983.

Dunn, Ashley. "Mountain Standoff." *Los Angeles Times*, August 28, 1992.

Ehrman, Bart D. *Jesus: Apocalyptic Prophet of the New Millennium.* Oxford, UK: Oxford University Press, 1999.

Eller, Donnelle, and Gwyne Skinner. "White Supremacy Group Has Waterloo Members." *Northern Iowan*, November 8, 1985.

Ferris, Kirby. *A Mountain of Lies: The Apprehension and Arrest of Idaho's Randy Weaver.* Stinson Beach, CA: Rapid Lightning Press, 1993.

Fitzgerald, Frances. *The Evangelicals: The Struggle to Shape America.* New York: Simon & Schuster, 2017.

Flynn, Kevin, and Gary Gerhardt. *The Silent Brotherhood: Inside America's Racist Underground.* New York: Macmillan, 1989.

Foster, J. Todd, and Bill Morlin. "Weaver Discusses Surrender at Ruby Ridge." *Spokesman-Review* (Spokane, WA), August 29, 1992.

Fowler, Veronica. "Ultra-Right Farm Groups Taking Root." *Des Moines Register*, September 29, 1985.

Frazier, Ian. "Grim Reapers." *New York Review of Books*, February 9, 2023.

Fuson, Ken, and Marie McCartan. "After the Showdown." *Des Moines Sunday Register*, September 13, 1992.

Gibbs, Nancy. "Apocalypse Now." *Time*, July 1, 2002.

Gibson, James William. *Warrior Dreams: Paramilitary Culture in Post-Vietnam America.* New York: Farrar, Straus and Giroux, 1994.

Goodman, Barak. *Ruby Ridge: Every Knee Shall Bow.* PBS documentary in *American Experience* series, 2023.

Grafton, Anthony. "The Millennia-old History of the Apocalypse." *The New Republic*, July 15, 2014.

Graham, Ruth, and Charles Homans. "Trump Is Connecting with a Different Kind of Evangelical Voter." *New York Times*, January 8, 2024.

Green, Larry. "Seeds of Discontent." *Los Angeles Times*, June 1, 1987.

Guinn, Jeff. *Waco: David Koresh, the Branch Davidians, and a Legacy of Rage.* New York: Simon & Schuster, 2023.

Hamm, Mark S. *Apocalypse in Oklahoma: Waco and Ruby Ridge Revenged.* Boston, MA: Northeastern University Press, 1997.

Herbers, John. "Armageddon View Prompts a Debate." *New York Times*, October 24, 1984.

Hofstadter, Richard. *The Paranoid Style in American Politics and Other Essays.* Cambridge, MA: Harvard University Press, 1996.

Hummel, Daniel G. *The Rise and Fall of Dispensationalism: How the Evangelical Battle over the End Times Shaped a Nation.* Grand Rapids, MI: Eerdmans, 2023.

"An Idaho Resort Town Grapples with Bigotry and Bombings." *Chicago Tribune*, October 5, 1986.

Jackson, Jeffrey. *Death & Taxes.* Documentary film, 1993.

Jess, Fred. "ETC." *Bee and Herald* (Jefferson, IA), August, 1983.

Johnson, Denis. "The Militia in Me." *Esquire*, July 1, 1995.

Katz, David S., and Richard H. Popkin. *Messianic Revolution: Radical Religious Politics to the End of the Second Millennium.* New York: Farrar, Straus and Giroux, 1998.

Keating, Kevin. "FBI Sniper Can't Be Tried." *Spokesman-Review* (Spokane, WA), November 1, 1997.

Kermode, Frank. *The Sense of an Ending: Studies in the Theory of Fiction.* Oxford, UK: Oxford University Press, 1966.

Keyes, David. "Weavers Inspire Hate and Admiration." *Bonner County (Idaho) Daily Bee*, August 27, 1992.

Kirban, Salem. *Satan's Angels Exposed.* Huntingdon Valley, PA: Salem Kirban, Inc., 1980.

Kitchener, Caroline, and Abdallah Fayya. "History Is Testing Evangelicals. Again." *The Atlantic*, March 14, 2018.

Knickerbocker, Brad. "Why a 1992 Shooting in Idaho Has Become a Rallying Point." *Christian Science Monitor*, September 5, 1995.

Kristian, Bonnie. "The Surprising Power of Dispensationalism." *Christianity Today*, August 8, 2023.

Lamy, Philip. *Millennium Rage: Survivalists, White Supremacists, and the Doomsday Prophecy.* New York: Plenum Press, 1996.

LaRock, Christopher A. *John Todd: Beyond the Legend* (private publication), 2011.

Lawrence, D. H. *Apocalypse.* New York: Viking, 1982.

Lees, James H., and S. W. Beyer. "History of Coal Mining in Iowa." *Iowa Geological Survey Annual Report* 19, no. 1 (1909). https://doi.org/10.17077/2160 -5270.1149.

Levitas, Daniel. *The Terrorist Next Door: The Militia Movement and the Radical Right.* New York: St. Martin's Press, 2002.

Lewis, Sinclair. *Elmer Gantry.* New York: Penguin Books, 1967.

Lindsey, Hal. *The Late Great Planet Earth.* Grand Rapids, MI: Zondervan, 1970.

———. *The 1980's: Countdown to Armageddon.* King of Prussia, PA: Westgate Press, 1980.

———. *There's a New World Coming.* Eugene, OR: Harvest House Publishers, 1984.

Lippman, Walter. *Drift and Mastery: An Attempt to Diagnose the Current Unrest.* New York: Mitchell Kennerley, 1914.

Lobsinger, Caroline. "County Postpones School Opening Day." *Bonner County (Idaho) Daily Bee*, August 27, 1992.

MacFarquhar, Neil. "From the Past, a Chilling Warning about the Extremists of the Present." *New York Times*, May 1, 2021.

Maddow, Rachel. *Prequel: An American Fight Against Fascism.* New York: Penguin Random House, 2023.

Mallon, Thomas. "Possessed." *The New Yorker*, November 1, 2009.

Marsden, George M. *Fundamentalism and American Culture.* Oxford, UK: Oxford University Press, 2006.

Martin, William. "Waiting for the End." *The Atlantic*, June 2, 1982.

McCarthy, Colman. "Chill in Iowa." *Washington Post*, October 12, 1984.

McGinn, Bernard. *Anti-Christ: Two Thousand Years of the Human Fascination with Evil.* New York: Columbia University Press, 1999.

McLean, Mike, and Caroline Lobsinger. "Weavers' Son Found Dead." *Bonner County (Idaho) Daily Bee*, August 25, 1992.

Miller, Dean. "Boundary Sheriff Candidate Opposed to Mixed Marriages." *Spokesman-Review* (Spokane, WA), May 21, 1988.

———. "Court Hears Ex-Friend's Testimony." *Spokesman-Review* (Spokane, WA), May 19, 1993.

———. "Sheriff's Race Focus of Primary." *Spokesman-Review* (Spokane, WA), May 21, 1988.

Morlin, Bill. "ATF Informer Says FBI's Spy Blew His Cover." *Spokesman-Review* (Spokane, WA), September 9, 1995.

———. "Feds Foiled Aryan Plot." *Spokesman-Review* (Spokane, WA), July 27, 1994.

———. "Feds Have Fugitive 'Under Our Nose.'" *Spokesman-Review* (Spokane, WA), March, 8, 1992.

———. "Marshal Killed Weaver's Son at Ruby Ridge, Tests Confirm Bullet Came from Federal Agent's Gun, Says Sheriff." *Spokesman-Review* (Spokane, WA), October 23, 1997.

Nash, Roderick Frazier. *Wilderness and the American Mind.* New Haven, CT: Yale University Press, 1967.

O'Leary, Stephen D. *Arguing the Apocalypse: A Theory of Millennial Rhetoric.* Oxford, UK: Oxford University Press, 1994.

"One Marshal Dead, Others Confront Fugitive in Idaho." *New York Times*, August 23, 1992.

Ostling, Richard. "Religion: Armageddon and the End Times." *Time*, November 5, 1984.

Ostling, Richard N., and Joan K. Ostling. *Mormon America: The Power and the Promise.* New York: HarperCollins, 1999.

Pagels, Elaine. *Revelations: Visions, Prophecy, and Politics in the Book of Revelation.* New York: Viking, 2012.

Perlstein, Rick. "I Thought I Understood the American Right. Trump Proved Me Wrong." *New York Times Magazine*, April 11, 2017.

Pew Research Center. "Section 3: War, Terrorism, and Global Trends." June 22, 2010. https://www.pewresearch.org/politics/2010/06/22/section-3-war-terrorism-and-global-trends/.

Pierce, William Luther. *The Turner Diaries.* National Alliance publication, 1978. https://archive.org/details/turner-diaries_202402.

Plowman, Edward E. "The Legend(s) of John Todd." *Christianity Today*, February 2, 1979.

Public Religion Research Institute. "Understanding QAnon's Connection to American Politics, Religion, and Media Consumption." May 5, 2021. https://prri.org/research/qanon-conspiracy-american-politics-report/.

Reed, Christopher. "White Supremacy Fights On in the Rockies." *The Guardian*, August 31, 1992.

Reorganized Church of Jesus Christ of Latter Day Saints. Circular no. 8: *A Brief History and Financial Summary of the Gallands Grove, Iowa, District.* https://www.latterdaytruth.org/pdf/100776.pdf.

Rhodes Production System. *Ruby Creek Massacre* (documentary film), 1992. https://www.youtube.com/watch?v=RaZZHiB_1xc.

Rhodes, Steve. "Ex-C.F. Family Involved in Mountain Standoff." *The (Waterloo, IA) Courier*, April 5, 1992.

Ribuffo, Leo P. *The Old Christian Right: The Protestant Far Right from the Great Depression to the Cold War.* Philadelphia: Temple University Press, 1983.

Robertson, Pat. *The New World Order.* Dallas, TX: Word Publishing, 1991.

Rogan, Joe. Interview with Special Forces veteran Mike Glover. *The Joe Rogan Experience*, episode 1931, January 26, 2023.

Ronson, Jon. *Scandalous: Ruby Ridge.* Fox Nation documentary film, 2020.

———. *The Secret Rulers of the World.* World of Wonder documentary series, 2001.

———. *Them: Adventures with Extremists.* New York: Simon & Schuster, 2002.

Rossing, Barbara R. *The Rapture Exposed: The Message of Hope in the Book of Revelation.* New York: Basic Books, 2004.

Rushdoony, Rousas John. *The Nature of the American System.* Vallecito, CA: Chalcedon/Ross House Books, 1965.

Russonello, Giovanni. "QAnon Now as Popular in U.S. as Some Major Religions, Poll Suggests." *New York Times*, August 12, 2021.

Sandeen, Ernest R. *The Roots of Fundamentalism: British and American Millenarianism, 1800–1930.* Chicago: University of Chicago Press, 1970.

Schell, Jonathan. "Comment." *The New Yorker*, May 10, 1981.

Schram, Martin, and John M. Goshko. "Jerry Falwell Vows Amity with Israel." *Washington Post*, September 11, 1981.

Shephard, Alex. "How Tucker Carlson Lost It." *The New Republic*, September 16, 2021.

Smith, Erin A. "*The Late Great Planet Earth* Made the Apocalypse a Popular Concern." *Humanities* 38, no. 1 (Winter 2017).

Smith, Hendrick. "Pentagon Papers." *New York Times*, July 3, 1971.

Southern Poverty Law Center. "William Pierce." SPLC website, 2025. https://www.splcenter.org/resources/extremist-files/william-pierce/.

Stack, Peggy Fletcher, and David Noyce. "Worst Speech in LDS History." *Salt Lake Tribune*, March 5, 2023.

Stern, Kenneth S. *A Force Upon the Plain: The American Militia Movement and the Politics of Hate.* New York: Simon & Schuster, 1996.

Stock, Catherine McNicol. *Rural Radicals: Righteous Rage in the American Grain.* Ithaca, NY: Cornell University Press, 1996.

Sutton, Matthew Avery. *American Apocalypse: A History of Modern Evangelicalism.* Cambridge, MA: Harvard University Press, 2014.

———. "The Capitol Riot Revealed the Darkest Nightmares of White Evangelical America." *New Republic*, January 14, 2021.

Thompson, Hunter S. *Generation of Swine: Tales of Shame and Degradation in the '80s.* New York: Summit Books, 1988.

Toobin, Jeffrey. *Homegrown: Timothy McVeigh and the Rise of Right-Wing Extremism.* New York: Simon & Schuster, 2023.

Trickey, Erick. "Long Before QAnon, Ronald Reagan and the GOP Purged John Birch Extremists from the Party." *Washington Post*, January 15, 2021.

Turk, David S. "William Degan: A Look Back at the Quincy Hero on the 30th Anniversary of Ruby Ridge." *Patriot Ledger* (Quincy, MA), August 24, 2022.

Turkewitz, Julie, and Eric Lichtblau. "Police Shooting of Oregon Occupier Declared Justified." *New York Times*, March 9, 2016.

United States Department of Justice. *Department of Justice Report on Internal Review Regarding the Ruby Ridge Hostage Situation.* Washington, DC: 1994. https://www.justice.gov/sites/default/files/opr/legacy/2006/11/09/rubyreportcover_39.pdf.

United States Senate. "The Federal Raid on Ruby Ridge: Hearings before the Subcommittee on Terrorism, Technology, and Government Information of the Committee on the Judiciary," Sept. 6–Oct. 19, 1995. (Serial No. J-104-41).

"Unsolved Murders." *Spokesman-Review* (Spokane, WA), February 19, 1995.

"The Untold Story of Ruby Ridge with Survivor Sara Weaver" (Sara Weaver interview). *Good Simple Living* podcast, n.d. https://www.youtube.com/watch?v=5ddUlMu1DMU.

Walker, Jesse. *The United States of Conspiracy.* New York: Harper Collins, 2013.

Walter, Jess. "The Prodigal Dream." *Spokesman-Review* (Spokane, WA), November 29, 1992.

———. *Ruby Ridge: The Truth and Tragedy of the Randy Weaver Family.* New York: Harper Perennial, 2002.

Walter, Ray. "Paperback Talk." *New York Times*, March 16, 1981.

Watson, Kimberley. "Mormons in Space." Religious New Service, July 26, 2017.

Weaver, Randy. "Randy Weaver speech at Kerrville, Texas, 2003." https://www.youtube.com/watch?v=PN_uL4lzwFY.

———. *Vicki, Sam, and America: How the Government Killed All Three.* Provo, UT: Sunrise Publishing, 2003.

Weaver, Randy, and Sara Weaver. *The Federal Siege at Ruby Ridge.* Marion, MT: Ruby Ridge, Inc., 1998.

Weaver, Sara. *From Ruby Ridge to Freedom.* Kalispell, MT: Overboard Books, 2012.

Weber, Timothy P. *Living in the Shadow of the Second Coming: American Premillennialism 1875–1982.* Grand Rapids, MI: Zondervan, 1983.

Weland, Mike. "Weavers Prefer Isolation." *Bonners Ferry (Idaho) Herald*, May 6, 1992.

Wessinger, Catherine. *Oxford Handbook of Millennialism.* Oxford, UK: Oxford University Press, 2011.

Westover, Tara. *Educated.* New York: Random House, 2018.

Wilkinson, Alissa. "Satan, the Pope, and Dungeons and Dragons." *Vox*, November 8, 2016.

Wills, Garry. *A Necessary Evil: A History of American Distrust of Government.* New York: Simon & Schuster, 1999.

———. *Nixon Agonistes: The Crisis of the Self-Made Man.* New York: HarperCollins, 1970.

———. *Reagan's America: Innocents at Home.* New York: Doubleday, 1987.

———. *Under God: Religion and American Politics.* New York: Simon & Schuster, 1990.

———. "Where Evangelicals Came From." *New York Review of Books*, April 20, 2017.

Wojcik, Daniel. *The End of the World As We Know It: Faith, Fatalism, and Apocalypse in America.* New York: New York University Press, 1997.

Zeskind, Leonard. *Blood and Politics: The History of the White Nationalist Movement from the Margins to the Mainstream.* New York: Farrar, Straus and Giroux, 2009.

NOTES

PROLOGUE

3   *The root cellar was stocked*: Walter, *Ruby Ridge*, 135.

3–4   *All three of the Weavers' dogs*: Weaver and Weaver, *The Federal Siege at Ruby Ridge*, 47.

4   *Fresh game would be welcome*: Senate Judiciary Subcommittee Hearings, Kevin Harris testimony, September 26, 1995.

4   *Even though it was built on the cheap*: Brown and Brown, *First Canary*, 145.

4   *A woodstove brought from Iowa*: Weaver, *From Ruby Ridge to Freedom*, 8.

4   *Randy explained to neighbors*: Senate Judiciary Subcommittee Hearings, Ruth Rau testimony, September 20, 1995.

4   *Instead of building downhill*: Weaver and Weaver, *The Federal Siege at Ruby Ridge*, 20.

4   *She told Midwestern friends*: Bock, *Ambush at Ruby Ridge*, 32.

5   *Before they even started framing the house*: Walter, *Ruby Ridge*, 52.

5   *Fortress*: Keyes, "Weavers Inspire Hate and Admiration."

5   *Compound*: The FBI and US Marshals both used the terms *compound* and *Weaver compound* throughout their operation and the ensuing trial.

6   *They monitored their driveway*: Department of Justice Report on Internal Review Regarding the Ruby Ridge Hostage Situation (henceforth below, "*DOJ Report*"), IV, B.

6   *As the dogs paced fretfully*: Walter, *Ruby Ridge*, 166.

6   *Based on her reading of scripture*: Senate Judiciary Subcommittee Hearings, Kevin Harris testimony, September 26, 1995.

7   *For a decade*: Dundon, "Survivalists Make Plans for Time of 'Great Tribulation.'"

7   *After finishing their breakfast*: Weaver, *From Ruby Ridge to Freedom*, 16.

7   *Taking a break*: Brown and Brown, *First Canary*, 93.

8   *The previous winter*: Weaver and Weaver, *The Federal Siege at Ruby Ridge*, 21.

8   *"Hey Dad, come out here"*: Senate Judiciary Subcommittee Hearings, Randy Weaver testimony, September 6, 1995.

8   *Buddy, a small brown border collie*: Weaver, *From Ruby Ridge to Freedom*, 50.

8   *Ten-year-old Rachel came last*: Walter, *Ruby Ridge*, 167.

8   *Randy later testified*: Weaver and Weaver, *The Federal Siege at Ruby Ridge*, 47.

8   *He weighed less than eighty pounds*: Senate Judiciary Subcommittee Hearings, Randy Weaver testimony, September 6, 1995.

8   *His favorite book*: Brown and Brown, *First Canary*, 81.

8   *Trotting behind Striker*: Walter, *Ruby Ridge*, 135.
8   *He carried a light .223*: Senate Judiciary Subcommittee Hearings, Kevin Harris testimony, September 26, 1995.
9   *He carried a shotgun*: Walter, *Ruby Ridge*, 167.
9   *She watched Elisheba*: Burkett, *The Right Women*, 108; Weaver and Weaver, *The Federal Siege at Ruby Ridge*, 48.
10 *"Freeze, Randy!"*: Weaver and Weaver, *The Federal Siege at Ruby Ridge*, 38. The particulars of this highly contested episode are assembled from the recollections and testimony of Randy Weaver, Kevin Harris, the US marshals on the scene, and the DOJ's internal review of the case. Since there is little agreement about the precise order of events, I have used my best judgment about who is likely to know (or recall, or tell) the truth regarding any particular detail. More citations are provided in the chapter devoted to the events of August 21, 1992.
10 *"I realized immediately"*: Letter signed by Randy, Kevin, Sara, and Rachel that was smuggled out of cabin during the siege by Jackie Brown.
10 *Seeing the man at a distance*: Senate Judiciary Subcommittee Hearings, Kevin Harris testimony, September 26, 1995.
10 *"You shot my dog"*: Ibid.
11 *"I'm coming, Dad!"*: Senate Judiciary Subcommittee Hearings, Randy Weaver testimony, September 6, 1995.
11 *"Bird-dogging"*: Senate Judiciary Subcommittee Hearings, Kevin Harris testimony, September 26, 1995.
11 *Seeing Sam go down*: Ibid.
11 *"I'm hit. I'm hit."*: Senate Judiciary Subcommittee Hearings, Arthur Roderick testimony, September 15, 1995.
11 *Cooper fired on Kevin*: Walter, *Ruby Ridge*, 171.
11 *Cooper hurried over to Bill Degan*: Senate Judiciary Subcommittee Hearings, Arthur Roderick and David Hunt testimony, September 15, 1995.
12 *Vicki and the girls began desperately shouting*: Weaver and Weaver, *The Federal Siege at Ruby Ridge*, 48.
12 *"Sam is dead"*: Ibid.
12 *"We went berserk"*: Senate Judiciary Subcommittee Hearings, Randy Weaver testimony, September 6, 1995.
12 *"ambush"*: Walter, *Ruby Ridge*, 171, 175.
12 *Up at the cabin, Sara Weaver changed*: Weaver and Weaver, *The Federal Siege at Ruby Ridge*, 49.
12 *For a few minutes Randy and Vicki sat*: Senate Judiciary Subcommittee Hearings, Randy Weaver testimony, September 6, 1995.
13 *In the afternoon the weather turned*: Weaver and Weaver, *The Federal Siege at Ruby Ridge*, 50.
13 *After a while, Vicki took Elisheba in her arms*: Walter, *Ruby Ridge*, 179.
13 *In her diary she recorded*: Ronson, *Them*, 73.
13 *"Sirens from everywhere"*: Senate Judiciary Subcommittee Hearings, Randy Weaver testimony, September 6, 1995.

INTRODUCTION
14 *"Watching, waiting, and working for the millennium"*: Boyer, *When Time Shall Be No More*, 12.
14 *In a large-scale telephone survey*: "Understanding QAnon's Connection to American Politics."
14 *Today, the number of Americans who profess*: Russonello, "QAnon Now as Popular in U.S. as Some Major Religions."
15 *And he causeth all . . . to receive a mark*: Revelation 13:16–17, KJV.

15 *In 2010, a Pew survey*: Pew Research Center, "Section 3: War, Terrorism, and Global Trends."

17 *The Weaver tract was actually on Caribou Ridge*: Weaver and Weaver, *The Federal Siege at Ruby Ridge*, 18. It was Bill Morlin, writing for the Spokane *Spokesman-Review*, who appears to have first used the phrase "Ruby Ridge."

CHAPTER ONE

26 *Colliers like Samuel Jordison mined the coal*: Lees and Beyer, "History of Coal Mining in Iowa."

27 *In 1878, thirteen Coalville miners*: Reorganized Church of Jesus Christ of Latter Day Saints, *A Brief History and Financial Summary.*

27 *In the years since 1844*: Ostling and Ostling, *Mormon America.*

27 *In a report to church authorities*: Reorganized Church of Jesus Christ of Latter Day Saints, *A Brief History and Financial Summary.*

27 *They raised hogs, cattle, corn, and soy*: Weaver, *From Ruby Ridge to Freedom*, 1; Walter, *Ruby Ridge*, 14.

28 *They often gathered for large midday meals*: Walter, *Ruby Ridge*, 15.

28 *For fun, they took long road trips*: Weaver, *Vicki, Sam, and America*, 17.

28 *Her younger sister Julie*: Fuson and McCartan, "After the Showdown."

28 *At Fort Dodge Senior High in 1967*: *1967 Dodger* (Yearbook of Fort Dodge Senior High).

28 *She received straight A's*: Ibid.; Walter, *Ruby Ridge*, 18.

29 *The RLDS church, which renamed itself*: Ostling and Ostling, *Mormon America*, 343.

29 *In her senior year of high school*: Weaver and Weaver, *The Federal Siege at Ruby Ridge*, 12.

30 *Clarence and Wilma met*: Online obituary for Wilma J. Weaver, Caldwell Parish Funeral Home.

30 *Clarence, who sold Chevrolets, was deeply patriotic*: Weaver and Weaver, *The Federal Siege at Ruby Ridge*, 12.

30 *In 1959, when Randy was eleven*: Ibid., 13.

30 *In winter, he played pickup hockey*: Brown and Brown, *First Canary*, 139.

30 *"He was so easy to talk to and fun to be with"*: Associated Press, "Fugitive Showed No Racism in Iowa High School."

30 *"He was fun-loving"*: Fuson and McCartan, "After the Showdown."

31 *Wilma and Clarence were Presbyterians*: Zeskind, *Blood and Politics*, 301.

31 *Presbyterian, Baptist, United Brethren*: Fuson and McCartan, "After the Showdown."

31 *Even in a place where almost everyone*: Walter, *Ruby Ridge*, 21.

31 *"[Randy] always believed in God"*: Brown and Brown, *First Canary*, 139.

31 *"What shall be the sign of thy coming"*: Matthew 24:3, KJV.

32 *"When ye shall see all these things"*: Matthew 24:33–34, KJV.

32 *Along with a friend*: Weaver and Weaver, *The Federal Siege at Ruby Ridge*, 13.

32 *Off hours, he drank Schlitz*: Walter, *Ruby Ridge*, 21.

32 *It was there that Vicki first noticed him*: Fuson and McCartan, "After the Showdown."

32 *During a party at a local ballroom*: Brown and Brown, *First Canary*, 140.

33 *"the first time I saw her"*: Goodman, *Ruby Ridge: Every Knee Shall Bow.*

33 *Like Vicki, Randy was short*: Brown and Brown, *First Canary*, 139.

33 *When his job driving the school bus ended*: Weaver and Weaver, *The Federal Siege at Ruby Ridge*, 13.

33 *A childhood spent hunting small game*: Ibid., 12; Aho, *This Thing of Darkness*, 55.

34 *His discharge papers*: *DOJ Report*, IV, B. Weaver's full DD-214 is reproduced in Brown and Brown, *First Canary*, 78.

34 *Westmoreland responded by requesting another 200,000*: Smith, "Pentagon Papers."

34 *Randy was promoted to sergeant*: Ronson, *Scandalous: Ruby Ridge.*

34 *She had graduated*: Brown and Brown, *First Canary*, 141.

34   *Randy was honorably discharged*: Aho, *This Thing of Darkness*, 55.
34–35   *Before long, he would change his mind*: Weaver and Weaver, *The Federal Siege at Ruby Ridge*, 13.
35   *When the US Marshals commissioned*: DOJ Report, IV, B.
35   *"a Green Beret from Vietnam"*: That particular example is from *The Joe Rogan Experience*, an interview with Special Forces veteran Mike Glover.
35   *A month after Randy's discharge*: Walter, *Ruby Ridge*, 24.
36   *He wanted to try for a job at the FBI*: Ibid.
36   *Randy applied for G.I. Bill benefits*: Aho, *This Thing of Darkness*, 55.
36   *Not long after their wedding*: Walter, *Ruby Ridge*, 25.
36   *Amway's real product is a potent rhetoric*: General information on culture of Amway from conversation with David J. Harris of Harvard.
37   *"you've got to believe"*: "Amway Founders Fundamentals," promotional video featuring Richard DeVos.
37   *The fundamentalist leanings of many Amway sellers*: Walker, *The United States of Paranoia*, 203.
38   *Back in Coalville*: Walter, *Ruby Ridge*, 24.
38   *That changed abruptly in the early '70s*: Burgmaier, *The Farm Crisis*.
38   *The surge in demand*: Braun, "China's U.S. Grain Haul."
39   *In 1973, after just two quarters*: Aho, *This Thing of Darkness*, 55.
39   *Vicki, still working as a secretary*: Brown and Brown, *First Canary*, 141.
39   *They weren't even thirty, but*: Walter, *Ruby Ridge*, 31.
39   *Randy was often in the front driveway*: Ibid., 27.
39   *Vicki, whose life would be directly shaped*: Weaver and Weaver, *The Federal Siege at Ruby Ridge*, 13.
39   *From her father, she inherited*: Walter, *Ruby Ridge*, 32.
40   *Mormons consume (and produce) science fiction*: Watson, "Mormons in Space."
40   *Mormon authors have been blending sci-fi*: Bowman, "Everybody Loves Star Wars."
40   *"We believe in miracles and angels"*: Ibid.
40   *"sometime between leaving Middle-earth"*: Mallon, "Possessed."
40   *"From almost any page"*: Chambers, "Big Sister Is Watching You."
41   *Randy was never much of a reader*: Weaver and Weaver, *The Federal Siege at Ruby Ridge*, 13.
41   *"My wife and I, if you knew us"*: Senate Judiciary Subcommittee Hearings, Randy Weaver testimony, September 6, 1995.
42   *Randy was the handy, always-goofing dad*: Weaver, *From Ruby Ridge to Freedom*, 3.
42   *"She was the kind of mother"*: Fuson and McCartan, "After the Showdown."
42   *The kids raced Hot Wheels*: Weaver, *From Ruby Ridge to Freedom*, 3.
42   *On weekends the family*: Ibid., 1.

CHAPTER TWO
43   *During those mid-'70s summers*: Ronson, *Them*, 101.
44   *For a long stretch, they settled into the padded pews*: "Cedarloo Baptist Church Dedication Set."
44   *The author of Ezekiel*: Boyer, *When Time Shall Be No More*, 25.
45   *This backdating allows Daniel's author*: McGinn, *Anti-Christ*, 14.
45   *Written about six decades after the crucifixion*: Pagles, *Revelations*, 163.
45   *Revelation is modeled closely on Daniel*: Boyer, *When Time Shall Be No More*, 21, 26.
45   *As one theologian has noted*: Rossing, *The Rapture Exposed*, 82.
46   *"Come up hither"*: Revelation 4:1, KJV. (All subsequent citations from Revelation are from the King James Version.)
48   *"If it is imagery"*: Lawrence, *Apocalypse*, 4.
48   *"language that will peel the skin"*: Thompson, *Generation of Swine*, 296.

NOTES

49   *Historians of religion*: Boyer, *When Time Shall Be No More*, 36.
49   *For John, it is obviously a stand-in*: Ibid., 43.
49   *The Beast most likely represents the emperor Nero*: Ibid., 44.
50   *"anti-Roman propaganda that drew"*: Pagles, *Revelations*, 16.
50   *It was a time when someone like John of Patmos*: Ibid., 46.
51   *"But of that day and hour knoweth no man"*: Matthew 24:26, KJV.
51   *"were devices by which religious groups"*: Cohn, *The Pursuit of the Millennium*, 19.
52   *As early as the second century*: Boyer, *When Time Shall Be No More*, 47.
52   *Augustine, the most influential*: Grafton, "The Millennia-old History of the Apocalypse."
52   *At the Council of Ephesus in 431 CE*: Boyer, *When Time Shall Be No More*, 49.
52   *Martin Luther went so far as to claim*: Ibid., 61.
52   *Inside the tidy house on University Avenue*: Walter, *Ruby Ridge*, 31.
52   *"the thrilling doctrine"*: Sutton, *American Apocalypse*, 329.
53   *"preaching of the gospel"*: Weber, *Living in the Shadow of the Second Coming*, 14.
53   *This assumption—that history is slowly tending*: Marsden, *Fundamentalism and American Culture*, 49.
53   *"God made me the messenger"*: Wojcik, *The End of the World As We Know It*, 21.
54   *Surveying the social and technological advances*: Weber, *Living in the Shadow of the Second Coming*, 14.
54   *"America in the early nineteenth century"*: Sandeen, *The Roots of Fundamentalism*, 42.
55   *Cotton Mather, for instance*: Wojcik, *The End of the World as We Know It*, 21; Weber, *Living in the Shadow of the Second Coming*, 13.
55   *A half century later, during the chaotic years*: Sandeen, *The Roots of Fundamentalism*, 5.
55   *In 1798, prophecy watchers*: Weber, *Living in the Shadow of the Second Coming*, 14.

CHAPTER THREE

57   *In the United States, the turn*: Ernest R. Sandeen's *The Roots of Fundamentalism: British and American Millenarianism, 1800–1930* is the definitive history of early fundamentalism; see p. 123.
58   *Those new ideas*: Boyer, *When Time Shall Be No More*, 86.
58   *Despite generating several million words*: Akenson, *Exporting the Rapture*, 425.
58   *A proper full-scale biography*: Ibid., 292.
59   *Darby's father made a fortune*: Wessinger, *Oxford Handbook of Millennialism*, 517.
59   *He graduated from Trinity College*: Akenson, *Exporting the Rapture*, 12.
59   *The Plymouth Brethren, who defined themselves*: Ibid., 145, 287.
60   *"tight discipline, compelling propaganda"*: Ibid., 287.
60   *He favored days-long sessions*: Ibid., 435.
60   *Even so, it would fall*: Katz and Popkin, *Messianic Revolution*, 144.
60   *Using only his own "literalist" reading*: Sandeen, *The Roots of Fundamentalism*, 64.
60   *Adherents of this reading*: Boyer, *When Time Shall Be No More*, 88; Akenson, *Exporting the Rapture*, 292.
61   *With all true believers beamed to safety*: Katz and Popkin, *Messianic Revolution*, 143.
62   *"unchristian delusion"*: Sandeen, *The Roots of Fundamentalism*, 95.
62   *As a result of the prophetic*: Sutton, *American Apocalypse*, 20.
62   *Darby did not give much credit*: Akenson, *Exporting the Rapture*, 292.
63   *Doubters regard it as a modern heresy*: Kristian, "The Surprising Power of Dispensationalism."
63   *Compared to the contortions*: Boyer, *When Time Shall Be No More*, 88.
63   *In the fall of 1862, Darby sailed*: Akenson, *Exporting the Rapture*, 431.
63   *Over the next two decades, he made six more*: Boyer, *When Time Shall Be No More*, 90.
64   *"gather churches out of churches"*: Sandeen, *The Roots of Fundamentalism*, 73.
64   *His ideas found early traction*: Ibid., 75.

64   *In the United Kingdom, the Darbyite charge*: Akenson, *Exporting the Rapture*, 426.
64   *The new apocalyptic faith*: Boyer, *When Time Shall Be No More*, 90.
64   *"tinker and patch up a world system"*: Sutton, *American Apocalypse*, 34.
64   *"I don't find any place"*: Boyer, *When Time Shall Be No More*, 94.
64   *Scofield, who had experienced a conversion*: Ibid., 97.
65   *"the sounds of the theological war"*: Sutton, *American Apocalypse*, 24.
65   *"the most resilient popular theological movement"*: Hummel, *The Rise and Fall of Dispensationalism*, 8.
65   *It came from The Fundamentals, a popular series*: Sutton, *American Apocalypse*, 83.
65   *"to do battle royal for the faith"*: Marsden, *Fundamentalism and American Culture*, 107.
66   *"How did people who set out to preserve"*: Wills, *Under God*, 135.
66   *Seminarians and leading churchmen*: Ribuffo, *The Old Christian Right*, 85.
66   *"How the Higher Critics have sneered"*: Sutton, *American Apocalypse*, 50.
67   *One consequence of H. L. Mencken's*: Ibid., 177.
67   *"Now for the first time"*: Boyer, *When Time Shall Be No More*, 102.
67   *The formal establishment of Israel in 1948*: Ibid.
68   *Under the widespread assumption*: Ibid., 145.
68   *"Only when Christ comes again"*: Kitchener and Fayya, "History Is Testing Evangelicals. Again."
68   *"had almost no role in shaping"*: Sutton, *American Apocalypse*, 66.
68   *In the 1920s and '30s, as Fundamentalism spread*: Ibid., 137.
68   *"eleven o'clock on Sunday morning"*: Martin Luther King Jr. on NBC's *Meet the Press*, April 17, 1960.
69   *Inside the house on University Avenue*: Walter, *Ruby Ridge*, 31.
70   *"We are living the latter days"*: Ibid., 180.
70   *While mainline denominations*: Ibid.
70   *For those Americans who did not approve*: Sutton, *American Apocalypse*, 342.
70   *Not since the nineteenth century*: Ibid.
70   *His own prediction*: Fitzgerald, *The Evangelicals*, 376.
70   *"When we moved in here"*: Rhodes, "Ex-C.F. Family Involved in Mountain Standoff."

CHAPTER FOUR
71   *One afternoon in 1978*: Walter, *Ruby Ridge*, 28.
71   *More than all the other apocalyptic*: Aho, *This Thing of Darkness*, 62; Brown and Brown, *First Canary*, 142.
71   *Born in Texas in 1929*: Wojcik, *The End of the World as We Know It*, 38.
72   *"the intellectual and ideological 'Vatican'"*: Weber, *Living in the Shadow of the Second Coming*, 238.
72   *After graduating, Lindsey preached at UCLA*: Marsden, *Fundamentalism and American Culture*, 241.
72   *By the late '60s, Lindsey was running*: Wojcik, *The End of the World as We Know It*, 38.
72   *Alongside the Bible*: Smith, "The Late Great Planet Earth Made the Apocalypse a Popular Concern."
73   *In his book, the pre-Tribulation Rapture*: Boyer, *When Time Shall Be No More*, 127.
73   *"Scarlet O'Harlot"*: Lindsey, *The Late Great Planet Earth*, 122.
73   *Lindsey claimed that his imagined*: O'Leary, *Arguing the Apocalypse*, 143.
74   *Estimating a generation*: Lindsey, *The Late Great Planet Earth*, 54.
74   *"the fuse of Armageddon"*: Ibid., 44.
74   *"Gog," the evil kingdom*: Ibid., 94.
74   *The ten-horned Beast*: Ibid., 82.
74   *Seeing college kids doing yoga*: Ibid., 124.
74   *"I've been taking trips and I've really seen God"*: Ibid., 126.

74–75　*"will make the regimes of Hitler, Mao"*: Ibid., 166.
75　*Armageddon was coming*: Boyer, *When Time Shall Be No More*, 127.
75　*Horses with lion heads that spit fire*: Ibid.
75　*Fire and brimstone that melt the flesh*: Ibid., 128.
75　*A Green Beret friend told Lindsey*: Lindsey, *The Late Great Planet Earth*, 26.
75　*"hot rods of the apocalypse"*: Davis, *City of Quartz*, 1.
76　*The Late Great Planet Earth was published*: Walter, "Paperback Talk."
76　*Quickly spilling beyond the prophecy shelves*: O'Leary, *Arguing the Apocalypse*, 144.
76　*Cheaply printed prophecy almanacs*: Grafton, "The Millennia-old History of the Apocalypse."
76　*The first bestseller in the New World*: Wojcik, *The End of the World as We Know It*, 23.
76　*During the golden age of televangelism*: Sutton, *American Apocalypse*, 344.
76　*"Are the Last Days Almost Here?"*: Ibid.
76　*The Late Great Planet Earth was published in 1970*: Wojcik, *The End of the World as We Know It*, 37.
77　*Scholars now reckon*: O'Leary, *Arguing the Apocalypse*, 137.
77　*At one point, Lindsey had three separate titles*: Wojcik, *The End of the World as We Know It*, 37.
77　*"probably the single most read"*: Ehrman, *Jesus: Apocalyptic Prophet of the New Millennium*, 7.
77　*Among other distinctions, he was the first*: Aho, *Far-Right Fantasy*, 88.
77　*By one recent tally*: Wills, "Where Evangelicals Came From."
77　*In 1978, the year Vicki brought home a copy*: Cover of the 1978 edition.
79　*"God didn't send me to clean"*: Boyer, *When Time Shall Be No More*, 299.
79　*While earlier fundamentalists*: Lindsey, *The Late Great Planet Earth*, 118.
79　*"The Bible," Lindsey claimed, "supports building"*: Boyer, *When Time Shall Be No More*, 252.
79　*Ronald Reagan was reportedly*: Ibid., 141.
79　*"step aside and let the prophets"*: Lindsey, *The Late Great Planet Earth*, 8.
80　*Along with new works, older tracts*: Boyer, *When Time Shall Be No More*, 6.
80　*By one conservative estimate*: Wessinger, *Oxford Handbook of Millennialism*, 516.
80　*Many more, having absorbed dispensational*: Hummel, *The Rise and Fall of Dispensationalism*, 326.
80　*The Late Great Planet Earth lit a fire*: Aho, *This Thing of Darkness*, 62; Brown and Brown, *First Canary*, 142.
80　*"You've got to read this book"*: Walter, *Ruby Ridge*, 28.

CHAPTER FIVE
82　*In one, she saw herself and Randy*: Brown and Brown, *First Canary*, 142.
82　*Something about the vibrancy of these images*: Walter, "The Prodigal Dream."
83　*In 1978, the Weavers brought two-year-old Sara*: Ibid.
84　*By the late 1970s, Randy had developed the habit*: Walter, *Ruby Ridge*, 28.
84　*"We were crazy born-again legalists"*: Ibid., 32.
84　*Stands of small white crosses*: Frazier, "Grim Reapers."
85　*Iowans had begun killing themselves*: Burgmaier, *The Farm Crisis*.
85　*Following the Dust Bowl*: Levitas, *The Terrorist Next Door*, 171.
85　*Under Presidents Eisenhower and Nixon*: Ibid., 172.
85　*During most of the '70s*: Corcoran, *Bitter Harvest*, 8.
86　*"hedgerow to hedgerow"*: Ibid.
86　*"They almost hauled you in"*: Levitas, *The Terrorist Next Door*, 173.
86　*Soaring inflation tripled the price*: Corcoran, *Bitter Harvest*, 8.
86　*At the same time, in the space of little more*: Levitas, *The Terrorist Next Door*, 173.
86　*When farmers rushed to sell off*: Zeskind, *Blood and Politics*, 73.
86　*Between 1981 and 1988*: Ibid.

87   *In a place where almost every aspect of the economy*: Burgmaier, *The Farm Crisis*.
87   *"The sharp report"*: Corcoran, *Bitter Harvest*, 11.
87   *By the early '80s, Iowa ranked forty-ninth*: Burgmaier, *The Farm Crisis*.
87   *In 1979, at the start of the crisis*: Ibid.
87   *Over the course of a decade*: Green, "Seeds of Discontent."
88   *At Sambo's, talk of Jewish bankers*: Walter, "The Prodigal Dream."
88   *He started sleeping with a pistol*: Walter, *Ruby Ridge*, 37.
88   *Since well before the American Revolution*: *Under the Eye of Power* (2023) by Colin Dickey provides a comprehensive and thoughtful survey of American conspiracism.
89   *"While the liberals may view belief"*: Rushdoony, *The Nature of the American System*, 157.
89   *"No Western nation is as religion-soaked"*: Bloom, *The American Religion*, 30.
90   *Even before the Internet*: Barkun, *A Culture of Conspiracy*, 44.
90   *Previous generations of American Christians*: Boyer, *When Time Shall Be No More*, 72, 95, 107.
90   *In the late 1970s, seated in his booth*: Walter, *Ruby Ridge*, 40.
90   *Again and again, people around them*: Weaver and Weaver, *The Federal Siege at Ruby Ridge*, 13.
90   *As Randy later told it*: Ibid., 14.
91   *Besides the fact that this certainly*: *DOJ Report*, II, A.
91   *Once, during a living room debate*: Walter, *Ruby Ridge*, 41.
91   *"talked about a lot of crazy stuff"*: Walter, "The Prodigal Dream."
91   *In 2023, Sara Weaver would use a more contemporary formulation*: Sara Weaver interview, *Good Simple Living* podcast.
91   *"It is possible"*: Lippman, *Drift and Mastery*, 1.
92   *Even as the farm crisis battered*: McCarthy, "Chill in Iowa."
92   *She grew her hair long*: Walter, *Ruby Ridge*, 26.
92   *Convinced of an impending financial crisis*: Ibid., 27.

CHAPTER SIX
93   *For reasons that remain vague*: Ronson, *Scandalous: Ruby Ridge*.
94   *"I have never taken to the hills"*: Lindsey, *The Late Great Planet Earth*, 1.
94   *"felt all the organized churches"*: Cummins, "Fugitive Won't Budge, Friends Say."
94   *"some kind of friction between my folks"*: Weaver, *From Ruby Ridge to Freedom*, 4.
94   *At various times, she has alluded*: Ronson, *Scandalous: Ruby Ridge*; Sara Weaver interview, *Good Simple Living* podcast.
94   *Years later, having been born again*: Sara Weaver interview, *Good Simple Living* podcast.
95   *"This was the first domino"*: Weaver, *From Ruby Ridge to Freedom*, 5.
95   *"That was how and when it started"*: Ibid.
95   *"Apparently some people were offended"*: Weaver and Weaver, *The Federal Siege at Ruby Ridge*, 14.
95   *After Woody's letter to the IRS*: Ibid.
95   *"I know there are people who want"*: Dundon, "Survivalists Make Plans for Time of 'Great Tribulation.'"
95   *Unchurched, the Weavers began*: Brown and Brown, *First Canary*, 142; Walter, "The Prodigal Dream."
95   *As mainline churches shrank*: Boyer, *When Time Shall Be No More*, 4.
96   *Abiding the conspiratorialist's first commandment*: Arbanas, "Friend: Weaver Became Racist."
96   *"knew there was something unusual"*: Lindsey, *The Late Great Planet Earth*, 31.
96   *Vicki delved into Christian apocrypha*: Brown and Brown, *First Canary*, 143.
96   *Some of the people who joined*: Walter, *Ruby Ridge*, 26.
96   *One Sambo's regular*: Arbanas, "Friend: Weaver Became Racist."

96   *"Randy and I cried together many times"*: Walter, "The Prodigal Dream."

97   *She was the resident theologian*: Walter, *Ruby Ridge*, 32.

97   *While the adults discussed prophetic signs*: Weaver, *From Ruby Ridge to Freedom*, 40.

97   *Some days, the group drove*: Dundon, "Survivalists Make Plans for Time of 'Great Tribulation.'"

97   *The television, once an important source*: Weaver, *From Ruby Ridge to Freedom*, 5.

97   *"Sam got rid of his stuff"*: Ibid.

97   *The Weavers' dishes were decorated*: Walter, *Ruby Ridge*, 39.

98   *"I guess you could say"*: Fuson and McCartan, "After the Showdown."

98   *"Events in history are no accident"*: Boyer, *When Time Shall Be No More*, 265.

98   *In 1981, at the height of the doomsday craze*: Chandler, *Doomsday*, 255.

99   *The true purpose of public education*: Fuson and McCartan, "After the Showdown."

99   *Since homeschooling without a teaching certificate*: Walter, "The Prodigal Dream."

99   *The Klan cooked up elaborate rituals*: Aho, *This Thing of Darkness*, 94.

99   *As the Weavers' conspiratorial faith*: Walter, *Ruby Ridge*, 99.

100 *While old Iowa friends*: Associated Press, "Weaver Turned Racist in the West, Friend Says."

100 *"How can you believe that?"*: Walter, "The Prodigal Dream."

100 *One Iowa banker*: Burgmaier, *The Farm Crisis*.

100 *In 1977, a group of farmers*: Levitas, *The Terrorist Next Door*, 168.

101 *In the winter of 1979*: Ibid., 171.

101 *Preaching armed resistance*: Ibid., 169.

101 *After a decade of steep decline*: Levitas, *The Terrorist Next Door*, 168.

101 *During the farm crisis, the magazine*: Lamy, *Millennium Rage*, 126; Ronson, *Them*, 104.

102 *Its masthead included several staffers*: Crothers, *Rage on the Right*, 26; Walker, *The United States of Paranoia*, 203.

102 *After his arrest, Timothy McVeigh*: Toobin, *Homegrown*, 57.

102 *The aesthetics of the movement*: Belew, *Bring the War Home*, 3.

102 *While the Klan and earlier far-right organizations*: Ibid.

102 *They claimed that paper money*: Fowler, "Ultra-Right Farm Groups Taking Root."

103 *Because one of the ways*: Levitas, *The Terrorist Next Door*, 3.

103 *While most Posse adherents*: Corcoran, *Bitter Harvest*, 29.

103 *"the chief executive of this government"*: Ibid., 27.

103 *Its roots, like so much else*: Crothers, *Rage on the Right*, 66; Levitas, *The Terrorist Next Door*, 169.

103 *After long sessions*: Levitas, *The Terrorist Next Door*, 24.

104 *The Posse movement first spread*: Ibid., 8.

104 *In Portland, Henry Lamont Beach*: Coates, *Armed and Dangerous*, 105.

104 *In North Idaho*: Levitas, *The Terrorist Next Door*, 8.

105 *"official who violated the law and the Constitution"*: Ibid., 2.

105 *It would not be long before presidential hopeful*: Zeskind, *Blood and Politics*, 74.

105 *Instead of sound legal advice*: Levitas, *The Terrorist Next Door*, 186.

105 *"The farmers were the first victims"*: Lamy, *Millennium Rage*, 127.

105 *Posse literature told farmers*: Corcoran, *Bitter Harvest*, 27.

105 *In 1982, William Gale co-led paramilitary training*: Levitas, *The Terrorist Next Door*, 184.

106 *At a permanent base*: Zeskind, *Blood and Politics*, 73.

106 *By the mid-'80s, according to Daniel*: Levitas, *The Terrorist Next Door*, 9.

106 *A surprising twist in all of this*: Ibid., 10.

106 *A 1986 advisory sent to federal law*: Coates, *Armed and Dangerous*, 105.

106–107 *"for an invasion of the United States"*: Fowler, "Ultra-Right Farm Groups Taking Root."

107 *Along with another Deere employee*: Eller and Skinner, "White Supremacy Group has Waterloo Members."

NOTES

107 *Even late in his life*: Randy explained both his atheism and constitutional ideas in 2007 at a speech given to reporters during the standoff at the New Hampshire home of Ed and Elaine Brown, in 2007. https://www.youtube.com/watch?v=UD-5t5NBsVk.

CHAPTER SEVEN

108 *The weekly "Church Notices" section*: "Church Notices," *The (Waterloo, IA) Courier.*
109 *Todd, a tall, slender man*: Walter, *Ruby Ridge*, 43.
109 *Friend and neighbor Carolee Flynn*: Walter, "The Prodigal Dream."
109 *He claimed to have been*: Barkun, "Conspiracy Theories and the Occult," 703.
110 *"the most powerful witchcraft bloodline"*: LaRock, *John Todd*, 1.
110 *As young man, he explained*: Walker, *The United States of Paranoia*, 187.
110 *It was a particular preoccupation*: Ibid.
110 *This conspiracy involved the Rockefellers*: Barkun, *A Culture of Conspiracy*, 57.
110 *Todd's remit within the Illuminati*: LaRock, *John Todd*, 11.
110 *Flattering his churchgoing audiences*: Barkun, "Conspiracy Theories and the Occult," 703.
111 *Under the influence of Todd's preaching*: Barkun, *A Culture of Conspiracy*, 57.
111 *As Todd told it, the Illuminati set him up*: Walker, *The United States of Paranoia*, 190.
111 *Todd dropped famous names*: "The Testimony of John Todd" cassette, available on YouTube.
111 *His story, which blended endtimes*: Barkun, *A Culture of Conspiracy*, 55.
112 *His matter-of-fact, oddly charming talks*: Walker, *The United States of Paranoia*, 188; Plowman, "The Legend(s) of John Todd."
112 *"As a framework for thought"*: Johnson, "The Militia in Me."
112 *"The world is dominated by an evil"*: Cohn, *The Pursuit of the Millennium*, 21.
113 *In this and other instances*: LaRock, *John Todd*, 20.
113 *Chick Publications claims*: Wilkinson, "Satan, the Pope, and Dungeons and Dragons."
113 *He began to fall out of favor*: Walker, *The United States of Paranoia*, 191.
114 *His claims were taken seriously enough*: Plowman, "The Legend(s) of John Todd."
114 *In 1979, Christianity Today*: Ibid.
114 *"Is witch-turned-evangelist John Todd"*: Ibid.
115 *Even the John Birch Society*: Walker, *The United States of Paranoia*, 196.
115 *On the other side of street, so to speak*: Ibid.
115 *"Our group embraced everything"*: Barkun, "Conspiracy Theories and the Occult," 704.
115 *"arguably the most heavily armed"*: Ibid., 703.
115 *In 1985, the FBI raided*: Walker, *The United States of Paranoia*, 208.
116 *He received probation*: Barkun, "Conspiracy Theories and the Occult," 704.
116–117 *Along with his family*: Walker, *The United States of Paranoia*, 206.
117 *"a number of individuals in Cedar Falls"*: "Call the Courier." *The (Waterloo, IA) Courier.*
117 *"I remember very clearly"*: Arbanas, "Friend: Weaver Became Racist."
117 *"When ye therefore shall see the abomination"*: Matthew 24:15–21, KJV.
118 *"And I will call for a sword"*: Ezekiel 38:21, KJV.
118 *In a city as small as Cedar Falls*: Walter, *Ruby Ridge*, 44.
118 *The young woman's parents*: Ibid.
118 *As it turned out, the Cedar Falls PD*: Cummins, "Fugitive Won't Budge, Friends Say."
118 *Shannon Brasher, a man apparently given*: Dundon, "Hang Gliding Man Fulfills Quest to Fly."
119 *Dundon was greeted warmly*: Dundon, "Survivalists Make Plans for Time of 'Great Tribulation.'"
119 *"The Bible teaches"*: Ibid.
120 *"We reject idolatry"*: Ibid.
120 *"That was a straight-up lie"*: Senate Judiciary Subcommittee Hearings, Randy Weaver testimony, September 6, 1995.

120 *Randy did the same*: Walter, *Ruby Ridge*, 44.

120 *"not on what is seen"*: 2 Corinthians 14:18, New International Version.

CHAPTER EIGHT

123 *"We're servants and what the lord tells us"*: Dundon, "Survivalists Make Plans for Time of 'Great Tribulation.'"

123 *At the start of the summer, the house sold*: Walter, "The Prodigal Dream."

123 *By then, all talk of "the group"*: Cummins, "Fugitive Won't Budge, Friends Say."

123 *God told Vaughn Trueman*: Walter, *Ruby Ridge*, 46.

124 *More names were added*: Weaver and Weaver, *The Federal Siege at Ruby Ridge*, 15.

124 *It would be hard to find a pair*: Ibid., 14.

124 *"Vicki and I had come to the conclusion"*: Ibid., 15.

125 *"He was excited, and so were we"*: Weaver, *From Ruby Ridge to Freedom*, 7.

125 *Dragging their furniture and possessions*: Cummins, "Fugitive Won't Budge, Friends Say."

125 *Randy sold his Harley*: Weaver and Weaver, *The Federal Siege at Ruby Ridge*, 15.

125 *DeEtta Lisby, a Cedar Falls neighbor*: Cummins, "Fugitive Won't Budge, Friends Say."

125 *"I prayed," she wrote*: Walter, *Ruby Ridge*, 55.

126 *In 1982, looking upon what many*: Dundon, "Survivalists Make Plans for Time of 'Great Tribulation.'"

126 *The whole family took a field trip*: Weaver, *From Ruby Ridge to Freedom*, 8.

126 *Vaughn Trueman marveled*: Arbanas, "Friend: Weaver Became Racist."

126 *By the time they left Iowa, she had accumulated*: Weaver, *From Ruby Ridge to Freedom*, 8.

126 *Carolee Flynn watched in distress*: Walter, "The Prodigal Dream."

126 *Randy traded the family station wagon*: Weaver and Weaver, *The Federal Siege at Ruby Ridge*, 16.

127 *The day before they left*: Weaver, *From Ruby Ridge to Freedom*, 8.

127 *Of all the family they left behind*: Weaver and Weaver, *The Federal Siege at Ruby Ridge*, 16.

127 *Randy's father Clarence visited once*: Fuson and McCartan, "After the Showdown."

127 *"Turned out to be Randy Weaver"*: Jess, "ETC."

128 *"Our goal and our dream," wrote Randy*: Weaver and Weaver, *The Federal Siege at Ruby Ridge*, 16.

128 *In North Idaho, along with Mennonites*: Aho, *Politics of Righteousness*, 22.

128 *Vicki, who, in keeping with Deuteronomy*: Sara Weaver interview, *Good Simple Living* podcast.

128 *They made a road trip out of it*: Weaver, *From Ruby Ridge to Freedom*, 9.

128 *They got a room at a local motel*: Walter, *Ruby Ridge*, 51; Weaver, *From Ruby Ridge to Freedom*, 11.

129 *"deep clear lakes"*: Senate Judiciary Subcommittee Hearings, Larry Craig statement, September 5, 1995.

129 *Idaho has long been a bastion*: Conley, *Idaho Loners*, ii.

130 *"I'm as conservative as any person"*: Shephard, "How Tucker Carlson Lost It."

130 *At the local market, Vicki and Sara*: Brown and Brown, *First Canary*, 138.

130 *"There are a lot of people here"*: Walter, *Ruby Ridge*, 51.

130 *Whether or not Randy and Vicki*: Belew, *Bring the War Home*, 3.

131 *While most Americans still associated the Old South*: Aho, *This Thing of Darkness*, 152.

131 *Once the Weavers had departed*: Walter, *Ruby Ridge*, 61.

131 *At the time the Weavers lived there*: Johnson, "The Militia in Me."

131 *In 1986, activists selected Kootenai County*: Aho, *Politics of Righteousness*, 7.

132 *The Lord had promised Randy*: Walter, *Ruby Ridge*, 51.

132 *"When we drove up to see [the land]"*: Walter, "The Prodigal Dream."

132 *For five thousand dollars*: Weaver and Weaver, *The Federal Siege at Ruby Ridge*, 18.

132 *The man who sold them the land*: Weaver, *From Ruby Ridge to Freedom*, 11.

NOTES

132 *The family would winter*: Walter, *Ruby Ridge*, 54.
132–133 *The word appears 245 times*: Nash, *Wilderness and the American Mind*, 13.

CHAPTER NINE

134 *A Gallup poll from the early 1980s* : Boyer, *When Time Shall Be No More*, 2.
134 *A 1982 cover story*: Martin, "Waiting For the End."
134 *"most of the prophecies"*: Sutton, *American Apocalypse*, 355.
135 *"never, in the time between"*: Herbers, "Armageddon View Prompts a Debate."
135 *"It seems careless"*: Wills, *Under God*, 15.
135 *"Ever since [Fundamentalism's] rise"*: Sandeen, *The Roots of Fundamentalism*, ix.
136 *Seated in the audience*: Ostling, "Religion: Armageddon and the End Times."
137 *"I do not know how many future generations"*: Schell, "Comment."
137 *"I have read the Book of Revelation"*: Gibbs, "Apocalypse Now."
138 *It did not help that*: Barkun, *A Culture of Conspiracy*, 40.
139 *"the missing link between the occult"*: Robertson, *New World Order*, 181.
139 *the great "dekooking"*: Wills, *Nixon Agonistes*, 253.
139 *As has been abundantly reported*: Perlstein, "I Thought I Understood the American Right."
139 *Barry Goldwater perfected and demonstrated*: Trickey, "Long Before QAnon, Ronald Reagan and the GOP."
140 *"The Nightmare of God"*: Berrigan, *The Nightmare of God*.
140 *"Alice in Wonderland wearing a dragon mask"*: Lewis, *Elmer Gantry*, 130.

CHAPTER TEN

141 *Gordon Wendell Kahl grew up in North Dakota*: Corcoran, *Bitter Harvest*, 43.
141 *He signed up for the army*: Ibid., 44.
141 *He returned home, married his girlfriend*: Jackson, *Death & Taxes*.
141 *Kahl's gathering impression*: Corcoran, *Bitter Harvest*, 46.
141 *Hitler, who kept a portrait of Ford*: Maddow, *Prequel*, 84.
142 *The Protocols, which presents itself*: Barkun, *A Culture of Conspiracy*, 40.
142 *The version that circulates today*: Ribuffo, *The Old Christian Right*, 10.
142 *It proved especially popular*: Aho, *This Thing of Darkness*, 82.
142 *"believer in the Word of God"*: Sutton, "The Capitol Riot Revealed the Darkest Nightmares."
142 *After reading Ford's book*: Corcoran, *Bitter Harvest*, 46.
143 *As with so many who would go on*: Ibid., 49.
143 *"tithes to the synagogue of Satan"*: Zeskind, *Blood and Politics*, 74.
143 *He traveled to American Agriculture Movement*: Corcoran, *Bitter Harvest*, 24.
143 *"We are a conquered and occupied nation"*: Ibid., 25.
143 *The following year, he was charged*: Ibid., 54.
143 *The court recognized its own*: Ibid., 55.
144 *He painted a sheriff's star*: Jackson, *Death & Taxes*.
144 *When Kahl received a fresh summons*: Corcoran, *Bitter Harvest*, 56.
144 *"engage in a struggle to the death"*: Ibid., 68.
145 *"as much to serious national concern"*: Adler, *After the Tall Timber*, 92.
145 *"I'd rather die on my feet"*: See, for instance, the speech he gave at the New Hampshire home of Ed and Elaine Brown, in 2007, available on YouTube, https://www.youtube.com/watch?v=Fs6QcPjpEbk.
145 *In the years before the Ruby Ridge siege, Vicki*: See, for instance, her letter to the Aryan Nations dated June 12, 1990, reproduced in Brown and Brown, *First Canary*, 160.
146 *In the winter of 1981*: Zeskind, *Blood and Politics*, 75.
146 *He told anyone who would listen*: Corcoran, *Bitter Harvest*, 57.
146 *Theoretically a fugitive*: Ibid., 63.
146 *He publicly threatened*: Ibid., 71.

146 *"I haven't shot anybody since World War II"*: Ibid., 59.
147 *The three men in Kahl's party*: Ibid., 77.
147 *The meeting in Medina was attended*: Ibid., 78.
148 *Bradley Kapp, the young deputy*: Ibid., 82.
148 *"believed Kahl when he said"*: Ibid.
148 *"It's not worth getting killed over"*: Ibid., 93.
148 *Yorie shot first*: Ibid., 98.
149 *Kahl disappeared into a large underground network*: Ibid., 158.
149 *The Marshals Service posted a $25,000 reward*: Ibid.
150 *As with Samuel Weaver's dog Striker*: Ibid., 139, 141.
150 *Chasing various leads*: Ibid., 163.
151 *From their perspective, the vast manhunt*: Ibid., 162.
151 *The full details of his itinerary*: Ibid.
151 *"Prairie fog has chilled the trail"*: Jackson, *Death & Taxes.*
151 *"a struggle to the death"*: Zeskind, *Blood and Politics*, 75.
152 *"declared war on the people"*: Corcoran, *Bitter Harvest*, 145.
152 *"I know where you can find Gordon Kahl"*: Ibid., 233.
152 *Robertson met an agent*: Ibid., 236.
152 *"You're one of them"*: Ibid., 237.
153 *On June 3, 1983, FBI agents*: Ibid., 241.
153 *Unsure whether Kahl had even been hit*: Ibid., 245.
154 *As word of his death*: Levitas, *The Terrorist Next Door*, 5.
154 *The fact that his body*: Jackson, *Death & Taxes.*
154 *"Give me liberty or give me death"*: Corcoran, *Bitter Harvest*, 245.
154 *The Spotlight proceeded to spend several years*: Toobin, *Homegrown*, 78.
154 *In Martin's telling*: Martin, *Terror on Ruby Ridge*, 4, 26.
155 *Along the way, she became friendly*: Brown and Brown, *First Canary*, 148.
155 *"Since the name Gordon Kahl"*: Zeskind, *Blood and Politics*, 78.

CHAPTER ELEVEN

156 *The family celebrated by moving*: Weaver, *From Ruby Ridge to Freedom*, 13.
156 *"I feel like . . . we had to get this house built"*: Walter, "The Prodigal Dream."
156 *Pine and cedar mill scraps were free*: Brown and Brown, *First Canary*, 145.
156–157 *Vicki insisted that they pawn her diamond*: Weaver and Weaver, *The Federal Siege at Ruby Ridge*, 19.
157 *One corner was set aside for Vicki's sewing*: Ibid., 19, 22.
157 *With the rush of building behind them*: Walter, "The Prodigal Dream."
157 *mene, mene, tekel, upharsin*: Daniel 5:25, KJV.
157 *"Jesus is telling me," she wrote*: Walter, *Ruby Ridge*, 59.
158 *After a small earthquake hit the Northwest*: Ibid., 54.
158 *A 1984 poll showed that 39 percent*: Boyer, *When Time Shall Be No More*, 144.
159 *"One Evil Empire down"*: Wills, *Reagan's America*, 29.
159 *Randy had wanted to build below the spring*: Weaver and Weaver, *The Federal Siege at Ruby Ridge*, 18.
159 *"basic survival was a full-time job"*: Weaver, *From Ruby Ridge to Freedom*, 15.
159 *During the brief summers*: Weaver, *From Ruby Ridge to Freedom*, 25.
159 *She foraged herbs to dry*: Ibid., 24.
160 *According to Sara, nobody in the family*: Ibid., 23.
160 *"readin', writin', arithmetic"*: Walter, *Ruby Ridge*, 54.
160 *"Everybody knows the government"*: Weland, "Weavers Prefer Isolation."
160 *Randy used one of the animals*: Weaver, *From Ruby Ridge to Freedom*, 18; Weaver and Weaver, *The Federal Siege at Ruby Ridge*, 12.

160 *They spent their free time*: Weaver, *From Ruby Ridge to Freedom*, 23.

160 *A hoop swing hung*: Goodman, *Ruby Ridge: Every Knee Shall Bow*.

160 *Later, he and Randy installed*: Weaver, *From Ruby Ridge to Freedom*, 17.

161 *In the evening, when work was finished*: Fuson and McCartan, "After the Showdown."

161 *Sara remembers the thrill*: Weaver, *From Ruby Ridge to Freedom*, 23.

162 *There was a two-seater outhouse*: Weaver and Weaver, *The Federal Siege at Ruby Ridge*, 19; author's interview with Mike Weland, October 18, 2023.

162 *Besides the cabin, the largest structure*: Weaver, *From Ruby Ridge to Freedom*, 236.

162 *Randy took short-term jobs*: Weaver, *From Ruby Ridge to Freedom*, 27; Brown and Brown, *First Canary*, 145; Walter, *Ruby Ridge*, 61.

162 *"as lazy as they come"*: Walter, *Ruby Ridge*, 133.

163 *Sara recalls the family of five*: Weaver, *From Ruby Ridge to Freedom*, 28.

163 *Harris's father had died*: Senate Judiciary Subcommittee Hearings, Kevin Harris testimony, September 26, 1995.

163 *In exchange for long hours*: Weaver and Weaver, *The Federal Siege at Ruby Ridge*, 20; Weaver, *From Ruby Ridge to Freedom*, 21.

163 *After a chance meeting with Vicki*: Senate Judiciary Subcommittee Hearings, Kevin Harris testimony, September 26, 1995.

163 *On the day he was leaving*: Ibid.

163 *Years later, Randy would publicly refer*: See, for instance, the speech he gave at the New Hampshire home of Ed and Elaine Brown, in 2007, available on YouTube, https://www.youtube.com/watch?v=Fs6QcPjpEbk.

163 *In 1984, he lived with the family*: Senate Judiciary Subcommittee Hearings, Kevin Harris testimony, September 26, 1995.

164 *They also explained their newfound conviction*: Walter, *Ruby Ridge*, 61.

164 *"Weaver likes to talk"*: Senate Judiciary Subcommittee Hearings, Kevin Harris testimony, September 26, 1995.

164 *In letters and occasional phone calls*: Walter, *Ruby Ridge*, 61.

164 *In the early 1970s, when Randy was coming*: Ibid., 62.

165 *Once they were well settled in their new home*: Walter, *Ruby Ridge*, 59.

165 *"You can't tell me," she wrote*: Ibid., 16.

165 *In fact, it was Brigham Young*: Stack and Noyce, "Worst Speech in LDS History."

165 *When the family arrived in 1983, Boundary County*: Stern, *A Force Upon the Plain*, 21.

165 *In the mid-'80s, after a string*: "An Idaho Resort Town Grapples with Bigotry and Bombings."

166 *But drop that same person*: Weaver, *From Ruby Ridge to Freedom*, 19.

166 *While fundamentalist ministers were often*: The definitive study of racism in the early fundamentalist movement is Leo P. Ribuffo's *The Old Christian Right*.

166 *"paramilitary political-religious cults"*: Aho, *This Thing of Darkness*, 123.

167 *The creed that united these assorted outfits*: A comprehensive overview of British Israelism and Christian Identity can be found in Michael Barkun's *Religion and the Racist Right*.

167 *While the notion that Anglo-Saxons are descended*: Barkun, *Religion and the Racist Right*, 122.

168 *William J. Cameron, the Canadian-born editor*: Ribuffo, *The Old Christian Right*, 12.

168 *If the basic premise of racism*: Barkun, *Religion and the Racist Right*, 159.

169 *Like Randy and Vicki, most people who arrived*: Aho, *Politics of Righteousness*, 85.

169 *"Yahweh is White Power!"*: Goodman, *Ruby Ridge: Every Knee Shall Bow*.

169 *"God deals with nations"*: Schram and Goshko, "Jerry Falwell Vows Amity with Israel."

170 *"We are Identity, but we are not Christians"*: Fuson and McCartan, "After the Showdown."

170 *One Iowa friend speculated*: Walter, "The Prodigal Dream."

170 *Julie Jordison saw her big sister's evolving*: Walter, *Ruby Ridge*, 18, 41.

NOTES

CHAPTER TWELVE

172 *When the Weavers moved into their cabin*: Weaver, *From Ruby Ridge to Freedom*, 19.
172 *It was also Terry Kinnison who sold them*: Ibid.
172 *Late in the fall of 1984*: Arbanas, "Friend: Weaver Became Racist."
172 *"a huge slapstick barn"*: Ibid.
172 *The whole deal was done off the books*: Arbanas, "Weaver's Ex-Neighbor Testifies."
172 *Based on some of the harsh things*: DOJ Report, IV; Miller, "Court Hears Ex-Friend's Testimony."
173 *the conflict might have begun*: Ibid.
173 *Sara would later recall the Kinnisons*: Weaver, *From Ruby Ridge to Freedom*, 19.
173 *The Weavers countersued*: Walter, *Ruby Ridge*, 94.
173 *"May the God of Abraham rebuke them"*: Ibid.
173 *As a parting shot*: Ibid., 64.
174 *Kinnison himself reported*: Miller, "Court Hears Ex-Friend's Testimony."
174 *He testified that they would kill*: DOJ Report, IV.
174 *"when [their] home will be under siege"*: Ibid., IV.
174 *One Bonners Ferry resident speculated*: Ibid., II.
174 *Randy told an FBI investigator*: Senate Judiciary Subcommittee Hearings, Randy Weaver testimony, September 6, 1995.
175 *During the Secret Service investigation*: Walter, *Ruby Ridge*, 63.
175 *On a cold winter day in 1985*: Walter, *Ruby Ridge*, 70.
175 *The whole mess was just a campaign*: Weaver, *From Ruby Ridge to Freedom*, 20; DOJ Report, IV.
175 *He added, however, that law enforcement*: DOJ Report, IV.
175 *We hereby make a public notice*: Ibid., III.
176 *"Please," she wrote, "let me apologize"*: Walter, *Ruby Ridge*, 64.
176 *Randy had become increasingly outspoken*: Miller, "Court Hears Ex-Friend's Testimony."
176 *A forest ranger friend of the Wohalis*: DOJ Report, IV.
177 *A friend described these men*: Brown and Brown, *First Canary*, 149.
177 *"Whatever God you serve"*: Miller, "Court Hears Ex-Friend's Testimony."
177 *"have three weapons brought to bear"*: DOJ Report, IV.

CHAPTER THIRTEEN

178 *"a bit on the goofy side"*: Weaver and Weaver, *The Federal Siege at Ruby Ridge*, 26.
178 *Some of his ideas were genuinely alarming*: DOJ Report, IV.
178 *"interested in learning more"*: Weaver and Weaver, *The Federal Siege at Ruby Ridge*, 27.
179 *At the Aryan Nations, the main uniform*: Aho, *This Thing of Darkness*, 154.
179 *The heart of the compound*: Day, "Welcome to Hayden Lake."
181 *In the year 2000, with legal support*: Definitive histories of the Aryan Nations can be found in Levitas, *The Terrorist Next Door*, and Zeskind, *Blood and Politics*.
181 *Back when Butler had started the Aryan Nations*: Belew, *Bring the War Home*, 4.
181 *It is difficult to get reliable numbers*: Ibid.
182 *Vietnam veterans made up an outsize part*: Ibid.
182 *Like the most ardent members*: Zeskind, *Blood and Politics*, 93.
183 *When Randy Weaver and Frank Kumnick*: Walter, *Ruby Ridge*, 76.
183 *Among them was a gangly middle-aged man*: Zeskind, *Blood and Politics*, 96.
183 *Pierce cannily built the National Alliance*: Southern Poverty Law Center, "William Pierce."
183 *Despite his prolific organizing*: Pierce, *The Turner Diaries*, available online as a PDF.
185 *"What will you do if the govt comes"*: Zeskind, *Blood and Politics*, 31.
185 *One tally puts the novel's body count*: Berger, "Alt History," *The Atlantic*, September 16, 2016.
185 *"William Pierce doesn't build bombs"*: Blythe, "The Guru of White Hate."
186 *Rev. Butler had personally baptized*: Levitas, *The Terrorist Next Door*, 106.

186 *As with so many on the apocalyptic far right*: Ibid., 105.
186 *"radicalize American yeomanry"*: Zeskind, *Blood and Politics*, 96.
186 *In a small tin barn in Metaline Falls*: Ibid., 97.
187 *They robbed an armored car in Seattle*: Ibid., 98.
187 *An Order member named Bruce Pierce*: Flynn and Gerhardt, *The Silent Brotherhood*, 210.
188 *It was an impressively planned attack*: Ibid., 237.
188 *The cash and the ruthlessness*: MacFarquhar, "From the Past, a Chilling Warning."
189 *Over the next few months*: Zeskind, *Blood and Politics*, 99.
189 *One fugitive shot and killed a Missouri highway patrolman*: Flynn and Gerhardt, *The Silent Brotherhood*, 386.
189 *They also seized hundreds of guns*: Zeskind, *Blood and Politics*, 99.
189 *In all, it was a bit of a mess*: Flynn and Gerhardt, *The Silent Brotherhood*, 385.
189 *The blockbuster trial in Fort Smith*: Ibid., 386.
190 *"Should you fall, my friend"*: Ibid., 388.
190 *Like the "don't eat the brown acid" warnings*: Walter, *Ruby Ridge*, 77.
190 *Aside from the fact that nobody*: Weaver and Weaver, *The Federal Siege at Ruby Ridge*, 26.

CHAPTER FOURTEEN
191 *When they parted*: Senate Judiciary Subcommittee Hearings, Kenneth Fadeley testimony, September 7, 1995.
191 *"Gus," whose real name was Kenneth Fadeley*: Ibid.
192 *At trial, Randy's defense*: Walter, *Ruby Ridge*, 300.
192 *For several years of dangerous undercover work*: Senate Judiciary Subcommittee Hearings, Herb Byerly testimony, September 7, 1995.
192 *Two years after the Ruby Ridge siege*: Senate Judiciary Subcommittee Hearings, Kenneth Fadeley testimony, September 7, 1995.
192 *One of the schemes he laid out for Gus*: Senate Judiciary Subcommittee Hearings, Herb Byerly testimony, September 7, 1995.
193 *Kumnick said that he could use his position*: Morlin, "Feds Foiled Aryan Plot."
193 *Kumnick laid this all out for Gus*: Ibid.
193 *"Of course, it's funny"*: Ibid.
194 *Agents gathered tips and compiled lists*: Walter, *Ruby Ridge*, 68.
194 *By the time the ATF*: DOJ Report, IV.
194 *Because of the bombings*: Senate Judiciary Subcommittee Hearings, Herb Byerly testimony, September 7, 1995.
195 *On an icy day in January of 1987*: Ibid.
195 *Kumnick, who had already met*: DOJ Report, IV.
195 *Randy, who had been cooped up*: Weaver and Weaver, *The Federal Siege at Ruby Ridge*, 27.
196 *The informant remembered meeting Randy*: Ibid.
196 *The three men greeted each other*: Walter, *Ruby Ridge*, 77.
197 *He quizzed Gus*: Ibid., 83.
197 *He repeatedly brought up the notion*: DOJ Report, IV.
197 *He spun his various schemes*: Morlin, "Feds Foiled Aryan Plot."
197 *In his harebrained way*: Walter, *Ruby Ridge*, 85.
197 *Away from his blustery friend*: Ibid., 87.
198 *Vicki had spent the afternoon shopping*: Ibid.
198 *"I hope he kills half of them"*: Ibid., 88.
198 *"So much for the stud finder"*: Weaver and Weaver, *The Federal Siege at Ruby Ridge*, 27.
198 *"I remember getting the impression"*: Weaver, *From Ruby Ridge to Freedom*, 34; DOJ Report, IV.
198 *One such young man*: Weaver, *From Ruby Ridge to Freedom*, 34, 83, 104.
199 *At the '87 Congress, it was Randy*: Senate Judiciary Subcommittee Hearings, Kenneth Fadeley testimony, September 7, 1995.

NOTES

CHAPTER FIFTEEN

200 *After five years in Idaho*: Walter, *Ruby Ridge*, 95.

200 *They sold one of their horses*: Brown and Brown, *First Canary*, 147.

200 *It sat along a deep, fast-flowing creek*: Weaver, *From Ruby Ridge to Freedom*, 32.

200 *"all of our time wasn't spent"*: Ibid., 33.

201 *The kids collected*: Ibid.; Brown and Brown, *First Canary*, 147.

201 *The weavers had become part of*: Brown and Brown, *First Canary*, 148.

201 *One family felt so inspired*: Brown and Brown, *First Canary*, 147, 149.

201 *The families quickly became close*: Ibid.

201 *Around the same time*: Walter, *Ruby Ridge*, 95.

202 *Steve Tanner, one of the Weavers'*: Senate Judiciary Subcommittee Hearings, Ruth Rau testimony, September 20, 1995.

202 *Since the deal was off the books*: Ibid.

202 *Vicki might have been naturally suited*: Walter, *Ruby Ridge*, 132.

202 *"If a grizzly bear comes and hurts"*: Fuson and McCartan, "After the Showdown."

203 *As Sara remembers it*: Weaver, *From Ruby Ridge to Freedom*, 31.

203 *As for the decision to run*: August 2018 interview with John Lamb, available on YouTube, https://www.youtube.com/watch?v=xD5sudxGgTo.

204 *As a campaign gimmick*: Weaver, *From Ruby Ridge to Freedom*, 33.

204 *Asked by a reporter if he would permit*: Miller, "Sheriff's Race Focus of Primary."

204 *"I question whether they should pass"*: Ibid.

204 *"was not to let federal agents come"*: August 2018 interview with John Lamb, available on YouTube, https://www.youtube.com/watch?v=xD5sudxGgTo.

204–205 *"Boundary County Sheriff Candidate"*: Miller, "Boundary Sheriff Candidate Opposed to Mixed Marriages."

205 *While the other candidates for sheriff*: Ibid.

205 *"the Jews running the world"*: Ibid.

205 *Apart from that, Randy's strategy*: Brown and Brown, *First Canary*, 148.

205 *He partly blamed the media*: Walter, *Ruby Ridge*, 97.

205 *Afterward, one voter told*: Fuson and McCartan, "After the Showdown."

205 *"but was kept from entering the office"*: The Phoenix Liberator, November 3, 1992, http://phoenixarchives.com/liberator/1992/1192/110392.pdf.

206 *A month after the election*: DOJ Report, IV.

206 *Nineteen eighty-nine was supposed to be a banner year*: Hamm, *Apocalypse in Oklahoma*, 16.

206 *Along with a special celebration*: "Aryan Leader Will Still Meet Skinheads."

206 *Randy once again ran into Kenneth*: Walter, *Ruby Ridge*, 100.

206 *Randy also introduced the Gus*: Senate Judiciary Subcommittee Hearings, Kenneth Fadeley testimony, September 7, 1995.

207 *In particular, Byerly hoped*: DOJ Report, IV.

207 *Chuck Howarth was a former Klansman*: Senate Judiciary Subcommittee Hearings, Herb Byerly testimony, September 7, 1995.

207 *David Trochmann was a conspiracy theorist and Identity Christian*: Ibid.

208 *As it happened, the Weavers*: Senate Judiciary Subcommittee Hearings, Kenneth Fadeley testimony, September 7, 1995.

208 *As Fadeley looked on*: "Unsolved Murders," *Spokesman-Review*.

208 *When Vicki began to cry*: Walter, *Ruby Ridge*, 101.

208 *According to notes Fadeley wrote*: Senate Judiciary Subcommittee Hearings, Kenneth Fadeley testimony, September 7, 1995.

209 *Randy asked what kind of weapons*: Ibid.

209 *By scouring local shops*: Weaver, *From Ruby Ridge to Freedom*, 40.

209 *According to Randy, Fadeley pointed*: Weaver and Weaver, *The Federal Siege at Ruby Ridge*, 28.

209 *This time, it was Fadeley*: Senate Judiciary Subcommittee Hearings, Herb Byerly testimony, September 7, 1995.
209 *In truth, the ATF wanted to delay*: Walter, *Ruby Ridge*, 104.
209 *Randy asked where the finished product*: Senate Judiciary Subcommittee Hearings, Herb Byerly testimony, September 7, 1995.
210 *"I cut 'em as short as you could"*: August 2018 interview with John Lamb, available on YouTube, https://www.youtube.com/watch?v=xD5sudxGgTo.
210 *"We talked about other things"*: Weaver and Weaver, *The Federal Siege at Ruby Ridge*, 28.
210 *"Other than that, we don't have to be"*: DOJ Report, IV.
210 *"Four or five a week?"*: Ibid.
210 *But in the meantime, winter was coming*: Weaver and Weaver, *The Federal Siege at Ruby Ridge*, 28.

CHAPTER SIXTEEN
211 *then the Last Judgment begins*: Blake, "A Vision of the Last Judgment."
213 *After a year and a half*: Weaver, *From Ruby Ridge to Freedom*, 36.
213 *She was fourteen now*: Ibid.
214 *"Cut off thine hair"*: Jeremiah 7:29 (KJV), quoted in Walter, *Ruby Ridge*, 111.
214 *The ATF was all ready*: Walter, *Ruby Ridge*, 106.
214 *"Don't be doing any business"*: August 2018 interview with John Lamb, available on YouTube, https://www.youtube.com/watch?v=xD5sudxGgTo.
214 *"If you want to believe someone else"*: Walter, *Ruby Ridge*, 108.
214 *By then, the ATF had moved*: Ibid.
214 *The informant handed over the cash*: Weaver and Weaver, *The Federal Siege at Ruby Ridge*, 29.
215 *"I will kill him. I will kill him."*: February 2018 interview with Roger Roots and John Lamb, available on YouTube, https://www.youtube.com/watch?v=PmgtMpE7uYM.
215 *They asked Gus why his VIN*: Walter, *Ruby Ridge*, 112.
215 *He counted himself lucky*: Morlin, "ATF Informer Says FBI's Spy Blew His Cover."
215 *A splashy figure at Hayden Lake*: Ibid.
216 *It was three men*: Ibid.
216 *Meanwhile, with Fadeley out of circulation*: Senate Judiciary Subcommittee Hearings, Herb Byerly testimony, September 7, 1995.
217 *Three weeks after Byerly*: Weaver and Weaver, *The Federal Siege at Ruby Ridge*, 29.
217 *The agents, dressed in their office clothes*: Weaver, *From Ruby Ridge to Freedom*, 41.
217 *On their way out of town*: Brown and Brown, *First Canary*, 148.
217 *Randy emerged wearing*: Senate Judiciary Subcommittee Hearings, Herb Byerly testimony, September 7, 1995.
217 *"one of those kids in school"*: February 2018 interview with Roger Roots and John Lamb, available on YouTube, https://www.youtube.com /watch?v=PmgtMpE7uYM.
217 *If Randy would provide them*: DOJ Report, IV.
218 *Randy flushed with anger*: Senate Judiciary Subcommittee Hearings, Herb Byerly testimony, September 7, 1995.
218 *As a first-time offender*: Walter, *Ruby Ridge*, 118.
218 *"Aryan Nations & all our brethren"*: Brown and Brown, *First Canary*, 161.
219 *She tacked copies to the doors*: Brown and Brown, *First Canary*, 159.
219 *On December 13, 1990, the US Attorney*: DOJ Report, IV.
220 *"Ambush City"*: Senate Judiciary Subcommittee Hearings, Herb Byerly testimony, September 7, 1995.
220 *This involved leaving the kids*: Brown and Brown, *First Canary*, 161.
220 *Crossing the bridge, with Randy*: DOJ Report, IV.
221 *"Nice trick," Randy said to Byerly*: Senate Judiciary Subcommittee Hearings, Herb Byerly testimony, September 7, 1995.
221 *Vicki showed up with a security guard*: Brown and Brown, *First Canary*, 164.

221 *Having put so much effort*: DOJ Report, IV.

222 *He somehow thought that if he lost*: Walter, *Ruby Ridge*, 126; DOJ Report, IV.

222 *And since the only thing they had*: Weaver, *From Ruby Ridge to Freedom*, 46.

223 *Before letting him go, the magistrate explained*: DOJ Report, IV.

223 *Randy said that he would like Everett Hofmeister*: Brown and Brown, *First Canary*, 164.

224 *After a long family meeting*: Walter, *Ruby Ridge*, 118.

224 *"You ain't going anywhere"*: August 2018 interview with John Lamb, available on YouTube, https://www.youtube.com/watch?v=xD5sudxGgTo.

224 *"null and void in my mind"*: Randy Weaver speech at Kerrville, Texas, 2003.

224 *"I'll keep writing as long as someone"*: Walter, *Ruby Ridge*, 127.

224 *From the court's perspective*: Ibid., IV.

225 *Both were written*: Ibid.

226 *"The stink of your lawless government"*: Ibid.

226 *Vicki's letter to the Queen*: Ibid.

226 *"to stay home"*: Weaver and Weaver, *The Federal Siege at Ruby Ridge*, 34.

227 *It was a colleague*: DOJ Report, IV.

228 *"believes that this charge"*: DOJ Report, IV.

228 *The Marshals office in Idaho*: Ibid.

228 *"wait-and-see attitude"*: Senate Judiciary Subcommittee Hearings, David Hunt testimony, September 15, 1995.

228 *He had brought in hundreds of fugitives*: Ibid.

228 *Evans had been the top marshal*: Walter, *Ruby Ridge*, 129.

229 *With the Weavers, everything*: Senate Judiciary Subcommittee Hearings, David Hunt testimony, September 15, 1995.

229 *He also reached out*: Goodman, *Ruby Ridge: Every Knee Shall Bow*.

229 *When news that Randy was officially a fugitive*: February 2018 interview with Roger Roots and John Lamb, available on YouTube, https://www.youtube.com/watch?v=Pmgt MpE7uYM.

229 *At forty-one, she had not been*: Weaver and Weaver, *The Federal Siege at Ruby Ridge*, 34.

229 *"I wouldn't do that"*: Ibid.

229 *"in any other manner which was convenient"*: Ibid.

230 *We, the Weaver family, have been shown*: DOJ Report, IV.

230 *"I was astounded"*: Senate Judiciary Subcommittee Hearings, David Hunt testimony, September 15, 1995.

230 *But at the time, the Marshals*: Fuson and McCartan, "After the Showdown."

230 *"If the kids can't live in peace"*: Senate Judiciary Subcommittee Hearings, David Hunt testimony, September 15, 1995.

CHAPTER SEVENTEEN

231 *For news of the outside world*: Brown and Brown, *First Canary*, 81.

231 *Vicki continued to weave rugs*: Fuson and McCartan, "After the Showdown."

231 *Maurice Ellsworth grimly joked*: Senate Judiciary Subcommittee Hearings, Maurice Ellsworth testimony, September 15, 1995.

232 *While Hunt tried in vain*: Walter, *Ruby Ridge*, 143.

232 *In Ron Evans's initial request*: DOJ Report, IV.

233 *"That is when they started treating us"*: Senate Judiciary Subcommittee Hearings, Ruth Rau testimony, September 20, 1995.

233 *While Randy shouted about ZOG*: Walter, *Ruby Ridge*, 116.

233 *Ruth Rau's later testimony*: Senate Judiciary Subcommittee Hearings, Ruth Rau testimony, September 20, 1995.

233 *They donned swastika armbands*: Brown and Brown, *First Canary*, 150; Senate Judiciary Subcommittee Hearings, Ruth Rau testimony, September 20, 1995.

233 *"soaping the windows"*: Senate Judiciary Subcommittee Hearings, Randy Weaver testimony, September 6, 1995.

234 *"set the marshals up"*: Senate Judiciary Subcommittee Hearings, Ruth Rau testimony, September 20, 1995.

235 *"was set to stand them off"*: Senate Judiciary Subcommittee Hearings, Ed Torrance testimony, September 20, 1995.

235 *"feds came after him"*: Ibid.

235 *I was just waiting for someone"*: Senate Judiciary Subcommittee Hearings, Randy Weaver testimony, September 6, 1995.

235 *When, during the long runup*: Mike Weland, "Weavers Prefer Isolation." Randy's other conditions can be found in the *DOJ Report*, IV.

235 *"I call it the paranoid style"*: Hofstadter, *The Paranoid Style in American Politics*, 3.

236 *The notion that evil elites*: Boyer, *When Time Shall Be No More*, 171.

237 *"[Randy] was paranoid"*: Walter, *Ruby Ridge*, 132.

237 *They brought books*: Ibid., 135.

237 *"I wish the Master"*: Ibid., 134.

238 *In a chipper letter*: Rhodes, "Ex-C.F. Family Involved in Mountain Standoff."

238 *Kevin Harris came and went*: Walter, *Ruby Ridge*, 135.

238 *They brought milk, bags of groceries*: Fuson and McCartan, "After the Showdown."

238 *People they had never even met*: Walter, *Ruby Ridge*, 136.

238 *Richard Butler, who had beaten*: Ibid., 140.

238 *"sit in our home and chat"*: Weaver, *The Federal Siege at Ruby Ridge*, 34.

239 *"we are all fine"*: Rhodes, "Ex-C.F. Family Involved in Mountain Standoff."

239 *In April, the Griders*: Walter, *Ruby Ridge*, 136.

239 *In June, they had a party for Vicki's forty-second birthday*: Ibid., 139.

239 *In response to the accusation*: Ibid., 144.

239 *"I have no way of knowing for sure"*: Walter, "The Prodigal Dream."

239 *Hunt asked Jeppeson*: DOJ Report, IV.

239 *"Dave Hunt was just playing"*: Weaver, *The Federal Siege at Ruby Ridge*, 35.

240 *"Our situation is not about shotguns"*: Aho, *This Thing of Darkness*, 57.

240 *"Things aren't looking good"*: Rhodes, "Ex-C.F. Family Involved in Mountain Standoff."

240 *That September, Bantam Books*: Boyer, *When Time Shall Be No More*, 329.

240 *A few months later, the influential dispensationalist*: Sutton, *American Apocalypse*, 361.

240 *Another popular title released that year*: Barkun, *A Culture of Conspiracy*, 52.

240 *A front-page story in the New York Times*: Boyer, *When Time Shall Be No More*, 329.

241 *It did not put them at ease to hear*: Weaver, *From Ruby Ridge to Freedom*, 46.

241 *After thirty-six difficult hours*: Weaver and Weaver, *The Federal Siege at Ruby Ridge*, 34.

241 *"Elisheba Anne Weaver, Born Oct. 24"*: Fuson and McCartan, "After the Showdown."

241 *In keeping with Old Testament guidelines*: Weaver, *From Ruby Ridge to Freedom*, 46.

241 *When Sara got her period*: Ibid.

241 *Through Allen Jeppeson, he assured*: Walter, *Ruby Ridge*, 144.

241 *"Your lawless One World Beast Courts"*: DOJ Report, IV.

242 *She also demanded that Hunt answer for*: Walter, *Ruby Ridge*, 144.

242 *The Justice Department later deemed*: DOJ Report, IV.

242 *For his part, Randy insisted*: Weaver and Weaver, *The Federal Siege at Ruby Ridge*, 34.

242 *"I respect courage and would have trusted"*: Senate Judiciary Subcommittee Hearings, Randy Weaver testimony, September 6, 1995.

242 *Echoing this, Allen Jeppeson*: Senate Judiciary Subcommittee Hearings, Allen Jeppeson testimony, September 20, 1995.

242 *"I was looking for Jesus Christ"*: Senate Judiciary Subcommittee Hearings, Randy Weaver testimony, September 6, 1995.

242 *When the snows came*: DOJ Report, IV.

CHAPTER EIGHTEEN

243 *When winter loosened its grip*: DOJ Report, IV.
243 *It started in March*: Morlin, "Feds Have Fugitive 'Under Our Nose.'"
244 *"He's sitting up there"*: Coates, "Standoff with Police Enters Second Year."
244 *According to Sara, the racket*: Weaver, From Ruby Ridge to Freedom, 43.
244 *One magazine ran a picture*: Ibid.
244 *The case received so much publicity*: Walter, Ruby Ridge, 152.
244 *"It is the duty of the Marshals"*: Associated Press, "Marshals Know He's There But Leave Fugitive Alone."
245 *"Holed Up on a Mountaintop"*: As shown in Goodman, Ruby Ridge: Every Knee Shall Bow.
245 *"the Marshal Service is sending a message"*: Rhodes, "Ex-C.F. Family Involved in Mountain Standoff."
245 *"I have to wonder what the feds"*: Stern, A Force Upon the Plain, 23.
245 *"[Randy's] kind of under house arrest"*: Rhodes, "Ex-C.F. Family Involved in Mountain Standoff."
245 *According to Randy, Geraldo's producers*: Weland, "Weavers Prefer Isolation."
245 *The news clippings they had already*: Ibid.
246 *"may have been shot at"*: DOJ Report, IV ("Chronology of events").
246 *In late March, he called a meeting*: Walter, Ruby Ridge, 149.
246 *"While time may have initially been"*: DOJ Report, IV.
246 *Trying for a Hail Mary*: Senate Judiciary Subcommittee Hearings, Maurice Ellsworth testimony, September 15, 1995.
247 *What would happen if he were*: Ibid.
247 *"Mr. Randall has indoctrinated his family"*: DOJ Report, IV.
248 *"to wait until Mr. Randall leaves his house"*: Ibid.
248 *Jurgensen, who was a competent carpenter*: Walter, Ruby Ridge, 157.
249 *As it was, the Marshals were spending*: Ibid.
249 *In April, Roderick*: Ibid., 152.
249 *Footage of the Weavers*: DOJ Report, IV.
249 *Watching the family that spring*: Ibid; Senate Judiciary Subcommittee Hearings, Arthur Roderick testimony, September 15, 1995.
249 *Kevin and Sam took it apart*: Senate Judiciary Subcommittee Hearings, Kevin Harris testimony, September 26, 1995.
249 *Roderick thought that Harris*: Senate Judiciary Subcommittee Hearings, Arthur Roderick testimony, September 15, 1995.
249 *Through mutual friends*: Author's interview with Mike Weland, October 18, 2023.
250 *"Vicki was the strength"*: Cole, "Weaver Isn't on a Crusade."
250 *"everyone thought of Vicki as the head"*: Ibid.
250 *"You really ought to interview"*: Ibid. (Original interview is with James Aho, subsequently quoted by Michelle Cole.)
250 *"Right now the only thing they can take"*: Weland, "Weavers Prefer Isolation."
250 *Henry Hudson would be sitting*: DOJ Report, IV.
251 *If there was violence*: Ibid.
251 *He was a longtime SOG member*: Senate Judiciary Subcommittee Hearings, Arthur Roderick testimony, September 15, 1995.
251 *He played hockey in the winter*: Turk, "William Degan: A Look Back."
251 *At a party in Boston*: Letter by Karen Degan, read into record during Senate Judiciary Subcommittee Hearings, September 15, 1995.
252 *"Zeroing" guns after shipping*: DOJ Report, IV.

CHAPTER NINETEEN

253 *They did not expect to see any*: DOJ Report, IV.
254 *Meanwhile, the "observation team"*: Ibid.

NOTES

254 *Harris had spent much of that spring*: Senate Judiciary Subcommittee Hearings, Kevin Harris testimony, September 26, 1995.

255 *Roderick wanted to get a better look*: Senate Judiciary Subcommittee Hearings, Arthur Roderick testimony, September 15, 1995.

256 *Having gotten closer to the cabin*: DOJ Report, IV.

256 *"typical vehicle response"*: Senate Judiciary Subcommittee Hearings, Dave Hunt testimony, September 15, 1995.

256 *The observation team watched*: DOJ Report, IV.

256 *"The dogs are on us"*: Ibid.

257 *One of them yelled, "Freeze, Randy!"*: Senate Judiciary Subcommittee Hearings, Arthur Roderick testimony, September 15, 1995.

257 *"I'm coming, Dad!"*: Senate Judiciary Subcommittee Hearings, Randy Weaver testimony, September 6, 1995.

257 *"You shot my dog, you sonofabitch"*: Senate Judiciary Subcommittee Hearings, Kevin Harris testimony, September 26, 1995.

257 *Roderick would later find a bullet hole*: Senate Judiciary Subcommittee Hearings, Arthur Roderick testimony, September 15, 1995.

257 *Kevin Harris, shooting from the hip*: Senate Judiciary Subcommittee Hearings, Kevin Harris testimony, September 26, 1995.

257 *Unlike the Weavers, the marshals*: Senate Judiciary Subcommittee Hearings, Arthur Roderick testimony, September 15, 1995.

258 *Cooper testified under oath*: Senate Judiciary Subcommittee Hearings, Larry Cooper testimony, September 15, 1995; Morlin, "Marshal Killed Weaver's Son."

258 *A subsequent investigation*: Morlin, "Marshal Killed Weaver's Son."

258 *They could agree on one thing*: DOJ Report, IV; Larry Cooper interview for US Marshals Museum, October 24, 2013, https://www.youtube.com/watch?v=Nc5-BH6-vGg.

258 *When, two days later*: Senate Judiciary Subcommittee Hearings, Arthur Roderick testimony, September 15, 1995.

258–259 *In a similar fashion, Randy would later suggest*: August 2018 interview with John Lamb, available on YouTube, https://www.youtube.com/watch?v=xD5sudxGgTo.

259 *Up at the observation post*: Goodman, *Ruby Ridge: Every Knee Shall Bow*.

259 *Passing through the fern meadow*: DOJ Report, IV.

259 *He pulled off Degan's shirt*: Walter, *Ruby Ridge*, 173.

260 *"Yahweh! Yahweh!"*: Ibid.

260 *"I have one officer dead"*: Recording of 911 call from Goodman, *Ruby Ridge: Every Knee Shall Bow*.

260 *Meanwhile, Vicki changed into jeans*: Weaver and Weaver, *The Federal Siege at Ruby Ridge*, 38.

260 *They half-expected to be shot*: Ibid.

260 *The three marshals still crouching*: Larry Cooper interview for US Marshals Museum, October 24, 2013, https://www.youtube.com /watch?v=Nc5-BH6-vGg.

260 *The three men, who had been out*: Walter, *Ruby Ridge*, 178, 179.

261 *"pinned down"*: DOJ Report, IV.

261 *Whatever was really happening*: Ibid.

261 *They made it to the meadow*: DOJ Report, IV.

261 *Unable to find a light switch*: Larry Cooper interview for US Marshals Museum, October 24, 2013, https://www.youtube.com/watch?v=Nc5-BH6-vGg.

261 *The exhausted officers brought their weapons*: DOJ Report, IV.

262 *Even if it had not been*: Ibid.

262 *The FBI called up SWAT units*: Ibid.

262 *"performed a good pincer move"*: Senate Judiciary Subcommittee Hearings, Arthur Roderick testimony, September 15, 1995.

262 *"like someone hunting rabbits"*: Senate Judiciary Subcommittee Hearings, Larry Cooper testimony, September 15, 1995.

263 *As it happened, Mueller had been*: DOJ Report, IV.

264 *"clearly... willing to shoot at"*: Ibid.

264 *Once Harris and the family retreated*: Ibid.

264 *Earlier that afternoon, a mile up the hill*: Weaver and Weaver, *The Federal Siege at Ruby Ridge*, 48.

264 *When it started to rain*: Weaver, *From Ruby Ridge to Freedom*, 55.

264 *"It sounded like every patrol car"*: Senate Judiciary Subcommittee Hearings, Kevin Harris testimony, September 26, 1995.

265 *In the dark, Kevin and Randy*: Weaver, *From Ruby Ridge to Freedom*, 56.

265 *On the local radio*: Weaver and Weaver, *The Federal Siege at Ruby Ridge*, 39.

265 *When he came back inside*: Weaver, *From Ruby Ridge to Freedom*, 56.

CHAPTER TWENTY

266 *A few hours before that flight left*: DOJ Report, IV.

266 *Neither Potts nor Rogers wanted*: Ibid.

266 *By 6:30 p.m., an advance team*: Ibid.

267 *"could be the subject of deadly force"*: Ibid.

267 *He received preliminary approval*: Walter, *Ruby Ridge*, 184.

267 *By the next morning, the advance team*: DOJ Report, IV.

268 *Idaho governor Cecil Andrus*: Ibid.

268 *In Bonners Ferry, the first day of the school year*: Lobsinger, "County Postpones School Opening Day."

268 *With the FBI in charge*: Zeskind, *Blood and Politics*, 304; DOJ Report, IV.

268 *He watched in distress*: Ibid.

269 *Back at the ski condo on Saturday*: Ibid.

269 *A few days later, they left Idaho*: Walter, *Ruby Ridge*, 227.

269 *"Weaver/Harris group"*: DOJ Report, IV.

270 *"well trained and capable of firing"*: Ibid.

270 *Saturday, the day after the shootout*: Weaver, *From Ruby Ridge to Freedom*, 57.

270 *Why had nobody come up the hill*: Ibid.

271 *They tried to remain*: DOJ Report, IV.

271 *The night before, they had set*: Weaver, *From Ruby Ridge to Freedom*, 57.

271 *Vicki was determined*: Walter, *Ruby Ridge*, 198.

271 *They placed boxes of ammo*: Ibid., 199.

271 *By 10:30 that morning*: DOJ Report, IV, Part F.

271 *The Weavers could then pick up*: Ibid.

271 *The other would carry a small assault team*: Ibid.

272 *At 2:40 p.m., a draft of the plan*: Ibid.

272 *One veteran agent, Michael Kahoe*: Associated Press, "FBI Agent Gets Prison Term for Destroying Ruby Ridge Report."

273 *"serious constitutional infirmities"*: DOJ Report, IV, Part F.

273 *"to assist HRT personnel"*: Ibid.

273 *Gene Glenn, who was technically running the show*: Ibid.

273 *"If you see 'em, shoot 'em."*: Hamm, *Apocalypse in Oklahoma*, 24.

273 *In the early afternoon*: DOJ Report, IV, Part F.

274 *"long-range precision fire"*: Ibid.

274 *It consisted of two men*: Ibid.

274 *Kevin took the opportunity*: Walter, *Ruby Ridge*, 199.

274 *"I wanted to go see my boy"*: Senate Judiciary Subcommittee Hearings, Randy Weaver testimony, September 6, 1995.

274 *It was the sixth such flight*: DOJ Report, IV, Part F.
275 *Just as they turned to go back*: Ibid.
275 *Other snipers in the area*: Ibid.
275 *It felt, he said, like being kicked*: Weaver and Weaver, *The Federal Siege at Ruby Ridge*, 39.
275 *"to spit in the coward's face."*: Ibid.
275 *"What happened?"*: Senate Judiciary Subcommittee Hearings, Randy Weaver testimony, September 6, 1995.
276 *The sniper reasoned*: DOJ Report, IV, Part F.
276 *"Like a washrag"*: Weaver, *From Ruby Ridge to Freedom*, 59.
277 *The baby was covered in blood*: Ibid.
277 *It took a few seconds for everyone to register*: Ibid., 60.
277 *For the benefit of his daughters*: Ibid.
277 *After placing a blanket*: Ibid.
277 *Sara removed his shirt*: Ibid.
277 *"They were shooting at us"*: Ibid., 61.
278 *"After dad put his shirt and jacket"*: Ibid.

CHAPTER TWENTY-ONE
279 *At 6:30 that evening, half an hour after*: DOJ Report, IV, Part F.
280 *"maybe one of the children could run out"*: Walter, *Ruby Ridge*, 199.
280 *Some of the snipers, crouched in the woods*: DOJ Report, IV, Part H.
280 *"the world is nothing"*: Fuson and McCartan, "After the Showdown."
280 *Sara cut off his shirt*: Weaver, *From Ruby Ridge to Freedom*, 65.
280 *Starting a little after 9:00 p.m.*: Walter, *Ruby Ridge*, 208.
280 *Randy locked the front door*: Weaver, *From Ruby Ridge to Freedom*, 60.
281 *"Can't do it, buddy"*: Senate Judiciary Subcommittee Hearings, Randy Weaver testimony, September 6, 1995.
281 *Rachel took over care of Elisheba*: Burkett, *Right Women*, 108.
281 *Randy piled furniture*: Weaver, *From Ruby Ridge to Freedom*, 61.
281 *Two APCs rolled*: DOJ Report, IV, Part H.
281 *"We kept our silence"*: Weaver, *From Ruby Ridge to Freedom*, 61.
281 *Realizing the obvious*: DOJ Report, IV, Part H.
282 *"Whoever grabbed that telephone"*: Senate Judiciary Subcommittee Hearings, Randy Weaver testimony, September 6, 1995.
282 *In the afternoon, the APCs returned*: DOJ Report, IV, Part H.
282 *What looked to the Weavers*: Weaver, *From Ruby Ridge to Freedom*, 66.
282 *One indication of just how badly*: Walter, *Ruby Ridge*, 214.
282 *They assumed that the pious people*: DOJ Report, IV, Part H.
282 *When their questions were met*: Walter, *Ruby Ridge*, 214.
282 *People who had been hanging back*: Rhodes Production System, *Ruby Creek Massacre*.
283 *One man approached the phalanx*: McLean and Lobsinger, "Weavers' Son Found Dead."
283 *When they had to go to the bathroom*: Walter, *Ruby Ridge*, 224.
283 *Agents were installing listening devices*: DOJ Report, IV, Part H.
283 *Terrified for her father's life*: Weaver, *From Ruby Ridge to Freedom*, 68.
283 *"I stayed close to my rifle"*: Ibid.
283 *One morning, he suggested that Vicki*: Walter, *Ruby Ridge*, 215.
284 *"psychological warfare"*: Weaver and Weaver, *The Federal Siege at Ruby Ridge*, 40.
284 *"You killed my fucking wife!"*: Ibid., 214.
284 *The Weavers came to believe*: DOJ Report, IV, Part H.
284 *Down in the meadow, at the sprawling encampment*: Ibid.
284 *"I didn't want to negotiate"*: Senate Judiciary Subcommittee Hearings, Randy Weaver testimony, September 6, 1995.

284 *The FBI started to worry*: DOJ Report, IV, Part H.

284 *"Get the fuck out of here!"*: Ibid.

285 *"Sensing some sort of trick"*: Weaver, *From Ruby Ridge to Freedom*, 71.

285 *The aggressive rules of engagement*: DOJ Report, IV, Parts F and H.

285 *On Wednesday afternoon*: DOJ Report, "Chronology of Events."

285 *Instead of responding*: Walter, *Ruby Ridge*, 232.

286 *With Kevin and Randy dictating*: Walter, *Ruby Ridge*, 229.

286 *The day after they recorded this testimonial*: Ibid., 231.

287 *Jackie and Tony Brown, the Weavers' close friends*: Brown and Brown, *First Canary*, 41.

287 *John Trochmann, who would harness*: Burkett, *Right Women*, 106.

287 *Near the bridge, she and other women*: Ibid.

287 *Tom Metzger, a former grand dragon*: Zeskind, *Blood and Politics*, 305.

288 *In Colorado, an Identity pastor*: Stern, *A Force Upon the Plain*, 35.

288 *Willis Carto's Spotlight reported tirelessly*: Zeskind, *Blood and Politics*, 305.

288 *People parked haphazardly*: Hamm, *Apocalypse in Oklahoma*, 25.

288 *There were skinhead crews*: Ibid.

288 *Members of the Aryan Nations*: Zeskind, *Blood and Politics*, 304.

288 *Someone handed out photocopies*: Stern, *A Force Upon the Plain*, 26.

288 *Richard Butler, who had encouraged Randy*: *Ruby Ridge: American Experience*, PBS Documentary.

288 *To underscore the continuity*: Hamm, *Apocalypse in Oklahoma*, 25; Belew, *Bring the War Home*, 198.

288 *"'There's a family not far from here'"*: Westover, *Educated*, 8.

289 *Like many others, young Tara Westover*: Ibid., 209.

289 *When local contractors arrived*: Rhodes Production System, *Ruby Creek Massacre*.

290 *Some believed that Bill Grider*: Bock, *Ambush at Ruby Ridge*, 77.

290 *One canny promoter wandered the crowd*: Stern, *A Force Upon the Plain*, 34.

291 *"Knowing that there were people"*: Weaver and Weaver, *The Federal Siege at Ruby Ridge*, 61.

291 *"White Supremacy Fights On"*: Reed, "White Supremacy Fights On."

291 *"no one was injured in the shooting"*: Weaver and Weaver, *The Federal Siege at Ruby Ridge*, 71.

291 *The Friday night canard*: "One Marshal Dead, Others Confront Fugitive in Idaho."

291 *The cabin, sided in three-quarter-inch plywood*: See, for instance, Associated Press, "Marshal Slain at Remote Idaho Cabin."

292 *With a single pan of the camera*: Most signs mentioned are visible in Rhodes Production System, *Ruby Creek Massacre*. Also a good list from: Stern, *A Force Upon the Plain*, 24.

292 *A group of men from Portland*: Goodman, *Ruby Ridge: Every Knee Shall Bow*.

293 *In Ruby Creek Massacre*: Rhodes Production System, *Ruby Creek Massacre*.

293 *"We are truly convinced"*: Weaver and Weaver, *The Federal Siege at Ruby Ridge*, xvi.

294 *On Wednesday, four days after Vicki*: Hamm, *Apocalypse in Oklahoma*, 26.

294 *One local vet kept a stern vigil*: Rhodes Production System, *Ruby Creek Massacre*.

CHAPTER TWENTY-TWO

295 *Gritz— "rhymes with whites"*: Walter, *Ruby Ridge*, 234.

295 *Elected officials harnessed that pain and the spectacle*: Zeskind, *Blood and Politics*, 295.

296 *"Do you see the sign, scent, stain, and mark"*: Stern, *A Force Upon the Plain*, 30.

296 *Among them was Randy's friend Tony Brown*: Brown and Brown, *First Canary*, 62, 71.

296 *At the same time, Kirby Ferris*: Bock, *Ambush at Ruby Ridge*, 87.

296 *On Wednesday evening, five days after*: DOJ Report, IV, Part H.

297 *At the protest by the creek*: Walter, *Ruby Ridge*, 234.

297 *A few "Gritz for President" signs*: Stern, *A Force Upon the Plain*, 30.

297 *Then, on Friday—a full week*: Rhodes Production System, *Ruby Creek Massacre*.

298 *"I want to talk to Bo Gritz in person!"*: DOJ Report, IV, Part H.

298 *By then, the FBI's behavioral scientist*: Ibid.
298 *A subsequent review of notes and interviews*: Ibid.
299 *The crowd, visibly relieved*: This entire scene is recorded in Rhodes Production System, *Ruby Creek Massacre.*
300 *"I'm ready to get my gun and my clips"*: Dunn, "Mountain Standoff."
300 *Standing at the edge of the crowd*: Walter, *Ruby Ridge*, 246.
300 *"Arise, O Israel! It is time for war!"*: Rhodes Production System, *Ruby Creek Massacre.*
300 *This time, he was joined*: Brown and Brown, *First Canary*, 73.
300 *Who, she wondered, were they at war with?*: Ibid., 90.
300 *"Only if I can wear it backwards"*: Ibid., 92.
300 *As the little delegation approached*: Ibid.
300 *Instead, Gritz and Randy spoke*: DOJ Report, IV, Part H.
300 *Gritz explained that Spence*: Foster and Morlin, "Weaver Discusses Surrender at Ruby Ridge."
301 *Although Sara would not let Gritz or McLamb*: Weaver and Weaver, *The Federal Siege at Ruby Ridge*, 62.
301 *Kevin, who had been smoking*: Brown and Brown, *First Canary*, 92.
301 *Worried that Jackie would be searched*: Ibid.
301 *Borrowing a knife*: Ibid., 99.
301 *As if imparting a sacrament*: Rhodes Production System, *Ruby Creek Massacre.*
301 *Once she was finally alone*: Brown and Brown, *First Canary*, 100.
302 *Sara, still convinced that anyone who stepped*: Weaver and Weaver, *The Federal Siege at Ruby Ridge*, 62.
302 *At this, Gritz lost his cool*: Walter, *Ruby Ridge*, 242.
302 *Jaundiced and weakened*: Weaver and Weaver, *The Federal Siege at Ruby Ridge*, 62.
302 *By late morning, everyone inside*: DOJ Report, IV, Part H.
302 *Around six that evening*: Brown and Brown, *First Canary*, 105.
302 *Promising not to let the body*: Weaver and Weaver, *The Federal Siege at Ruby Ridge*, 63.
302 *Then she mopped up a puddle*: Brown and Brown, *First Canary*, 105; DOJ Report, IV, Part H.
303 *Jackie joined Vicki's body*: Brown and Brown, *First Canary*, 108.
303 *Randy, however, said that they needed*: DOJ Report, IV, Part H.
303 *Besides, the departure of Kevin*: Weaver and Weaver, *The Federal Siege at Ruby Ridge*, 63.
303 *They both wore FBI wires*: Walter, *Ruby Ridge*, 248.
304 *"They can kill us if they have to"*: Ibid., 249.
304 *Unlike the day before, they refused*: Walter, *Ruby Ridge*, 249.
304 *McLamb asked them to sign a letter*: Walter, *Ruby Ridge*, 249; Stern, *A Force Upon the Plain*, 33.
305 *He opened the door*: Walter, *Ruby Ridge*, 249.
306 *They put Elisheba in a fresh diaper*: Weaver and Weaver, *The Federal Siege at Ruby Ridge*, 63.
306 *For the first time in over a week*: Walter, *Ruby Ridge*, 250.
306 *Randy, who was wearing faded jeans*: Ibid.
306 *Her mother's ruby wedding ring*: Fuson and McCartan, "After the Showdown."
306 *"Unbelievably," she later recalled*: Weaver and Weaver, *The Federal Siege at Ruby Ridge*, 63.
306 *His wound was cleaned*: Walter, *Ruby Ridge*, 251.
306 *Rachel, Sara, and Elisheba climbed*: Weaver, *From Ruby Ridge to Freedom*, 76.
306 *"It looked like a scene"*: Goodman, *Ruby Ridge: Every Knee Shall Bow.*
308 *The sisters were escorted*: Weaver and Weaver, *The Federal Siege at Ruby Ridge*, 65.
308 *Passing through the crowd*: Weaver, *From Ruby Ridge to Freedom*, 80.
308 *In a motel room in Sandpoint*: Ibid.

EPILOGUE
309 *The first to have his say*: Rhodes Production System, *Ruby Creek Massacre.*
310 *"[Randy] told me to give you guys"*: Ibid.

NOTES

310 *"objective reasonableness"*: DOJ Report, IV.
311 *Five years later, a Boundary County*: Keating, "FBI Sniper Can't Be Tried."
311 *In the meantime, just two months*: Belew, *Bring the War Home*, 202.
311 *"the tender mercies"*: Crothers, *Rage on the Right*, 45.
311 *"The blood of these innocent ones"*: Knickerbocker, "Why a 1992 Shooting in Idaho Has Become a Rallying Point."
311 *The meeting in Estes Park*: Stern, *A Force Upon the Plains*, 35.
311 *The Colorado gathering is commonly cited*: Belew, *Bring the War Home*, 4, 5.
313 *"If there was no persecution"*: Walter, *Ruby Ridge*, 350.
315 *Opposing factions formed*: Walter, *Ruby Ridge*, 363.
315 *Between the cost of surveillance*: Stern, *A Force Upon the Plains*, 39.
315 *While the Davidians disagreed*: Guinn, *Waco*, 136.
316 *Whereas Vicki claimed prophetic vision*: Ibid., 80.
316 *At Waco, one FBI negotiator*: Katz and Popkin, *Messianic Revolution*, x.
316 *Once again, the FBI*: Guinn, *Waco*, 135.
317 *For a time, he considered killing*: Walter, *Ruby Ridge*, 391.
317 *After his arrest, he described*: Toobin, *Homegrown*, 5.
318 *In 1998, Randy traveled to Waco*: Ronson, *Them*, 90.
318 *"I tell you what, boys," he said*: Ronson, *The Secret Rulers of the World* documentary, episode 1, "The Legend of Ruby Ridge."
318 *"Absolutely," came the reply*: February 2018 interview with Roger Roots and John Lamb, available on YouTube, https://www.youtube.com/watch?v=PmgtMpE7uYM.
318 *After the siege, Sara, Rachel, and Elisheba*: Weaver, *From Ruby Ridge to Freedom*, 83.
318 *In his later years, he identified*: February 2018 interview with Roger Roots and John Lamb, available on YouTube, https://www.youtube.com/watch?v=PmgtMpE7uYM.
320 *Finicum had pledged*: Turkewitz and Lichtblau, "Police Shooting of Oregon Occupier Declared Justified."
321 *"I almost feel [that my parents] were"*: Sara Weaver interview, *Good Simple Living* podcast.
321 *When, in 2024, the time rolled around*: Graham and Homans, "Trump Is Connecting with a Different Kind of Evangelical Voter."
322 *John of Patmos was firmly*: Pagels, *Revelations*, 107.
322 *"As a formal school of theology"*: Kristian, "The Surprising Power of Dispensationalism."
322 *"And we realize, to our horror"*: Lawrence, *Apocalypse*, 11.
323 *die "by suicide"*: The Perpetuation of Our Political Institutions: Address Before the Young Men's Lyceum of Springfield, Illinois January 27, 1838, by Abraham Lincoln.

INDEX

ABOUT THE AUTHOR

CHRIS JENNINGS is the author of *Paradise Now: The Story of American Utopianism*. A former editorial staffer at *The New Yorker*, he grew up in New York City and graduated from Deep Springs College and Wesleyan University. Jennings lives in Inverness, California, with his family.